Building Microsoft® SQL Server® 7 Applications with COM

Sanjiv Purba

Wiley Computer Publishing

John Wiley & Sons, Inc.

NEW YORK · CHICHESTER · WEINHEIM · BRISBANE · SINGAPORE · TORONTO

To my father, Parkash Singh Purba

Publisher: Robert Ipsen
Editor: Robert M. Elliott
Managing Editor: Angela Murphy
Text Design & Composition: Publishers' Design and Production Services, Inc.

Designations used by companies to distinguish their products are often claimed as trademarks. In all instances where John Wiley & Sons, Inc., is aware of a claim, the product names appear in initial capital or all capital letters. Readers, however, should contact the appropriate companies for more complete information regarding trademarks and registration.

This book is printed on acid-free paper. ☉

Published by John Wiley & Sons, Inc.

Published simultaneously in Canada.

This publication is designed to provide accurate and authoritative information in regard to the subject matter covered. It is sold with the understanding that the publisher is not engaged in professional services. If professional advice or other expert assistance is required, the services of a competent professional person should be sought.

The content of this book is based on **Beta 3** of **Microsoft SQL Server 7**. There may have been changes made to the product since this release. Therefore, screen shots and examples may not be identical to the final product.

For current information about **Microsoft SQL Server 7**, you should visit www.microsoft.com/

Library of Congress Cataloging-in-Publication Data:

Purba, Sanjiv.
    Building Microsoft SQL Server 7 applications with COM / by Sanjiv
  Purba.
      p. cm.
    Includes bibliographical references and index.
    ISBN 0-471-19233-3 (pbk. : alk. paper)
    1. Client/server computing   2. SQL server.   3. Database
  management.   4. COM (Computer architecture)   III. Title.
  QA76.9.C55P86   1999
  005.75′85—dc21   98-44489

Printed in the United States of America.

10 9 8 7 6 5 4 3 2 1

Contents

Preface

Microsoft's latest release of SQL Server is version 7 , which strategically positions this database product to support mission-critical applications across the enterprise, thus competing head to head with Oracle, Informix, Sybase, and DB2 in the Windows environment. This latest release incorporates 2+ years of design and is intended to establish the basic architecture for this strategic product for the next decade. This is reflected in the new leading digit in the version number from the previous release. SQL Server is an important link within the overall Microsoft Enterprise product direction, which includes COM+ (formerly COM and Microsoft Transaction Server), ActiveX, Visual Studio, and the family of BackOffice Servers and products.

SQL Server 7 offers important enhancements over version 6.5 that go beyond incremental functional improvements, and instead offers more enterprise wide capability and a more elegant approach to database management. Installing and configuring a powerful database has never been easier. SQL Server offers auto-configuration, dynamic memory management, dynamic space management, self-tuning and tighter integration with the operating system. Each of these capabilities allows the database engine to configure itself to the physical environment and improve its performance with virtually no administrative intervention. There are also improvements in the utilities that interact with SQL Server through more functionality and a higher level of visualization. All this means less administrative time in the development environment, which leaves more time for actual development activities.

Another significant improvement in this release is a higher degree of scalability. This is achieved in three notable ways. The previous realistic database limit was 200 GB which, though substantial, was not enough to support data intensive organizations at the enterprise level. This limit has been increased to the 1+ Terabyte range. Version 6.5 also supported hundreds of concurrent users, while the new release has the capability to support thousands. Windows NT, Windows 95, and Windows 98 can all support SQL Server right out of the box starting with the new release. Applications can thus scale from the desktop to the enterprise using the same database platform and virtually the same code. Enhancements to job scheduling capabilities, job execution, profiling tools, and tuning tools support operational efforts in critical production environments where every second of response time is expensive.

There are substantial performance and other functional improvements to the product. These include improvements to the Query Processor and support for parallel and distributed query operations. Other improvements include Big IO, Small IO, new more efficient page formats, new more efficient row formats, trigger improvements, unicode datatype support (e.g., support for multi-languages), text datatype improvements, and image datatype improvements. Table indexing operations have also improved with the introduction of more index types, and better selection and concatenation of the indexes on a table. SQL Server also supports universal data access through OLE DB, full-text search, English Query, web assistant, active server pages, OLAP Server/Plato, and improved general data warehousing support. Microsoft is building a beachhead in the lower end of the data warehousing market with these last few initiatives. Many of the overall limitations in SQL Server 6.5 have either been eliminated or the thresholds have been increased throughout the new release.

Another significant improvement in SQL Server is an expanded support for row-level locking. This improvement allows SQL Server 7 to support Enterprise Resource Planning packages (ERP) such as SAP, PeopleSoft, and Baan. These applications are a large part of the enterprise applications market, which was previously going untapped by SQL Server due to the lack of row-level locking capability and the performance impacts that ensued as a result of this. Coupled with the other Microsoft tools, SQL Server's popularity will increase substantially in this market increasing general demand for these types of skills. Microsoft Corporation recently implemented a large enterprise-wide SAP implementation using SQL Server in their own offices. Application packages in other markets, such as imaging and workflow, will also benefit from this enhancement.

History

SQL Server's commercial history can be traced back to 1987, when it was released in a joint collaboration between Microsoft and Sybase Corporation. Sybase Corporation developed the initial database engine, then sought Microsoft's marketing channels to rapidly build a market presence. Until the early 1990s, they were virtually the same product offering. However, since 1994/1995, Microsoft and Sybase took their version of SQL Server in different directions. Although there are still a significant amount of similarities between their core engines, the two products are diverging dramatically with their current releases.

Microsoft has focused a tremendous amount of resources on building their version of SQL Server on top of Windows NT. There is a tight integration between these two popular products. The success of Microsoft SQL Server is tightly linked to that of Windows NT in the future. Many studies show that Windows NT is becoming the Enterprise Operating System of choice, positioned to surpass UNIX before the year 2000. This will continue to increase the popularity of SQL Server as well. Published TPC-C tests in magazines at the time of writing show that SQL Server performs well compared to other database servers. SQL Server performs particularly well in terms of response time and product cost compared with other database vendors. The last few years has demonstrated Microsoft's commitment towards expanding this client base. Windows NT, which originally supported the Intel chip in virtually all of its implementations, can now point to other highly successful ports of the operating system to Compaq, Data General, Digital (DEC), Hewlett Packard, NCR, Wang, and Tandem environments. Windows NT on the 64 bit DEC Alpha platform has provided powerful performance results for many types of applications running under SQL Server. Support for Windows 95 and Windows 98 included in SQL Server 7 also extend this user base to the desktop.

The buzzword for the early 1990s was "open systems." These were seen as a panacea to the proprietary nature of mainframe systems, and helped spawn a "best of breed" approach for building technology, data, and application architectures. For example, this could involve connecting the best database with the best protocol with the best development language for a given environment. Usually this approach meant buying products from several different vendors and integrating the architecture through customization. In recent years, there has been a departure from the "best of breed" approach towards a single vendor provide all approach due to the complexity of the integration effort. Systems "openness" is still a desirable goal, however, many organizations do not want to assume the risk of integrating products from different vendors. Their choice is to allow the product vendor to be the integrator instead. This trend has seen the collapse or stagnation of vendors who were once highly popular choices. There has also been an increase in the size of the major players who are in a position to offer organizations an end to end technical solution. Some of the major companies that fit into the top tier of this category include IBM, Oracle, and Microsoft. Second tier companies include Informix, Sybase, DEC, SUN, and Forte.

Understanding Database Servers

Database servers are a large component of the n-tier architecture model and the client/server model. Database Servers typically reside on a server platform running on top of a 32+ bit operating systems, such as Windows NT, UNIX, AIX, or MVS. They service applications running on client platforms on top of 16 bit or 32 bit operating systems. The n-tier architecture model supports a continuum of architectures ranging from "thin server-fat client" to "fat server-thin client", and anywhere in between. As shown in Figure P.1, these tools act as guardians of corporate data in any one of these architectures. The "thin" and "fat" terminology that is commonly used today refers to the amount of processing or business logic occurring on the client or the server. In a thin client model, the application interface resides on the client platform and captures or displays information to the user. The data is transferred to the fat client where the processing occurs. In a fat client model, the user interface still captures and presents data to the user, however, the processing also occurs on the client platform. In this model, the thin server acts as a data repository with minimal or no processing. Between these extremes, the business processing can be partitioned between the client and server platforms. The next generation application model extends the basic client/server model by including a web-browser on the client platform. Although this model, offers many advantages over the strictly thin/fat client/server model, the role of the database server is just as important. It is still the guardian of corporate data.

At a high level, a database server consists of the following components: a data repository, a database engine consisting of a query parser and optimizer, relational database compatibility, SQL (SEQUEL) dialect, database extensions and a security framework. Distributed database servers allow components to be invoked remotely. One of the major enhancements of database servers over traditional databases is the programmable database engine. This integrates an SQL dialect with database extensions to maintain applications within the database server repository. Applications running on client platforms can invoke applications stored within the database server in this architecture. This provided dramatic improvements to client/server applications by moving processing logic to the database server platform, thus reducing data transfer volumes over local area networks and wide area networks. The database extensions or enhancements provide the capability of writing powerful applications that imbed SQL commands with procedural constructs. In the future, procedural constructs are expected to be supported through standard languages such

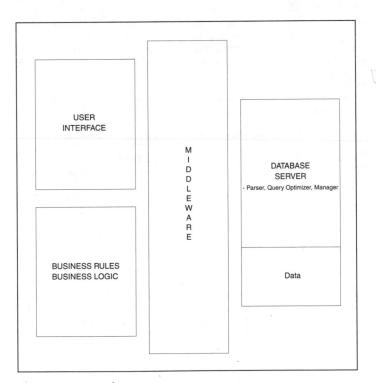

Figure P.1   Database servers.

as JAVA and C++. It is also expected that Microsoft will incorporate the Visual Basic script into many of their products, including SQL Server. Such moves will allow components or applets to be distributed and redistributed freely across different technical requirements. Currently, the database extensions are, in essence, proprietary.

Selecting a Database Server

The major database servers available in the market are capable of handling many different types of environments and industries. Each of them can cite success stories and unique experiences. Organizations that are entering a technology selection phase should realize that there are important differentiating factors between the database vendor products that are available in the marketplace. The selection criteria identified in this section can be used to help distinguish between the different options. The list of selection criteria can be augmented with a specific weight value based on the specific priorities of your own business organization. If this approach is undertaken, it is important to involve a mix of corporate sponsors, users, and technical staff to ensure that there is strong agreement on the criteria selection elements and their relative weights. It is not uncommon to start with an initial list of 6 to 12 potential products. Using the important criteria, it is possible to drop many of the potential candidates to end up with a list of about four finalists. Some common selection criteria that has been used to select a winner from this list is shown in Table P.1.

Table P.1   Criteria for Selecting a Database Server

SELECTION CRITERIA	DESCRIPTION
Product Costs and Total-Cost-Of-Ownership	This includes license fees, development license, runtime fees, support costs, and any other costs associated with using the products. It is also useful to include training costs, as well. It is important to compare the true costs of the products being considered. Do not forget currency conversion in the event that the products are being offered from different countries.
Ease of Use	Effort required in using the product in development, testing, and production environments.
Ease of Learning	Effort required in learning to use the product in different environments.
Data Capacity	The amount of data that can safely be managed by the product. This varies widely between a few hundred gigabytes and into the terabytes.
Scalability	Ability for the product to scale to larger hardware platforms and larger requirements.
Performance	Application performance under different transaction volumes and technology architectures.
User Connections	Number of concurrent users supported by the product.
Hardware Requirements	Hardware requirements for the server and client components. This also has a direct bearing on product cost. Some products require significantly more hardware and high end operating systems to execute.
Internet/Intranet Support	Support for web-based applications.
Openness	Compatibility with other products.

Vendor Cultural Fit	Cultural fit between the vendor and the client organization culture. This is important, as new product adoptions generally require extensive cooperation between both the vendor and the client organization. If values are shared between the two, they are more likely to be successful. For example, clients weary of assuming risk are likely to select a large, stable product vendor, while clients looking for competitive advantage and who can react quickly to events may find it preferable to work with a lean and mean, aggressive vendor. It is important to assess compatibility with a vendor's local resources and support capabilities.
Vendor Support Quality	Quality of technical and business support. Hours of help line operation.
Compatibility with Current Environment	Technical capability of the product to fit into the current technical architecture. For example, will the product require additional modeling or development tools.
Product Popularity	Is the product a market leader?
Vendor Stability	The financial and technical stability of the vendor. A determination if they are expected to survive independently, or if there is some knowledge of who they are likely to merge with or be acquired by. Some leading products lose technical ground because they are acquired by a competitor for mercenary purposes and future investment dries up.
Application Functionality	Surprisingly, the application functionality has the same importance as some of the other factors, but not predominantly so. This is because vendors often leapfrog each other, and the functionality picture can change fairly quickly.

Before making a final decision, it is important to recognize that the database vendors have a tendency to leapfrog each other in terms of technology. A solid advance by one vendor is often followed by an advance by a rival vendor. It is therefore appropriate to ask when a missing feature will actually be required in an application environment before taking an otherwise suitable vendor off the list. It is also important to interview database vendors to get a clear understanding of the future direction of their products. It is also not always necessary to select the product with the largest capacity. Organizations that have 2 GB of data and 40 users, and who do not have a strategic plan to substantially grow in the future, may be effectively supported by a database that is capable of holding no more than 100 GB of data.

Why Microsoft SQL Server?

The largest SQL Server 6.5 sites in the world at the time of writing are in the 500 Gigabyte range with multiple servers. However, by running SQL Servers concurrently it is possible to support larger application environments. Multiple cascading SQL Server engines support retail databases in the 2.5 terabyte range for decision support with up to 20,000 concurrent OLTP users. . SQL Server performs well on Compaq Proliant Pro 5000 machines with multiple processors. There is also strong excitement for the DEC AlphaServer 8000 support (support for 12 platforms with 64 bit processors running NT and multiple SQL Server engines). SQL Server enjoys the best TPC-C scores under Windows NT at the time of writing. TPC-C benchmarks show a Compaq ProLiant 5000 system will support in excess of 10 Million transactions per day. It has a low $100 per user license cost. It is well on the way to becoming one of the three big database vendors, behind IBM and Oracle. For these reasons, SQL Server has successfully serviced many businesses around the world in a broad range of industries.

In the past few years, SQL Server has proven its ability to support the needs of an ever widening group of users in corporate enterprises. Products that can support this level of the organization must be able to meet strict criteria, including the following:

- Fit within an overall technical architecture
- Scale in terms of data volumes and concurrent user connections
- Offer high concurrency
- Be highly reliable
- Be highly secure
- Be supported by a financially sound vendor

Microsoft SQL Server scores well in all these categories. Microsoft SQL Server has also enjoyed high public satisfaction for three additional reasons:

1. Integration with Microsoft products.
2. Good price/performance ratio.
3. Strong feature set.

However, until recently, SQL Server has been viewed as a departmental database incapable of supporting the enterprise as a whole.

The major historical deficiencies that have been identified by users of SQL Server include the following:

- Scalability, in terms of database size (practical limit of 200 GB for a single server), number of users, and transaction capability
- Consistent pricing—large hikes have left some customers unsure of what the future will bring
- Lack of row level locking
- Tied to INTEL chip (e.g., DELL and Compaq)
- Limitation of Windows NT to scale to the Enterprise

SQL Server 7 along with Microsoft's other strategic products address all of these concerns. In particular, the combination of SQL Server with Wolfpack, Microsoft Transaction Server, and Visual Basic can produce mission critical application for the enterprise. Other Microsoft products, such as SMS and Visual SourceSave also fill in some of the gaps previously identified by users in the areas of systems management. SQL Server 7 is also capable of running under Windows 95, so the product suite is capable of offering application scalability from the desktop to large clustered systems capable of supporting up to the terabytes range of data.

Microsoft has worked aggressively with hardware manufacturers to build support for Windows NT. A notable success has been with the 64 bit DEC Alpha hardware platform that performs well in data intensive applications. Windows NT also runs well in Unisys environments with six high-end processors. Other supported platforms include Dell PowerEdge 6100, Compaq Proliant 5000, NCR WorldMark 4300, HP NetServer LX Pro, SNI Primergy 560, Digital Prioris SZ 6200MP, and NCR WorldMark 4300S. These new environments will add to the popularity of Windows NT (which at the time of writing are exceeding yearly UNIX shipments by over 100,000 copies). With the emergence of true 64-bit memory addressing (2 to the power of 64 bits), SQL Server will be able to support many objects directly in main memory with dramatic performance improvements.

Microsoft's Enterprise Strategy

As shown in Figure P.2, Microsoft SQL Server (code named Sphinx) is a key component of the Microsoft enterprise architecture strategy. Microsoft Transaction Server (MTS), a product widely released in 1997, is another key component of the architecture that is required to scale a Microsoft architecture solution to enterprise levels. The Transaction Server supports scalability and trans-

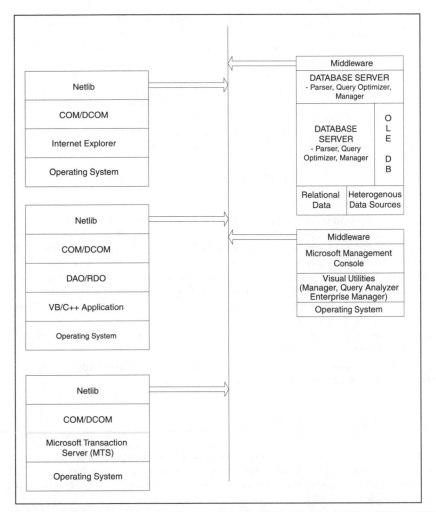

Figure P.2 Microsoft Enterprise architecture strategy.

action processing on top of the Distributed Component Object Model or DCOM. MTS is a TP Monitor (code-named Viper), like CICS, IBM Encina, and Tuxedo. Enhancements to Visual Basic in Release 5 enable it to support interaction with a database server, n-tier architecture, and object oriented technologies. Visual C++ is a good companion for the Windows bound VB and is far more portable. Microsoft is also offering additional products, including the following:

Wolfpack (clustering support, failover). Microsoft Cluster Server (MCS) is also called WolfPack. It supports high application availability and 2 node failover—one server can takeover for a failed one through shared channels (hot standby). Symmetric Virtual Server can work with SQL Server so that two servers can be active concurrently in the architecture—doing different work until they are needed for the failover. Massively Parallel Clusters are expected to be available in a few years to support additional hardware attachments to an existing environment to improve performance.

Microsoft Transaction Server (MTS). This product acts as a TP monitor and an Object Request Broker (ORB). Objects use DCOM to interact with other objects. Supports transaction management, process isolation, security, resource pools, and networking. Components are plugged into MTS. Applications can work directly against the database, or with some modifications, can go through MTS. This is a critical tool in Microsoft's overall strategy to build distributed, mission-critical applications for the Enterprise. Works with MTS, OLE DB, and DCOM to offer relational/object functionality.

OLE DB. This product provides universal data access. It can access data sources, beyond relational databases (a limit of ODBC) including multimedia stores. Prior to OLE DB, separate APIs required to access different relational data sources. OLE DB requires a single API and a unified object model. It is expected to be incorporated into SQL Server as a query processor based on OLE DB. SQL Server can use 1 or more OLE DB engines to process queries against other data sources (e.g., flat files, Excel spreadsheets). SQL Server bundles the responses and the return set to the client platform.

DCOM/COM. This middleware approach offers a binary interface standard and defines interfaces to objects using IDL (Interface Definition Language). Both VB and C++ can both build DCOM objects within the Microsoft product suite.

ACTIVEX. Offers component based support for object access across the Internet. OLE DB and ActiveX(ADO) are an alternative to ODBC, DAO, and RDO. DAO and RDO are two programming models, the first is best for manipulating ISAM files, while the latter is suitable for relational table access.

DAO. An access approach is created for JET database engine and is used with Microsoft Access, the desktop database. This approach works best in single user environments. DAO uses COM objects to interface with the Jet database. Access supports ISAM, but is weak with relational databases.

RDO. This access approach is created for relational database access. It is a wrapper around ODBC API, and is itself a COM object.

Falcon. This product integrates with SQL Server Distributed Transaction Coordinator to handle transactions spread across multiple NT Servers—message queuing.

Database Server Options

Database Server technology has expanded in the past few years to include support for data warehousing, Internet/Intranet/Web solutions, large object/image, motion, Object persistence, and OO support. The major database server players are in the midst of releasing new versions of their products, as shown in Table P.2.

Purpose of This Book

The purpose of this book is to support readers in developing enterprise wide distributed n-tier applications in a Windows NT environment. Over the past decade, the original Windows desktop operating system laid the groundwork for the emergence of Windows NT (New Technology). NT has matured from a workgroup operating system into one that is positioned to scale to the enterprise over the next few years. Since SQL Server is positioned to play a critical role in this integrated environment, this book focuses on both the big "enterprise" picture as well as the details of the product.

This book focuses on the Microsoft SQL Server environment, product enhancements over previous versions of the product, system commands, Transact SQL, performance, tuning, and administration processes. In addition to technical information about SQL Server, this book also takes a broader view of this powerful tool in the context of the standard systems development life cycle (SDLC), specifically identifying SQL Server involvement in various phases. Enhancements to the SQL Server engine, such as utilizing the world wide web, internet/intranet, application portability, interoperability, components, and data warehousing are also covered in this book. Other Microsoft SQL Server products that are required to build enterprise solutions, such as Microsoft Transaction Server, Visual Basic, and DCOM are also discussed in this book—based on experience

Table P.2   Database Servers from the Major Vendors

DATABASE SERVER	DESCRIPTION
IBM DB2 Universal Database Enterprise Extended Edition	Multimedia support, supports web users, support for Windows NT, Sun Solaris, AIX, and OS/2. Native support for Java Database Connectivity (JDBC) and Java-based applets. IBM DB2 Universal Database supports large objects (LOBs), offers a 4GL C/C++, JAVA extensions: text, image, video, fingerprints
Informix Universal Server	Object relational database, support for non-relational datatypes (e.g. images, video, and sound), extensions called Datablades that involve 3rd party vendors for such functionality as digital media, document management, world wide web, database optimization, mapping, data warehousing. Supports large objects (LOBs), no 4GL, supports C/C++, JAVA. Supports 15+ DataBlade extensions.
Oracle 8.0	Object Oriented support, database table partitions, transaction queuing, pooled user connections, parallel replication, parallel administrative tasks (e.g. loading without user impact into protected partitions), enhanced data warehouse support, and support for hundreds of terabytes of data. Future support for Server-side C++, JAVA, and JDBC. Part of Oracle's Network Computing Architecture. Supports large objects(LOBs), offers a 4GL, C/C++, PL/SQL, and support for text, spatial, video.
Sybase Adaptive Server 11.5 (ASE 11.5)	Replaces Sybase SQL Server System 11. Deploys distributed component based applications. Future support for JAVA. Predictable performance improvements. Supports mixed workload environments Sybase Adaptive Server family offers distributed application support and Extended data type support. Common Language Processor. Stored procedures are forward compatible. Optimized data store. Adaptive Component Architecture. Customer-Centric computing. OLTP/DSS/mixed-workload—Adaptive Server Enterprise. Mobile computing—SQL Server Anywhere. Distributed data marts—Adaptive Server IQ.
Computer Associates OpenIngres	Supports multiple OS environments, such as NT, UNIX, and OpenVMS. Access to DB2, SQL Server data. GUI based database administration. Rule-based configuration, highly configurable, online backups, distributed configurations.
Computer Associates Jasmine	Pure Object oriented database works with relational data through gateways. Supports multimedia applications through support for text, video, sound, and spatial data. Object oriented databases store true objects and complex data. POET OQL is another example of an object oriented database.

from development projects. This book focuses on providing substantial examples that demonstrate algorithms and components that are useful on development projects.

Intended Audience

This book is intended to meet the needs of Information Technology (IT) professionals, including those who are new to the client/server development architecture (and hence have little database server knowledge) and want to learn SQL Server, those professionals who have used a competitor's database server (e.g. Oracle, Sybase), and those professionals who have used earlier versions of SQL Server.

IT Directors, technical managers, consultants, analysts, developers, architects (e.g. technical, application, and data), testers, DBAs, data analysts, data designers, and students will find this book useful for increasing their knowledge base in general, and to support application projects in particular.

Organization of the Book

This book is divided into 5 parts containing 20 chapters and an additional appendix. The objectives of each part of the book are introduced prior to a listing of the chapters that are contained in that section.

Part 1: Quick Start

This part of the book provides the reader with installation instructions, a description of the enhancements in the new release, an introduction to n-tier architecture, an introduction to COM/MTS, and a quick tour of the important features of SQL Server. A two-part primer is also included to provide the reader with a view of the important SQL Server commands and features. The rest of the book expands the roadmap. Part 1 also provides a complete system development lifecycle and identifies SQL Server linkages to phases and activities. The organizational roles required to support SQL Server throughout the SDLC are also described in Part 1.

Chapter 1 provides the reader with the opportunity to install and get SQL Server up and running rapidly. This chapter also provides a quick tour of the more useful utilities that are packaged with SQL Server, as well as providing a quick walkthrough of the SQL Server environment itself. This chapter focuses on providing the reader with the information that is necessary to start profiting from SQL Server by filtering out second stage topics.

Chapter 2 provides an introduction to the basics of n-tier architecture, beginning with a comparison of 2-tier versus 3-tier architecture. This is expanded to n-tier architecture. This chapter also examines Microsoft's Component Object Model (COM), COM+, Microsoft Transaction Server (MTS), and distributed architecture. This chapter lays the foundation for using SQL Server in distributed n-tier applications.

Chapter 3 provides a primer or tutorial that is used in the rest of the book to expand on specific areas of the SQL Server environment. This chapter, along with Chapter 4, take the reader through the major steps required to build a data based application. This chapter begins by examining activities that are essential for starting database type projects and proceeds to build the requirements for a sample application including a simplified schema for a logical data model. The chapter converts the logical data model into a physical data model, describing the activities required to do this, and then builds a script to create the physical tables corresponding to the data model. The reader is also shown how to create user defined databases to house the user defined tables. This is done through a combination of batch scripts and using SQL Server 7's powerful wizards. The database and table scripts are executed to create database objects, and the reader is shown how to add and retrieve information from the user defined database tables.

Chapter 4 is the second part of the primer or tutorial that was started in Chapter 3. This chapter examines SQL Server architecture, databases, and database objects. While Chapter 3 focused on creating databases and database tables, this chapter focuses on basic Transact-SQL commands to manipulate information within the database tables. As part of this examination, reader's are shown the basics of joins, subqueries, views, stored procedures, triggers, and cursors that form the basis of using SQL Server from an application perspective.

Chapter 5 provides a methodology focus to the SQL Server specific topics introduced in the first four chapters. The information contained in this chapter is based on experiences gained on data based projects, and is vital for ensuring that development project leveraging SQL Server in distributed, n-tier environments are implemented.

Part 2: Building the Application Framework

This part of the book describes how the physical environment should be configured before installing SQL Server. Other topics discussed in this part of the book include data types, data validation, referential integrity, the data definition language, the data manipulation language, and data control language.

Chapter 6 examines the SQL Server environment from a technical perspective to build on the knowledge gained in the first four chapters. This includes managing configuration values, database options, and set commands. Each of these are enhanced in SQL Server 7, and each affect the inner functioning of SQL Server. This chapter also examines the activities that are required to establish a working database environment based on SQL Server.

Chapter 7 examines data storage and representation in the SQL Server environment. This involves a rigorous examination of SQL Server datatypes and a comparison to the ANSI standard. This chapter also examines methods for validating data, ensuring referential integrity, and maintaining overall data quality.

Chapter 8 expands on the primer presented in Chapter 3 for creating databases and database objects. This involves an examination of the common Data Definition Language (DDL) commands, such as CREATE, ALTER, and DROP

Chapter 9 expands on the primer presented in chapter 4 for manipulating data and database objects. This involves an examination of the common Data Manipulation Language (DML) commands, such as SELECT, INSERT, UPDATE, and DELETE.

Chapter 10 examines the new features in SQL Server 7 for administering security through login ids, roles, userids, and domain ids. Permission management through the GRANT and REVOKE commands is also discussed in this chapter. This chapter examines batch script approaches and using the powerful administration wizards that are available to assist DBAs.

Part 3: Incorporating Advanced Features

This part of the book examines leveraging more advanced features incorporated into SQL Server, including writing stored procedures, system functions, triggers, and advanced data manipulation techniques. This includes joins, views, subqueries, and server-side cursors.

Chapter 11 examines stored procedure management using batch scripts and the administrative tools that are packaged with SQL Server. This chapter examines the control-of-flow language that includes procedural constructs such as if-else, while, and case. Stored procedures are a basis of distributed systems, including n-tier architecture.

Chapter 12 examines the functions that are built into the SQL Server environment. These include date/time manipulation, mathematical processing and text processing.

Chapter 13 examines how to leverage the different types of triggers to maintain referential integrity in a database. New features available for triggers in SQL Server 7 are also discussed in this chapter.

Chapter 14 examines the different types of joins, subqueries, views and server side cursors that are supported by SQL Server to support distributed, n-tier systems.

Part 4: Build Advanced Applications Using COM, Internet/Intranet, Visual Basic, and MTS

This part of the book provides tutorials for building several n-tier applications. This includes building an n-tier application using Visual Basic, COM, and MTS. Another tutorial demonstrates how SQL Server can be leveraged with the Internet, WWW, and Interdev. The other tutorial demonstrates building client applications to leverage SQL Server.

Chapter 15 demonstrates how to build an n-tier application using COM and SQL Server based on specific user requirements, a data model, and an object model. The application is built on top of MTS using Visual Basic.

Chapter 16 examines the principles that are followed in building usable user interfaces in distributed n-tier environments. This discussion involves leveraging SQL Server transaction and locking abilities in a multi-user environment of this architecture.

Chapter 17 demonstrates how to build applications that leverage internet/intranet technology through the use of COM, SQL Server, and Active Server Pages (ASP).

Part 5: Deploying Production-Ready N-Tier Applications and System Administration

This part of the book examines the activities that are required to complete the final phases of the application lifecycle and prepare it for production. This includes testing, optimization, and deployment. SQL Server administrative commands are also examined in this part, including the detailed options of ISQL, BCP and DBCC. The GUI utilities that are available with SQL Server are also examined in detail.

Chapter 18 provides an approach for preparing an application for implementation.

Chapter 19 focuses on system administration through SQL Server utility dialogues including the Enterprise Manager, Query Analyzer, and the administrative wizards that are packaged with SQL Server 7.

Chapter 20 focuses on SQL Server utilities and tools that are used for ongoing maintenance of SQL Server based systems.

Appendix A examines the essential relational data modeling concepts necessary to leverage the examples contained in this book.

Acknowledgments

I want to thank Microsoft for developing and supporting a solid product that has satisfied clients worldwide. I also want to thank Microsoft for supporting my efforts in writing this book through access to beta versions of the product. In particular I would like to thank Graham Flint, a manager in the Microsoft Toronto office, and Ken Headrick, Enterprise Channel Account Manager.

My special thanks go to Stephen D'Silva, Senior Consultant and technology leader with Deloitte Consulting, for providing nearly 100 percent of Chapter 15, "Building a COM-based N-tier Application." My special thanks also go to Charles Dow, Practice Leader for OO Technologies with Deloitte Consulting, for providing nearly 100 percent of Chapter 17, "Connecting SQL Server to the Internet."

I also want to thank the following individuals for their valuable assistance over the years in very many different areas that are important:

James Fehrenbach, Peter Fernie, Francis Renaud, Gord Shields, Franca Del Bel Belluz, Ted Wallace, Christine Stephens, Shashela Tushingham, Wayne Thomas, Wayne Martin, Bruce Anderson, Dipak Karia, and Emilie Herman.

I would also like to thank my parents, Parkash and Inderjit Purba, my aunt Dr. Sudarshan Puri, my grandparents, Amrit Gurcharan Singh and Rajwant Kaur Puri, my sisters, Minni Coombs and Nina Jaiswal, my wife's grandmother, Naseeb Kaur (Bebe), my wife Kulwinder, and my sons, Naveen Parkash and Neil Ravi.

PART

one

Quick Start

Part One of this book provides the reader with a roadmap for exploring the Microsoft SQL Server features that support real-world application development. This includes examining the business context of the product, the SQL Server environment, distributed application development capabilities, and enhanced functionality in SQL Server 7 over earlier versions of the product.

Chapter 1 introduces the reader to the SQL Server environment and provides a quick start for readers learning SQL Server or who want to learn about some of the inherent improvements in this powerful product. The reader is also assisted in installing SQL Server and taking a first tour of the product and its new features.

Chapter 2 examines 2-tier, 3-tier, and n-tier application architecture. COM, COM+, DCOM, ActiveX, and the Microsoft Transaction Server (MTS) are also discussed in this chapter. This technology forms the infrastructure of n-tier applications that are capable of scaling to thousands of concurrent users.

Chapter 3 is a primer that provides a quick overview of common SQL Server functions and shows how to use them to build a sample application. The reader is introduced to database creation and manipulation commands within the SQL Server environment that are accessible through Transact-SQL, wizards, and GUI-based utilities.

Chapter 4 is the conclusion of the primer that began in the previous chapter. It explores more complex database objects such as stored procedures, triggers, views, and table joins. System help procedures are also covered.

Chapter 5 examines methodologies, techniques, standards, and approaches for building n-tier database-oriented applications using SQL Server and COM.

CHAPTER
1

Getting Started

Microsoft SQL Server is a database server that supports applications in a variety of environments, including n-tier client/server, data warehousing, Internet, and object-oriented environments. SQL Server offers data services to local and remote client platforms. As shown in Figure 1.1, clients residing in several locations issue service requests to SQL Server and then receive responses in return. Essentially, applications on client platforms issue requests to database servers through an internal or external network. The database server inspects the security access of the requester, inspects the syntax of the request, parses it, optionally optimizes the execution of the request (if an execution plan does not already exist), and then proceeds to execute it. The database server returns a response to the client platform either in the form of a message indicating that some work was performed or in some cases not performed to any data that satisfies the request. Responses from database servers are referred to as result sets. As the figure shows, the SQL Server product and the related databases generally reside on the same platform. Client platforms communicate with SQL Server over a local area network (LAN) or a wide area network (WAN). It is also possible to install several SQL Server engines on the same platform or have them installed on different geographically distributed platforms. Applications on a client platform can communicate with any of the database servers in the configuration. Database servers can also pass requests to one another using "remote procedure calls" or messaging middleware products. Each SQL Server is identified by a specific name that is selected by the user(s) at installation time.

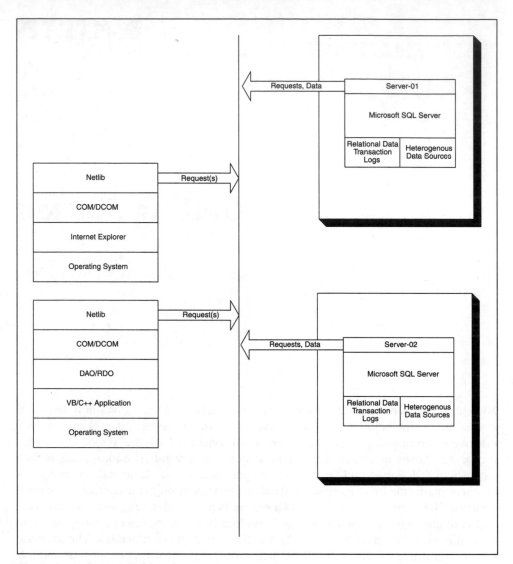

Figure 1.1   SQL Server and servicing requests.

The Road Map

For the purposes of classification, it is useful to divide the substantial features incorporated into Microsoft SQL Server and the surrounding environment into categories that include the operating environment and storage architecture, development environment, engine architecture, enhanced services, features and add-ons, and client platform services. These categories are described in Table 1.1.

Table 1.1 SQL Server Environment Categories

CATEGORY	DESCRIPTION
Operating environment and storage architecture	This consists of the SQL Server environment itself. This category encompasses the physical environment including file structures (formerly devices and segments), database objects, and transaction logs. Utilities and system procedures are also included in this category.
Development environment	This consists of features that support development activities within the SQL Server environment, such as stored procedures, triggers, views, DDL, DML, and the control-of-flow language. These are contained in the SQL Server Transact-SQL dialect.
Engine architecture	The engine architecture consists of the parser, normalization, query optimizer, SQL manager, procedure and statement execution, query execution, DDL, and OLE DB.
Enhanced services, features, and add-ons	This consists of recent advances in SQL Server such as data warehousing, data replication, transaction server, and World Wide Web support.
Client platform services	This consists of the middleware that supports connectivity between client platforms and the SQL Server engine. This category also encompasses front-end, multitier development tools such as Visual Basic, PowerBuilder, and modeling tools.

What You Get

After installing Microsoft SQL Server you have access to the tools shown in Table 1.2 through the main Windows menu under Start-Programs. These are graphical tools that are far simpler and more efficient to use than traditional text-based tools for accessing the database server environment.

Table 1.2 SQL Server Tools

COMPONENT	DESCRIPTION	USAGE
Books Online	Provides access to help information and other technical reports.	Adhoc
Client Network Utility	Network configuration and protocols for the client.	Occasional
Enterprise Manager	This is an administration tool to manage database objects and the operating environment. In the recent release of SQL Server, this tool is linked with the Microsoft Management Console (MMC). This tool is frequently used by database administrators (DBAs) during development and ongoing operations.	Frequent
MSDTC Administrative Console	The Distributed Transaction Console is used to distribute transactions across a set of SQL Servers. This tool is frequently used by DBAs or librarians to deploy applications.	Occasional
Profiler	Formerly called SQL Trace. This tool runs traces, analyzes deadlocks, and assists in identifying badly constructed queries. This tool is frequently used by DBAs to monitor ongoing efficiency within the database environment. It is also used during the development life cycle to optimize and tune the application.	Frequent
Query Analyzer	Formerly called ISQL/w. This tool is used to run queries and commands against SQL Server, displays returned information, and provides costing information about commands. This tool is frequently used by DBAs and other development resources.	Frequent
Readme.txt	This contains release notes about SQL Server.	Occasional
Server Network Utility	This tool provides network configuration and protocols for the database server.	Occasional
Service Manager	This tool provides the ability to start, stop, and pause SQL Server. This tool is frequently used by DBAs. It is possible to configure NT to start SQL Server automatically.	Frequent
Uninstall SQL Server 7	This tool removes SQL Server from the environment. It is a relatively clean way of removing the product from your hard disk.	Occasional

What's New in SQL Server 7

Microsoft SQL Server release 7 supports larger databases, integrates with more Microsoft products aimed at supporting the enterprise, such as Microsoft Transaction Server (MTS) and OLE DB, and supports n-tier application development. The internal architecture of SQL Server 7 is object oriented and component based. SQL Server 6.5 was a significant enhancement over SQL Server 6, which was a tremendous step up from SQL Server 4. Until the release of SQL Server 6.5, Microsoft SQL Server shared the same core engine with Sybase SQL Server. However, the functionality of version 6.5 diverged noticeably away from Sybase SQL Server because of Microsoft's stronger focus on functional enhancements, such as limited row-level locking, direct data warehousing support, and data replication. SQL Server 7 is arguably an important milestone in SQL Server's history. It positions Microsoft as a serious database server player that can support the enterprise as a whole in terms of the key criteria that are discussed in this section.

Capacity

Microsoft SQL Server has been an NT-based database product. Since NT has historically been a workgroup or departmental operating system, Microsoft SQL Server capacity has been more or less sufficient to handle the requirements of those size environments. Capacity can be measured in terms of database size, throughput, and concurrent user connections. Concurrency is a key attribute—as load is measured not by the number of users that can use the application, but by the number of users who are simultaneously using the application. In terms of capacity, SQL Server can now support over 1 TB of real data. The throughput of the database in terms of TCP-C numbers and other client information demonstrates impressive growth over version 6.5 and against the competition. SQL Server can now also support concurrent user connections that number in the thousands.

Scalability

Microsoft SQL Server is positioned to scale from a stand-alone database server to an enterprise-wide SQL Server capable of supporting over 1 TB of data and hundreds and thousands of concurrent users. This degree of scalability is supported without a corresponding strain on the hardware resources. Adding user connections and increasing storage requires nominal increases of other supporting resources. Due to the scalability improvements in NT, SQL Server is now also able to leverage an increasing number of engines, from 8 to 32 depending on the hardware capability.

Interoperability

By its very nature, Microsoft SQL Server is restricted to Microsoft operating systems, at the exclusion of others, such as UNIX, MVS, OS/2, and MAC OS. However, the industry momentum is clearly behind Microsoft and many organizations are committing to Microsoft Enterprise solutions. This is a huge market in itself. Within this family, SQL Server is highly interoperable between the NT family, Windows 95, and Windows 98.

SQL Server's interoperability is tightly integrated with these operating systems. NT, specifically, is successfully supporting a range of hardware platforms, notably the DEC Alpha 64-bit series. This is an especially exciting enhancement in terms of mobile, desktop, and large environment support. SQL Server can replace applications of the access database where it is a requirement to support databases in the desktop and in large clustered environments as well. This is also supported by new physical formats (e.g., for pages, rows, extents, data files, and transaction logs) for the data architecture. Also watch for NT's and Windows 95/98's continued penetration into computer platforms that support other types of electronic products.

Integration

An important benefit of SQL Server is its tight integration with other Microsoft Enterprise solutions. COM+ (formerly COM and MTS), ActiveX, Microsoft SQL Server, Visual Basic, Visual C++, SourceSave, NT, SMS, OLE DB, Internet Information Server (IIS), Internet Studio, and the Web tools provide the infrastructure for enterprise strength solutions. There is also tight integration with modeling tools such as the Visual Data Modeler. Integration with OLE DB supports access to heterogeneous data, including relational tables and flat files, as shown in Figure 1.2.

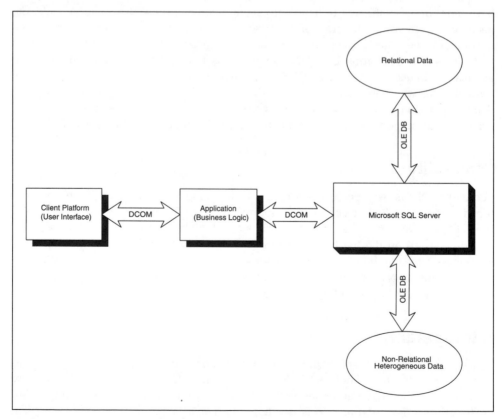

Figure 1.2 SQL Server and OLE DB.

Ease of Use

Microsoft SQL Server is possibly one of the easiest database servers to use and administer. The product offers a high level of self-tuning, automation, wizards, and graphical tools. These are enabled during the entire project life cycle. Many activities can be performed in several ways, including the use of the visual tools, scripts, or traditional text-based interfaces. The visual tools also allow generation of traditional text-based scripts. The following features support SQL Server's ease of use:

Dynamic space management allows databases to dynamically size themselves without DBA involvement. SQL Server blurs many of the tasks between DBAs and developers, freeing up resources to do other work on the project.

Data files grow and shrink automatically. This feature can be turned off or severely limited when files are created in order to protect disk space.

There are many wizards to assist in completing major activities. These include administration, performance, security, and object management.

Graphical tools simplify interaction with the database (e.g., graphical show plan, command syntax is color coded in the query analyzer).

The query analyzer suggests indexes for best access based on a costing algorithm.

Automated configuration of memory disk space. Resources are requested by SQL Server as they are required.

Performance

Until this latest release, many of my colleagues did not consider Microsoft SQL Server to offer exceptionally high performance in larger database environments. Oracle, DB2, and Sybase were perceived as better performers in high-load environments as long as enough hardware was allocated to the solution. However, Microsoft SQL Server offers dramatic performance improvements in its utilities, database engine, integration with NT, and data structures, including the following:

- Improvements to the query optimizer through better statistics management and algorithms. The query processor also uses OLE DB to support distributed queries. The query processor is optimized to support star query joins.
- Large database support (more than 1 TB).
- Large I/O support (I/O block size increase 400 percent).
- Page sizes have increased from 2 KB to 8 KB, extents use 64 KB blocks, and scans use 64 KB blocks. I/O size has increased to 64 KB for scans.
- Smart I/O leverages the large I/O improvements to improve throughput and performance.
- Indexing strategy improvements now use multiple indexes on a table to improve performance. Statistics are also generated automatically.
- Other improvements include parallel index creation, multiple covered indexes, and join indexes.

- Join improvements include hash strategies, merge strategies, nested loop joins, and single queries leverage multiple join types.

- Support for smart Read Ahead. Improved caching.

- Improved query optimization (e.g., index intersection, hash joins, parallel query execution).

- Improved query costing model improves the accuracy of building query plans.

- Parallel querying within a query through use of multiple processors. Large, complex queries perform better than in previous versions of the product.

- Supports multiple-index filtering for faster queries.

- Unused indexes are dropped to improve table scan performance.

- Parallel reads. Parallel queries are supported through intra-query parallel execution, where a query can leverage multiple processors.

Architecture

Microsoft SQL Server is based on a highly componentized architecture. Architecture enhancements to this release include

Full row-level locking or "dynamic" locking support on data and index pages. Version 6.5 supported limited row-level locking capability. This is a much requested feature that will go a long way toward enhancing the popularity of this product. Locking automatically scales between row, page, and table locks based on contention for data. Row locks require the most resources to maintain so they are the least desirable from a performance perspective. However, row locks reduce data contention, so they are useful under heavy transaction loads to improve system performance. Full dynamic row-level locking allows SQL Server to support many enterprise resource planning (ERP)-type packages, such as PeopleSoft, FileNet, and SAP. Locks can now be applied at the row, page, or table level. Row-level locking is available at the data row and index level. The choice of lock is automatically selected by SQL Server but can be overridden by the DBA.

Internal SQL Server architecture is now based on OLE DB-DCOM components. This is a major enhancement for extensibility of SQL Server, and integration with Microsoft's enterprise development tool suite. OLE DB provides access to both SQL Server and non-SQL Server (e.g., Excel) data.

An increase in addressable main memory space. This is important because database objects such as tempdb can be moved directly into main memory for improved performance. Data and procedure cache sizes can also be increased. There is also support for 1 GB of RAM for improved response time and calculations.

Dynamic memory optimizes memory allocation. Large memory support for more than 4 GB is available for NT 5.0 systems.

SQL Server 7 is compliant with ANSI/ISO information schema standard.

Support for both 3-tier and n-tier architecture.

Some system tables have been removed. These include sysprocedures, sysre-storedetail, syssegments, systasks, sysusages, syslocks, syskeys, and syshistory.

The full path to database objects consistently contains four components: server.database.owner.object.

New system procedures and system tables in both the master and the model database.

New disk format and storage subsystem for more efficient data storage and access capabilities. The new data structures offer a better opportunity to scale.

Administration

Microsoft SQL Server contains many administrative enhancements including

- Backup and Restore support more efficient on-line backup. Incremental backup support is also available.
- Improvements to DBCC performance and added functionality.
- Improved bulk data loading.
- Transaction log enhancements improve backup/recovery procedures.
- Utilities modified to support new higher limits of SQL Server.
- Many new administration wizards are available, including profiling, index tuning wizard, graphical query analyzer, and version update utility to upgrade version 6.5 databases.
- Improvements to event/alert functions.
- New storage structures are based on files and file groups. Old storage structures were segments and devices.
- Scripting supports improvements to job scheduling.
- Improvements to multisite administration.
- Improvements to database security levels.
- On-demand memory allocation, on-demand disk, auto-update statistics, improved statistics generation, and query plan auto-recompilation.
- Improvements in SQL Server Enterprise Manager.

Functionality

Microsoft SQL Server supports enhancements to its core functionality including

- The Unicode datatype is supported for better multilingual support. This is available through ODBC, OLE DB..
- Support for variable-length character fields with a maximum size of 8 KB.
- Support for physical row-order scans.

- Improvements to trigger use. Multiple triggers can be fired at the table level, increasing support for component-based development. Recursion is supported by triggers.

- Columns can be added/removed from tables without having to unload and load the data.

- LRU strategy is replaced by a clocking method. Pages that are dormant are marked for reuse. Improvements to the Read Ahead system to improve parallelization.

- The physical layout of the SQL Server files has changed from the previous version. This requires an upgrade of files to version 7. The upgrade actually occurs very quickly.

- The concept of devices is removed from SQL Server 7, allowing databases to automatically be allocated additional disk space.

- Elimination of general limitations (e.g., naming size).

- Improvements to ISQL/w (renamed ISQL Server Query Analyzer), including graphical views of joins and index access.

- Implementation of a new utility called Microsoft English Query. This allows users to submit database requests in English. This is a useful enhancement to the user interface and will lead to other user-friendly applications.

- Improvements to SQL Trace (now called SQL Server Profiler) to allow real-time monitoring of the database for specific events.

- Support for stored procedures not using Transact-SQL, but VBA, and working with MTS. This improves application portability, and the ability to freely distribute application components.

- Introduction of a Visual C++ SQL Server stored procedure debugger.

- Two-node clustering and support for up to eight processors (requires two copies of SQL Server).

- Transaction management through tight integration with MTS. Better distributed transaction support and management tools.

- Support for message queuing.

- Enhancements to the select statement (e.g., TOP n | [PERCENT n).

Data Warehousing, Replication, and eCommerce

SQL Server 7 continues to integrate data warehousing, replication, and eCommerce into the core database product. Enhancements in this area include

Distributed management object (DMO) support.

Replication improvements. These include multisite updates, transactional replication, snapshot replication, merge replication, and heterogeneous support. Types of replication that are supported include master-slave, tight linkage, and loose linkage.

Data warehousing enhancements. These include Plato, PivotTable Service (PTS), English Query, Microsoft Management Console (MMC), universal data access through OLE DB and ADO, and data transformation services. SQL Server data warehouse changes are augmented by OLAP hooks into Excel and VB. Improved data warehouse support also includes data transformation services based on COM architecture. Plato is a multidimensional database management system. Support for Panorama ROLAP.

Linguistic search for data.

Support for tabular data streams (TDSs).

Improvements to the Query Processor supports decision support and data warehousing applications.

Improvements to database replication and heterogeneous database support and subscriptions. Replication will improve from a single update site to multiple subscribers to a model where more than one site can be updated.

Leverages Internet Information Server (IIS), Microsoft Proxy Server, and Site Server. Web Assistant to put data on a website.

Database object encryption for Internet data transfer.

Another benefit offered by SQL Server is its return on investment or its cost/performance ratio. SQL Server offers a winning combination of functionality compared with the price of a working solution. However, it is important to watch this ratio, as it has eroded in the past two years. This erosion may continue into the future.

Generally Painless Installation

This section describes the installation process for Microsoft SQL Server 7. SQL Server can be installed on a stand-alone platform or in a LAN environment. The former approach is useful for readers who are learning the product for the first time. The latter approach is the preferred method for work environments.

It is important to note the term "generally" painless installation. In most cases, installation is straightforward. However, the occasional system can experience difficulties for a variety of reasons, including the following:

Operating system problem.

Internet Explorer version is older than the operating system.

Service pack missing.

Configuration issues, such as not enough RAM, insufficient disk space, or insufficient processing power.

 Make a bootable disk of your computer before starting the install process. This can be done through the Start-Setting-Control Panel-Add/Remove Programs option.

Follow the Prompts

As a prelude to installing SQL Server, the following steps should be followed:

1. Sign on to Windows NT/95/98 as an administrator.
2. Create a Windows NT/95/98 user account (with administrator privileges) for SQL Executive.
3. Create a Windows NT/95/98 user account (with administrator privileges) for SQL Server.

Installing SQL Server generally consists of a straightforward set of activities that can be painlessly completed by the installer. The product is installed under a Windows NT Server platform, or in a small number of cases under Windows NT Client. It is also supported by Windows 95 and Windows 98. The first step is to insert the CD ROM containing SQL Server in the CD ROM drive and select Run. Enter the drive letter that corresponds to the CD ROM drive (e.g., d:), and select OK. The system responds with a list of folders for different environments, such as Alpha, Clients, I386, Mips, Odbc_sdk, Ppc, Ptk, and Sqlbks65. For example, open the I386 folder by double clicking on it to install SQL Server under an Intel platform. Find the setup icon and click on it. Click on the Continue button to get past the welcome window that appears. On the first installation of SQL Server, you will be prompted to enter your name and organization information. The product ID is typically found on a small label attached to the back of the CD ROM case. There are three versions of SQL Server: desktop, standard, and enterprise.

Follow the instructions that appear in the active window. The following options are available:

Install SQL Server and utilities. Select this option to install SQL Server and commonly used utilities. This is the option to use on the first use of the CD ROM.

Upgrade SQL Server. Select this option if an earlier version of SQL Server is installed on the system.

Install utilities only. Select this option to install the utilities, without the database. This can be done if the utilities were removed or not initially installed.

Change network support. Select this option to change the network infrastructure support.

Add a language. Select this option to add support for a different human language (e.g., French).

Rebuild the master database. Select this option to rebuild the master database if it has become corrupted or erroneously changed.

Set server options. Select this option to modify the root directory (c:\mssql by default), master database path (c:\mssql\data\master.dat by default), or error log path (c:\mssql\log\errorlog by default). The suboptions allow toggling of starting the server at boot time, auto-starting the executive at boot time, auto-starting the mail client, Windows NT event logging, and SQL performance monitor integration.

Click on the Change Options button to initiate the changes immediately. This change will not affect the data in the SQL Server engine.

Set security options. Select this option to set the security options. This window allows the login security mode to be established as standard, Windows NT integrated, or mixed. A login ID and domain can also be established. An audit level can be established to audit successful or failed logins. It is also possible to identify mappings between characters.

Remove SQL Server. Select this option to remove SQL Server from the environment. This approach is preferable to other manual methods of removing the engine. The reason for this is that other methods may recover the disk space occupied by the tool; however, the Windows environment still believes that SQL Server is installed on the computer system. In the version of the software that was tested, you will be prompted with another Window and asked whether to proceed. Removal of SQL Server takes a few seconds. You must remove the file setup.exe manually.

Reinstallation of SQL Server can then be done in one of two ways: on top of the existing SQL Server programs or from scratch into a new environment.

Click on the text corresponding to the desired radio button option (e.g., click anywhere on Install SQL Server and Utilities) and click on the Continue button to display the corresponding window to proceed with the option.

Installation Options

Table 1.3 explains options that can be selected at SQL Server installation during the execution of the setup program. Generally the default options are acceptable for most installations. However, in some cases, for performance reasons, customized options can provide much needed improvements in application performance. Many of the options can be modified after installation, however, this generally requires the master database and user databases to be rebuilt. Use the SETUP program to change the configuration after SQL Server is installed.

Client and Server on the Same Platform

Microsoft SQL Server can be installed on a stand-alone platform. Select the Install SQL Server and Utilities button and click on the Continue button. A basic installation that uses the NFS file format with no external clients is the simplest way to get started using the product quickly and is sufficient for the examples in this book.

Client and Server on Different Platforms

The primary difference between implementing SQL Server on a single platform versus a distributed environment is the need to prepare the client platforms in the latter case. The client platform will typically have a front-end application development tool installed, such as Visual Basic or Visual C++. Clients communicate with SQL Server through the network using one of the protocols shown in Table 1.3.

Table 1.3 Installation Options

OPTION	DESCRIPTION
Licensing mode	Per server licensing: can do a one time change to per seat licensing. Charges are based on the number of users able to connect to the server. The server limits the connections centrally. Per seat licensing: charges are based on each supported seat.
Master device positioning	This is the master database that contains system tables, information about the entire database, and system procedures in earlier versions of SQL Server. The default location is c:\MSSQL\DATA. The physical name of the master database is master.dat. Minimum size is 25 MB. This should be increased if there is an expectation to add more tables, datatypes, or stored procedures. A size of 35 MB is recommended by the author.
Installation path	Default path is C:\MSSQL
Character sets	The default character set specifies the combination of numbers, letters, and special symbols that are supported by SQL Server. The character sets available for installation include **ISO 8859-1.** This is the default character set. It is used for compatibility with Sybase. **Code page 850.** This character set supports multiple languages for European, North American, and South American countries. **Code page 437.** This character set supports enhanced U.S. English characters.
Sort orders	It is possible to specify case-sensitive sort orders. On the whole these are slower than a nonsensitive sort order. Information is stored in the SQL Server environment (e.g., system databases, system tables, user tables, result sets) based on the sort order that is selected. The sort order can be changed after installation. This also requires the master database to be rebuilt and the user databases to be unloaded, re-created, and reloaded. In general, changing the sort order after installation is an expensive operation.
Network support	Named pipes are the default option. It is possible to select additional Net Libraries from the following list: Multi-Protocol, NWLink IPX/SPX, TCP/IP sockets, Banyan VINES, AppleTalk ADSP, and DECnet sockets.
Auto-start options	The default is a manual start-up of SQL Server and SQL Executive. This can be changed so that both these servers start up automatically when the NT system is brought up.

NT Server Is not the Same as NT Client

The Windows SQL Server engine should be installed under NT Server if it is intended to support client platforms within the application environment. It is also possible to install SQL Server under NT Client in a stand-alone configuration. SQL Server can also be installed under Windows 95 and Windows 98. Client platforms that issue service requests to SQL Server can run a more diverse range of operating systems including NT Server, NT Client, Windows 95, Windows 98, and Windows 3.x.

After Successful Installation

A successful installation updates the Windows NT Registry with the following key: HKEY_LOCAL_MACHINE\software\Microsoft\server_nm. A successful installation creates the following applications in a Windows environment. These can be seen either as a folder or as an option in the Start menu. The relevant components available in the SQL Server menu structure include Books Online, Client Network Utility, Enterprise Manager, MSDTC Administrative Console, Profiler, Query Analyzer, Server Network Utility, and Service Manager. These applications are explored in more detail later in this chapter. Table 1.4 shows the databases that are created by the installation. Each database

Table 1.4   Default Databases after Installation

DATABASE NAME	PHYSICAL DATA FILES (DATA + LOG FILES)	MINIMUM INSTALL SIZE	DESCRIPTION
Master	Master.mdf Mastlog.ldf	9.0 MB	The master database contains logical information about the database environment.
Model	Model.mdf Modellog.ldf	2.0 MB	The model database is the template that is used to build user-defined databases. Any changes made to the model database are propagated to the databases created subsequent to the change.
Msdb	Msdbdata.mdf Msdblog.ldf	4.5 MB	Contains alert and job information.
Tempdb	Tempdb.mdf Templog.ldf	9.0 MB	The temporary database is a very active area. It is used as working storage by many commands, such as sorts, group by, and order by. It is also possible to create temporary tables and procedures in this area.
Pubs	Pubs.mdf Pubs_log.ldf	2.0 MB	This is a sample application.
Northwind	Northwnd.mdf Northwnd.ldf	9.0 MB	This is a sample application.

has a physical data file (.mdf extension) and a corresponding log file (.ldf extension). The minimum install size combines the size of the database file and the log file.

 Client/Server installations can occur on a single machine. In such an event, the client and server separation is logical rather than geographical. This is entirely consistent with the client/server model.

A successful SQL Server installation on a Server platform creates a physical Mssql7 (you can override this name) directory under the root. Table 1.5 shows the important level 1 subdirectories that are created under \Mssql7.

Note that the executable files in the binn subdirectory correspond to the applications that are described later in this chapter. For example, Sqlmangr is the executable for SQL Server Service Manager and Sqlservr is SQL Server. Some of these applications can also be invoked by double clicking on their names in the Windows NT Explorer. Some dependent applications will not start using this technique; however, the operating system displays an appropriate error message if you make such an attempt.

Upgrading from a Previous Version of SQL Server

Most SQL Server features are available automatically, thus allowing the process of upgrading to be done incrementally. SQL Server databases prior to version 6 should first be upgraded to SQL Server 6.5. To upgrade SQL Server 6.5 to SQL Server 7, unload the data from your current databases and reload the data into the SQL Server 7 databases. This is required because of the new row-level locking capability in SQL Server 7. This can take a great deal of time and may have to be done on a weekend or at night. However, tests have shown that the upgrade process is very efficient, so do not be surprised if it takes a fraction of the allocated time. SQL Server 7 also offers a better storage architecture in terms of efficiency, so your converted database may require up to 30 percent less space. A general rule of thumb is to allocate about 1 hour for every 1 GB of data being converted. You can expect to get better performance by improving the hardware on the system. SQL Server is packaged with a Version Upgrade Wizard that should be used to upgrade from SQL Server 6.5 to SQL Server 7. The upgrade wizard performs a checksum calculation to ensure that the data is transferred correctly.

When upgrading from version 6.5 to version 7, keep a DB6.5 compatibility level for user-defined databases. System databases should be set to version 7's compatibility levels with the new system procedure sp_dbcmptlevel 65. Most SQL Server 7 commands are enabled for user databases even if they are left at a version 6.5 compatibility level.

The following steps should be followed to upgrade a version 6.5 server to version 7:

1. Backup current database.
2. Increase resources and establish settings.
3. Upgrade databases.
4. Check permissions.
5. Check output logs.

Table 1.5 SQL Server Subdirectory Structure

SUBDIRECTORY NAME	DESCRIPTION
Backup	Contains backup copies of files.
Bin	Contains protocol files.
Binn	Contains application and utility executables, including isql, bcp, Sqltrace, Sqlservr, Sqlmangr, Webwiz70.
Books Server.	Contains online information and literature on SQL
Charsets	Supports a combination of character sets that can be selected at installation time.
Data	Contains the database and log files after installation. The extension of the files is .mdf or .ldf. For example, Master.mdf is the physical repository for the master database. Mastlog.ldf is the repository for the master database log file. Other files in this directory include Model.mdf and Modellog.ldf for the model database and model database log, respectively. Msdbdata.mdf and Msdblog.ldf for the Msdb database contains scheduling information and support for SQL Executive. Tempdb.data and Templog.dat are the temporary database and associated log file, respectively.
Include	Contains include files.
Lib	Contains library files.
Log	Contains error log files. Previous log files are archived by a sequence numeric extension. Browse these files for error information about an SQL Server session.
Repldata	Contains replicated data.
Samples	Contains samples for a variety of environments including DBLib and Odbc.
Snmp	Contains the Mssqlmib file.
Symbols	Contains system files.
Upgrade	Contains applications to upgrade from previous versions of the product.
Install	Installation files for SQL Server. This includes Transact-SQL scripts and commands to create and populate the system databases and contents. It is possible to browse many of these files and view the Transact-SQL code as examples.

6. Run system procedures.

7. Set compatibility levels.

8. Plan for removal of SQL Server 6.5 from the hard disk.

9. Configure the new SQL Server environment.

 Use chkupg.exe from the operating system or from graphical tools to inspect the capability of a data server environment. Display the results from running this command.

Installing Microsoft Visual Database Tools

After installing SQL Server, it is useful to install supporting tools or utilities such as the Microsoft Visual Database Tools. This tool set is packaged with some versions of SQL Server and with other Microsoft Visual Suites. It requires Microsoft Internet Explorer 3 to install correctly. Internet Explorer can be found and downloaded from the Microsoft Web site (www.microsoft.com) and must be installed on the platform before Visual Database Tools can be successfully installed. A successful installation of this product will update the Start menu options, allowing the tool to be selected graphically.

To use the Microsoft Visual Database Tools application, it is necessary to create a connection to SQL Server. This is done by selecting New-Project from a pulldown menu. Ensure that the Projects tab is selected and enter a Project Name. Enter any valid name and select a location on the disk drive for physical storage. Press OK to proceed to the next dialogue.

Press the New button beside the DSN name and select the SQL Server driver. Enter a name for the source and write down the location of the driver so that it can be selected for other projects. Select the Next button until a dialogue that prompts for the Server name appears on the screen. Enter the name of the active SQL Server, which in this example is Server-01. Any description can be entered in the Description field. Press the Enter key to proceed to the next dialogue. For simplicity, trusted security can be selected to simplify the logon process. Press the Next button to proceed to the next dialogue box where you can modify the default database. Click on the Change the default database to checkbox and select Master as the default database. Leave the other values alone and press the Next button until the ODBC Microsoft SQL Server Setup dialogue appears. Click on the Test Data Source button to ensure that a valid connection can be established. Press OK to complete the operation, which will create a data source in the Select Data Source dialogue box. Select the data source that was just created so that it appears in the DSN Name field. Press the OK button. Notice that the project that was just created appears in the hierarchy on the left of the Microsoft Developer Studio.

Starting Microsoft SQL Server

From the Windows NT Server environment, SQL Server can be started through one of the components available through the SQL Server menu options. SQL Server start-up and stop operations are controlled through an easy to understand traffic light metaphor. To start the engine, select the SQL Service Manager option to display the window shown in Figure 1.3. Use your mouse to click on the Start/Continue option to start SQL Server. If the envi-

Figure 1.3   SQL Server Manager dialogue.

ronment is sound, and SQL Server was successfully installed, the green light will go bright showing that the server is active. It is possible to select specific SQL Servers in a multi-server environment by selecting a service from the pulldown menu. (See Figure 1.3.)

SQL Server can also be configured to start automatically when the operating system is booted. This is done through an SQL Server installation option or through operating system commands. Microsoft SQL Server can be started in several basic modes: automatic, manual, and single-user. The first two are used most often, the difference being how they are started. The single-user mode is used for some administrative purposes, for example, when recovering a master database that is corrupted.

Stopping Microsoft SQL Server

SQL Server is stopped by selecting the SQL Service Manager option and double clicking on the Stop option with the name of the database server selected. Another method of shutting down the server is to use the Shutdown command from the Query Analyzer (formerly ISQL/w) dialogue. Shutting the computer down without a standard shutdown causes SQL Server to undergo exception processing when it is restarted, including rolling the transaction logs forward.

Inspecting the Errorlog File

A text-based session/errorlog file is maintained by SQL Server throughout a session. Different session logs are separated by sequential numbers. These files are stored in the \mssql\log directory by default. The log files have a root name of errorlog. Older versions of Errorlog have a name of the form errorlog.x, where x starts at 1 and increases sequentially. The current errorlog file does not have a suffix and is locked while SQL Server is running. Figure 1.4 is a sample errorlog. It is a good practice to review this file because it contains valuable information. SQL Server tests each database and flags errors if they are encountered. The date and time stamp provides statistical information concerning the length of time the actions require.

```
98/08/13 17:57:43.28 kernel  Microsoft SQL Server 7.00-7.00.517 (Intel
                                                                   X86)

   Jun 19 1998 17:06:54
   Copyright (c) 1988-1998 Microsoft Corporation
   Enterprise version on Windows

98/08/13 17:57:43.51 kernel  Copyright © 1988-1997 Microsoft
                                                       Corporation.
98/08/13 17:57:43.54 kernel  All rights reserved.
98/08/13 17:57:43.56 kernel  Logging SQL Server messages in file
'C:\MSSQL7\log\ERRORLOG'.
98/08/13 17:57:43.72 kernel  initconfig: Number of user connections
                                         limited to 32767.
98/08/13 17:57:43.76 kernel  SQL Server is starting at priority class
                                         'normal'(1 CPU detected).
98/08/13 17:57:44.05 kernel  User Mode Scheduler configured for thread
                                                          processing
98/08/13 17:57:46.58 server  Directory Size: 2559
98/08/13 17:57:46.89 spid1   Using dynamic lock allocation. [2500] Lock
                                  Blocks, [5000] Lock Owner Blocks
98/08/13 17:57:46.91 kernel  Attempting to initialize Distributed
                                         Transaction Coordinator.
98/08/13 17:57:53.44 spid1   Starting up database 'master'.
98/08/13 17:57:53.48 spid1   Opening file C:\MSSQL7\data\master.mdf.
98/08/13 17:57:53.60 spid1   Opening file C:\MSSQL7\data\mastlog.ldf.
98/08/13 17:57:53.98 spid1   Loading SQL Server's Unicode collation.
98/08/13 17:57:54.21 spid1   Loading SQL Server's non-Unicode sort order
                                         and character set.
98/08/13 17:57:54.74 spid1   Starting up database 'model'.
98/08/13 17:57:54.76 spid1   Opening file C:\MSSQL7\DATA\model.mdf.
98/08/13 17:57:54.94 spid1   Opening file c:\mssql7\data\modellog.ldf.
98/08/13 17:57:55.36 spid1   1 transactions rolled forward in database
                                         'model' (3).
98/08/13 17:57:55.37 spid1   0 transactions rolled back in database
                                         'model' (3).
98/08/13 17:57:55.52 spid1   Clearing tempdb database.
98/08/13 17:57:55.83 spid1   Creating file C:\MSSQL7\DATA\TEMPDB.MDF.
98/08/13 17:57:56.18 spid1   Closing file C:\MSSQL7\DATA\TEMPDB.MDF.
98/08/13 17:57:56.35 spid1   Creating file C:\MSSQL7\DATA\TEMPLOG.LDF.
98/08/13 17:57:56.42 spid1   Closing file C:\MSSQL7\DATA\TEMPLOG.LDF.
98/08/13 17:57:56.78 spid1   Opening file C:\MSSQL7\DATA\TEMPDB.MDF.
98/08/13 17:57:56.83 spid1   Opening file C:\MSSQL7\DATA\TEMPLOG.LDF.
98/08/13 17:57:57.69 spid1   Closing file C:\MSSQL7\DATA\TEMPDB.MDF.
98/08/13 17:57:57.80 spid1   Closing file C:\MSSQL7\DATA\TEMPLOG.LDF.
98/08/13 17:57:57.90 spid1   Starting up database 'tempdb'.
```

(Continues)

Figure 1.4   Sample ErrorLog.

```
98/08/13 17:57:57.92 spid1  Opening file C:\MSSQL7\DATA\TEMPDB.MDF.
98/08/13 17:57:58.01 spid1  Opening file C:\MSSQL7\DATA\TEMPLOG.LDF.
98/08/13 17:57:58.42 spid1  Server name is 'CATOR2W207'.
98/08/13 17:57:58.63 spid6  Starting up database 'msdb'.
98/08/13 17:57:58.69 spid6  Opening file C:\MSSQL7\DATA\msdbdata.mdf.
98/08/13 17:57:59.15 spid6  Opening file c:\mssql7\DATA\msdblog.ldf.
98/08/13 17:57:59.28 ods    Using 'SSMSSH70.DLL' version '7.0.517' to
                                              listen on ''.
98/08/13 17:57:59.46 ods    Using 'SSMSSO70.DLL' version '7.0.517' to
                                              listen on '1433'.
98/08/13 17:57:59.60 ods    Using 'SSMSRP70.DLL' version '7.0.517' to
                                              listen on 'CATOR2W207'.
98/08/13 17:58:02.56 spid7  Starting up database 'pubs'.
98/08/13 17:58:02.74 spid7  Opening file C:\MSSQL7\DATA\pubs.mdf.
98/08/13 17:58:03.32 spid7  Opening file c:\mssql7\DATA\pubs_log.ldf.
98/08/13 17:58:04.64 spid7  1 transactions rolled forward in database
                                              'pubs' (5).
98/08/13 17:58:04.79 spid7  0 transactions rolled back in database
                                              'pubs' (5).
98/08/13 17:58:04.91 spid8  Starting up database 'Northwind'.
98/08/13 17:58:05.03 spid8  Opening file C:\MSSQL7\DATA\northwnd.mdf.
98/08/13 17:58:05.35 spid8  Opening file C:\MSSQL7\DATA\northwnd.ldf.
98/08/13 17:58:06.22 spid8  1 transactions rolled forward in database
                                              'Northwind' (6).
98/08/13 17:58:06.24 spid8  0 transactions rolled back in database
                                              'Northwind' (6).
98/08/13 17:58:07.05 spid6  8 transactions rolled forward in database
                                              'msdb' (4).
98/08/13 17:58:07.06 spid6  0 transactions rolled back in database
                                              'msdb' (4).
98/08/13 17:58:07.24 spid1  Recovery complete.
98/08/13 17:58:07.38 spid1  SQL Server's Unicode collation is:
98/08/13 17:58:07.41 spid1      'English' (ID = 1033).
98/08/13 17:58:07.45 spid1      comparison style = 196609.
98/08/13 17:58:07.48 spid1  SQL Server's non-Unicode sort order is:
98/08/13 17:58:07.51 spid1      'nocase_iso' (ID = 52).
98/08/13 17:58:07.54 spid1  SQL Server's non-Unicode character set is:
98/08/13 17:58:07.56 spid1      'iso_1' (ID = 1).
98/08/13 17:58:07.69 kernel Warning: override, autoexec procedures skipped.
98/08/13 18:50:54.20 spid1  Closing file C:\MSSQL7\DATA\northwnd.mdf.
98/08/13 18:50:54.53 spid1  Closing file C:\MSSQL7\DATA\northwnd.ldf.
98/08/13 18:50:55.37 spid1  Closing file C:\MSSQL7\DATA\pubs.mdf.
98/08/13 18:50:56.06 spid1  Closing file c:\mssql7\DATA\pubs_log.ldf.
98/08/13 18:50:56.92 spid1  Closing file C:\MSSQL7\DATA\msdbdata.mdf.
98/08/13 18:50:57.38 spid1  Closing file c:\mssql7\DATA\msdblog.ldf.
```

Figure 1.4 *(Continued)*

Signing On

It is only possible to sign on to Microsoft SQL Server if the engine has been started and is running in the operating system environment. Several methods are available to sign on and issue requests to SQL Server, as shown in Table 1.6.

 Microsoft SQL Server and Sybase SQL Server historically share the same engine, but there have always been differences. For example, Sybase SQL Server uses the syntax isql-Uuserid-Ppassword to sign on. The minor difference in the syntax between the two products is the use of the "-" in Sybase and the "/" in Microsoft SQL Server.

Administrative Applications

This section describes some of the more useful user-friendly visual tools that are installed as part of the SQL Server setup process. The applications provide a graphical and user-friendly method of interacting with the SQL Server. An interactive alternate method usually exists to work directly with SQL Server without going through the user-friendly tool. However, the first method is easier to learn, more intuitive, and generally

Table 1.6 Signing onto SQL Server

METHOD	DESCRIPTION	ACTIONS
ISQL utility	This is a text-based interactive utility that is the underlying engine of the more advanced methods of executing SQL and Transact SQL commands and system procedures.	Transfer control to the operating systemprompt by selecting the Start button and finding the icon to bring up DOS.Type: isql **/U**userid **/P**password **/i**file.txt (e.g., isql **/U**sa **/P**password **/ i**script1.txt)isql uses the DB-Library interface. isql can be replaced with osql which uses the ODBC interface.
SQL Server Query Analyzer	This interactive GUI utility allows execution of SQL and Transact SQL commands and systems procedures. The results appear in a tab within the overall dialogue window. Another tab allows manipulation of query and trace flags. This was formerly the isql/w utility.	Select File-Connect from the main menu to display a Connect to SQL Server prompt. Enter the name of the database server for the connection, which in this example is Server-01. The List Servers button can be used to select from a list of database servers. Choose one of the Connection options (e.g., stick with the default). Enter "sa" as the login name. Leave the password. This is shown in Figure 1.5. Click on the Connect button.

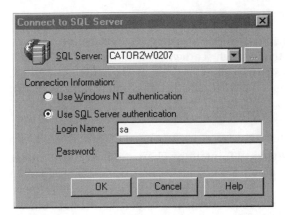

Figure 1.5 Connect to SQL Server.

faster when it is mastered. Each of these important SQL Server Administrative tools are discussed later in this book.

Microsoft SQL Server Service Manager

The SQL Server Service Manager is used to start, pause, and stop SQL Server applications, namely SQL Server Agent, SQL Servers, and MSDTC. This is an intuitive interface that uses a traffic light metaphor. By default the application itself is found under Start-Programs-Microsoft SQL Server-SQL Server Service Manager. Selecting this option displays the dialogue box shown in Figure 1.6. The Server list box displays the names of the servers that are available on the system. The Services list box displays a list of services that can be selected. In this example, the name of SQL Server was established as Server-01 at installation time. This is selected in the figure. The service to start the server is MSSQLSERVER, which is also selected in this example. Double click on Start/Continue (green light) to start the server. Under normal circumstances, the green light will be selected and SQL Server will start to run.

The hypertext at the bottom of the dialogue box reflects the successful launch of SQL Server; in this example it reads

Figure 1.6 SQL Server Service Manager.

```
\\SERVER-01 - MSSQLServer - Running
```

Once SQL Server is running, the SQL Server Service Manager dialogue box can be closed by clicking the "x" symbol in the top right corner of the box. The traffic light metaphor is still visible in the Windows status line. A server can also be paused by clicking on the Pause option (yellow light) or shut down by clicking on the Stop option (red light).

SQL Server Query Analyzer

The SQL Server Query Analyzer is a graphical form of the character-based ISQL utility with a few more integrated tools. In previous versions of SQL Server it was called ISQL/w. This application supports execution of any command statements that can be issued directly through the character-based ISQL command. Under the default installation, this application is available under Start-Programs-Microsoft SQL Server-SQL Server Query Analyzer. Selecting this option displays the Connect to SQL Server dialogue which is used to connect to an active server, as shown in Figure 1.7. As shown in this example, Server-01, which was started using the SQL Service Manager, is selected in the pulldown list. Selecting the Use Windows NT Authentication will activate Windows trusted security. Selecting Use SQL Server Authentication requires entry of a login name and password. This example uses the installation defaults for both of these fields. Login name is sa (system administrator). The password is empty by default. The List Servers option displays the available servers. Clicking on the Connect button creates the link between the application and the active SQL Server.

The SQL Server Query Analyzer application, as shown in Figure 1.8, appears after a successful logon. This application consists of a large dialogue window and a nested dialogue that has three tabs. There is also a pulldown menu and a toolbar. The default toolbar options allow a query to be cleared, a script to be loaded from disk, a query to be saved, query options to be established, a database to be selected, the current query to be executed, a result set to be cleared, a query to be executed, an SQL Statement Execution Plan to be displayed, and the execution of a running query to be halted.

The three tabs on the Query Analyzer are Query, Results, and Plan. The Query tab is used to issue requests to SQL Server. SQL Server displays the results to the active query in the Results tab. The third tab, Plan, displays the SQL Statement Execution Plan. The

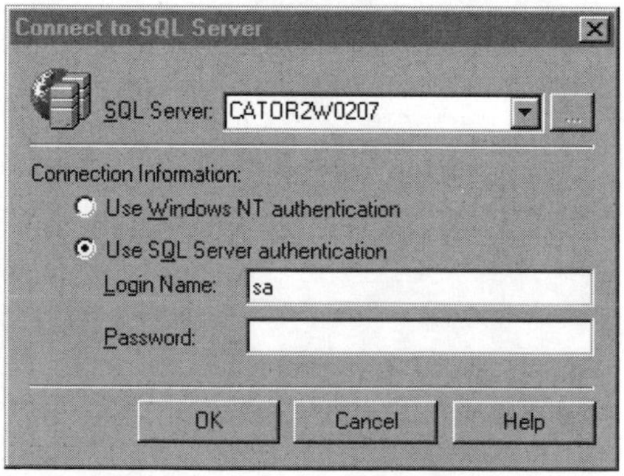

Figure 1.7 Connect to SQL Server.

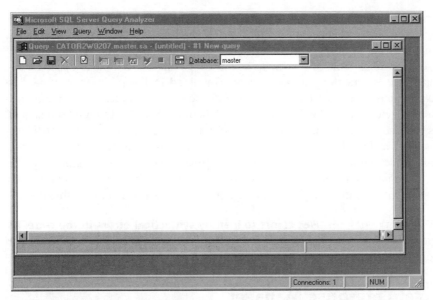

Figure 1.8   SQL Server Query Analyzer.

latter displays the graphical execution plan in the Plan tab. Clicking on the graphics drills down into further details. This command can be invoked through the Query-Execute With Graphical Showplan option from the pulldown menus.

The Query pulldown option also contains several other useful commands when the Query tab is selected (on top of the others). The Object Help option searches the default database for the object that is selected. For example, typing sysobjects, selecting it, and choosing Query-Object Help displays information about the sysobjects system table, as well as its fields, datatypes, lengths, and null acceptability. The other command, Query-Set Options, displays a dialogue that allows options to inspect statistics about queries to be established.

The options in this dialogue fall into two groups: query flags and format options. Query options include No Count Display, No Execute, Parse Query Only, Show Query Plan, and Show Stats Time. The No Execute option is useful in evaluating the cost and plan of a query without the risk of executing it (and possibly bringing down the server). Show Query Plan and Show Stats Time are useful in evaluating query plans. Another option that can be set using this dialogue is rowcount. When the value is 0, all the rows in response to a query are returned. A value greater than 0 places a limit on the number of rows that are returned by a query. This is useful in many instances. Some queries can literally return hundreds or thousands of rows. In other cases, it is useful to only return the first 10 or 20 rows of sorted data. A final example is a scrolling application that can only accept a screen full of information at a time. Format Options allows customization of the results through such options as Result Output Format, Right Align Numerics, Print Headers, and Output Query. Result Output Format establishes the format of the printed data, allowing column alignment and delimiters. Selecting Print Headers causes column headings to print in the output. Selecting Output Query prints the original SQL query in the output.

You can use the Query Analyzer as a text editor. The text can be coded directly into the top window and saved using the File-Save As option from the pulldown menu. If you only want to execute a portion of the code that is displayed in the window, highlight the text and select the execute button or choose Query-Execute Query from the main pulldown menu.

Sometimes it is necessary to repeatedly issue different SQL commands during a development cycle. An example of this might be inserting data into a table and issuing another command to select the number of rows contained in the table. Of course it is possible to type one command, execute it, clear the screen type in a second command, clear the screen, and reenter the first command. A better method is to type both sets of commands into the save screen. Using the mouse, only the commands that are to be executed should be highlighted, and the Query-Execute (or click on the Execute button) option should be selected. Executing the second command then requires highlighting the appropriate commands and repeating the execution sequence. The first set of commands can be reissued without any rekeying by changing the commands that are highlighted.

 The query analyzer uses colors to identify syntactical errors in the code. As you code Transact-SQL statements in this tool, watch for colors that flag for potential syntactical mismatches.

SQL Server Enterprise Manager

This application is used to administer SQL Server and is a snap on to the Microsoft Management Console (MMC). Figure 1.9 shows the functions that can be administered with

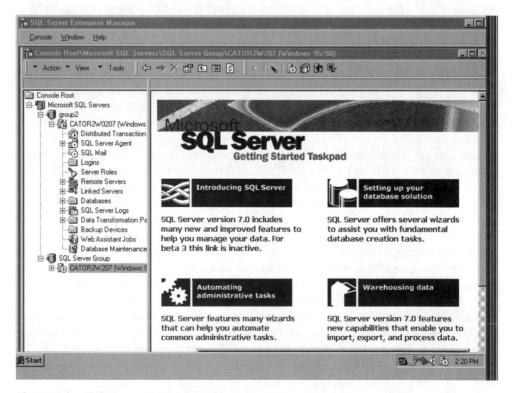

Figure 1.9   SQL Server Enterprise Manager.

this dialogue. This includes creating and maintaining database objects such as databases, tables, stored procedures, and triggers. The figure shows an expanded version of the contents of an SQL Server in the left hierarchy. The options shown on the right side of the screen can be selected. This application is also used to register the server and maintain user profiles. Although the majority of the functions offered by this utility can be performed with a combination of the Query Analyzer (SQL/w) and batch commands in the operating system, the Enterprise Manager simplifies the interface and offers DBAs a consistent method for completing their job functions. It is more object-oriented in its operation than the previous versions of the tool. Some of the version 6.5 functionality has moved to the Visual Database Tools application.

Selecting one of the database objects in the left hierarchy shows an additional level of detail for that type of object. For example, selecting the database level displays the databases that are available in the environment. This is shown in Figure 1.10. This example contains several databases that were created with the Create Database Wizard.

Selecting one of the databases displays the dialogue box shown in Figure 1.11. This is a very useful feature that can be used instead of several system procedures. The panels in this folder provide a view of such things as the tables contained within the database, the size of the database, the amount of free space available, and details about the transaction log. This is a huge improvement over earlier versions of SQL Server that required the use of multiple commands to produce the same information.

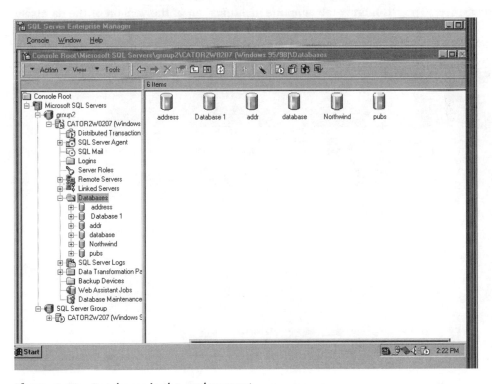

Figure 1.10 Databases in the environment.

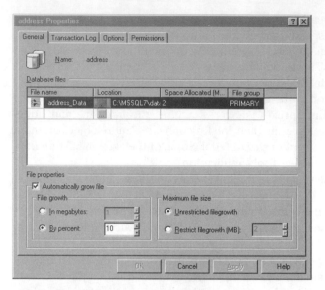

Figure 1.11 Details about a database.

SQL Server Client Network Utility

This dialogue consists of three tabs, DB Library, Net Library, and Advanced, as shown in Figure 1.12. The DB Library tab supports identification of the version of the database middleware that links an application to the Net Library. The Net Library tab supports identification of the Net Library software. It also supports identification of the default

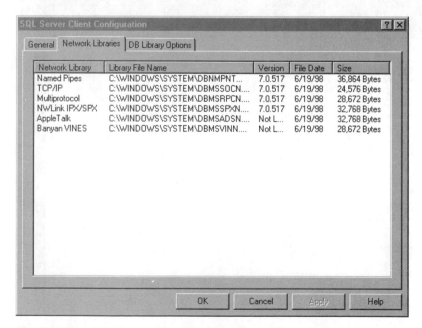

Figure 1.12 SQL Server Client configuration utility.

network (e.g., Named Pipes, TCP/IP Sockets, and Banyan Vines). The Advanced Tab supports identification of servers, DLLS, and a connection string.

SQL Performance Monitor

As shown in Figure 1.13, this application reports performance statistics about SQL Server in a graphical format. This is another tool for database administrators to use in analyzing the SQL Server environment. The pulldown menu supports alerts, logs, and reports. Data for the chart can be displayed from the current server or from a log file. Charts can also be exported to files.

SQL Server Profiler

As shown in Figure 1.14, this application can be used to trace events in a database server. This application was called SQL Trace in SQL Server 6.5. The General tab must be used to start using this application. It is necessary to enter a mnemonic name and a source to establish a trace. This will prompt you to register a database server name (e.g., Server-01 with an sa logon ID). The results of a trace can be displayed on the screen or saved into a file. The Events tab is used to identify the events that are captured by this application as they occur in the registered database server. Some examples of these events are Connect, Disconnect, ExistingConnection, RPC:Starting, ErrorLog, Insert, and Delete. The Trace Criteria tab is used to identify the event criteria, including an Application Name, ConnectionID, CPU, Database ID, Duration, Event Text, Host Name,

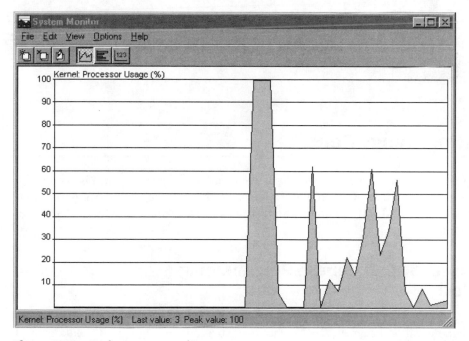

Figure 1.13 Performance monitor.

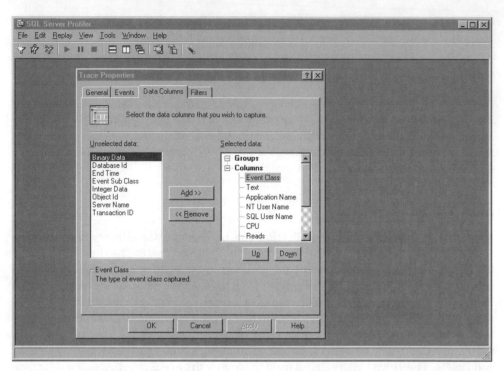

Figure 1.14 SQL Server Profiler.

Host Process ID, NT Domain Name, Index ID, Object ID, Owner ID, Reads, Writes, Severity, SPID, and SQL User Name. The last tab, Output Data, is used to select data from the previous list.

Getting Things Done

A variety of methods are available to issue commands or requests in the Microsoft SQL Server environment. A few examples are discussed here, however, the two-part primer starting in Chapter 3 and extending into Chapter 4 provides a more detailed discussion of this topic.

Transact-SQL: Database Programming Dialect

Transact-SQL is the programming language built into the SQL Server engine. It consists of a data definition language (DDL), data manipulation language (DML), data control language (DCL), and control-of-flow language. The control-of-flow language consists of programming constructs such as if, while, case, and built-in functions. Transact-SQL also supports database objects such as stored procedures, triggers, views, cursors, datatypes, and user-defined datatypes. Transact-SQL is accompanied by system procedures that interact with the SQL Server environment and the system tables.

Transact-SQL was introduced with the first commercially available version of SQL Server in 1987. It has been consistently enhanced with new releases of the product. For example, the first version of SQL Server did not support interstored procedure communication through updated parameter values. In fact, stored procedures could not update parameter values from the calling stored procedure. This required creative programming through the creation of temporary tables to hold values that different stored procedures were required to access. This required a lot more table reads and writes.

The Transact-SQL syntax is based on the ANSI SQL '92 dialect. This dialect supports extensions to the standard but is based primarily on Sequel. Application partitioning has always been a problem with client/server applications and will continue to be a lesser problem with network applications. The reason for this is that the client dialogue is traditionally not the same as the database server programming dialect. This means that once a module is designed and programmed to reside on the client or the database server, it is not possible to move the module between these two tiers because of the programming language inconsistencies. There is a chance that Microsoft may choose VBA-Script as the Transact-SQL standard syntax to act as a host to standard Sequel DDL, DML, and DCL dialects and for the extensions. While this will not allow stored procedures to be more portable between database products, such as SQL Server and Oracle, the change will allow greater code reuse between the client and the server tiers within a Microsoft environment.

Finding Out Who's Using the System

In a multiuser environment, it is necessary to identify users who are consuming SQL Server resources and to communicate with them in the event that the environment must be modified. A system procedure, sp_who, locates this information in the system tables and displays it to the requester. System procedures are a set of utilities or programs that interact with the Microsoft SQL Server environment and system tables to perform useful housekeeping functions and report on SQL Server internals. To test this system procedure you must log into an active SQL Server engine. This command can be executed from the SQL Server Query dialogue. The command sp_who is typed in the Query tab, the command is highlighted with the mouse, and the execute option is selected from the toolbar. The results of these actions are shown in Figure 1.15.

Finding Your Way around the Microsoft SQL Server Environment

Commands issued in the SQL Server environment operate on the default database(s). It is also possible to qualify a command or destination with a path that consists of

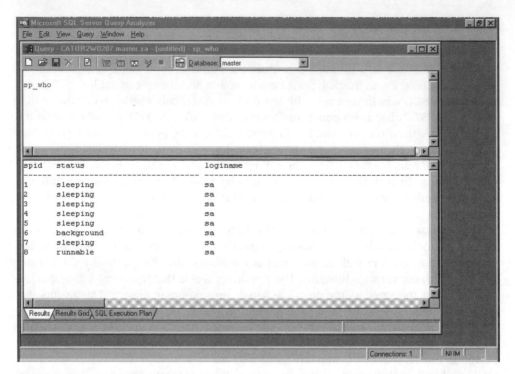

Figure 1.15   sp_who results.

server.database.owner.object. For example, pubs.dbo.stores references the stores table that is owned by the dbo in the pubs database. The database and owner are not required if you are the owner of a database object, and if the database is in the path. For example, suppose that the default database is Master. The command Select * from stores displays the following message: Invalid object name stores. This is because the stores table cannot be found by SQL Server, even though it exists in the pubs database. The table is found by providing a complete path, as follows: Select * from pubs.dbo.stores. We could also locate the table with the command Select * from pubs..stores.

Limitations and Ceilings

Microsoft SQL Server is capable of satisfying the requirements of the business enterprise as a whole. Many of the limits in version 6.5 have been eliminated or their capacity has been greatly increased. Table 1.7 shows the limits SQL Server places on various features of the product.

Table 1.7 Limitations and Ceilings

COMPONENT	MAXIMUM LIMIT
Databases per server	32,767
Database size	200 GB (version 6.5) 1 TB (version 7)
Device fragments	32
Tables per database	2 billion
Number of columns per table	250 (version 6.5) 1024 (version 7)
Tables in a query	16
Physical disks per databases	32
Indexes per table	249 + 1 clustered index
Characters in a database object name	30 (version 6.5) 128 (version 7)
Row length (for text data)	1962 bytes (version 6.5) 8060 bytes (version 7)
Addressable memory	2 to 3 GB
Nested stored procedure	32 (version 6.5)
Page size	2 KB (version 6.5) 8 KB (version 7)
Bytes per index, foreign key, primary key	900
Columns for group by and order by	16 (version 6.5) No column limit (but a disk size limit)
Columns per index, foreign key, primary table	16
Columns for a select	4096
Columns per insert	250 (version 6.5) 1024 (version 7)
Files/database	32 (version 6.5) 32,767 (version 7)
Nested subqueries	16 (version 6.5) 64 (version 7)
Nested trigger levels	16 (version 6.5) 32 (version 7)
An extent	8 pages (nonfragmented)
Page size	2 KB (version 6.5) 8 KB (version 7)
Foreign key constraints per table	31 (version 6.5) 63 (version 7)
Tables per Select	16 (version 6.5) 32 (version 7)

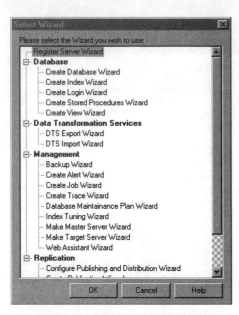

Figure 1.16   Select Wizard dialogue.

New Wizards

The new version of Microsoft SQL Server offers a plethora of helpful wizards to guide you in completing various activities. As shown in Figure 1.16, wizards are divided into broad categories that include database, data transformation services, management, and replication. Wizards are a good place to start, but eventually the graphical tools support a more power-user-oriented approach for conducting the same activities. Here is a list of the wizards that are available to you: Create Backup, Create Alert, Create Database, Create Diagram, Create Index, Create Job, Create New Data Service, Create SQL Server Login, Create Stored Procedures, Create Trace, Create View, Database Maintenance Plan, DTS Export, DTS Import, Full_text Indexing, Index Tuning, Make Master Server, Make Target Server, Register Servers, Upgrade, and Web Assistant. Chapter 3 provides examples of using some of the basic wizards. These are the wizards that are available from the primary wizards dialogue, which will probably be expanded by Microsoft over time. Other wizards are also available throughout the SQL Server environment.

It is necessary to select a server context before using the wizards. This can be done by selecting a server in the dialogue box on the right of the screen. Wizards can be invoked from the pull down menu or the menus icons on the Enterprise Manager dialogue box.

Hardware Requirements

The hardware requirements for running earlier versions of Microsoft SQL Server are the following: Intel 486+, DEC Alpha, MIPS chips, 16 MB RAM minimum, >32 MB RAM recommended; 100 MB disk space. It is possible to save some disk space by running SQL Server books from the CD ROM, NTFS, or FAT file system. SQL Server 6.5 requires Windows NT Server 3.51+. A workstation version of SQL Server can run on Windows NT Workstation 3.51+. SQL Server 7 is more demanding of resources. It requires Windows NT 4.x or higher, Windows 95 or higher, and Internet Explorer 4 or higher. My testing shows that running SQL Server 7 on anything less than a 133 MHz Pentium with 24 MB RAM is highly unproductive. Even 24 MB is underpowered and should be 64 MB or more.

Test Environment

Research for this book was completed on a variety of Intel-based platforms, including both low-end and high-end systems. Name brands of the hardware are not included in Table 1.8, as I believe that the limitations encountered during testing were more a function of the power of the hardware as opposed to the vendor.

The low-end, 75 MHz platform was capable of running Microsoft SQL Server under Windows NT 4 with one connection. Upgrading to NT 5 Beta or Windows 98 brought the performance down significantly. This required a transfer to a faster machine. Upgrading to a 133 MHz platform made a significant difference in performance. The 350 MHz system with 128 MB RAM provided a great improvement in performance that was immediately evident during the implementation process, startup, and issuing of complex queries.

Table 1.8 Experiences with Different Platforms

TECHNICAL ARCHITECTURE	EXPERIENCE
75 MHz, Windows NT, 16 MB RAM	Significant memory problems and slow performance. Significant installation problems.
Pentium, 133 MHz, 32 MB RAM	Easy installation. Acceptable performance for noncritical environments.
Pentium II, 233 MHz, 32 MB RAM	Easy installation. Good overall performance.
Pentium II, 350 MHz, 128 MB RAM	Easy installation. Excellent overall performance. My minimum preference for a development environment.

A 10 GB HARD DISK SOFTWARE INCOMPATIBILITY ISSUE?

After suffering through the poor performance on a low-end Pentium, it was necessary to upgrade the machine. I chose a 350 MHz Pentium II with a 16 GB hard disk to ensure there was more than an adequate supply of power and capacity. Installing SQL Server 7 was painless in that environment. However, an interesting concern was raised when trying to install older Windows-based software that was running well under Windows 95. A graphics package that installs and works fine under Windows 95 could not install on a disk that had 14 GB free space because it could not recognize the 14 GB of free space and instead seemed to read it as 14 MB. A possible workaround that I did not try was to install a lot of software until 999 MB of disk space was free, at which point the package could be installed.

An Ethernet LAN supported the database server and client platforms. SQL Server 6.5 and SQL Server 7 Beta were used to test the code provided in this book. The database server was executed on Windows NT Server. SQL Server was tested under Windows NT 4, Windows NT 5, Windows 95, and Windows 98.

Summary

In this chapter you were introduced to the new Microsoft SQL Server environment. Enhancements made to SQL Server 6.5 were discussed in the context of portability, interoperability, scalability, ease of use, administration, architecture, and new functionality. This chapter also examined upgrading SQL Server 6.5 or implementing SQL Server 7. The reader was also provided with a walk-through of the GUI tools, wizards, and SQL Server environment. This chapter also examined limits and ceilings on SQL Server components. The chapter concluded by describing experiences under a diverse set of test environments.

Learning the Basics of N-Tier Applications and COM

This chapter discusses n-tier application architecture and its building blocks. This architecture is enabled by Microsoft's Component Object Model (COM) specification which serves as the foundation of object linking and embedding (OLE), ActiveX, dynamic data exchange (DDE), and the emerging COM+ standard. COM's language independence allows this specification to be implemented in a number of different languages including Visual C++, Visual Basic, and Java. COM's importance to Microsoft's enterprise direction cannot be overstated. It is the driving force behind Microsoft's future strategy and it forms the underpinnings of products such as Microsoft Office and BackOffice.

N-tier architecture and component-based development are currently the popular strategic directions for systems development initiatives. This architectural combination provides a good balance between achieving reuse while retaining the ability to customize functionality during the application development life cycle in order to support business competitiveness. Reuse, scalability, and portability are the three most important features and objectives of n-tier architecture.

Reuse refers to procedures, processes, documentation, and code. In the context of this discussion, the focus rests on the reusability of code. The higher the level of reuse, the lower the future development risks and costs to a development initiative. Reuse offers the capability to borrow solutions instead of building them from scratch. This cuts out the majority of the development life cycle and most of the testing effort. The focus shifts to tuning business rules and integrating reusable components. What is an acceptable level of code reuse? How is reuse measured in terms of codes, modules, applications, and systems? These are questions that must be answered by the executive management level in an organization. There are dramatic consequences as a result of this choice. It is not a good idea to start with an unachievable objective of, say, 75 percent reuse or higher in organizations that are just beginning to implement reuse programs. A more modest number in the 30 to 50 percent range is a good target for the first few projects designed around reusability.

Scalability refers to an application's ability to accommodate increasing numbers of concurrent users, processes, and data without degrading application performance or throughput. In traditional 2-tier architecture, and even going back to the mainframe world of the 1980s, it was always an expensive operation to add more devices, more power, and more resources. Scalability in n-tier applications is supported by fewer overall resources. Another benefit of the new tiered architectures is that specific resources can be increased while others are left alone.

Portability refers to the ability to migrate an application to a different application or technical architecture with minimal changes to the code. There are always tradeoffs in achieving high levels of portability, especially in terms of development effort and application performance. N-tier architecture supports portability, and the reuse and scalability benefits compensate for the time taken to achieve the goal of application portability.

Defining Tiered Architectures

What exactly is a tier? Why is it important? To understand the answer to these questions, it is necessary to break an application down into its discrete elements. All applications consist of one or more of the following: a set of modules that interact with the user, referred to as the user interface layer; a set of modules that represent the business rules that the application is supporting—referred to as the business logic layer; and a set of modules that manage access to the database, referred to as the data services layer. The collection of modules that comprise the user interface is a tier. The collection of modules that comprise the business rules is also a tier. Similarly, the collection of modules that comprise the data services is also a tier. The level of coupling, integration, and logical distribution of each of these layers determines the value of n in n-tier. The traditional client/server model consists of some combination of a database server and a graphical development tool such as Sybase/PowerBuilder, SQL Windows/Visual Basic, or Oracle/Oracle Forms. This is referred to as a 2-tier architecture and is shown in Figure 2.1.

2-tier architecture was successful in building usable client/server applications. The popularity of client/server architecture was also fueled by the downsizing of mainframe applications. Self-contained applications were converted to a client/server platform or small systems were built to start implementing the new technology. The 2-tier model worked well for small numbers of concurrent users, say less than 100, and with a small set of transactions. However, as the need to scale to a larger number of concurrent users, say 1000, arose or the need to support an increasing number of transactions emerged, 2-tier architecture was found to lack the flexibility to satisfy those strict objectives. 2-tier client/server development has supported production applications for close to a decade. However, several problems have been identified including a limita-

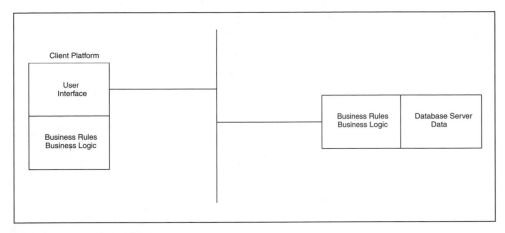

Figure 2.1   2-tier architecture.

tion on application scaling, required high network capacities because of high data transfer, and a lack of portability/interoperability. Client/server popularity was enhanced by workgroups. There are also problems with two-phase commits that affect traditional 2-tier architectures. These are rectified by a multiphase commit or commits that leverage messaging architectures.

3-tier architecture uncoupled the layers in the 2-tier model and specifically included business rules into a separate tier. This allows any of the tiers to be ported to different platforms in response to the need for more resources. 3-tier architecture continues to use the basic tools that were available for the 2-tier model, but with some notable exceptions. The most important of these is the Transaction Server, which has traditionally been the mainstay of the mainframe world through products such as CICS and Tuxedo. As shown in Figure 2.2, 3-tier architecture is effective in scaling to larger numbers of concurrent users with high volumes of data. 3-tier architecture replaces 2-tier fat clients with thin clients. The tiers are not tightly bound. With this increased ability to scale, another consideration has become the need to reuse working solutions.

Reuse in the information technology (IT) industry has been driven by comparisons to industries that grew during the last quarter of a century. The argument has been that if something like an automobile or a television set can be built from prepackaged components, then why can't the same process be used to build an application once and reuse it, much as an integrated circuit is reused. But what size application can conveniently be reused? Application packages such as PeopleSoft and SAP are examples of reuse at an aggregate level. But these do not lend themselves to what can be referred to as custom development. In particular, this approach, while valid in the markets that require them, does not satisfy the model of reusing the equivalent of an integrated circuit at the software level. To do this, each application would need to be much smaller and satisfy a limited subset of business requirements. The collection of these tiny applications would satisfy a complete business requirement. Objects and classes can satisfy this view. However, object technology is characterized by more than reuse, and in fact is commonly described by three characteristics:

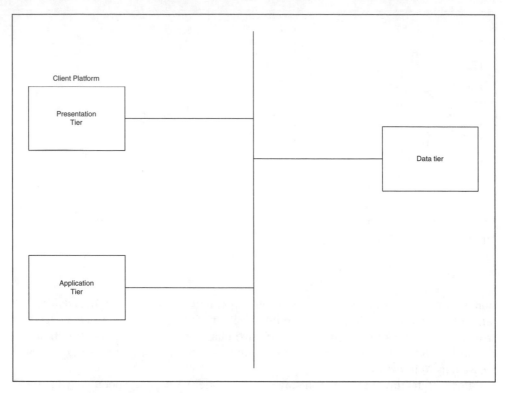

Figure 2.2   3-tier architecture.

Encapsulation. The behavior or methods of an object are available to other objects or classes through messages that are passed through an interface. The object's methods are the only way to access the data belonging to the object.

Polymorphism. The same message can be interpreted by different objects and can result in different behavior. An example of such a message can be "close door." One object may interpret this to mean to shut a hinged door, another object may send an electric signal to shut an electric door, and another object may cut an electric signal that is keeping a door open at a shopping plaza.

Inheritance. Objects acquire behaviors and attributes from higher level objects or parent objects. Changes to the behavior of a parent object are automatically inherited by the child objects.

The last characteristic, inheritance, can have side effects that are not desirable in some types of applications or in certain development environments. This is especially consistent with the fact that changes at the parent object level have an effect throughout all lower level objects inheriting the original behavior. Some teams are interested

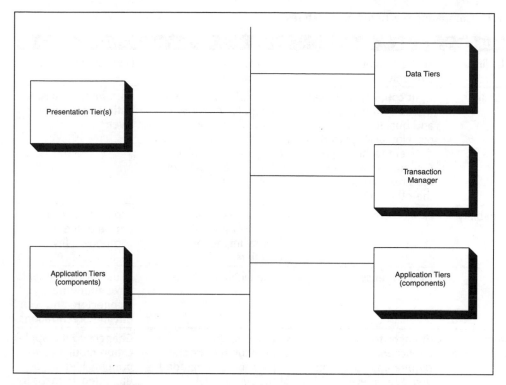

Figure 2.3 N-Tier architecture.

in leveraging encapsulation and polymorphism but do not want to leverage inheritance. A solution to this is the component. A component is objectlike, while not entirely an object. A component contains an interface that accepts and passes messages to other components. By design, a component is small, and the work that it does is very small as well. A collection of components makes an application in the traditional sense. As shown in Figure 2.3, components can be distributed throughout a 3-tier architecture.

In n-tier applications, data validation can be moved from the presentation layer or the data layer to the middle application tier.

Table 2.1 compares 2-tier, 3-tier, and n-tier architectures in the context of specific criteria that include scalability, portability, expandability, system maintenance, reuse, and response time. Notice that in some cases, the benefits from going from a 2-tier architecture to an n-tier architecture are reversed in the opposite direction. For example, the costs increase as you move from 2-tier to n-tier in the short term. However, in the longer term, the costs of 2-tier architecture turn out to be higher than the n-tier solution. Single-tier architecture is not covered in Table 2.1 because of its limited feature set. Web-based architectures are included in 3-tier architecture.

Table 2.1   Comparing the Tiered Architectures

FEATURES	2-TIER	3-TIER	N-TIER
Scalability	Scales to workgroup size only.	Scales to hundreds or thousands of users.	Highest scalability.
Portability	Tight coupling between the user interface, data, and business logic layers. Not easily ported to different technologies. A change in one tier requires changes to the other tiers.	User interface, data, and business logic layers separated into three logical tiers. Each tier can be migrated or replaced with minimal impact on the other tiers.	Portability is possible at the component level.
Exandability	Limited expandability.	Any of the tiers can be fed more resources with minimal impact on the other tiers.	Expandability supported at the component level.
Reuse	Limited reuse.	Reuse within the tiers.	Reuse of components throughout the architecture and with outside organizations.
System maintenance	Changes to the application usually require an application upgrade on every client platform.	Changes to the application require the application be upgraded at the server level.	Changes to the application require components libraries be upgraded, perhaps for as little as a single component upgrade.
Response time	Response time does not scale with increasing concurrent users. Adding resources reaches a ceiling.	Response time can be improved by adding users.	Response time can be improved by adding users.
Reliability	A fault can bring down the whole application for repair.	A fault can bring down a tier for repair.	A fault can bring down a component for repair.
Security	Not secure.	Security can be improved.	Multiple levels of security are available.
Costs (short term)	Low	Medium	High
Costs (long term)	High	Medium	Medium
Development ease	Straightforward development. Lots of human resources available at competitive prices.	Development requires strong architecture planning. Competition for human resources is intense.	Development requires strong architecture planning, component modeling, and component integration. Keen competition for human resources demands a premium.

Defining a Transaction

A transaction contains one or more activities that must be executed as a bounded unit of work. This means that all the activities must complete together or be backed out together. Each activity must also complete as part of a consistent and logical sequence of activities. The acronym ACID is used to describe transactions—atomicity, consistency, isolation, and durability.

Atomicity. A transaction must be self-contained and all its pieces must complete or rollback as a single unit.

Consistency. A transaction must always execute in the same order and produce results that are predictable.

Isolation. A transaction executes without being affected by other transactions or affecting other transactions in turn.

Durability. The results of a transaction last after the transaction is completed. The results are permanent.

In distributed 3-tier applications and n-tier applications, transaction integrity and efficiency requires additional attention from the developer because all the components involved in the successful completion of a transaction may be separated by huge geographical and physical distances. A live WAN or Internet connection cannot always be assumed, so provisions must be included in the architecture to handle this sort of error condition.

Components

A component consists of an interface definition, methods, and reusable code. Components provide business, administrative, or technical services to their clients with durable results. They are connected together to offer complete applications. Components are objectlike in that they encapsulate methods and data. Components differ from traditional objects in that the inheritance property is not enforced. Components can be included in class libraries and can also be delivered in executable forms or dynamic link libraries. They can run in a variety of methods, including the following: as an isolated server process, as a client process, as an SQL Server process, or as an IIS process. Components also support code reuse, can be fairly large in themselves in terms of the business rules they support, can be combined into sophisticated business frameworks, and can be assembled into applications. Components can also encapsulate business rules as COM in-process server components, which are faster than COM out-of-process components which are distributed.

Enterprise-level applications can be fully componentized or built on small independent, portable components. Components can be replaced or snapped into an application without forcing all of it to be changed. This results in a flexible solution because components can be interchanged with new versions or more desirable components without effecting the entire application. Components support transactions and will automatically join an existing transaction when the components run. Interface pointers are assigned to clients for COM objects. Examples of components are invoice, invoice_items, and movies in a video store rental application.

Component Object Model

The Microsoft object model is a specification that allows COM objects to be packaged as components. COM is also an infrastructure technology and an open binary standard. It is an open object model that is not language dependent and is supported by such diverse languages as C++, PowerBuilder, JAVA, and Visual Basic. COM objects can be implemented in DLLs or as executables and are seamless to clients. COM objects contain business rules that are accessed through messages that are passed to the component interface. Since COM is language independent, it is possible to mix and match COM objects within an application. All COM standard clients can use COM objects.

The COM specification emerged in 1993. It was introduced in OLE 2 and was intended to allow third-party software to request services from OLE clients. OLE is a specification that refers to compound documents. COM has grown to support MS Windows and MS Office. ActiveX is a specific implementation of COM that was introduced in early 1996.

Clients call a COM object which subsequently creates an object and initializes it with data. A moniker is a special type of COM object that creates and initializes only one other COM object. COM objects can load data from simple files and structured storage using OLE DB. OLE DB, which can read both SQL and non-SQL data, is now a part of the core COM architecture. A COM object itself supports multiple predetermined interfaces/objects. The interface definition consists of a COM CLASS (id, iid, clsid). In-process servers use COM for communication and to provide better response times than out-of-process servers. Out-of-process server examples include tools like Excel. Out-of-process remote servers support components that reside on different hardware platforms. DCOM, or distributed COM, is used to facilitate communication between the client and the component. In the in-process remote server, remote components run under MTS. DCOM is still used for communication. Figure 2.4 shows the types of COM interfaces that are available. Notice that the interface varies with the type of development language being used.

DCOM emerged in 1996 as a communication protocol. The original COM specification did not change substantially in the DCOM specification, but it did succeed in extending COM to distributed environments across networks. DCOM thus supports distributed objects. DCOM also supports distributed security through authentication and data encryption. It is intended to support thousands of clients. The DCOM and COM interfaces are communication protocols. Implementation details are hidden in both specifications. DCOM also supports ActiveX.

The new releases of Visual Basic require a basic understanding of COM fundamentals. COM interfaces should be published. Before the availability of COM interfaces, objects were required to access classes directly, which resulted in versioning problems. With COM, client application code does not get modified as long as the interface does

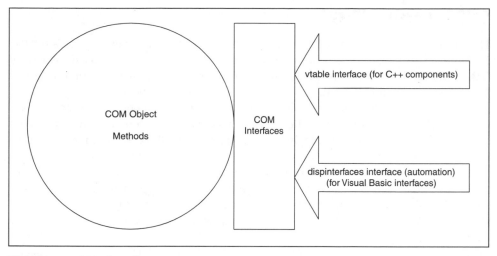

Figure 2.4   COM interfaces.

not change. COM objects implement one or more interfaces, and objects can be upgraded over time to support additional interfaces. COM uses a globally unique identifier (GUID) which is similar to a universal user identification number to distinguish between COM entities. Other useful identifiers are CLSID (coclass identifiers) and IID (interface identifiers). These identifiers are used to register server components on client machines using the Windows registry. VB also supports automatic garbage collection for COM objects.

IUnKnown is the standard interface inherited from other COM interfaces. This interface has three methods AddRef(), Release(), and QueryInterface(). Since COM supports polymorphism and versioning, COM clients can move between an object's exposed interfaces. vTable is the COM interface and a function pointer that is generated in the object. vTable pointers are passed to clients. The procedure for generating vTable binding in VB includes combining the compiler and the runtime version to generate a mapping layer. This leads to the vTable binding. COM also defines classes or coclasses. COM uses the interface definition language (IDL) to define interfaces and classes with C++ and Java. IDL is C-like, with object-oriented extensions. VB IDE can generate a type library from source code, which then generates vTable binding. Oleview.exe can be used on an as needed basis to generate IDL source. VB generates vTable at compile time. vTable binding is more efficient than IDispatch binding.

Multiple categories/collections of interfaces are supported by COM. Objects are allocated to categories. Interfaces can define standard memory layout for COM objects and the definition of client method calls. Resource dispensers channel access for nondurable, shared resources (e.g., database connections) through these. Components are loaded into SQL Server and the IIS.

DCOM versus CORBA

The primary competitor for COM is arguably the Object Management Group's (OMG) Common Object Request Broker Architecture (CORBA). CORBA was designed by OMG, with participation from Sun, DEC, HP, NCR, and Hyperdesk Corporation. Just as ActiveX is built on top of COM, and is a component-based solution, so too is JavaBeans built on top of the CORBA. JavaBeans offers another type of a component-based solution. Desktop components are called JavaBeans while server components are called Enterprise JavaBeans. CORBA is defined by Application Objects, Common Facilities, Object Request Brokers, and Object Services. The CORBA specification provides standards and a protocol for object request/message passing. CORBA defines object request brokers (ORBs) as the vehicle for request/message passing between objects. ORBs support application interoperability, and thus support heterogeneous environments. Table 2.2 identifies the primary differences between COM/DCOM and CORBA.

Object Request Brokers

Object request brokers are used by objects running in one system to request services from objects running in another system. CORBA and COM/MTS provide specifications to facilitate this communication, thereby providing heterogeneous platform support. In this architecture, a base client communicates with application components, which com-

Table 2.2 Comparing DCOM versus CORBA

FEATURES	COM/DCOM	CORBA
Request processing or placement	Offers multiple interfaces/ objects or components.	Follows a standard model of inheritance.
Counting references	Counts all referenced connected objects.	Does not count references.
Object identity	Referenced in the interface so that object references change over connections.	Unique and persistent object reference allows reconnection to objects.
Application program interfaces	2	2
Protocols	2	1
Language support	Open, but not wide in practicality. Has a strong Windows-based focus with support for VC++ and VB.	Wide. JAVA and C++ are strong proponents.

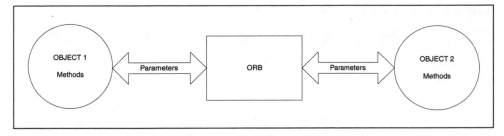

Figure 2.5 ORB communication.

municate through the resource dispenser with the resource manager. Another method of viewing this is that the presentation tier communicates with the ORB which communicates with the MTS. MTS in turn communicates with the business layer. MTS also communicates with the data layer. Figure 2.5 shows interobject communication through an ORB.

ORBs have four basic objectives: manage concurrency, resource pooling, security, and context management (e.g., execution environment) and thread management. ORBs process requests from objects to other objects and return responses to requesting objects. This is a software solution. ORBs also hide details and in the process become highly portable across environments. The data for ORBs can be drawn from a variety of data sources, including SQL and non-SQL data.

ActiveX

ActiveX is an object model that is built on top of COM. It leverages DCOM for out-of-server processes. ActiveX is Microsoft's answer to component-based development. JavaBeans is arguably the most vibrant competitor for ActiveX, but ActiveX can be designed to run faster in several popular configurations. JavaBeans, from JavaSoft, is a component-based architecture Application Program Interface (API) for Java. ActiveX takes full advantage of the Win32 environment and is language independent. COM-based components are called ActiveX controls if they are intended for desktop use. These control the use of the dispinterfaces specification when they are written in Visual Basic. ActiveX also controls the Windows registry and can execute as a native Windows application.

Table 2.3 compares JavaBeans and ActiveX. This information may change over time as both of these standards are actively evolving and being modified.

ActiveX components are invoked when a client calls CoCreateInstance. The local database registry is searched for the component named with the call. The active client consists of Internet Explorer that runs standard HTMLVBScript. Active Server consists of MTS and IIS. This holds business logic and Active Server pages. In some cases, it is preferred to use dynamic HTML instead of ActiveX.

Table 2.3   Comparing JavaBeans versus ActiveX

FEATURES	JAVABEANS (SUN)	ACTIVEX (MICROSOFT)
Major vendor alliances	IBM Netscape Sun Microsystems	Microsoft
Platform portability	Java and JavaBeans support cross-platform development. Platform independence.	Does not support cross-platform portability.
Internet/ WWW support	Optimized for Internet/ World Wide Web. Supports browser/nonbrowser environments.	Small OCX controls support effective transportation over the Internet. Part of the Active Platform development environment extends OLE to the Internet. Active platform = active desktop and active server.
Applet support	Component framework for applets.	Component framework.
Compilation support	Interpreted language	Compiles into Windows byte code that can be transferred across the network.
Security	JavaBeans works with the Java virtual machine. This is a highly secure architecture because applets run in the virtual machine. They do not have access to other files or applications on the client platform. This is an important safeguard against applets that are downloaded from diverse web servers.	There are security problems in the Internet environment. Intranet environments may be more secure. ActiveX allows access to files and applications on the client platform.
Response time	Downloaded to a Java virtual machine on a client platform. JavaBeans compiles into neutral J-Code. This makes it slow. Not as fast as ActiveX.	Optimized for Windows environments. Favors the Windows platform. Very efficient under this platform.
Connectivity	JavaBeans API connects with ActiveX and OpenDoc through bridges.	Integrates into MS Office.

Microsoft Transaction Server

This section provides a definition for the Microsoft Transaction Server (MTS), reasons to leverage it for your n-tier applications, and an architectural description of the product. MTS is a powerful tool for building server-centric, n-tier, Web-based applications that leverage COM objects. The COM supports the development of small, atomic components that encapsulate business logic. MTS is the container, or the glue, that pulls everything together. Components are installed under MTS, which expects single-user components but supports multiuser code. MTS is a part of the Microsoft Backoffice.

A Definition

MTS is a significant product initiative for Microsoft and the cornerstone of their corporate IT strategy. It plays a key role in the Windows Distributed interNet Applications Architecture (DNA) strategy that integrates client/server computing, web computing, and n-tier architecture. Microsoft Transaction Server 1.0 was released in early 1997 and was built on top of the COM. In fact, MTS simplifies the COM by allowing components to be atomic and not concerned about the details of transaction control. This normally requires a significant resource overhead that impacts performance as more concurrent users are added to the application. MTS was packaged with Windows NT Server Enterprise Edition and was in the Backoffice suite as well. It can be viewed as part ORB and part transaction processing (TP) monitor. As an ORB it can act as middleware in the DNA strategy. As a TP monitor it offers transactional component services, benefits from additional processors, and supports an increasing number of user connections to data.

Components are identified as transactional if they are to be linked into transactions with MTS and distributed transaction services (DTS). MTS uses the Distributed Object Model to manage objects and object sets. It also supports COM objects, ActiveX DLLs, and can run ActiveX objects. MTS performs transaction control for components. Components, because they are intended to be the building blocks of applications, cannot and should not determine when a transaction begins or ends. To support n-tier architecture, transactions must be stateless. MTS allows full rollback of failed transactions or a full commit of a successful one. It maintains a transaction across multiple objects and centralizes access to information. A component indicates success or failure to MTS. MTS also supports the concurrent execution of transactions by acting as a container for running components (e.g., VB, Internet Browser, Netscape on clients, MTS is a server-based container).

MTS is packaged with Windows NT Server, Enterprise Edition 4.0, Standard Edition 4.0, NT Workstation 4.0, and Windows 95. It also integrates with Information Server 4.x or higher, Message Queue Server 1.x (MSMQ) or higher, MS SNA Server 4.x (for mainframe access), and Oracle databases. NT Server 5.0 is based on an object architecture with a hierarchical folder organization.

MTS components call the MTS API so client components are not burdened with the need to do this. This is useful in the development phase, as client components can be written in single-user mode, but deployed in multiuser mode under MTS during testing and at implementation time. MTS controls component traffic across platforms and networks. It also supports transactional queues, processes, threads, and nested transactions within fully distributed environments with a distributed security service.

Components use the ItransactionContext and COM IobjectContext interfaces. Transactions use DTC. MTS has an ODBC Resource Dispenser component that load balances data requests. Server components must be registered in the MTS run-time environment. MTS can be leveraged to build COM servers. MTS is not visible to clients but does receive client calls. The relationship between MTS and other Microsoft technologies is as follows: DCOM–MTS–COM–Object–RDO/DAO/ADO–ODBC–MS SQL Server.

Why MTS

Distributed TP monitors do not historically support client/server tools. This has resulted in limited scalability in terms of concurrent users in client/server applications. Since MTS is part ORB, part TP monitor, and part middleware, it is Microsoft's solution to the scalability problem. MTS allows you to build server-centric application architectures that are component oriented. The end result is a reduced need for infrastructure support. Other benefits that are offered by MTS include

Ease of maintenance.

Increased application scalability.

Increased security.

Support for Internet/Intranet based apps. MTS also works well with Web-based architectures.

Use objects anywhere on a network. Clients and MTS are usually on different platforms.

The resource dispenser: manages shared state data (e.g., ODBC resource dispenser manages shared connections).

Supports the component models requirement for transaction protection.

Automatic transaction support.

Role-based security.

Cross database support.

Database connection pooling.

Component-oriented run-time environment.

Examples of this solution include a validation module or a calculator that can be reused in different technical or operating environments.

MTS Architecture

MTS is a transaction-oriented environment. MTS objects are in-process COM objects or components, which must be a DLL, a class factory implementation for object creation, or a type library that is used to describe component interfaces. MTS architecture consists of three primary components: MTS Explorer, Management Console Support, and Automatic Client Installation Utility. The MTS Explorer can browse a loaded component's methods and interfaces. The activity of MTS objects can be viewed through MTS Explorer. The MTS Explorer is the window into the MTS run-time environment and allows component methods to be reviewed and attributes to be established.

An MTS client communicates with mtx.exe (the container), the MTS Executive (mtxex.dll), and MTS objects. The Microsoft Management Console can be used to administer IIS, MTS, and Index Server. The MTS architecture also includes the following: MTS Executive (DLL that provides run-time services to components), server processes, user components, resource managers, resource dispensers, Distributed Transaction Coordinator (DTC), and Transaction Server Explorer. The Microsoft Transaction Server Executive is a DDL that serves TS components and runs in the background. The MTS can be given its own server platform. The COM is the MTS interface mechanism. Figure 2.6 shows the interaction MTS in a broader architectural context. Figure 2.7 shows the architecture between IIS Active Server Pages (ASPs), a Web browser, MTS, and SQL Server.

The MTS holds stateless objects for next to no cost and is a key enabler for application scalability in environments that leverage the MTS. Performance improvements are also gained by grabbing resources and holding them for a minimal amount of time. Set-Complete signals that the MTS does not have to maintain state. The MTS provides context, thread management services. The MTS also relies on multiple server processes to facilitate scalability. Objects that disappear when they have no state to maintain save system resources. The MTS wraps around the MTS objects that it instantiates. Like some CICS sessions, components do not remember their state if they work with the MTS. Components should be created and released as quickly as possible. Single instances of objects can be pooled. Components support 3-tier architecture. They can be

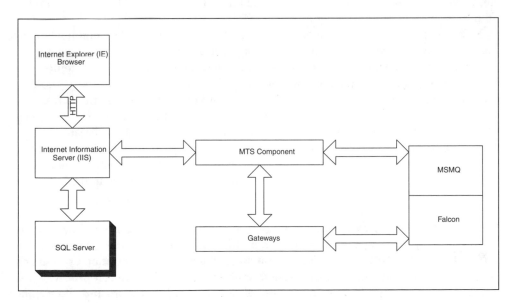

Figure 2.6 MTS architecture.

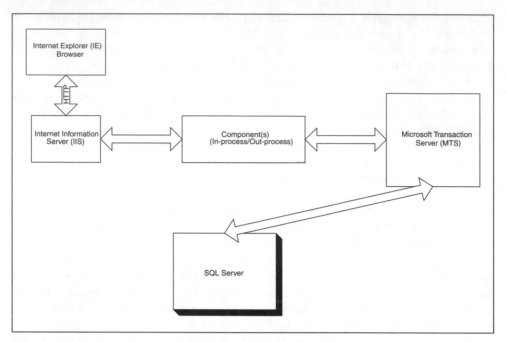

Figure 2.7 MTS and component architecture.

implemented on application servers with good performance because stateless components generate fewer database calls than stateful ones do. The MTS itself maintains state information for components.

MTS controls the creation, maintenance, and destruction of COM component instances. MTS manages transactions that span physical boundaries (e.g., physical components and databases). These components are instantiated in the same context by using the CreateInstance function, which is like VB's CreateObject. SetAbort() combination. Components are registered with MTS and are identified as requiring a transaction, supporting a transaction, and independent of a transaction. MTS shares resources among clients and provides administrative support. Packages should be created before the registration is done. DLL files can be dragged right into an open package after it is created, and thus completes the registration process. It is useful to register components with the MTS run-time environment after they are created and compiled into DLLs using the MTS Explorer.

MTS has a problem with temp tables, as only one userid is used by all connections. A work-around to this problem is to leverage individual user-defined tables in a user-defined database. Connection information establishes uniqueness. MTS also has a problem with multiple selects in a stored procedure. A work-around to this problem is to use one select per stored procedure and allow components to manage the sequence of stored procedure calls.

Microsoft Windows NT Server Client Access License (CAL) is required by platforms running MTS components. MTS Server components can be written in a variety of languages as long as they support ActiveX DLLs. MTS Clients can be supported by any language that calls COM/DCOM objects, such as VB, VBScript, Java, and C++.

MTS objects are created using CoCreateInstance for C++ or CreateObject (VB). MTS creates an associated context object (with an IObjectContext interface) and the MTS object. The MTS object communicates with the MTS Executive through the context object interfaces and methods by getting a pointer to the IObjectContext interface of the context object (done through the GetObjectContext API). The methods in IObjectContext include those shown in the following list [both release resources and support just-in-time activation (JIT)]. These methods should be executed after obtaining a context object:

SetComplete. Component is ready to commit.

SetAbort. Component is ready to roll back.

IsCallerInRole. Implement security using this method.

CreateInstance. This method is used to create an object in the current ObjectContext.

There are a few other objects of interest at this time. The SharedPropertyGroupManager object is used to manage shared property groups. The SharedPropertyGroup object is used to manage shared properties. The SharedProperty object processes shared properties. MTS objects use these methods to communicate with the MTS Executive. Clients hold interface pointers to components.

The following syntax represents a simplified set of components to support a video rental store's business process:

```
IRentVideo
    methods: Rent, Return, Reserve

Rent(ItemNo){
If (MovieVideo) UpdateVideoRentalAgreement(ItemNo)
    Else If (MovieEquipment) UpdateEquipRentalAgreement(ItemNo)
    Else
        GeneralRentalAgreement(ItemNo)
    AdjustInventory(ItemNo)
PrintInvoiceCopy (ItemNo)

Return (ItemNo)
}

Return(ItemNo) {
    ScanItem(ItemNo)
    AdjustInventory(ItemNo)
}

Reserve(ItemType) {
```

```
    ItemNo = SearchInventory(ItemType)
    If (ItemAvailable)
        ReserveItem(ItemNo)
    Else
    ErrorHandle()
}
```

When components are created, MTS captures the instantiation of the component and spawns context objects to keep context information, such as security data, participation of transactions, and execution thread information, and to allow the component to talk with MTS. Context objects expose the IObjectContext COM interface and its underlying methods which can be used by components to use MTS. IObjectContext has methods to commit or abort a transaction, enable transactions, disable transactions, and security verification. Each of these methods is applied to the calling component. SetAbort(), transaction failed; SetComplete(), transaction successful. Figure 2.8 shows the interaction of these methods and components. Invoke SetAbort() or SetComplete() at the end of each method. IObjectContext supports methods such as Activate(), Deactivate(), CanBePooled().

The MTS run-time environment requests a reference to IObjectContext through GetObjectContext(), a global method. Programming code in components invokes this method. The IObjectContext pointer interface is returned to the context object. Figure 2.9 shows the interfaces that are exposed to MTS.

Not all components implement IobjectContext. In such cases the component does not receive Activate() and Deactivate() messages. The Implements keyword in VB is used to implement the IObjectContext interface. IObjectContext::CreateInstance() creates an instance of a component in the same transaction as the invoking component. The context object acts as a pipeline to MTS. IIS provides scalable Web services for Internet service providers (ISPs), security enhancements, support for eCommerce, and the capability to run ActiveX components. ASP runs inside MTS. Applications run in separate memory buffers so they do not impact the Web server.

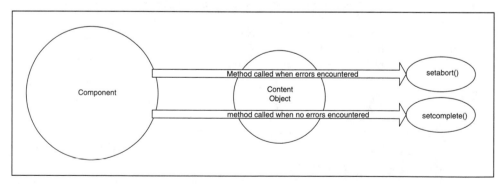

Figure 2.8   SetAbort and SetComplete.

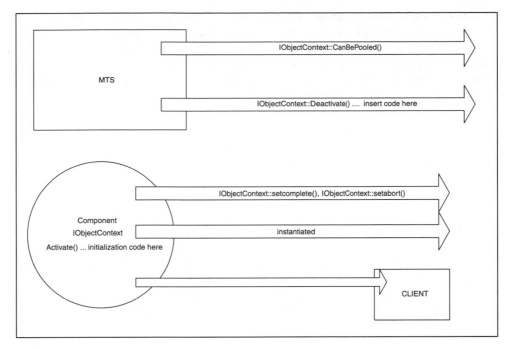

Figure 2.9 MTS and COM.

COM+

COM+ is the next generation of COM. COM+ introduces an object virtual machine, supports binary interoperability, and simplifies application architecture. COM+ is tightly integrated with MTS. COM+ retains COM functionality, run-time enhancements, and object services. COM-based applications can port to COM+ with minimal changes. This technology is expected to be bundled with Windows NT 5 and was included on the NT 5 Beta 2 product.

Summary

This chapter introduced concepts that facilitate the development of n-tier, distributed applications using SQL Server and COM. The benefits and weaknesses of 2-tier, 3-tier, and n-tier architecture were evaluated. COM, DCOM, and ActiveX were reviewed as component enabling technologies. Component-based architecture supports reusability and code sharing within the same organization, or across organizations. MTS was also introduced in this chapter as a key Microsoft technology that enables enterprise-wide n-tier architecture by supporting a larger concurrent user base through stateless components.

N-tier, distributed applications are built on the foundations defined in this chapter. The technical architecture consists of Microsoft Transaction Server (MTS), Windows (in its various instances), Visual Basic, C++, and SQL Server. COM provides the specification for component communication. DCOM provides the hooks needed for component communication in distributed environments. We also learned that COM and MTS are being bundled into the NT operating system.

CHAPTER 3

Primer for Building an Application: Part A

This chapter provides the reader with an overview of the commonly used functions and features of Microsoft SQL Server 7. It also presents a development life cycle using SQL Server as one of the core tools in the development environment. In the application design phase, we define a logical data model and then convert it into a physical data model. Two methods for building applications are demonstrated: using the wizards, and building and running scripts using the visual tools and utilities. The application primer continues in Chapter 4. This chapter examines techniques for enhancing applications through the use of stored procedures, triggers, views, joins, subqueries, and table creation options. These are discussed in more detail later in the book in the context of more complex objects and their support for n-tier architecture using COM.

Where to Start?

It is useful to begin with a conceptual understanding of a business problem before building a technology solution. This section describes the activities that should be considered before the development cycle begins.

Prepare for Development

Application development is supported by a variety of technical environments—from a single workstation to an elaborate combination of best-of-breed hardware and software combinations. Chapter 1 described the process for setting up the hardware platforms for a test/development environment and installing Microsoft SQL Server within that environment. This is the first step toward building a full development environment, which is usually sufficient for the purpose of learning SQL Server. However, a full development environment in a business setting must consider a wider set of tools included in the following categories.

Project Management and Estimating Tools

These tools are critical to project success, despite the power and usefulness of the other tools. Project management tools are used by project managers to track team resources, build a project plan or schedule, track milestones, track deliverables, and track time spent on activities. Project management tools also require extensive reporting functions, including a full Gantt chart, milestone dates, resource list, resource list by activity, resource list by activity by week, picture of current work done, and resource overallocations, among others. Examples of project management tools include Microsoft Project, Project Workbench, and Timeline. Estimating tools are used along with a best-practices database to assign roles and durations to activities in a project plan based on a set of criteria (e.g., project complexity, extent of politics, and experience of the team members). For example, the best-practices database may contain data to suggest that a certain activity (e.g., review project plan) requires two days of work effort by a project manager and a business analyst. The database may also suggest that the same activity with an experienced team could require 1.5 days of work effort, while an inexperienced team may require five days of effort. Every activity in the project plan would have a similar estimate. Project managers generally use the estimating tool to build a first draft project plan and then customize the estimates based on their own experiences, knowledge of the project team, and knowledge of the project requirements. The value of the tools in this category is proportional to the complexity and size of the project. Larger projects require more rigor and discipline.

Change Management

This category includes tools for source code management, version control, object promotion, and the handling of change requests. Without good tools in this category, projects requiring multiple resources will start to trip over each other. Source code will also get lost, especially if there is team turnover in the environment. It is not unusual for someone to leave all their source files on a local hard disk that accidentally gets cleaned up before source files can be transferred. Within the Windows NT environment, some examples of change management tools include Microsoft SourceSave and PVCS. The latter is the more powerful of the two tools; the former is used in environments of all sizes and is gaining in popularity. It is also a Microsoft product and tightly integrated with the other Microsoft tools.

Systems Management

This category includes asset management and object distribution in a distributed client/server environment. Systems management (and change management) tools and techniques are more thorough in the traditional mainframe environment. However, both categories have suffered weak tools in the distributed client/server environment. Systems management tools are also used to deploy applications. This situation continues to improve over time. Within the Windows environment, Microsoft SMS is a solid candidate for this category.

Development Tools

This category includes all tools used for developing applications, including 3GL and 4GL tools that are capable of functioning in any of the tiers of an n-tier architecture. This category includes such tools as Microsoft Visual Basic, Visual C++, Delphi, Power-Builder, SQL Windows, and Oracle 2000.

Database

This category refers to the database and database servers that manage business data. Common industry choices for database servers include Microsoft SQL Server, Oracle 8, Sybase SQL Server, DB2, and Informix. This category also includes data warehouse products such as Teradata and Red Brick. Another subcategory includes object databases, such as Jasmine. Recent additions to this category include universal servers from vendors such as Informix, IBM, and Sybase. Universal servers support object relational data models and nonrelational datatypes.

Modeling Tools

This category identifies tools for modeling parts of a business domain. There are a wide variety of models, including data models, process models, and object models. In terms of data models, there are logical and physical data models. Logical data models are used to describe business entities, fields, and constraints. They are intended to be independent of a particular database. For example, the same logical data model can be implemented under SQL Server or Oracle. Physical data models are derived from logical data models and are fine tuned for specific implementation tools. For example, in an SQL Server environment, physical tables may all be derived from logical entities with the addition of a last_changed datetime (timestamp) field. CASE tools are often included in this category. Examples of tools in this category include Erwin, System Architect, and S-Designer. Modeling tools such as Select and Rational Rose support object-oriented environments. Microsoft offers the recently released Visual Data Tools as a good entry in this category.

Middleware

This category identifies components that connect the other components together in an environment. Middleware supports interoperability and portability in heterogeneous environments. Middleware comes in proprietary flavors (e.g., Sybase Open Client) or industry standards (ODBC). Within an SQL Server environment, ODBC and the new OLE DB are good choices for database-related middleware. Additional middleware components are also required throughout the rest of the systems architecture.

Transaction Monitors

This category identifies products that support multiple, concurrent users and which manage transactions in distributed environments. Examples include CICS, Encina, and the new Microsoft Transaction Server (MTS). The latter supports SQL Server and is discussed later in this book. MTS is an important enabler for Microsoft's quest to support the enterprise.

Testing Tools

This category identifies products used to test and debug applications in both real-time and batch mode. Testing tools that can simulate a high number of virtual users are useful to test an application's concurrency and its capability to support increasing concurrent user loads. The tools should also support the creation of test scripts and test data. Examples of these tools include SQA Suite and Platinum Final Test. In some cases, test tools or test harnesses are custom developed by project teams to test an application through the development life cycle.

Network

This category includes LANs and WANs. It also includes communication protocols, communication cards, wiring, hubs, routers, brouters, and bridges. The Internet and intranets are also playing a large role in this area. For this reason, a common network protocol is TCP/IP under Ethernet or Token Ring.

Hardware

This category includes the platforms required to support development, test, and production environments. Within the Windows environment, common examples include Compaq Proliant, Dell, DEC Alpha, Unisys, and HP platforms. Platforms for servers are often configured with multiple CPUs and high levels of random access memory (RAM).

The selection of the proper tools is only the first step toward building a working development environment. Tools must be complemented with a development methodology and techniques to promote project success. Development methodologies and techniques are discussed in Chapter 5. In addition to selecting and implementing the tools identified in the previous categories, it is also necessary to design the application.

Some organizations are now opting for a single integrator-based solution, as opposed to a best of breed solution. The single integrator-based solution reduces the risk of integration between different products and also allows fewer vendor contact points to exist to better resolve issues. Such a solution assumes that the single vendor (or fewer vendors) approach will provide the solutions required to satisfy the ongoing requirements of an enterprise. This approach assumes that the selected vendors have the financial and investment resources to grow into the future. Microsoft clearly fits this description (as does Oracle, IBM, Compaq, and HP). Table 3.1 shows a Microsoft-centric technical solution consisting of the following tools in the major product categories.

Table 3.1 Microsoft-based Technology Architecture

PRODUCT CATEGORY	SUGGESTED TOOL
Development tools	Visual Basic, VC++
Database	SQL Server
Modeling tools	Rational Rose, Visual Modeler
Middleware	ODBC, OLE DB
Transaction monitors	MTS
Testing tools	SQA Team
Network	Token Ring, Ethernet, Intranet, Internet
Hardware	Dell, Compaq, HP
Project management and estimating tools	MS Project, MS Excel, MS Word, MS Powerpoint
Change management	SourceSave
System management	SMS

GUI versus Batch

GUIs have gained popularity since their inception in the early 1970s as a product of a systems experiment at Xerox Corporation. The hardware revolution of the last few years, as well as dropping RAM and disk drive prices, has resulted in desktop systems that are now many times more powerful than they were in the early 1990s. The Internet, intranet, and World Wide Web technology has also made GUIs more technically feasible and desirable. When SQL Server was first released in 1987, much of the administrative and development activities were completed in character mode, outside of a GUI environment. This capability still exists within SQL Server through the isql utility. Fortunately GUI tools have also evolved to perform many of the same activities graphically. The basic challenge then is to determine which approach to use and in which situations.

Many developers use SQL Server Enterprise Manager to build the first draft of database objects. The SQL Server system tables can then be used to generate and save scripts for the database objects within a database. The scripts that are generated are saved in the operating system environment and maintained in the normal project change management channels. The scripts are a valuable tool in supporting system upgrades. This approach can be generalized even further. Scripts should be used to maintain a copy of the system and data. GUI tools should be used to invoke the scripts.

Design the Application

The application built in this chapter intentionally begins with a small set of relational tables so that you can get started with using SQL Server 7. The business requirement is to build an application that manages address information for members along with a description of the products that they have ordered. The application should be flexible enough for multiple businesses to use, such as a mail-order clearing house that offers a wide range of products to its customers. The solution requires several data entities, as shown in Figure 3.1. The member entity contains basic information about a member. Members can support multiple addresses, for example, a billing address, shipping address, and a summer address. A second entity, address, is used to manage this information. There is a one-to-many relationship between the member-address entities. A third entity consists of a commonly used code entity. The address_type entity contains a description of the type of address that is stored in the address entity. The cardinality between the address-address_type is 1:1. A second code table, member_type, is used to track the type of member for marketing purposes. Another table, orders, contains detailed information about ordered items for members. Another code table, product_type, contains a description of the item being ordered.

The logical data model can be converted to a physical model under a specific database server product. A physical data model is optimized, as much as possible, for a specific physical product solution. Thus a single logical data model can generate multiple physical models, different for SQL Server, Oracle, Informix, and Sybase. The following tables contain the fields, datatypes, width, and constraints for each of the relational tables that are required to satisfy the business case. For the purposes of this example, only a small set of datatypes are used: character (width), integer, datetime, and money.

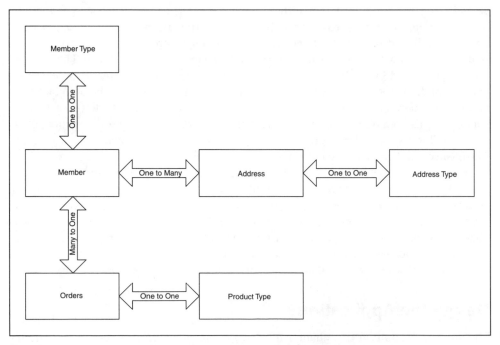

Figure 3.1 Logical data model for member addresses and orders.

Table 3.2 Member Table

FIELD NAME	DATATYPE AND WIDTH	CONSTRAINTS	INDEX
Member_no	Integer		Primary
Last_name	Character(30)		
Initial	Character(1)		
First_name	Character(30)		
Home_phone	Character(15)	Format validation on the graphical user interface (GUI)	
Business_phone	Character(15)	Format validation on the GUI	
Cell_phone	Character(15)		
Fax	Character(15)	Format validation on the GUI	
Email__address	Character(30)		
Web_site	Character(30)		
Preference	Character(80)		
Member_since	Datetime		
Member_type	Character(1)	Must exist in member_type table	Foreign

Table 3.2 maintains information for each member in the database. The member_no is an integer whose value is automatically generated by the application in a sequential fashion. The remaining column fields contain other personal information about the customer.

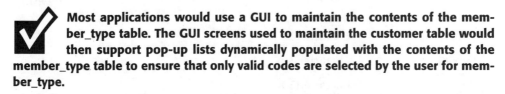 **Most applications would use a GUI to maintain the contents of the member_type table. The GUI screens used to maintain the customer table would then support pop-up lists dynamically populated with the contents of the member_type table to ensure that only valid codes are selected by the user for member_type.**

Table 3.3 contains a description of the member type. This table joins with the customer table on the member_type field.

Table 3.4 contains address information for each member, with the capability to support multiple addresses in a one-to-many relationship. Unique rows in this table are based on a compound member_no + address_type key. A member can only have one

Table 3.3   Member_Type Table

FIELD NAME	DATATYPE AND WIDTH	CONSTRAINTS	INDEX
Member_type	Character(1)		Primary
Description	Character(40)		

record of a given address_type. If a business requirement is to support multiple occurrences of the same address type, another field, sequence_no, could be inserted into this table. This would create a key of member_no + address_type + sequence_no. Note that the fields city, state_province, and country are also good candidates for code tables which would dynamically populate pop-up lists on the screen that supports the address table.

Table 3.5 contains a list of items ordered by a member that are on order. The key to the table concatenates the fields member_no + request_date + sequence_no. The table supports multiple requests by the same member with the same request date. The table also tracks the date by which the order must be supported.

Table 3.6 contains a list of address code types (e.g., shipping address, mailing address, billing address, summer address) and their descriptions.

Table 3.7 contains a list of product types and their descriptions.

 All examples and work shown in this book should be performed on a test server to protect your business data. Before starting, back up any information that you want access to in the future.

Table 3.4   Address Table

FIELD NAME	DATATYPE AND WIDTH	CONSTRAINTS	INDEX
Member_no	Integer	Referential integrity with member table	Primary
Address_type	Character(1)	Referential integrity with address table	Primary
Street1	Character(30)		
Street2	Character(30)		
City	Character(30)		
State	Character(20)		
Country	Character(15)		
Zip_pc	Character(10)		

Table 3.5   Orders Table

FIELD NAME	DATATYPE AND WIDTH	CONSTRAINTS	INDEX
Member_no	Integer	Customer_no must exist in customer table	Primary
Request_date	Datetime	Cannot be earlier than current date	Primary
Sequence_no	Integer	Generated sequentially	Primary
Product_type	Character(80)		
Units	Float		
Required_date	Datetime	Must be greater than current date	
Date_delivered	Datetime		
Comments	Character(100)		
Amount collected	Money		
Downpayment	Money	Must be positive	

Table 3.6   Address_Type Table

FIELD NAME	DATATYPE AND WIDTH	CONSTRAINTS	INDEX
Address_type	Character (1)		Primary
Description	Character(15)		

Table 3.7   Product_Type Table

FIELD NAME	DATATYPE AND WIDTH	CONSTRAINTS	INDEX
Product_type	Character (5)		Primary
Description	Character(20)		
On-hand	Float		
Unit price	Money		

Scripting the Tables

There are several methods to generate the physical database environment within Microsoft SQL Server. The common ones include the following:

Create an ASCII file containing Transact-SQL commands that are executed to create the tables in an SQL Server database using the isql batch command or the isql/w GUI utility. The notepad application in Windows can be used to create this file, as can many other program editors.

Use a data modeling tool (e.g., Microsoft Developer Studio, S-Designer, Erwin) to model the logical data model, convert it to a physical data model, and generate the database tables automatically.

Create the tables interactively using SQL Server Enterprise Manager.

 Create a subdirectory called \test in the root using the Windows NT Explorer applet. Save the code you build directly into this database. Also ensure that the SQL Server directory is in the path if you intend to use character entry mode.

Regardless of the method that is used to actually build the contents, the basic Transact-SQL script to generate these tables is included in this section. This is a first iteration of the database creation script. It begins by dropping the tables (code to check if the tables exist will be incorporated into these commands later in the primer), then creating the tables and fields. Successful compilation of this script will create empty tables in the database identified in the first "use" statement. This script will be iteratively enhanced in this chapter. Notice the use of the command "go" throughout the script. This command ends what is called a *batch* in SQL Server and so acts as a delimiter between batches. Commands in a script file are automatically assumed to be in a batch by SQL Server. They are not executed until a go is encountered. This has some subtle impacts that will be shown later. Another point to notice is that this script can be enhanced in several ways:

Adding clustered indexes

Adding rules and constraints

Identifying primary and foreign keys

Establishing default values for fields

Creating triggers

 If the pubs database was not installed with SQL Server, jump to the section in this chapter that describes how to create a database and follow the instructions. Return here, modify the command in script1.txt that currently reads "use pubs" to "use test1db," and continue as before.

COMMENTS IN THE CODE

Text that is surrounded by the codes /* */ are viewed as comments by the SQL Server parser. Comments take the form: /* this is a comment */. The complementary symbols can also be on different lines in the text. A comment can be placed on one line using the prefix codes – (dashdash). Comment text is not used to calculate query strategies by SQL Server. If the text is included inside a stored procedure, trigger, or view, it is compiled into the SQL Server system tables. If the comments are included outside database objects in a script file they are not compiled into the SQL Server system tables. An interesting side effect of this is that comments not compiled into the system tables cannot be generated using SQL Server's GUI tools because they do not exist in the environment. They only exist in the text scripts. This is acceptable as long as the scripts are maintained as a true original copy of the database objects. However, if the database system tables are ever to be used to generate table creation scripts for the current database environment, all comments should be moved into the database object creation blocks. Historically SQL Server placed rigid limits on the size of stored procedures. Thus it was desirable to avoid using space to store comments in the system tables. These limits have changed dramatically, so this is no longer the case.

A Reusable Script Template

It is useful to reuse script templates to keep yourself from starting from scratch each time you create a script. A standard script template that I prefer to reuse consists of the following:

```
/**************************************************************/
/* Filename:                                                */
/* Author:                                                  */
/* Description:                                    */
/**************************************************************/
use <database_name>
go


/*********************************************/
/* Drop the tables before recreating them. */
/*********************************************/
drop table <table_name1>
drop table <table_name2>
<table_list>
go


/******************************/
/* Create the table          */
/******************************/
create table table_name1
(
   field_names         datatype
)
go
```

```
/*********************************/
/* Create the table            */
/*********************************/
create table table_name2
(
   field_names          datatype
)
go
```

Creating Tables in a Database

Source Listing 3.1 uses the PUBS database, that is created when you install Microsoft SQL Server. It is possible to uninstall or delete this database, so if it does not exist, skip to the section in this chapter that shows you how to create a user-defined database. There are several methods to determine if a database exists, which will be reviewed shortly. For now, if the script executes successfully, assume that the database exists.

Run this script from the SQL Server Query Analyzer, as shown in Figure 3.2. Successful execution of this script will create the tables in the PUBS database.

```
/****************************************************************/
/* Filename: \dbcreat.txt                                     */
/* Author:    Sanjiv Purba                                    */
/* Description:                                               */
/* Use the pubs database to hold the tables being created.    */
/****************************************************************/
use pubs
go

/**********************************************/
/* Drop the tables before re-creating them. */
/* Ignore the information message if the     */
/* tables do not exist.                      */
/**********************************************/
drop table member
drop table member_type
drop table address
drop table orders
drop table address_type
drop table product_type
go

/*****************************/
/* Create the member table.  */
/*****************************/
create table member
(
   member_no          int,
   last_name          char(30),
   initial            char(1),
```

(Continues)

Source 3.1   Creating tables.

```
    first_name          char(30),
    home_phone          char(15),
    business_phone      char(15),
    cell_phone          char(15),
    fax                 char(15),
    email_address       char(30),
    web_site            char(30),
    preference          char(80),
    member_since        datetime,
    member_type         character(1)
)


/********************************/
/* Create the member_type table. */
/********************************/
create table member_type
(
    member_type         character(1),
    description         character(30)
)


/***********************/
/* Create the address. */
/***********************/
create table address
(
    member_no           int,
    address_type        char(1),
    street1             char(30),
    street2             char(30),
    city                char(20),
    state               char(20),
    country             char(15),
    zip_pc              char(10)
)


/***************************/
/* Create the orders table. */
/***************************/
create table orders
(
    member_no           int,
    request_date        datetime,
    sequence_no         integer,
    product_type        char(1),
    units               float,
    required_date       datetime,
    date_delivered      datetime,
    comments            char(100),
    amount_collected    money,
    downpayment         money
)
```

(Continues)

Source 3.1   *(Continued)*

```
/***********************************/
/* Create the address_type table. */
/***********************************/
create table address_type
(
    address_type        char(1),
    description         char(15)
)
go


/***********************************/
/* Create the product_type table. */
/***********************************/
create table product_type
(
    product_type        char(5),
    description         char(30),
    on_hand_qty         float,
    Unit_price          money
)
go
```

Source 3.1 *(Continued)*

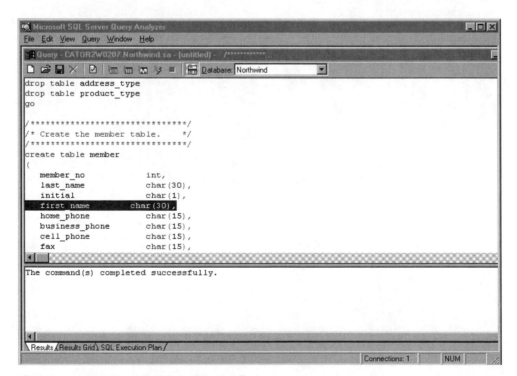

Figure 3.2 Running a batch script visually.

The "isql–Usa–P function can be used to execute the script from the native operating system.

To view the tables that you just created with the preceding script, use the following code in the Query Analyzer or by using the ISQL utility:

```
use pubs
go
select * from sysobjects
go
```

Batches and the Go Command

The command word go ends a batch and results in the execution of all the Transact-SQL code related to that batch. For this reason, the position and number of go commands in a script can produce different results. For this example, try using the following code directly with the SQL Server Query Analyzer tool:

```
use pubs
go

drop proc tmp
/* a 'go' command is ordinarily used to end a batch at this point */

create proc tmp
as
PRINT 'This is a test of the go batch command'
go

EXEC tmp
go
```

Executing this script results in the following error message appearing in the Results tab if the Query Analyzer tool is being used to run the script:

```
Server: Msg 111, Level 16, State 111
     CREATE PROCEDURE must be the first command in a query batch.

use pubs
go
select * from sysobjects where
go
```

Inserting a go command immediately after the drop proc command solves the error and causes the error message to go away. There are also many other examples where using or not using a go batch command separator makes a difference in the results that are achieved. The easiest way to know when to use a go is to separate Transact SQL commands into logical units of work. The go command should be used to execute one logical unit of work from another. In this example, there are four logical units of work:

Establish the default database.

Drop the old stored procedure from the sysmessages table.

[Re]-create the stored procedure.

Execute the stored procedure.

But remember, it is still possible to combine some of the units of work into a single batch. In this example, combining the first and second logical units of work would still achieve the same result. However, trying to combine the third and fourth will not work, and results in the following message being displayed:

```
Cannot add rows to Sysdepends for the current stored procedure because
it depends on the missing object tmp. The stored procedure will still be
created.
```

Building the Physical Database and Transaction Logs

The script defined earlier to create tables for an application used an existing database—pubs—to store the user tables. This section describes how to create and size a new database, modify the script file to use the new database, and generate the tables directly into the new database. Databases are used to store SQL Server objects, which include tables, indexes, user-defined datatypes, stored procedures, and triggers. Every database also consists of a transaction log which can be physically stored with the database itself or separated on a different device altogether. The transaction log for a database is constantly managed whenever there is activity against the database. For example, when a record is inserted into the database, a version is also written to the matching transaction log. Similarly an update in the database will cause one or two records to be written to the transaction log. The first record is the original record, the second record is the updated one. Transaction logs are used to synchronize a database if there is some sort of error occurring in SQL Server. Part of the initial processing that SQL Server performs when it is booted up is to process the transaction logs and to recommit completed transactions against the matching databases. Incomplete transactions are rolled back and not committed to the database.

"Committing" a transaction refers to completing Transact-SQL commands against a database, writing the results out to the physical database, and writing the associated start transaction-data end transaction markers to the associated transaction logs. Transactions that were contained in the transaction log without an end transaction marker are incomplete, so they are rolled back or removed from the database when SQL Server boots up after a crash.

Building a Database Environment Using Wizards

SQL Server 7 contains some helpful wizards that will get you working quite quickly. Users of earlier releases will notice a difference in the reduction in the steps required to create databases. Some of the useful wizards include

Create Database Wizard. To create a user-defined database.

Create Stored Procedures Wizard. To create stored procedures.

Create Index Wizard. To create indexes.

Create Login Wizard. To manage logins and permissions.

Create View Wizard. To create views.

A big improvement in the new release of Microsoft SQL Server is the ease with which databases can be created and administered almost right out of the box. Prior versions of the product required more work, especially in terms of creating devices, estimating sizes, and choosing between file formats. The Create Database Wizard provides an easy to follow interface that does most of the work for you. Figure 3.3 shows the activities that are followed to use the wizards to build the application environment. The major activities for doing this include Create the Database, Select the Default Database, Build the User Tables, and Build the Stored Procedures.

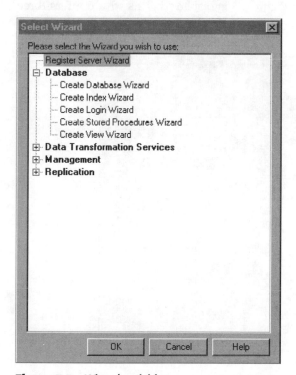

Figure 3.3   Wizard activities.

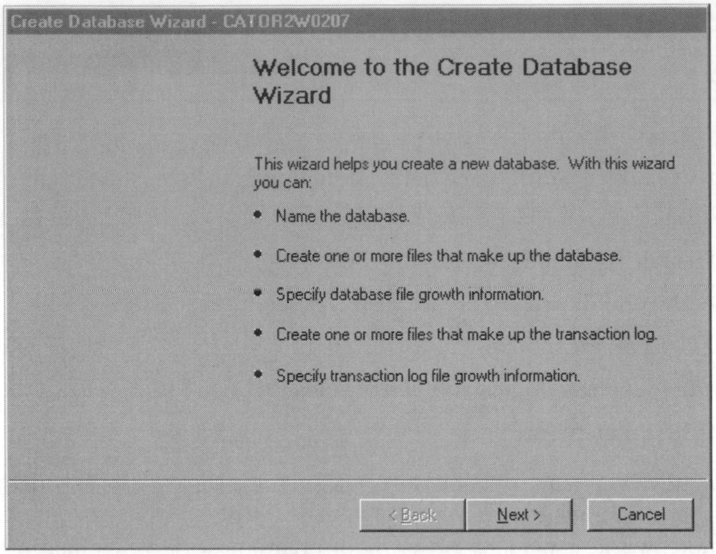

Figure 3.4   Create Database Wizard.

Figure 3.4 shows the wizard that is displayed when the Create Database Wizard option is selected in the Enterprise Manager dialogue. A successive sequence of dialogues allows you to provide a name to the database, a file location, a file location for the transaction log, until the dialogue in Figure 3.5 is displayed. This wizard offers three tabs. The first tab on the left provides access to database information, the middle tab

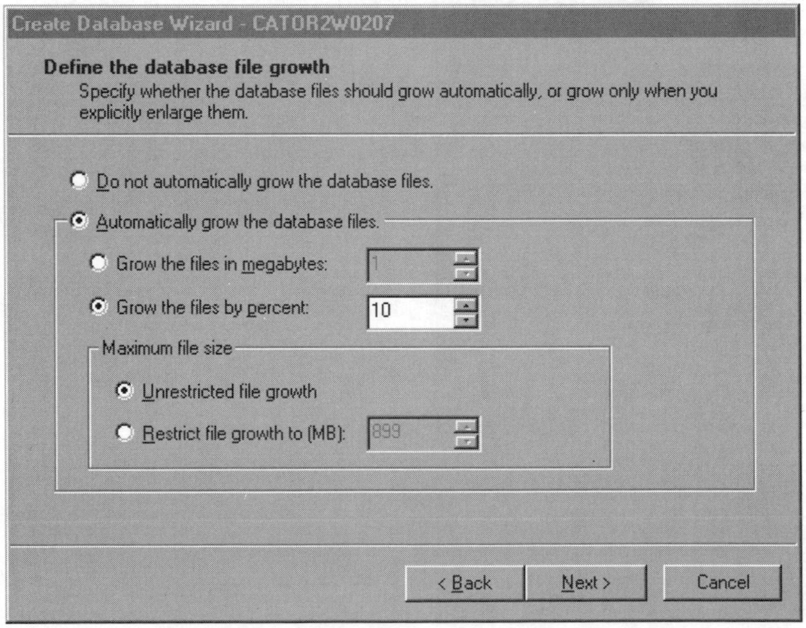

Figure 3.5   Adjust database information.

provides an opportunity to administer the transaction log, and the third tab allows database options to be adjusted.

A Note about the Database Naming Process through the Create Database Wizard

In the version of SQL Server 7 that was used for testing, this wizard created a database name, but added a preceding blank character. This can be observed by using the sp_databases system procedure to display the following information. The first three databases—Address, Database, Database 1—were created using the wizard. The names that were saved into the sysdatabases system table for these databases have a preceding blank character and one of the databases, Database 1, has an embedded blank.

```
DATABASE_NAME           DATABASE_SIZE          REMARKS

Address                     2048                 NULL
Database                    2048                 NULL
Database 1                  2048                 NULL
master                      8448                 NULL
model                       1536                 NULL
msdb                        8192                 NULL
Northwind                   8704                 NULL
pubs                        2104                 NULL
tempdb                       560                 NULL
```

There are two methods of dealing with this. The first is to refer to the databases as Address, Database, or Database 1. This problem will undoubtedly be resolved in the future and should be a temporary workaround. The other method is to use another system procedure to rename the database. This is the preferable method, but it requires a few additional commands to complete, as shown in the following code:

```
sp_dboption " Database","single user", "true"  /* this is mandatory */
sp_renamedb " Database", "database"
sp_dboption "database","single user", "false" /* use new database name */
sp_databases
```

This displays the following output, showing that the database rename command was successful:

```
DATABASE_NAME           DATABASE_SIZE          REMARKS

Address                     2048                 NULL
Database 1                  2048                 NULL
database                    2048                 NULL
master                      8448                 NULL
model                       1536                 NULL
msdb                        8192                 NULL
Northwind                   8704                 NULL
pubs                        2104                 NULL
tempdb                      2560                 NULL
```

Using Scripts to Manage Databases in Pre-SQL Server 7

The database creation script will also show you how to drop the tables in the original pubs database. The script itself can be run in batch isql mode, using the GUI of the Query Manager. It is also possible to use the SQL Enterprise Manager to execute the command equivalents in the script.

For earlier versions of the product, some preliminary work must be done to establish the environment and prepare to create a database. Before a physical database can be constructed in Microsoft SQL Server, it is necessary to define multiple devices on the physical disk media. Devices are also used to store transaction logs or for backup purposes. This is called a *dump device*. Many separate devices can be allocated on a disk drive. It is useful to split devices across different controllers for performance reasons. Because of the near concurrent activity on a database and its transaction log, it is useful to split the two into different devices. An additional benefit of doing this is the ability to occasionally back up only the transaction log for recovery purposes instead of the larger data + transaction log if the two are not physically separated into different devices. Databases can be started on one device, but they can span multiple devices.

Understanding the Syntax

The uppercase portion of the command is a reserved word and should be entered with the spelling that is shown in the example. SQL Server is not sensitive to the case of these reserved words, so they can be entered in upper, lower, or mixed case. The lowercase words are user supplied with specific information prior to executing the command. The words in quotes should be entered with surrounding quotes. The words without quotes are numbers. It is worth noting that depending on the case sensitivity established at installation time, SQL Server may be sensitive to the case of the user-supplied words, so it is important to be consistent in use of upper, lower, or mixed case with these entries.

Both Chapters 3 and 4 deal with the SQL Server primer and provide simplified views of command syntax. A good number of the SQL Server commands have fairly complex command syntax with substantial numbers of options each. The primer does not focus on the options, choosing to focus on the commonly used formats of the commands instead. More complex command syntax is discussed later in this book. The command syntax for creating a device on a disk drive is shown in the following code fragment. Devices are required in pre-SQL Server 7:

```
DISK INIT
   NAME     = 'logical_device_name',
   PHYSNAME = 'physical_device_name',
   VDEVNO   = virtual_number_for_device,
   SIZE     = number_of_blocks (in 2K increments)
```

PHYSNAME is the fully qualified path and file name for the device. VDEVNO is unique for the device and is a number between 0 and 255 (where 0 is used for the master device). SIZE cannot be less than 512, and is generally expressed as a multiple of this number. In this case, 512 means that 512 blocks, each of a size of 2 KB are reserved for the device. The physical size would therefore be 512×2 KB = 1024 KB, which happens to be the same as 1 MB. There is a final option called virtual_address, but this is generally not used and will be covered elsewhere in this book.

```
In this example, the size of this device is then: 5120 * 2 K =  10240 K.
This is 10,240,000 bytes or 10MB:
   DISK INIT
   NAME     = 'address1',
   PHYSNAME = 'c:\mssql7\data\address1.dat',
   VDEVNO   = 7,
   SIZE     = 5120
```

Successful execution of this command displays the message: "The command(s) completed successfully." The Explorer application can be used to verify that the device was created. Find the location c:\mssql7\data using the explorer application. There should now be an entry for address1.dat with a size of 10,240 KB (or 10 MB) in the directory. The type of the file is DAT. The modified date will be the system date when the disk init command was executed.

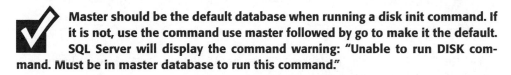

Master should be the default database when running a disk init command. If it is not, use the command use master followed by go to make it the default. SQL Server will display the command warning: "Unable to run DISK command. Must be in master database to run this command."

Use the system procedure sp_helpdevice to display information about the devices in SQL Server. This command displays the device_name, physical_name, description, status, cntrltype, and device_number of the created devices.

If you want to drop a device, it is first necessary to remove all the databases that use it first. A system procedure can be used to drop a device. It is also possible to use Microsoft Enterprise Manager to graphically manage devices, however, there were some inconsistencies in SQL Server 6.5 that make the system procedure the preferable method for dropping devices. The following syntax is used to drop devices:

```
sp_dropdevice logical_device_name[,DELFILE]
```

The DELFILE option removes the device from the disk drive and makes the disk space available for reuse. For example:

```
sp_dropdevice 'address1', DELFILE
```

Executing this command successfully displays several messages:

```
 File: 'c:\mssql7\data\address1.dat' closed
  Device dropped
  Physical file deleted
```

If you use the Windows Explorer, you will notice that the address1.dat file was removed from the disk drive.

Creating User Databases and Transaction Logs with Scripts

Databases and transaction logs are the basic data storage and processing vehicles in SQL Server. Both databases and transaction logs are stored on devices. A device can hold more than one database, and a database can span more than one device. Transaction logs can be stored with their database or split to a different device for a performance boost. SQL Server can support 32,767 databases, a large number that has increased even more in the production version of SQL Server 7. A database can be distributed across a maximum of 32 devices. The syntax for creating a database and a transaction log is shown here:

 The model database is used as a template to create user databases. Any objects that are created in the model database are also created in user databases created after the change. User-defined datatypes are often copied into this database, if they have a system-wide purpose.

```
CREATE DATABASE db_name
  [ON ddevice | DEFAULT=SIZE][,ddevice=size][,ddevice=size]repeats
  [LOG ON ldevice=size][,ldevice=size][,ldevice=size]repeats
  [FOR LOAD]
```

The [FOR LOAD] option holds the database until it is loaded. The size in this case is not in 2 KB pages, but rather given in megabytes.

Sample Scripts

The following example creates the database with a minimum size of 5 MB. It will take the entire disk space available. The LOG file will be created with a default size of 2 MB.

```
CREATE DATABASE address
ON address1
```

Successful completion of this command displays the following messages:

```
CREATE DATABASE: allocating 10 Mbytes on disk 'address1'
CREATE DATABASE: allocating 2 Mbytes on disk 'address1_log'
Recovering database 'address'
Recovery complete.
```

The next example shows how the address database will be created on the address1 device. The transaction log will be created on the address2 device:

```
CREATE DATABASE address
ON address1
LOG ON address2
```

Successful execution of this command displays the following messages:

```
CREATE DATABASE: allocating 10 Mbytes on disk 'address1'
CREATE DATABASE: allocating 10 Mbytes on disk 'address2'
Recovering database 'address1'
Recovery complete.
```

Dropping Databases

Dropping a database causes all the database objects within it to be dropped, as well as the corresponding transaction log file, even if it is on a different physical device. The syntax for dropping databases is

```
DROP DATABASE db_name1[, dbname2, dbname3, ....]
```

Sample Scripts

Following is one example of dropping a database:

```
DROP DATABASE address
go
```

Another example of dropping a database is

```
DROP DATABASE address, address_lines
go
```

Successful completion of a DROP DATABASE command displays the following message on the screen:

```
Deleting database file 'c:\mssql7\data\address1_log.dat'
```

Useful Help System Procedures

Microsoft SQL Server provides an extensive set of system procedures that inspect the system tables and provide help information for commands, functions, and the environment itself. The commands can be extremely subtle, in that a single parameter can dramatically alter the information returned by the help command. The basic syntax for invoking system procedures is as follows:

```
dbname..system_procedure  [parameter_list]
```

The following system procedures provide valuable information about devices and databases in the SQL Server environment:

sp_helpdevice. This help procedure inspects the system tables and displays the following information about devices available in the system—device_name, physical_name, description, status, cntrltype, fileid, and size.

sp_helpdb. This help procedure inspects database system tables and displays the following information about the databases defined in the system—name, db_size (in megabytes), owner (the owner of the database), dbid (unique for databases in the system), created (date the database was created), and status. The status column is important from an administrative perspective. Its value is set by a special command, set option parameters. This is important under many conditions, such as setting a database to single-user access to support fast batch copying with the bcp command.

sp_helpdb db_name. The sp_helpdb procedure with a database name as the parameter provides details about that database. The information returned includes name, db_size, owner, dbid, created, status, device_fragments, size (of each fragment), and usage (e.g., for data or the transaction log).

Completing the Script File to Create the Address Database

The information discussed in this section is used to construct a script file to create an address database. The following script file should be saved in a file with an appropriate name, for example, database.sql. The script file establishes the master database as the default database. It then drops the address database. This needs to be done in the event that the script is reexecuted. A warning message appears if the database does not exist, but this has no effect on the results. It is possible to insert additional code into the script to check that the address database exists before dropping it. The devices are dropped for the same reason. The script then creates two devices, one to hold a database, the other is its associated transaction log. The address database is then created. Two help commands are used to display intermediate results of the commands:

```
/**************************************************/
/* File Name: c:\database.txt                     */
/* Author:    Sanjiv Purba                        */
/* must establish the master database as default */
/**************************************************/
use master
go

/* drop the databases in case they exist */
drop database address
go

/* need the separate go's, otherwise a syntax error occurs. Drop these
devices if they previously exist. */
sp_dropdevice 'address1', DELFILE
go

sp_dropdevice 'address2', DELFILE
go

/* initialize three devices */
DISK INIT
    NAME = 'address1',
    PHYSNAME = 'c:\mssql7\data\address1.dat',
```

```
        VDEVNO = 7, SIZE = 5120
go


DISK INIT
    NAME = 'address2',
    PHYSNAME = 'c:\mssql7\data\address2.dat',
    VDEVNO = 8, SIZE = 5120
go

/* display the devices created so far */
sp_helpdevice

/* create the databases in the different devices that were created */
CREATE DATABASE address
   ON address1
   LOG ON address2
go

/* display the databases that have been created */
sp_helpdb
go

sp_helpdb address
```

Go Modifying the Table Creation Script

Since a separate database now exists for the address application (in either SQL Server
7 or pre-version 7), the associated script file can be modified to drop the address tables
from the pubs database, and re-create them in the address: database. The modified
script is shown in Source Listing 3.2.

```
/*********************************************************************/
/* Filename: \dbcreat.txt                                          */
/* Author:   Sanjiv Purba                                          */
/* Modification History:                                           */
/*    December   Sanjiv   Drop tables from pubs database           */
/*                        Recreate tables in address database      */
/*                                                                 */
/* Description:                                                    */
/* Change the default database and create tables to support the    */
/* Address application.                                            */
/*********************************************************************/

/* drop the address application tables from the pubs database */
use pubs
go
```
                                                          (Continues)

Source 3.2   Modified table creation script.

```
/* drop the tables in the pubs script, as they will not be used further */
drop table member
go
drop table member_type
go
drop table address
go
drop table orders
go
drop table address_type
go
drop table product_type
go

/* establish the address database as the new default database */
use address
go

/* drop the tables so that this script can be rerun. Ignore the */
/* information message if the tables do not already exist       */
drop table member
drop table member_type
drop table address
drop table orders
drop table address_type
drop table product_type
go

/*******************************/
/* Create the member table.    */
/*******************************/
create table member
(
    member_no          int,
    last_name          char(30),
    initial            char(1),
    first_name         char(30),
    home_phone         char(15),
    business_phone     char(15),
    cell_phone         char(15),
    fax                char(15),
    email_address      char(30),
    web_site           char(30),
    preference         char(80),
    member_since       datetime,
    member_type        character(1)
)
```

(Continues)

Source 3.2 *(Continued)*

```
/***********************************/
/* Create the member_type table.  */
/***********************************/
create table member_type
(
   member_type          character(1),
   description          character(30)
)


/*************************/
/* Create the address.   */
/*************************/
create table address
(
   member_no            int,
   address_type         char(1),
   street1              char(30),
   street2              char(30),
   city                 char(20),
   state                char(20),
   country              char(15),
   zip_pc               char(10)
)


/****************************/
/* Create the orders table. */
/****************************/
create table orders
(
   member_no            int,
   request_date         datetime,
   sequence_no          integer,
   product_type         char(1),
   units                float,
   required_date        datetime,
   date_delivered       datetime,
   comments             char(100),
   amount_collected     money,
   downpayment          money
)


/*****************************************/
/* Create the address_type table.        */
/*****************************************/
create table address_type
(
   address_type         char(1),
```

(Continues)

Source 3.2 *(Continued)*

```
    description          char(15)
)
go


/********************************************/
/* Create the product_type table.          */
/********************************************/
create table product_type
(
    product_type        char(5),
    description         char(30),
    on_hand_qty         float,
    Unit_price          money
)
go
```

Source 3.2   *(Continued)*

✓ It is possible to qualify every SQL command with the database and owner
name as follows: create table address.dbo.customer. This will save you from
having to change the default database name. This approach requires additional typing, however, so the method used in the script for changing the default database is preferred.

Adding Data to User-Defined Tables

Figure 3.6 shows the primary methods available to add data to user-defined tables: INSERT, VIEWS, BCP (batch copy procedure), and 3rd Party Tools. These are defined in the Data Manipulation Language (DML) of the ANSI '92 standard. The data is inserted into user-defined tables that are maintained within databases.

The different formats of the INSERT command are discussed in this section. The other methods are discussed later in this book. The basic syntax of this command is the following:

```
INSERT [INTO] table_name
(fieldname1, fieldname2, ....)
VALUES
(value1, value2, ....)
```

One example of the syntax for adding data to user-defined tables is

```
    INSERT INTO address_type
(address_type,description)
VALUES
    ('M', 'Mailing')
    go
```

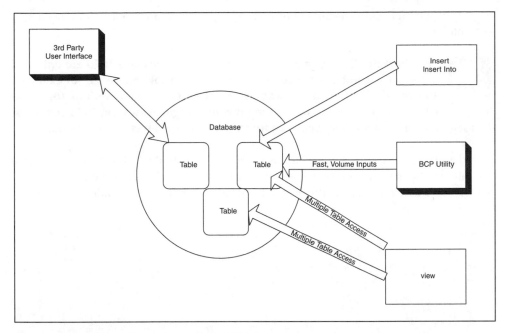

Figure 3.6   Adding data to user-defined tables.

```
    INSERT address_type
(address_type,description)
VALUES
    ('H', 'Home')
    go

    INSERT address_type
(address_type,description)
VALUES
    ('D', 'Delivery')
    go
```

A second example of this syntax is as follows:

```
INSERT address_type
    VALUES ('M', 'Mailing')

INSERT address_type VALUES ('D', 'Delivery')
go
```

SQL Server commands are case insensitive. SQL Server commands can be entered in upper case (e.g., VALUES), lower case (e.g., values), or mixed case (e.g., VALues).

Microsoft SQL Server displays a message (unless the option No Count Display is turned on) showing the number of rows that are affected by a command. In this case, the message is "(1 row(s) affected)". If the No Count Display option is selected, SQL

Server displays an acknowledgment of success (e.g., "The command(s) completed successfully").

The character field lengths that are specified in the table field are enforced when an attempt is made to insert data into the column fields. For example, the description field in the address was created with a length of 10. An attempt to insert a value that is greater than this length generates the following error message: "String/Binary data would be truncated Command has been aborted."

A data insert script can be used to insert data into the table. This saves reentry time and allows the database tables to be reconstructed at any time. Source Listing 3.3 inserts sample data records into the user-defined tables created into the address database.

```
/*******************************************************************/
/* Filename: \addrinsert.txt                                       */
/* Author:   Sanjiv Purba                                          */
/* Modification History:                                           */
/*                                                                 */
/* Description:                                                    */
/* Insert data into the user defined tables in the address db.     */
/* This script will add a single member to the database with all   */
/* the supporting data.                                            */
/*******************************************************************/
use address
go
/* Use the truncate command to drop data in the tables before inserting
   new data. The truncate command has advantages for efficiency, (e.g.
   it does not write to the log), over other commands to clear tables.
*/
TRUNCATE TABLE member
TRUNCATE TABLE member_type
TRUNCATE TABLE address
TRUNCATE TABLE orders
TRUNCATE TABLE address_type
TRUNCATE TABLE product_type
go


/***********************************/
/* Insert data into the member table */
/***********************************/
INSERT INTO member
(
    member_no,
    last_name,
    middle_initial,
    first_name,
```

(Continues)

Source 3.3   Insert data into user-defined tables.

```
    home_phone,
    business_phone,
    cell_phone,
    fax,
    email,
    web_site,
    preference,
    member_since,
    member_type
)
VALUES
(
    100,
    'Easy',
    ' ',
    'Bruce',
    '123-111-2222',
    '123-222-2222',
    '123-333-3333',
    '123-444-4444',
    'beasy@abc.com',
    ' ',
    'collectors plates',
    'Feb 01, 1994',
    '1'
)

/**************************************************/
/* Insert data rows into the member_type table */
/**************************************************/
INSERT INTO member_type
(member_type, description)
VALUES
('1', 'Collector Plates')

/**********************************************/
/* Insert data rows into the address table  */
/**********************************************/
INSERT INTO address
(
    customer_no,
    address_type,
    street1,
    street2,
    city,
    state_province,
    country,
```

(Continues)

Source 3.3   *(Continued)*

```
    zip_pc
)
VALUES
(
    100,
    'M',
    '123 Tobos Street',
    ' ',
    'New York City',
    'New York',
    'USA',
    '10111'
)

/*********************************************/
/* Insert data rows into the orders table */
/*********************************************/
INSERT INTO orders
(
    member_no,
    request_date,
    sequence_no,
    product_type,
    units,
    required_date,
    date_delivered,
    comments,
    amount_collected,
    downpayment
)
VALUES
(
    100,
    'Feb 1, 1999',
    1,
    'Pl101',
    1,
    'June 1, 1999',
    ' ',
    ' ',
    0,
    0
)

/*********************************************/
/* Insert data into the address_type table */
/*********************************************/
```

(Continues)

Source 3.3 *(Continued)*

```
INSERT INTO address_type
(address_type,description)
VALUES
('M', 'Mailing')
go


/*********************************************/
/* Insert data into the product_type table */
/*********************************************/
INSERT INTO product_type
(product_type,description,on_hand_qty, unit_price)
VALUES
('pl101M', 'Collector plate: early fall leaves', 100, 50)
go
```

Source 3.3   *(Continued)*

Using batch scripts to insert data into tables requires careful attention to referential integrity (RI) issues. Mistakes in RI can easily be made while coding a script (e.g., mistyping an I for a 1). Since the data is being inserted directly into the table, such errors may not be detected until they bring down a production application or produce incorrect reports. For production data, it is preferable to use validation programs to validate the data before inserting it directly into the table. Another method, which is covered in the next chapter, is to use table constraints for data validation.

Retrieving the Data

Data can be retrieved from tables using several different methods. The basic command for retrieving information from tables is the ANSI '92–compliant Select command. Figure 3.7 displays the results of issuing a select statement in the SQL Server Query Analyzer tool. The code is based on the following syntax:

```
SELECT ALL/DISTINCT/column_field_names
    FROM table/view hints
        WHERE clause
            ORDER BY clause
            GROUP BY clause
```

The Group By and Order By clauses group or sort output by the field that is specified. The default sequence for the Order By clause is the ascending sequence.

To select all the column fields, use the asterisk (*) to select all the column fields from a table, as in SELECT * from table_name.

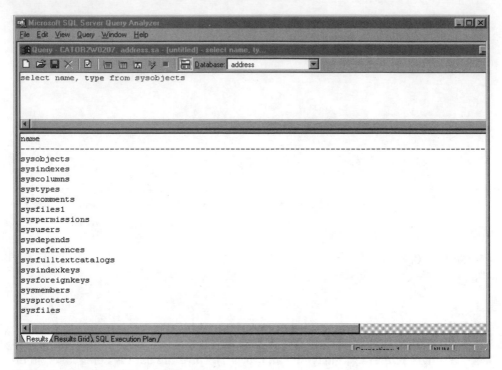

Figure 3.7 Output from a select statement.

Sample Scripts

The following example uses a wildcard (e.g., "*") to retrieve all the columns in a data record in the product_type user table in the default database. The absence of a WHERE clause selects all the data rows from the table.

```
SELECT * from product_type
    go
```

The following example uses a wildcard to retrieve all the columns in a data record in the member table. The WHERE clause is used to restrict the result set to only those data rows that have a member_type value of 1.

```
SELECT * from member
    WHERE member_type = '1'
go
```

 SQL Server accepts either double or single quotes around character values. Consequently, "R" and 'R' achieves the same result. However, SQL Server is insistent on matching the symbols, so "R' is not syntactically acceptable.

The following example specifies the inclusion of two specific columns in the result set, namely last_name and first_name. Other columns in the member table are ignored. Since there is no WHERE clause, all the data rows in the table are included in the result set.

```
SELECT last_name, first_name from member
go
```

The following example demonstrates how to insert a data row into a user table and subsequently retrieve it for display. This example specifies four column names that are intended to receive information. The VALUES portion of the statement specifies a value for each column that is specified in brackets '(...)', in the first part of the statement. The specified values match the order of the column names, and also remain consistent to the datatype of the column. Column names that are missing in the INSERT statement receive a value of NULL, IDENTITY, or DEFAULT depending on the script that was used to CREATE the table. Columns that are marked mandatory in the CREATE script must be included in the INSERT command. Rules and constraints are applied to the values contained in the INSERT statement. Violations cause the statement to be rejected. The second statement in the batch retrieves all the data rows from the product_type user table and orders them in ascending sequence by unit_price.

```
    INSERT INTO product_type
(product_type,description,on_hand_qty, unit_price)
VALUES
('pl101F', 'Collector plate: spring rivers', 100, 40)

    select * from product_type
ORDER BY unit_price
    go
```

 By default, the names of the table fields serve as column headings in the output. The table field name can be overridden by leaving a space and entering another name for the column heading, without surrounding quotes. An example of this is address_code code. Here code serves as the column heading.

Summary

This chapter was the first part of a two-part primer introducing the object maintenance commands in the Microsoft SQL Server environment. The chapter began with an examination of the products categories that are consistently required on application development projects including viewing development tools, databases, modeling tools, middleware, transaction monitors, testing tools, networking, hardware, project management and estimating tools, change management, and system management.

This chapter introduced the new wizards and examined some of the GUI interactive tools. A new "address" database was created. A small set of database tables were created and stored in an existing database (e.g., pubs) or the new address database. A sample logical application table schema was defined and converted to a physical format. The chapter also used the INSERT command to load test data into the relational database tables.

Primer for Building an Application: Part B

This chapter shows how to enhance the application defined in the previous chapter using additional Transact-SQL features. These features support a distributed, n-tier application that encapsulates either business logic or a database interface. Although stored procedures, triggers, and referential integrity are stored in a database data dictionary, these objects can form a distinct logical tier. Three broad application categories are examined in this chapter: the SQL Server environment; data validation through column constraints (e.g., primary, foreign, and identity); and complex database objects including joins, views, stored procedures, and triggers.

This chapter provides streamlined syntax that can be processed through scripts, graphical tools, and wizards. Subsequent chapters focus on more detailed versions of the command syntax.

The SQL Server Environment

Figure 4.1 combines a view of the operating environment, storage environment, development environment, engine architectures, Transact-SQL, client platform services, and other add-ons. As the figure shows, there are several types of client platforms. The first client platform example includes a 16/32-bit application developed in a tool such as Visual Basic 5/Visual C++ communicating directly to SQL Server through ODBC, VBO, or open client (middleware). The second client platform supports a 16/32-bit client appli-

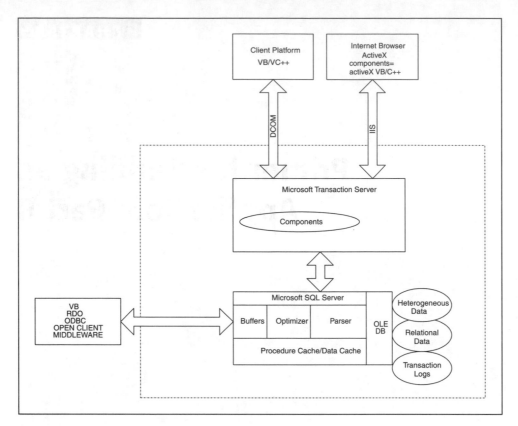

Figure 4.1   SQL Server environment.

cation that communicates with MTS through distributed common object management (DCOM). These are now based on an OLE DB and DCOM component model that is both extensible and scalable. In this example, MTS communicates with SQL Server and manages the user connections. The third client platform example supports a thin client application model that supports an Internet Explorer browser that executes ActiveX components through the Internet Information Server (IIS).

Figure 4.1 also shows that SQL Server consists of the following high-level components that are of relevance to this discussion: parser, query processor, databases, database objects, and transaction logs. The parser is the part of the SQL Server engine that interprets user command requests for syntactical correctness. The query processor is the part of the SQL Server engine that determines the most cost-effective method of responding to a request, including the access path and the indexes to traverse. The other database objects are discussed later in this chapter.

SQL Server Databases and Objects

Microsoft SQL Server architecture is heavily reliant on databases based on the relational data model. The databases contain information about the entire SQL Server environment and ongoing operations, including location of the data in the physical environment, user names and permissions, and configuration values that are used by SQL Server during execution. SQL Server is normally installed with the master, model, msdb, pubs, and tempdb databases. These are referred to as the system databases. The master database contains configuration information about the SQL Server environment. It also contains system procedures that are used to manipulate the environment and system tables (e.g., sp_who lists users signed into the system). The model database is used as a template to create new databases, called user databases. The pubs database contains user tables that support a sample application. The tempdb database is used for two main purposes. First, many SQL Server commands (e.g., Group By, Order By) use the tempdb as a temporary work area. Second, user applications can create temporary tables in the tempdb that automatically disappear at specific events (e.g., when the user creating them logs off the system).

Each database contains system tables that define the database itself. Databases also contain objects, such as tables, indexes, constraints, datatypes, user-defined datatypes, stored procedures, views, and triggers. Every database has a corresponding transaction log that plays a critical role in maintaining data consistency in the event of database server failure or disaster. Specific events are recorded to the transaction log on an ongoing basis. Various procedures also routinely sweep the transaction log. Because of this constant server interaction with the log, its location and use play a key role in application performance.

Each database in SQL Server contains the following system tables: sysobjects, sysindexes, syscolumns, systypes, syscomments, syspermissions, sysusers, sysdepends, sysreferences, sysindexkeys, sysforeignkeys, sysmembers, sysprotects, sysfileinfilegroups, and sysallocations. Table 4.1 shows that some system tables are present in both the master and the other databases. In some cases, the nonmaster databases contain system

Table 4.1 System Tables in all Databases

MODEL DATABASE SYSTEM TABLES	MASTER DATABASE SYSTEM TABLES	DESCRIPTION	EXTRACTING SYSTEM TABLE INFORMATION
Sysobjects	Sysobjects	Contains a row for every object within a database.	Select sysobjects. Select * from sysobjects.
Sysindexes	Sysindexes	Index information related to user tables.	Select sysindexes. Select * from sysindexes.
Syscolumns	Syscolumns	List of columns for defined tables.	Select syscolumns. Select * from syscolumns.
Systypes	Systypes	Contains the data types and the user defined datatypes.	Select systypes. Select * from systypes.

(Continues)

Table 4.1   *(Continued)*

MODEL DATABASE SYSTEM TABLES	MASTER DATABASE SYSTEM TABLES	DESCRIPTION	EXTRACTING SYSTEM TABLE INFORMATION
Syscomments	Syscomments	Contains text belonging to database objects such as stored procedures, triggers, and views.	Select syscomments. Select * from syscomments.
Syspermissions	Syspermissions	List of permissions for users active in the database.	Select syspermissions. Select * from syspermissions.
Sysusers	Sysusers	User list for the database.	Select sysusers. Select * from sysusers.
Sysdepends	Sysdepends	Contains dependencies for database objects.	Select sysdepends. Select * from sysdepends.
Sysreferences	Sysreferences	References or aliases.	Select sysreferences. Select * from sysreferences.
Sysindexkeys	Sysindexkeys	Primary keys designated for tables in the database.	Select sysindexkeys. Select * from sysindexkeys.
Sysforeignkeys	Sysforeignkeys	Foreign keys designated for tables in the database.	Select sysforeignkeys. Select * from sysforeignkeys.
Sysmembers	Sysmembers	Designated members for the database.	Select sysmembers. Select * from sysmembers.
Sysprotects	Sysprotects	Protected definitions.	Select sysprotects. Select * from sysprotects.
Sysallocations	Sysallocations	Physical space allocated to the database.	Select sysallocations. Select * from sysallocations.
Sysfileinfilegroups	Not available	Relationship to file groups.	Select sysfileinfilegroups. Select * from sysfileinfilegroups.

tables that do not occur in the master database. Table 4.2 contains a list of system tables that are contained only in the master database. Both tables contain a description and sample code to extract system table information from the data dictionary. To execute the sample code for a specific database, establish that database as the default, as follows: use database_name (e.g., use pubs).

 The master database should be routinely backed up. Be sure to test the backup copy by restoring it into a test environment.

Table 4.2 System Tables Unique to the Master Database Only

MODEL SYSTEM TABLES	MASTER SYSTEM TABLES	DESCRIPTION	EXTRACTING SYSTEM TABLE INFORMATION
Not available	Sysfiles1	Extended file list.	Select sysfiles1. Select * from sysfiles1.
NA	Sysdatabases	Databases defined in the environment.	Select sysdatabases. Select * from sysdatabases.
NA	Sysperfinfo	Performance information.	Select sysperfinfo. Select * from sysperfinfo.
NA	Sysprocesses	A list of processes active in the environment.	Select sysprocesses. Select * from sysprocesses.
NA	Sysxlogins	A list of remote logins.	Select sysxlogins. Select * from sysxlogins.
NA	Syslocks	A list of active locks on database objects.	Select syslocks. Select * from syslocks.
NA	Sysdevices	A list of device definitions for databases and transaction logs.	Select sysdevices. Select * from sysdevices.
NA	Sysmessages	User and error messages.	Select sysmessages. Select * from sysmessages.
NA	Sysconfigures	Configuration information.	Select sysconfigures. Select * from sysconfigures.
NA	Syscurconfigs	Current configuration values.	Select syscurconfigs. Select * from syscurconfigs.
NA	Sysservers	Remote servers known to the current SQL Server.	Select sysservers. Select * from sysservers.
NA	Syslockinfo	Detailed information about active locks.	Select syslockinfo. Select * from syslockinfo.
NA	Syslanguages	Languages known to the current SQL Server.	Select syslanguages. Select * from syslanguages.
NA	Syscharsets	Character sets supported by SQL Server.	Select syscharsets. Select * from syscharsets.
NA	Syscursorrefs	Cursor references.	Select syscursorrefs. Select * from syscursorrefs.
NA	Syscursors	Active cursors.	Select syscursors. Select * from syscursors.
NA	Syscursorcolumns	Columns belonging to the cursors.	Select syscursorcolumns. Select * from syscursorcolumns.
NA	Syscursortables	Tables accessed by active cursors.	Select syscursortables. Select * from syscursortables.

(Continues)

Table 4.2 *(Continued)*

MODEL SYSTEM TABLES	MASTER SYSTEM TABLES	DESCRIPTION	EXTRACTING SYSTEM TABLE INFORMATION
NA	Sysaltfiles	Alternate file lists.	Select sysaltfiles. Select * from sysaltfiles.
NA	Sysfiles	Files known to SQL Server.	Select sysfiles. Select * from sysfiles.
NA	Sysfilegroups	Files grouped together.	Select sysfilegroups. Select * from sysfilegroups.
NA	Sysarticles	Article information for the whole database environment.	Select sysarticles. Select * from sysarticles.
NA	Syspublications	Databases identified as publications for the purpose of replication.	Select syspublications. Select * from syspublications.
NA	Syssubscriptions	Databases subscribing to publications.	Select syssubscriptions. Select * from syssubscriptions.

Table 4.2 contains a list of system tables that exist only in the master database. To run the code that extracts information about the tables, utilize the Use Master command to change the default database to the master database and use the Query Analyzer to execute the command. You can also use a drop-down list in the Query Analyzer to change the default database name.

 Create objects in the model database if you want them to be automatically copied to new user databases.

Data Validation through Column Constraints

One form of data validation can be programmed directly into the SQL Server data dictionary through column constraints. This can be done when tables are created using the SQL Create command or when they are altered using the Alter command. Constraints also provide functionality that would otherwise need to be programmed. This is shown in Figure 4.2. This section examines the following table constraints:

Identity. At most, one column in every table can be assigned an identity constraint. This constraint automatically assigns a sequential number to a row being inserted into a table. This is used to satisfy applications that require a sequential counter (such as ticket number) to be incremented with every row that is inserted into a table. The identity constraint does not affect rows that are being modified, deleted, or selected.

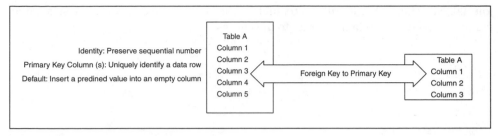

Figure 4.2 Column constraints.

Primary Key. This is one of two key constraints. This constraint is applied to one or more columns in a table. It guarantees that no more than one row with a specific combination of values for columns identified as "primary key" exist in the same table. This is a good way to guarantee key uniqueness.

Foreign Key and References. This is the second of the key constraints. This constraint can be applied to zero or more columns in a table. Columns that are marked with this constraint go through an extra step of validation before the row is inserted into the table. This involves examining another table, indicated in the foreign key constraint, and ensuring that the value exists in the foreign key table. The row is not inserted if there is a violation of this constraint.

Default. Only one default constraint can be attached to a column in a table. There is no limit on the number of columns that can be associated with default constraints. Default constraints provide a value to be inserted into a column if an insert command does not specify it.

Identity

The identity feature is identified for a maximum of one column in a table at the time it is created or altered. This column can be referred to with the logical name IDENTITY-COL in SQL code that accesses the table. It is important to realize that the values lost due to deleted rows are not automatically recovered. The examples in this section demonstrate how to take advantage of the identity constraint, how to use the timestamp datatype, how to delete a row, and how to override the identity constraint in an insert statement. The syntax for allocating an identity constraint to a table column is

```
CREATE TABLE table_name        IDENTITY (start, step)
```

Start determines the value inserted the first time a row is inserted after the identity constraint is applied to a column. The step value specifies the incremental value that is added to the sequential number for the next insert. This is a good way to leave numbering gaps in successive inserted rows in a table.

Sample Scripts

Source Listing 4.1 builds another small table to demonstrate a technique for creating a column with an identity feature. The example also extracts the inserted data from the journal_entry table. The journal_entry table is used to track text entries. The sequential number is used to maintain an order to the entries.

```
USE address
go

DROP TABLE journal_entry
go

CREATE TABLE journal_entry
(
    sequence_no     int       IDENTITY (2000, 1),
    description     char(80)
)
go

/* You do not need to specify the IDENTITY column name when inserting
rows into the table. The sequence_no will begin with 2000 and be
incremented by 1 on every insert */

insert journal_entry
(description) VALUES ('The first entry of the day')
go

/* insert two more records into the tables */
insert journal_entry
(description) VALUES ('The second entry of the day')
go

insert journal_entry
(description) VALUES ('The third entry of the day')
go

/* display the results */
select * from journal_entry
go

select description from journal_entry
go

/* use the logical name of the IDENTITY column to display the contents
of the table */

select IDENTITYCOL, description from journal_entry
go
```

Source 4.1   Using the IDENTITY constraint.

Source Listing 4.2 adds a timestamp to the journal_entry table.

```
USE address
go

DROP TABLE journal_entry
go

CREATE TABLE journal_entry
(
    sequence_no     int     IDENTITY (2000, 1),
    description     char(80),
    entry_time      timestamp
)
go

/* You do not need to specify a value for a column identified with the
timestamp datatype. There can only be one column per table with this
datatype. */

insert journal_entry
(description) VALUES ('The first entry of the day')
go

/* insert two more records into the tables */
insert journal_entry
(description) VALUES ('The second entry of the day')
go

insert journal_entry
(description) VALUES ('The third entry of the day')
go

insert journal_entry
(description) VALUES ('The fourth entry of the day')
go

/* display the results */
select * from journal_entry
```

Source 4.2   Using timestamp.

Source Listing 4.3 demonstrates how to delete records within a range in the journal_entry table. It then demonstrates how to insert a record with a specific value for the sequence_no. Notice that a specific Set command is required to do this.

```
select * from journal_entry
go

delete journal_entry
  where sequence_no > 2000 and sequence_no < 20004
go

select * from journal_entry
go

/* display the results */
select * from journal_entry
go

INSERT journal_entry
(sequence_no, description)
VALUES
(2002, 'this should not be accepted without a set identity_insert
command')
go
```

Source 4.3 Deleting records.

Without the SET command being issued, this command will display the following error: Attempting to insert explicit value for identify column in table journal_entry. The following code corrects this error:

```
SET IDENTITY_INSERT journal_entry on
go

INSERT journal_entry
(sequence_no, description)
VALUES
(2002, 'this value was explicitly inserted into the table')
go

SET IDENTITY_INSERT journal_entry off

select * from journal_entry
go
```

Primary Key Constraints

The primary key constraint can only be applied to one combination of key columns. This constraint identifies those values as the key columns for the table, optionally building an index on them. The syntax for the primary key constraint is

```
CREATE TABLE table_name
( [column_list     datatype ...] [PRIMARY KEY [CLUSTERED/NONCLUSTERED]]
)
```

Another example of the primary key constraint syntax is
```
CREATE TABLE table_name
(
     [column_list      datatype ...],

       CONSTRAINT PK_constraint_name PRIMARY KEY
[CLUSTERED/NONCLUSTERED] (column1, column2, ...)
)
```

Note that a clustered index is created by default on the column specified as primary key. Only one primary key constraint can be specified for a single table.

Sample Scripts

Source Listing 4.4 creates the journal_entry table, specifying the sequence_no column as both an identity constraint column and as a primary key column. This example also indicates that the column should generate a clustered index for the table.

```
USE address
go

drop table journal_entry
go

create table journal_entry
(
   journal_entry    int    IDENTITY (2000,1) PRIMARY KEY CLUSTERED,
   description      char(80),
   entry_time       timestamp
)
go

insert journal_entry   (description)
values (ëprimary key example entryí)
go
/* Run this batch 5 times before issuing the following code to see that
5 rows have been inserted into the table. */
select * from journal_entry
select a.id, b.rows
   from sysobjects a, sysindexes b
      where a.name = ëjournal_entryí and a.id = b.id
go
```

Source 4.4   Combining constraints.

In Source Listing 4.5, a primary key constraint is created using three columns as a combined key.

```
use address
go

drop table movie
go

create table movie
(
    movie_title      character (40),
    movie_type       character (20).
release_year     character (4),
actor1           character (20),
actor2           character (20),
director         character (20),
rating           int

    CONSTRAINT PK_movie PRIMARY KEY CLUSTERED (movie_title, movie_type,
release_year)
)    /* the PK represents primary key */
go
```

Source 4.5   A multi-column primary key constraint.

Foreign Key and References Constraints

The foreign key constraint can be applied a multiple number of times within a table. The purpose of this constraint is to define a relationship with the primary keys of other tables. The syntax for the foreign key constraint is

```
CREATE TABLE table_name
([column_name] FOREIGN KEY [columns] REFERENCES [reference_tables])
```

Another syntax for the foreign key constraint is

```
(    [column_names      datatypes ....],

CONSTRAINT constraint_name FOREIGN KEY [(column1, column2, ...)]
                REFERENCES [reference_tables(column1, column2, ...)]
)
```

Note that foreign key is validated with the tables identified in the references part of the command. References defines the table that supplies matching key columns.

Sample Scripts

Source Listing 4.6 demonstrates the use of the foreign key and references constraints.

```
USE address
go

drop table movie
drop table movie_type
go
create table movie_type
(
   movie_type     character(1) PRIMARY KEY,
   description    character(30)
)
go


create table movie
(
   movie_no        int IDENTITY (2000, 1) PRIMARY KEY CLUSTERED,
   movie_title     character (40),
   movie_type      character (1) REFERENCES movie_type (movie_type)
release_year    character (4),
actor1          character (20),
actor2          character (20),
director        character (20),
rating          int
)
go
/* the movie_type table should have a PRIMARY KEY to support the
REFERENCES constraint included on the movie_type column in the movie
                                                              table */

/* Insert data rows into the two tables. Start with the movie_type
                                                            table. */
insert movie_type
(movie_type, description)
VALUES
('S', 'Science Fiction')
go

insert movie
(
                                                    (Continues)
```

Source 4.6 Using foreign key and reference constraints.

```
movie_title,
movie_type,
release_year,
actor1,
actor2,
director,
rating
)
VALUES
(
     'Stare Wares',
     'S',
'1995',
'Gary Hamilton',
'Sue Rebecca',
' ',
5
     )
go

/* attempt to enter a movie_type that does not exist in the movie_type
                                                              table */

insert movie
(
movie_title,
movie_type,
release_year,
actor1,
actor2,
director,
rating
)
VALUES
(
     'T the Movie',
     'T',
'1995',
'Gary Hamilton',
'Sue Rebecca',
' ',
5
     )
go
```

Source 4.6 *(Continued)*

In Source Listing 4.7, a foreign key constraint is created for a slightly modified version of the movie table. A foreign key is created in the movie table. A primary key constraint is created on the fields that are referenced in the foreign table being inspected.

```
use address
go

drop table movie
drop table movie_type
drop table language
go

create table movie_type
(
   movie_type      character(1) PRIMARY KEY,
   description     character(30)
)
go

create table movie
(
   movie_no        int IDENTITY (2000, 1) PRIMARY KEY CLUSTERED,
   movie_title     character (40),
   movie_type      character (1) REFERENCES movie_type (movie_type)
release_year    character (4),
actor1          character (20),
actor2          character (20),
director        character (20),
lang_type       character (1),
rating          int

CONSTRAINT FK_language FOREIGN KEY (lang_type)
        REFERENCES language_type (lang_type)
)

create table language
(
   lang_type          char(1),
   description        char(20)

   CONSTRAINT PK_language PRIMARY KEY CLUSTERED (lang_type)
)
go

insert movie_type
(movie_type, description)
VALUES
```

(Continues)

Source 4.7 Modifying the movie table.

```
('S', 'Science Fiction')
go

/* Test the FOREIGN KEY constraint */
INSERT language
(lang_type, description)
VALUES
('E', 'English')
go

INSERT language
(lang_type, description)
VALUES
('F', 'French')
go

insert movie
(
movie_title,
movie_type,
release_year,
actor1,
actor2,
director,
lang_type,
rating
)
VALUES
(
    'Stares Wares',
    'S',
'1995',
'Gary Hamilton',
'Sue Rebecca',
' ',
'E',
5
    )
go

/* try to insert a language type that does not exist in the language
                                                          table */

insert movie
(
movie_title,
```

(Continues)

Source 4.7 *(Continued)*

```
movie_type,
release_year,
actor1,
actor2,
director,
lang_type,
rating
)
VALUES
(
    'Stares Wares',
    'S',
'1995',
'Gary Hamilton',
'Sue Rebecca',
' ',
'Z',
5
    )
go
```

Source 4.7 *(Continued)*

Note that it is also possible to use triggers to enforce referential integrity instead of constraints. Constraints are processed before triggers and are conceptually easier to implement because the validation procedure is saved with the table creation code. Constraints, however, are limited to referencing tables in the current database. Triggers do not have this limitation.

Default Constraints

Default constraints are associated with columns in a table. There can be zero or one defaults per column in a table. Default constraints are invoked if no value is supplied in an insert command for an associated field. The syntax for a default constraint is the following:

```
CREATE TABLE table_name
    column1   datatype   DEFAULT (value),
    column2   datatype   DEFAULT ('value'),
    column3   datatype   DEFAULT value,
column4   datatype   DEFAULT 'value',
column5   datatype   DEFAULT 'value',
column6   datatype   DEFAULT 'value'.
```

Sample Scripts

Source Listing 4.8 provides examples of engaging default constraints.

```
use address
go

drop table movie
drop table movie_type
drop table language
go

create table movie_type
(
   movie_type       character(1) PRIMARY KEY,
   description      character(30)
)
go

create table movie
(
    movie_no       int IDENTITY (2000, 1) PRIMARY KEY CLUSTERED,
    movie_title    character (40),
    movie_type     character (1) REFERENCES movie_type (movie_type),
release_year    character (4)     DEFAULT '1999',
actor1          character (20),
actor2          character (20),
director        character (20),
lang_type       character (1)     DEFAULT 'E',
rating          int               DEFAULT 4

CONSTRAINT FK_language FOREIGN KEY (lang_type)
         REFERENCES language_type (lang_type)
)

create table language
(
   lang_type           char(1),
   description          char(20)

   CONSTRAINT PK_language PRIMARY KEY CLUSTERED (lang_type)
)
go
```
(Continues)

Source 4.8 Using default constraints.

```
insert movie_type
(movie_type, description)
VALUES
('S', 'Science Fiction')
go

/* Test the FOREIGN KEY constraint */
INSERT language
(lang_type, description)
VALUES
('E', 'English')
go

INSERT language
(lang_type, description)
VALUES
('F', 'French')
go

insert movie
(
movie_title,
movie_type,
release_year,
actor1,
actor2,
director,
lang_type
)
VALUES
(
    'Mushy',
    'S',
'1999',
'Down Katrina',
'value',
'value',
'E'
    )
go
```

Source 4.8 *(Continued)*

Source Listing 4.9 demonstrates assigning three different types of defaults.

```
USE address
go

DROP TABLE sale
go

CREATE TABLE sale
(
    invoice_no      int,
    price           money       DEFAULT 0.00,
    sale_date       datetime    DEFAULT getdate(),
    comment         char (30)   DEFAULT 'Final Sale'
)
go

INSERT sale
(invoice_no, price) VALUES (110, 2.00)
go

INSERT sale (invoice_no) VALUES (111)
go

select * from sale
go
```

Source 4.9   Defining different default types.

Source Listing 4.10 demonstrates assigning three different types of defaults and an identity column.

```
USE address
go

DROP TABLE sale
go

CREATE TABLE sale
(
    invoice_no      int         IDENTITY,
    price           money       DEFAULT 0.00,
    sale_date       datetime    DEFAULT getdate(),
    comment         char (45)   DEFAULT 'Final Sale'
)
go

INSERT sale
(comment) VALUES ('testing default and identity constraints')
```

Source 4.10   Using defaults and identity constraints.

Complex Database Objects

The select statement is used to extract information from Microsoft SQL Server tables. This is a basic Sequel command that is the basis for many other types of information extraction or database objects. This includes

Joins. Mathematically join related columns in two or more relational tables to produce a result set.

Subqueries. Use the result set of one query to drive a result set off another query.

Views. Create a logical table that contains one or more columns from one or more tables.

Stored procedures. Select information from tables, save values to local variables, and conduct complex processing on the data.

Triggers. Attach to specific events in tables or columns.

Cursors. Process specific records in a result set.

Joins

Join commands are used to leverage basic mathematical set theory to manipulate information in more than one relational table. There are many types of joins, including full outer joins, left joins, right joins, equi-joins, and self-joins. This primer examines the commonly used equi-joins. The other types of joins will be discussed later in this book.

A simplified syntax for performing an equi-join on a flexible number of database tables is as follows:

```
SELECT [alias.]column_list
FROM table1 alias1, table2 alias2 ....
     WHERE selection_clause
Sample Script
```

Source Listing 4.11 uses three tables—movie, movie_type, and language—to demonstrate the equi-join.

```
create table movie_type
(
   movie_type      character(1) PRIMARY KEY,
   description     character(30)
)
go
create table movie
(
```
(Continues)

Source 4.11 Using the equi-join.

```
     movie_no          int IDENTITY (2000, 1) PRIMARY KEY CLUSTERED,
     movie_title     character (40),
     movie_type      character (1) REFERENCES movie_type (movie_type)
release_year      character (4)         DEFAULT '1999',
actor1            character (20),
actor2            character (20),
director          character (20),
lang_type         character (1)         DEFAULT 'E',
rating            int                   DEFAULT 4)


insert movie_type
(movie_type, description)

    SELECT a.movie_title, a.release_year, a.rating, b.description
        FROM movie a, movie_type b
        WHERE a.movie_type = b.movie_type
go
```

Source 4.11 (*Continued*).

 Joins are used extensively inside views to simplify and control SQL access by users to multiple tables.

Subqueries

Subqueries are similar to joins. Both retrieve information from multiple database tables. Subqueries tend to be more intuitive for some users than are joins. This section provides a brief introduction to subqueries. The syntax for subqueries is as follows:

```
SELECT column_fields FROM table_list
    WHERE [EXISTS/IN] (selection_clause)
```

In this example, the in command word can subquery:

```
SELECT movie_title, release_year, rating
        FROM movie
        WHERE lang_type IN (SELECT lang_type from language
            WHERE lang_type = 'E')
    go
```

Views

Views are yet another way of accessing information from one or more database tables. To the end-user, a view appears like any other database table. A view is a logical name that maps to a database schema. At the physical level, a single view may be drawing columns from a set of tables. Views can be customized to specific user needs, assigned their own security levels, and are easier to understand for users who are unfamiliar with the SQL model. A simplified syntax for the create view command is as follows (Note: the view is created in the default or current database):

```
CREATE VIEW owner.viewname [column_list]
    AS select_clause
```

Since views are similar to tables, information about them is also included in a number of system tables just like table information, including sysobjects. Views must be dropped, just as tables are dropped, before they are re-created in a database. A simplified syntax for the command to drop a view from a database is

```
DROP VIEW owner.viewname
```

Once a view is created, it is necessary to use SQL commands to utilize it. Since a view is like a table, the commands that have been discussed for tables—select, joins, and subqueries—can also be used with views. A simplified syntax to execute a view after it is created is as follows:

```
SELECT [*/column_names] from view_name where search_clause
```

Sample Scripts

The following example creates a view for a user who only requires a subset of fields in a table. Use a drop view command to drop the view before trying to create it to support iterative execution of the create view command. This code can be entered interactively or through a script file that is executed:

```
DROP VIEW movie_rating
go

CREATE VIEW movie_rating
AS
    SELECT movie_title, release_date, rating
        FROM movie
go

SELECT * FROM movie
go
```

 Using views to simplify SQL queries of a database does not come free. Someone needs to be charged with building and maintaining views for users to access. This can often become a full-time job. The caretaker of the views must understand the business application. Views also do not support triggers.

The following example leverages a view across two tables:

```
DROP VIEW movie_report
go
```

```
CREATE VIEW movie_report
AS
      SELECT a.movie_title, a.release_date, b.description
FROM movie a, movie_type b
          WHERE a.movie_type = b.movie_type
go

SELECT * FROM movie_report
Go
```

Leveraging Stored Procedures

Stored procedures are another important database object that were primarily responsible for driving the popularity of SQL Server when it was first released. Stored procedures support the thin client client/server model by compiling code directly into the database server dictionary. This innovation was a watershed when it was introduced in the late 1980s, and it forced vendors like Oracle to take notice and include stored procedures into their own product offerings. Stored procedures support the data definition language (DDL), data manipulation language (DML), and a control-of-flow dialect that supports the development of complex programs on the database server side. Figure 4.3 shows the process for using stored procedures. Stored procedures can be created in an external file or with the assistance of one of the SQL Server graphical administrative tools. My preference is to create stored procedures using a text

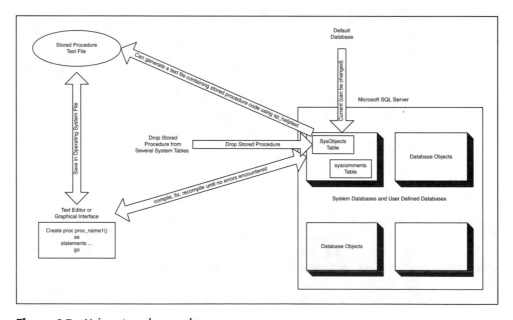

Figure 4.3 Using stored procedures.

editor and then put the script files through a process of change management. As the figure demonstrates, the major steps for creating a stored procedure are the following:

1. Build a path or change to the default database that will hold the stored procedure.

2. Drop the stored procedure if it already exists.

3. Write the stored procedure using a text editor or a graphical tool.

4. Compile the stored procedure into a SQL Server database.

5. Fix any compile errors and recompile the stored procedure until it compiles successfully.

6. Execute the stored procedure by name and provide any parameters that it expects to receive.

Stored Procedure Syntax

The syntax for writing stored procedures is

```
CREATE PROC[EDURE] proc_name
(
  @parameter        datatype,. . .
)
AS
DECLARE local_variable        datatype,. . .

Control-of-flow Statements

RETURN [return_code]
go
```

It is necessary to drop a stored procedure using the following syntax before creating it:

```
DROP PROCEDURE proc_name
go
```

Once a stored procedure is successfully compiled, it can be executed using the following syntax:

```
EXECUTE proc_name [parameters]
go
```

 Two names are relevant when working with stored procedures. The first name is that of the operating system file that contains the script for the stored procedure. The second name is the stored procedure name that is saved in the sysobjects table. An operating system file can contain many stored procedures.

Sample Scripts

Source Listing 4.12 creates a stored procedure in the default database under the object name insmovie.

```
/*————————————————————*/
/* ——— Code below this line is saved into insert1.sql ——— */
/*————————————————————*/

/* Filename: insert1.sql */

use address
go

/* drop the stored procedure*/
DROP PROC insmovie1
go

CREATE PROC insmovie1
AS
    SELECT 'this stored procedure will be enhanced to insert a movie'
    RETURN 0   /* 0 is a standard to indicate successful completion */
go

/*————————————————————*/
/* ——— Code above this line is saved into insert1.sql ——— */
/*————————————————————*/
```

Source 4.12   Creating a stored procedure.

As shown in Figure 4.4, the stored procedure can be executed from the Query Analyzer dialogue by including the following code in the window and selecting the Execute option:

```
Exec insmovie1
go
```

In Source Listing 4.13, the insmovie stored procedure is enhanced to insert a record into the language table. The stored procedure will be written to accept input parameters. The language table contains two fields: lang_type and description. Values must be supplied at run-time for each of these.

```
/* Filename: insert.sql */

/* drop the stored procedure if it exists. */
IF EXISTS (select name from sysobjects where name = "insmovie1")
BEGIN
    DROP PROC insmovie1
end
go
```

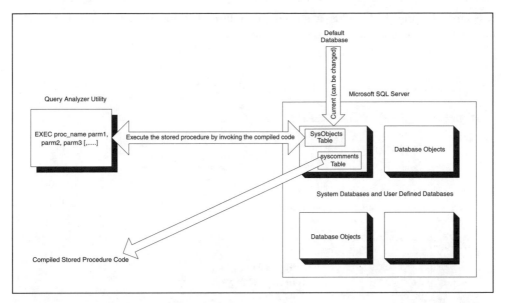

Figure 4.4 Executing a stored procedure.

```
CREATE PROC insmovie1
(
  @lang_type      char (1),
  @description    char (30)
)
AS
    INSERT INTO language
    (
        lang_type,
        description
    )
    VALUES
    (
        @lang_type,
        @description
    )
    RETURN 0  /* return a 0 code to the calling routine */
go

insmovie1 'M', 'Mandarin'
go

select * from language
go
```

Source 4.13 Enhancing the insmovie_stored procedure.

Source Listing 4.14 builds a stored procedure that inserts one record into the movie_type table and one record into the movie table.

```
/* Filename: insert1.sql */

/* Drop the stored procedure if it exists. */
IF EXISTS (select name from sysobjects where name = 'insmovie2')
    DROP PROC insmovie2
go

/*******************************/
/* Create the stored procedure */
/*******************************/
CREATE PROC insmovie2
(
    @movie_title      character (40),
    @movie_type       character (1),
@release_year      character (4),
@actor1            character (20),
@actor2            character (20),
@director          character (20),
@lang_type         character (1)
@rating            int,
@language          character (20)
)
AS
    DECLARE
    @return_code           int    /* variable names must begin with @ */

    insert language
    (
       lang_type,
       description
    )
    values
    (
       @lang_type,
       @description
    )

insert movie
(
movie_title,
movie_type,
release_year,
actor1,
```
(Continues)

Source 4.14 Inserting records into more than one table.

```
actor2,
director,
lang_type,
rating
)
VALUES
(
@movie_title,
@movie_type,
@release_year,
@actor1,
@actor2,
@director,
@lang_type,
@rating
        )


     RETURN 0    /* return a 0 code to the calling routine */
go
```

Source 4.14   *(Continued)*

Execute the insmovie2 stored procedure to store a record in the language table and the movie table. This example makes two assumptions: that an "H" code does not exist in the language table and so requires an insert; and that an "S" code exists in the movie_type table. We will examine methods of dealing with these situations from a programming perspective. If either of these assumptions is incorrect, the records will not be inserted correctly. However, the discussion that follows on triggers will handle the situation where an "S" does not exist in the movie_type table.

```
exec insmovie2 'The King's Folly', 'S', '1999', 'Neil Sector',
            'Victoria Tan', ' ', 'H', 5, 'Hindi'
go
```

Leveraging Triggers

Triggers are a special case of stored procedures and have different invocation procedures. Triggers are created like stored procedures, but are attached to columns in a table or to the table itself. Triggers are associated with specific events that can occur to data in a table. If a specified event occurs on a table or a specific column in a table, the trigger fires and the logic that it contains is processed and applied. This example provides a method of dealing with the "referential integrity" problem where a "reference" table does not contain a record with a key matching the row being inserted. There are three types of triggers that fire under three types of events: delete triggers fire when a delete operation occurs against a table or column; update triggers fire when an update operation occurs against a table or column; insert triggers fire when an insert operation

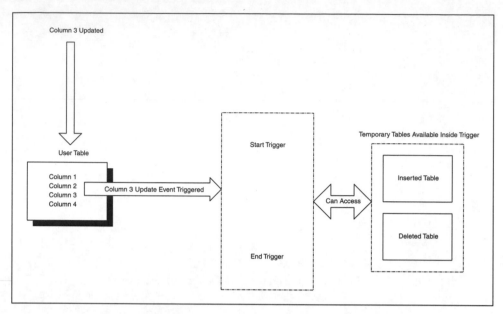

Figure 4.5 Manipulating triggers.

occurs against a table or column. As shown in Figure 4.5, triggers have access to two intermediate tables called "inserted" and "deleted." A set of control-of-flow and DML commands can be invoked during a trigger session. Insert operations use the inserted trigger table. Delete operations use the deleted trigger table. Update operations use the inserted and deleted trigger tables. These tables are referenced with the specific names "inserted" and "deleted" in the command section of triggers.

Earlier versions of Microsoft SQL Server only allowed one instance of each trigger type for a specific column or table. This meant that only one insert trigger could be allocated to a specific column. The same column could also have a delete trigger and an update trigger. SQL Server 7 allows multiple triggers to be created for the same event. This is a useful improvement that supports component-based development. Logic can be encapsulated and shared across columns. A streamlined syntax for creating triggers into a database is as follows:

```
CREATE TRIGGER owner.trigger_name
    ON owner.table_name
    FOR [INSERT/UPDATE/DELETE]/[INSERT/UPDATE]
    AS
        [IF UPDATE (column_field) [AND/OR column_field(s)]]
        commands
```

 The sp_configure system procedure can be used to set "nested triggers" to change the default nested level value.

Sample Scripts

The following example creates a trigger to fire when a record is inserted into the movie table:

```
use address
go

drop trigger trinsert_movie
go

CREATE TRIGGER trinsert_movie
ON movie
FOR INSERT
AS
    PRINT ('Inserting a record into the movie table')
go
```

Ensure that the trigger was parsed successfully into the database by examining the sysobjects system table. The following example uses a join command to extract and display the Transact-SQL code that belongs to the trinsert_movie trigger as it is stored in the data dictionary:

```
select * from sysobjects where name = 'trinsert_movie'
go

SELECT a.type, b.text
    FROM sysobjects a, syscomments b
        WHERE a.name = 'trinsert_movie' AND
            a.id = b.id
go
```

Test that the trigger fires when a movie record is inserted through the previous stored procedure:

```
exec insmovie2 'The Diamond Cube','S', '1999', 'Neil Sector',
            'Marsha Flanders', ' ', 'H', 5, 'Hindi'
go
```

Getting Help

There are many methods of getting help in the Microsoft SQL Server environment. This section looks at a list of useful system functions and global variables that are given values after commands are completed by SQL Server. The values in these variables can be inspected and appropriate action taken in response to the information that is provided by them.

System Functions

System functions are stored procedures that have the prefix sp_ and which query system tables to provide environment or system information to the user. SQL Server provides a comprehensive set of system functions that provide help to the user. They can be invoked anywhere that stored procedures or other SQL commands can be issued. Some of the more common help functions are presented in this section:

sp_help. This is a useful system procedure for getting help on database objects. sp_help is used to query the default database for database objects: Name, Owner, Type, Created_datetime, Parameter_name, Length, Precision, Scale, Param_order. Use the sp_help as follows: sp_help object_name.

sp_helptext. This system procedure is used to extract text from the syscomments table (unless the text is encrypted with the create command) for specific database objects such as stored procedures, triggers, and views. The text can be saved to operating system ASCII files to rebuild the generation scripts for the database objects.

sp_helpdb. This system procedure produces information about all the databases in the environment.

sp_helpdb database_name. This system procedure provides information about the specific database mentioned in the parameter.

sp_helplog. This system procedure displays information about a tables transaction log.

Leverage the Sysobjects System Table

Every SQL Server database has a sysobjects system table that contains a row for the objects that are stored within that database. Sysobjects can be examined for important information. For example, the type column can be inspected to determine the object type belonging to a row. The following examples are commonly used:

```
select * from sysobjects - to locate all the objects in a database
select * from sysobjects where type = 'S' -to locate all system procedures
                                                    in the database
select * from sysobjects where type = 'V' -to locate all view in the database
select * from sysobjects where type = 'U' -to locate all user tables in the
                                                    database
select * from sysobjects where type = 'P' -to locate all stored procedures
                                                    in a database
select * from sysobjects where type = "TR" -to locate all triggers in a
                                                    database
```

Global Variables

Global variables are used by Microsoft SQL Server to hold temporary status information about events. They are identified by the prefix @@. For example, the @@rowcount global variable contains the number of rows affected by the previous command. Table 4.3 contains a list of global variables supported by SQL Server that are commonly used.

Table 4.3 Global Variables

GLOBAL VARIABLE NAME	DESCRIPTION
@@total_read	Contains the total number of reads since the SQL Server booted up.
@@spid	Contains the server process ID of the current process.
@@rowcount	Contains the number of rows affected by the previous command.
@@io_busy	Contains the time spent on input/output operations since the SQL Server was booted up.
@@version	Contains the version number of the current database server.
@@isolation	Contains the transaction isolation level.
@@DBTS	Contains the current timestamp for the default database.
Db_name()	Displays the name of the default database.
Object_name(parameter)	Display the database object name.
Object_id(parm1, parm2)	Displays the object ID for the database object.

The values stored in global variables can be displayed using the select command with the following syntax:

```
SELECT @@version
go

SELECT @@rowcount
go

SELECT object_name (1)
/* displays sysobjects. This can be cross referenced with the sysobject
table contents that shows that the id for the sysobjects
table is (1) */
go

SELECT db_name()
go

SELECT object_id('sysobjects')
/* displays a value of 1, which is the object id (the reverse of
   object_name(1) */
go
```

Debugging Your Application

Useful commands for debugging stored procedures are the following. These can be selected from the graphical tools and will be discussed later in this book.

SET SHOWPLAN ON/OFF—builds a query processing plan.

SET STATISTICS IO ON/OFF—generates a list of logical/physical reads for tables in a command.

SET STATISTICS TIME ON/OFF—time required to parse and compile commands.

SET NOEXEC ON/OFF—builds a query plan, but does not execute it.

SET PARSEONLY ON/OFF—checks query syntax only.

Set noexec on can be used to inspect the stored procedure without actually running it. Each of these options can be selected from the MS Query Analyzer dialogue or entered interactively using ISQL.

Summary

This chapter focused on enhancing the basic topics that were introduced in Chapter 3, but with a stronger focus on object manipulation. Three broad SQL Server categories were discussed. This chapter also identified methods for retrieving system help and using global variables. The first category included an examination of the SQL Server environment itself. This included a review of system tables in both the model database and user defined databases.

The second category examined the declarative reference integrity options that SQL Server supports through column constraints. This includes primary keys, foreign keys, identity constraints, defaults, and references. The key constraints enforce data row uniqueness and rapid retrieval. The identity constraints enable automatic numbering based on a seed value. Defaults are used to insert information that is not provided by a user, and which is not mandatory. The references constraint is used to enforce referential integrity between two or more tables.

The last category consists of more complex database objects and complex processing including joins, views, stored procedures, and triggers. Joins are used to produce temporary tables by joining two or more tables based on specific criteria. Views are used to restrict access to specific columns in one for more tables. Stored procedures and triggers are used to support n-tier distributed architecture.

Leveraging the Project Life Cycle to Build N-Tier, COM Database Applications

This chapter focuses on full project life cycle development, project standards, and technical resource roles and responsibilities as they pertain to the SQL Server environment. An approach for designing and building n-tier, COM database applications is included in this discussion. Despite the large number of recent innovations and other technical enhancements incorporated into application development tools (e.g., syntax checkers, debuggers), the reality is that development projects that leverage SQL Server technology are still highly dependent on the traditional project life cycle activities and methodologies for their success. Neglecting the traditional processes, such as up-front analysis, team organizations, good design, and accurate requirements documentation and sign-off leave major exposures to the projects themselves. Arguably, the power of these tools is not going to replace the need to follow effective development methodologies and best practices. It is necessary, however, to augment the traditional approaches with submethodologies or approaches for designing and building component-based development and n-tier development. Both of these approaches are related, as n-tier architecture is characterized by a suite of components, each encapsulating different business rules.

Development projects generally follow a traditional application development life cycle that is based on a subset and specific ordering of the following standard phases: project initiation, requirements gathering, analysis, architecture, design, development, testing, implementation/deployment, and ongoing system maintenance. The relevant order of these phases and the activities within each of them vary with the technology and the development techniques being employed on the project. For example, GUI development tools support application prototyping and a high degree of user involvement. This enables a higher level of parallel development in the analysis/design and development phases in the life cycle. Testing and deployment activities can also be performed in a more parallel fashion because of the features supported by GUI-based technology. Another example where technology clearly impacts a project life cycle involves the ever-evolving client/server model that has arguably grown to encompass the thin Web browser client, Internet/intranet solutions, and n-tier architecture. These architecture models require a more integrated view of an organization's technology infrastructure and also require an initial planning that is not required in traditional 2-tier client/server environments. This chapter looks at each of the traditional project phases and relates them to SQL Server's requirements and dependencies in the context of n-tier architecture.

A Generic Project Life Cycle and Development Methodology

The generic project life cycle consists of standard phases or activities that are common to development projects in general. A development methodology is a specific implementation of the project life cycle that includes the experiences and knowledge of an organization gained over a wide range of projects, typically across a base of industries. Many development methodologies are available in the marketplace. Some are sold or licensed with a suite of modeling or management tools. Others are proprietary and represent a large investment on the part of organizations to gain a competitive advantage over other vendors. For example, larger consulting companies such as Deloitte Consulting, Ernst & Young, IBM, SHL Systemhouse, and Andersen Consulting have invested extensively in a suite of proprietary development methodologies that cover reengineering, strategy, client/server development, and ERP implementations (e.g., SAP, BAAN, and Peoplesoft). Each of these methodologies represent a full project life cycle, and they each include and focus on different techniques and practices. Many organizations periodically enhance their corporate methodologies with new project experiences every couple of years. Each development methodology encompasses different experiences and a different set of core philosophies. Organizations that focus on large, mega-development projects usually offer more extensive, recipe-like methodologies that are designed to reduce implementation risk and provide a standard corporate approach toward building and formatting the deliverables. Organizations that focus on quick-burn projects with tight implementation schedules and variable business requirements often leverage methodologies that consist of a streamlined set of guidelines and an iterative approach toward development that includes heavy user representation and sign-off. A project development methodology usually consists of the following:

Tasks and activities

Descriptions of each task and activity

Sample deliverables

Best practices

Tools used throughout the life cycle

Sample project plans

Techniques

Organizations that do not have proprietary methodologies and want to use one generally license an external methodology or use methodologies that accompany modeling tools. Examples of this are LDMS and Rational Rose.

> **The use of SQL Server is tightly integrated with the project life cycle. There are specific features that must be used at specific times throughout the life cycle. Similarly, there are also specific resource roles that are required throughout the project life cycle. The project plan should be used to plan at this level of detail.**

Subactivities within the SQL Server Environment

Following is a short list of subactivities within the SQL Server environment grouped by the standard project life cycle activities identified earlier.

Project Initiation

Project initiation tasks include confirming the mission of the project, steering committee composition, stakeholders, project scope, and milestone deliverable dates. This phase also oversees the establishment of a project office complete with standards, templates, status reports, an issue log, and a master copy of the project plan. At a physical environment level, project initiation involves understanding the enterprise-wide technology environment and standards, and the specific environment for the project. Seating arrangements also have to be arranged for the project team. Other activities include setting up phone mailboxes and e-mail lists.

The project manager generally builds a living project plan, identifies team roles, and allocates resources at this stage. The project plan has a higher level of detail for the near-term activities but high-level descriptions and sketchy details for phases that are further out in time. Resources should be allocated to tasks and deliverables and must become available to the project as they are needed according to the project plan.

SQL Server subactivities include

Ensure SQL Server licenses are purchased and are scaleable to the full development project and user teams.

Make a list of vendor contacts for the hardware and software.

SQL Server should be installed in a development environment.

Establish database standards.

Choose the project DBA. The DBA's involvement is critical in development projects.

Assemble the project team.

Build the project plan.

Conduct a kickoff meeting with full team and sponsors.

Brief vendors on project timeline and points of their assistance.

Requirement Gathering

Requirement gathering and early analysis activities are the most important activities in the life cycle. Invalid requirements negate the value of a system, no matter how brilliantly it is built. The project manager must ensure that requirements are gathered in their entirety for the application, technology, processes, and any other area that will impact the organization. The manager must ensure that the users buy into these requirements. A variety of techniques, including prototyping and storyboarding, should be used to ensure that the users and the project team agree on the interpretation of the requirements. This is an area of high risk since it is not uncommon for project teams and users to believe they are agreeing on the same requirements when, in fact, they actually have different interpretations.

SQL Server subactivities include

Determine if a modeling tool is to be used to generate the database scripts. If the answer is yes, a tool selection effort is required to select the modeling tool. The tool should be capable of supporting process models, data models, and/or object models that can generate SQL Server scripts.

Build high-level data and process models. Build an object model if it is needed.

Analysis/Architecture/Design

Analysis/architecture/design is often separated into distinct phases. System architecture, consisting of data, application, and technology, is the foundation of the IT solution that is to be developed. Building an architecture is a highly iterative process that involves repeated refinements and extensive product evaluations and selection processes. Architecture moves to a detailed level, based on the requirements that are captured in earlier phases. Design is started after the architecture is accepted by project management.

The project manager is responsible for ensuring that the appropriate level of expertise is available while the architecture is being developed. This is especially challenging when the architecture includes newer technologies, such as Internet/intranet, data warehousing, and object-oriented solutions. It is also important to receive active support and assistance from functional users as well as ensuring buy in from all stakeholders and those ultimately required to pay the bills. The project manager must understand the recommended architecture and design. The project manager, may rely on expert opinions in terms of defining the system architecture, but ultimately he is responsible and accountable for the recommendations.

SQL Server subactivities include

Establish environments for proof-of-concept activities to test risky application linkages.

Examine data quality.

Examine data sources.

Begin data conversion activities.

Identify rollout sites.

Build a logical data model.

Development

Development, regardless of the technology environment, involves managing technical resources through the process of building application code that functions in accordance with the business specifications. The project manager must ensure that developers adhere to standards and processes as well as unit testing their code.

SQL Server subactivities include

Strong involvement of DBA resources. The ultimate acceptance of an application often depends on the results of the database server environment.

Complete conversion of the logical data model to a physical data model.

Review database test scripts.

Benchmark application performance, including the database components.

Complete unit testing of all completed components.

Testing

This encompasses a series of testing methods, including functional testing, system testing, integration testing, regression testing, stress testing, and benchmarking. The project manager must ensure that the relevant users see the results of the tests. The project manager must also ensure that results are reported to senior management, who make a final decision to accept or reject the system.

SQL Server subactivities include

Testing involves an iterative approach of test, fix, and test again.

Functional testing.

Integration testing.

Regression testing.

Stress testing.

Implementation

Implementation involves all the activities necessary to implement the system for use by end users. This requires a tremendous amount of work in distributed client/server environments. Some tasks include ensuring the network is in place with the required protocols and bandwidth, implementing the production technology architecture, and ensuring the implementation of system management tools. Implementation also involves addressing disaster recovery concerns, contingency planning, and parallel system operations for a trial period.

SQL Server subactivities include

Get system signoff.

Verify data conversion.

Prepare sites for application implementation.

Maintenance

The project manager must conduct a review of the project and its major components, including the project plan, management style, performance of the team, and the performance of the users. The objective is to identify lessons learned from the experience and to share these with the organization to improve performance in future projects. If a formal methodology is in place, it is also useful to include the lessons learned within the methodology, either as additional tasks or as case studies. All the deliverables from the project should also be included in a central repository for future reference.

SQL Server subactivities include

Maintain an issue log.

Maintain a parallel test environment.

Approach for Building an N-Tier, COM Database Application

An n-tier, COM database application leverages the standard development life cycle but replaces some of the deliverables with those lending themselves to a component-based solution. The analysis phase produces an analysis model, interface specifications, CRC (class, responsibility, collaborators), domain object model, and a use case model. Architecture and design phases produce a functional model and an object model. Samples of these deliverables can be found in object-oriented methodologies. Some examples of these methodologies include the following: Objectory, Jacobson, OMT, Booch, and the Unified Method Language (UML). Industry momentum is currently behind the UML, supported by Rational Rose Corporation, which is a merging of Rational Software Corporation and Rose Software Corporation. Rational Rose Corporation also boosts the support of Booch, Rumbaugh, and Jacobson.

Selecting a Project Development Methodology

Not all development methodologies are equal. Project development methodologies that are being considered for a project should always have a successful track record. For example, if a methodology is required for a large client/server development project having a development staff of 100+ and a budget of $10 million over a two-year period, it is mandatory to ensure that the development methodology being considered was used successfully on a similar project, preferably in the same industry. Table 5.1 contains other important criteria to consider in making a development methodology.

Table 5.1   Project Methodology Criteria

CRITERIA	DESCRIPTION
Costs	All costs associated with adopting a development methodology including purchase cost, ongoing license costs, per seat costs, support costs, technical help costs, training costs, and consulting costs. Some consulting organizations provide their proprietary methodology packaged with consulting services.
Market penetration	Includes how well the product is known in the marketplace. This is also a representation of the vendor's standing. For example, methodologies from Rational Corporation have a number of solid market penetration features.
Resource availability	Availability of resources who have experience using the methodology on similar types of projects in similar industries. These resources can be available in the marketplace or through consulting organizations, possibly the vendor.
Cultural alignment:	Cultural similarities between the vendor supplying the methodology and the client that is licensing it. This is important to the eventual acceptance of the methodology within the corporate environment. Some methodologies are more flexible than others and may have a stronger focus on parts of the life cycle (e.g., testing) that are of interest to a particular client.
Sample deliverables	Methodologies that are deliverable-based seem to be easier to use than ones that are procedural. Deliverable-based methodology clearly identifies the types of deliverables produced at every step in the project life cycle. Samples of each deliverable, or at least the most important ones, should be available with the methodology. There should also be easy user access to the deliverables across the organization. This may include printed copies of the deliverables, CD ROM, and perhaps on a repository like Lotus Notes. Electronic access allows the deliverables to be periodically updated with new deliverables. This is a way of getting rapid results in a project
Linkage with other methodologies	The methodology's ability to integrate with other methodologies, for example, reengineering, object oriented, component-based development, data warehousing, and package customization are important for expandability into the organization.
Industry/ technology alignment:	The methodology's awareness of specific industries through specialized techniques (e.g., insurance, retail, telecom, banking) and specific technologies that include the Internet, object oriented, data warehousing, client/server, and component-based development.
Support for future trends	Methodologies that are deliverable based and from a stable vendor may be good candidates for long-term growth. The vendor must demonstrate future plans to grow the methodology, otherwise it could become obsolete in a few years. It is useful to understand the effort that is required to enhance the methodology.
Modularized	A methodology that is composed of a set of modules that communicate through deliverables is also expandable and flexible. Individual modules can be replaced with more relevant ones.

Deploying a Project Development Methodology in an Organization

Project methodologies are only useful if they are used consistently in the organization. This requires executive support, executive mandate, and a review mechanism to ensure that the selected methodology is deployed effectively and used consistently throughout the organization. The following activities should be included in a plan to deploy a methodology in an organization:

Identified as a corporate direction with support from the executive. Deployment of a development methodology will only be a success if it is accompanied by senior executive support and a communication plan. The support should come from a vice president or CIO level and should be a mandate. The communication plan should include the selection process that was used for the methodology, the strengths of the methodology, the reasons that a methodology is needed, short-term objectives, long-term objectives, a description of the implementation strategy, and the names of people in the organization who can answer questions and concerns. The focus of the communication plan must be to answer key questions, such as What's in it for the people using it? How will it help get the work done? Who's going to benefit from its implementation? What are the success stories? Resistance to methodologies until these questions are answered is not unusual. The senior executive mandate and the communication plan bring the methodology into focus and start building excitement in the organization.

Deployed throughout an organization. The methodology should be implemented electronically where possible, so that it is readily accessible and updatable. There should also be printed copies of the key parts of the methodology for those who do not have electronic access or who prefer paper. Lessons and customization to the methodology should be captured in a central information repository.

Readily accessible to those who are using it. The methodology must be readily accessible whenever it is needed. A few contacts who can answer questions must also be identified to the organization with a contact procedure, perhaps through a central help desk.

Successful pilot projects to serve as references. A methodology can be a complex body of work for those unfamiliar with its use. There will always be reluctance to adopt a different way of doing things. There may also be a perception that the methodology will increase the length of time required to do daily activities. A successful pilot project or series of pilot projects that clearly demonstrate the value of using the methodology, as well as some strong proponents who advocate its use, are vital for proceeding with the methodology.

Training on the methodology for existing resources and future resources. Formal training should be offered to anyone who is going to be using the methodology. Training should consist of a half-day orientation course and a more complex and thorough multiday training program for more advanced users. The orientation course should expand on the communication program and provide a high-level walkthrough of the methodology.

A quick-start program for using the methodology. A separate summary of how the methodology can be used in different phases of the life cycle is useful in easing the organization into using the methodology. This can consist of a small bound copy of the highlights accompanied by a one or two page graphical representation of the methodology activities and tasks.

Allowing for Change

Full life cycle development methodologies supply the process and the knowledge to build applications, deploy them, and to maintain them. Applications and the underlying technology used to build them are constantly changing or evolving. To remain useful, development methodologies themselves must continually evolve as well. For example, strictly mainframe methodologies are only capable of supporting a subset of the development initiatives that are underway today. Methodologies that are currently being considered by organizations should provide for the initiatives discussed in this section.

The Internet and the World Wide Web

The Internet is a hot area that has captured the attention of almost every leading software and hardware vendor in the IT industry. It factors strongly in future development initiatives, such as providing universal access to applications, allowing access to a database server, and supporting a more evolved client/server architecture model in all major industries. The next few years are also going to see the implementation of high-speed fiber-optic or high-speed cable modems that will increase data capacity and improve system response time. A few Internet browsers are emerging as the clear winners. These will determine the look and feel of the future desktop and impact the underlying operating system. Combined with applets that are written in languages such as JAVA, which offers enhanced security, the Internet will bring client/server applications to anyone with the capability to connect to the Internet.

The Internet is not a panacea that can solve all development problems, despite all the current excitement. The marketing hype surrounding the Internet (specifically the World Wide Web) is so strong that the general public is more enthusiastic about the Internet's possibilities than any other previous IT initiatives. Corporations are routinely setting up web sites and advertising their web addresses. Many products prominently display web addresses, but you have to dig and dig to find a mailing address or a phone number. However, this hype can be dangerous to development efforts. This is where the leadership, knowledge, and experience of the manager adds value to the project. Managers must educate themselves to distinguish between architectural alternatives offered by proven and stable technologies and the marketing hype of emerging technologies and wishful thinking. The manager, above all, is the wet blanket that keeps romance out of real solutions. Failure to do this results in many false starts and potentially damaging architectures. A methodology that sets realistic activities and expectations but has the capacity to embrace proven Internet solutions is a good step toward incorporating the Internet into application solutions. Vendors offering methodologies should be able to articulate their corporate plan to include Internet/intranet solutions into their solution.

Intranets

Intranets offer some of the advantages of the Internet, while restricting the user domain to a single corporation. This offers a solution to some of the limitations of the Internet, such as security and bandwidth considerations. The intranet/browser combination cannot be ignored in the future and will require changes to project management in terms of application development considerations and implementation rollout techniques. A browser on every desktop offers the potential to change the foundation of system management software and how some applications are developed and deployed. The provisions for Internet support should be considered for intranets as well.

Object-Oriented Techniques

Object-oriented techniques that include analysis, design, and development have had their supporters for many years. Object technology is gaining popularity and is expected to be used more extensively in the next decade. Project managers in distributed client/server projects must gain some knowledge and experience in this area in terms of understanding the limitations and advantages of using class libraries and objects. Another trend is to purchase business objects or components in an effort to save development time. While this can work wonderfully, it is important to consider that buying this type of commodity is like buying a wheel for a car or a transistor for a radio. The rule is buyer beware. It is important to have a quality assessment procedure in place, payment expectations, access to component source code, and confidence in the long-term viability and survival of the supplying vendor. Object-oriented techniques also have limitations in terms of team size that must be considered when planning the project. Component-based development that includes technical solutions, such as MTS, COM+, ActiveX, VB, and VC++, are becoming solid alternatives to pure object-oriented solutions offered by such tools as SmallTalk, C++, and VisualAge. Methodologies should support both of these types of initiatives.

Packages

Package solutions have become a strong alternative to 100 percent custom development. Many organizations are more likely to succeed in transforming their processes to match an existing package than the other way around. A common approach is to select a package that offers a good portion of the functionality required by an organization and customize the package for what is left. Project managers must ensure that a package solution was considered before committing to a custom solution.

Frameworks

Custom development has the capacity to precisely satisfy business requirements; however, there are a number of considerations that work against custom development including the amount of time it can take to completely develop, test, and implement a custom solution. Increasing the development effort also increases the risk in the development process. Custom development also requires a solid understanding of the business requirements. This involves interviewing business users that understand the business thoroughly, have the ability to articulate the requirements so that they can be documented, and have the time to do this work. Implementation risk can also result in runaway costs. Despite all this, custom development is a valuable approach that does solve many business problems.

A solution to the problems posed by custom development is to select a complete package such as PeopleSoft, Baan, or SAP. This solution leverages a known quantity, dramatically reduces development risk, and focuses on an implementation cycle that has been proven in other organizations. Package solutions are not without their own trade-offs. A packaged solution forces an organization to adapt to the package or introduce a list of enhancements. The costs with packaged solutions, though arguably more predictable, can still be significant and are not under the same independent competitive pressures and solutions built with traditional languages such as C or COBOL. The functionality of the package also depends on what the vendor wants to include in the future. Large customers are often able to influence the functionality that is included in future releases of a package. The very capability that makes packaged solutions attractive, that is, a proven solution, can in some cases remove competitive advantages between competitors, essentially defaulting to the same processes and the same technical solution. The usability of packaged solutions is generally a few years behind what can be built into customized solutions. For example, some leading vendor packages are still character based with no mouse interaction. Despite all this, packages are a valuable approach that can satisfy the needs of many customers.

Frameworks offer a solution that combines the best of the custom development approach and the package approach. Frameworks offer prebuilt industry- or technology-specific solutions that offer several advantages: reusable code, a quick start to development, reduced development risk, and the ability to leverage a partially proven solution. Project managers should evaluate frameworks based on criteria that include the popularity of the framework, success stories, cost, vendor commitment, and specific benefits in the context of a project.

Second-Generation Client/Server Tools

The next generation of client/server tools is moving away from a best-of-breed approach and more toward having a single vendor act as a system integrator. This is complemented by a 3-tier application architecture that consists of a presentation tier, business logic tier, and a physical database tier. Component libraries extend this model to n-tier architecture. These tiers support application portability and interoperability. The next generation of distributed client/server tools centralize system management tools, application and data partitioning, and abstraction from the physical layer. This affects traditional methodologies during several phases of the standard life cycle, including architecture, design, development, and testing.

Hardware Advances (64-Bit Processing)

Just as the IT industry is coming to terms with 32-bit processing, 64-bit processing is on the horizon. This will open all sorts of possibilities in terms of functionality, response time, and data capacity. Project managers should ensure that their hardware and software investments in the present will provide good value and not be wasted in the future. NT's successes on the DEC Alpha platform are sure to increase the penetration of 64-bit processing in high-demand environments. Industry benchmarks show that the DEC Alpha/NT combination provides significant improvements in high database activity environments. This will affect the potential architecture and design of applications that can leverage this technology. The addressing capability of a 64-bit platform with regard to main memory is several magnitudes higher than 32-bit processors. This has the capability to dramatically improve application and database performance.

Project Roles

Development projects are generally supported by a group of resources that can be mapped to project roles and an organization chart. This section focuses on the roles directly relevant to the use and support of SQL Server in the standard project development process. Examples of sample tools that are used to support the project roles are also identified in this section. Some of the tools are identified at the logical level, while others are identified at the product level. Table 5.2 identifies a range of tools and roles that are applicable across project life cycle activities.

Development Standards

Development standards should be established at the project level or preferably at the enterprise level. Standards typically cover all aspects of development including naming standards, development standards, database standards, and change management standards. It is useful to build the development standards based on deliverables that are packaged with a methodology. The following questions are pertinent to the establishment and ongoing use of standards in IT projects and are discussed in this section.

> **At what level should standards be established?** This question deals with identifying a list of divisions, groups, or areas that should have defined standards within the organization. It is also necessary to establish the level of detail in the defined standards.

> **How are standards defined?** This question deals with how standards are defined. Some popular choices include using IT service providers, such as the Meta Group and the Gartner Group, hiring an external consultant to lead or run the process,

Table 5.2 Project Roles Related to SQL Server

ACTIVITY	PROJECT ROLES RELATED TO SQL SERVER	SAMPLE TOOLS
Project initiation	Project manager Business users Executive sponsors	Project management Estimation tools Issues/change log
Requirement gathering	Project manager Business analysts	Modeling tools (e.g., Rational Rose, S-Designer)
Analysis/ architecture/ design	Database architects Database designers Database analysts Capacity planners Stress testers Network specialists	Modeling tools (e.g., Rational Rose, S-Designer) Test environment (e.g., SQA Test)
Development	Developers Database analysts Configuration management specialists Operations	SQL Server VB C++ MS Transaction Server Configuration Management
Testing	Users Developers Manager	SQA Test
Implementation	Operations Users Executive Sponsor	MS SMS
Maintenance	Users Developers Manager	Change Management SQL Server VB C++ MS Transaction Server

using the standards proposed by hardware/software vendors (e.g., Microsoft), and defining the different standards with teams composed of internal resources.

How are standards distributed to the development team and users? This question deals with the deployment delivery capabilities of the organization to ensure that those who require the standards are positioned to access them and that the standards are up to date, complete, and relevant.

How are standards updated or enhanced? This question deals with establishing "champions" or tactical teams that will keep track of the wider marketplace to determine when standards have become obsolete, outdated, or simply lax. The tactical teams are also responsible for ensuring that the standards are updated.

How are standards enforced? This question deals with how standards are enforced on project teams. It is one challenge to define standards, and it is just as difficult to ensure that standards are followed by project teams. This is especially true during project crunch times. The primary goal of application development teams is to complete and implement the application, and standards are sometimes neglected in such situations. Standards enforcement must also have teeth. The team or individuals responsible for enforcing standards should have the authority to enforce them.

Summary

This chapter made the argument that technological innovation is one consideration in developing n-tier database applications. The other consideration involves following a consistent methodology, identifying roles and responsibilities, aligning the standard life cycle with object-oriented or component techniques, and establishing usable standards.

This chapter also examined the full application life cycle in terms of component-based development and Microsoft SQL Server development and reviewed criteria for selecting a development methodology. Since methodologies are not static, some of the key features that are expected to require methodology support in the future were also identified in this chapter. SQL Server dependence on roles and activities in the standard life cycle were also reviewed.

PART

two

Building the
Application Framework

Part Two of this book provides the reader with a detailed discussion of specific SQL Server 7 features that are important for administering the environment and using SQL Server as a key tier in application development.

Chapter 6 examines configuration values, database options, and set commands. This chapter also examines the activities that must be completed to establish a database environment for SQL Server 7 and earlier versions.

Chapter 7 examines the types of datatypes that SQL Server supports. This chapter also examines common techniques for validating data and ensuring referential integrity and overall data quality.

Chapter 8 examines common data defintion language (DDL) commands including CREATE DATABASE, ALTER DATABASE, and DROP DATABASE.

Chapter 9 examines common data manipulation language (DML) commands including insert, update, delete, select tables. This chapter also provides examples of how the tools were used in the past.

Chapter 10 examines the NT security strategy, roles, login-IDs, user IDs, permissions, and domain IDs. This chapter provides examples for administering security using batch scripts and SQL Server 7 scripts.

CHAPTER
6

Getting Physical

Getting physical is much simpler with the most recent version of SQL Server where the design philosophy is to free up the DBA to do other work. Version 7 reduces the time required for mapping to the physical operating system environment. SQL Server achieves this by employing a number of new strategies, including

Dynamic resource management (e.g., main memory)

Presetting of configuration variables to provide good performance right out of the box

Generous inclusion of wizards to perform database creation, administration, and security activities

Abstraction from the physical environment (e.g., removal of raw partitions in favor of operating system files)

Chapters 1 through 5 provided an overview of the commonly used SQL Server features in client/server development projects. Part of the discussion involved creating a database called address in the physical environment after doing a complete installation of SQL Server under Windows NT/95/98. This chapter examines the activities that are completed in the physical SQL Server environment prior to the start of a development project. This includes installing SQL Server, creating SQL Server user databases, positioning transaction logs, potentially modifying configuration values, and understanding the database options.

Each database is mapped to a separate operating system file in the new version of SQL Server. This is also referred to as the primary data file, which contains all the significant system tables for that database. A database is always mapped to one and only one primary data file. Databases can also take advantage of zero or more secondary operating system files. Databases continue to leverage a separate transaction log file for database consistency and performance. This is an important enhancement and an improvement over having databases share operating system files. Database sizes no longer have to be predetermined because they can change as easily as the operating system file size changes. The primary data file has an .mdf extension. Secondary log files contain .ndf extensions. Log files have .ldf extensions.

SQL Server 7 allows specific files and indexes to be mapped to specific operating system files (called file groups). All files are initially allocated to a default file group. Recall that at the physical level, databases do not share the same operating system file. It is a useful strategy to allocate high-use tables to specific dedicated disk drives. It is also a good strategy to use different read-write heads in parallel for improved system performance. But before investing the effort to undertake this additional mapping effort, consider leveraging the other design initiative for SQL Server, namely reduced DBA tasks. Use the placement strategy after transaction analysis identifies the high-use tables.

Databases shrink automatically when a threshold of free space is found by a periodic background SQL Server process by removing free space. This is available through a database option in the Create Database Wizard. Initial file sizes are provided to SQL Server when databases are created. The automatic adjustment feature subsequently shrinks or expands the files until a preset threshold is reached or until disk space runs out in the event that no threshold was set. Automatic file maintenance parameters are specified after the product is installed. There is also another opportunity to do this through the administrative wizards. Despite the automatic file growth and shrinkage, it continues to be good development practice to accurately estimate data space requirements based on transaction analysis results. This allows the hardware to be sized correctly and also supports hardware planning initiatives.

SQL Server has dramatically changed its internal data structures. The basic unit of storage is still a page. However, pages are allocated or released automatically. Bitmaps have replaced linked lists to track information about each file. SQL Server keeps track of free space and reclaims it following record deletes.

Pages are now 8 KB in size instead of 2 KB. Pages have a 96-byte header that specifies page type, free space, and object ID. Page types can be data, index, log, text/image, global allocation map, page free space, and index allocation map. Figure 6.1 shows that each page contains a header, data rows, and a row-offset table. The row-offset table contains an entry for every data row in the table.

Extents continue to be the basic space allocation unit in SQL Server, except that they are now 64 KB bytes in size instead of 16 KB. Tables or indexes are now allocated one page of space at a time until they require more than one extent in space, at which time they are allocated one extent at a time. This reduces the amount of wasted free space. The one page allocation is part of a "mixed extent," which can be shared by objects within the same database. Extents that are dedicated to a single object with eight contiguous pages are called *uniform extents*.

You do not have to establish logical devices in SQL Server 7 in order to create a database.

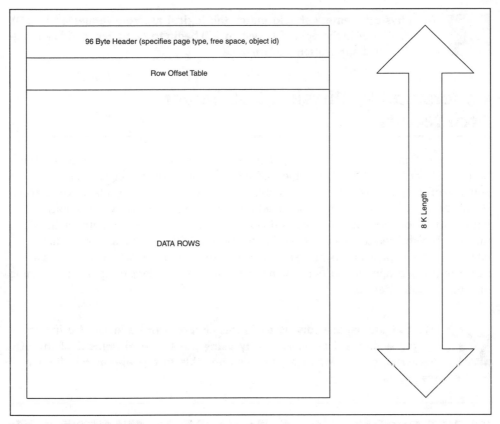

Figure 6.1 Components of a data page.

Tables with clustered indexes use linked lists to link data pages. The clustered index is implemented using a b-tree. Tables with no clustered indexes are implemented as heaps without linked lists.

Memory Utilization

Main memory is shared by many SQL Server commands and subsystems. The primary users of this space include transaction logs, recovery systems, query processor, procedure cache, buffer pool, and lock manager. SQL Server 7 periodically inspects SQL Server's memory requirements and the amount of free memory in the operating system environment. If free memory is available and required, SQL Server allocates it to the buffer cache. SQL Server will also relinquish memory to the operating system if it is not required. In SQL Server 7, locks require 96 bytes (up from 60 bytes), opening a database requires 2.880 KB, an open database object requires 276 bytes (up from 240 bytes), user connections require 24 KB (down from 44 KB). The decrease in user connections supports higher scalability of concurrent users.

The physical memory should match the logical memory requested by SQL Server otherwise the operating system will begin to swap pages. This will adversely affect application performance.

Understanding Physical SQL Server Architecture

As shown in Figure 6.2, the logical SQL Server architecture consists of databases. Databases are composed of database objects. The lowest level of the physical environment consists of the physical disk space and main memory. Database objects move between the disk space and the main memory that is allocated to SQL Server when it starts up. A large portion of the main memory is divided into a procedure and data cache. Main memory is also used to support locks and temporary tables. The manner in which procedures and database objects move between disk space and the main memory has a dramatic impact on application performance and so is the subject of application tuning efforts and optimization.

Most of the features discussed in this chapter can be invoked using batch scripts within isql or isql/w, or by using the GUI environment of the SQL Server Enterprise Manager. It is also possible to mix and match the use of both of these tools.

PHYSICAL FACTS (PRE-SQL SERVER 7)

1 page = 2 KB = 2048 bytes
32 segments/database
The disk init command adds rows to the sysindexes table in the master database.
4 MB = 2048 × 2 KB pages
1 MB = 1024 KB = 512 × 2 KB
Space is allocated to databases in 0.5 MB or 256 contiguous 2 KB pages.
1 extent = 16 KB or 8 × 2 KB pages. Extents are used for tables and indexes.
1 allocation unit = 32 extents
Database space information is stored in sysusages.

The basic process for creating database objects starts at the highest abstract level but also requires input from network specialists and operations resources regarding the physical environment. As shown in Figure 6.3, the process consists of a sequence of steps that must be customized for the type of database object being created.

The logical and physical environments within the SQL Server environment are shown in Table 6.1. At one end of the spectrum is the data that is stored in logical database objects. At the other end of the spectrum are the physical databases, which are stored on devices, on segments, and on disk. Figure 6.4 shows the physical environment objects.

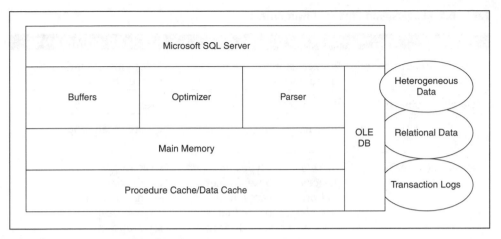

Figure 6.2 SQL Server architecture.

> You are not required to calculate disk size in SQL Server 7 before creating a database. For earlier versions, calculate the disk size by taking the total space required in megabytes and dividing it by 2 to produce a number in pages. This is the number provided to the disk init command. Thus 1 MB = 1024 KB = 512 × 2 KB; 10 MB = 10240 KB = 5120 × 2 KB.

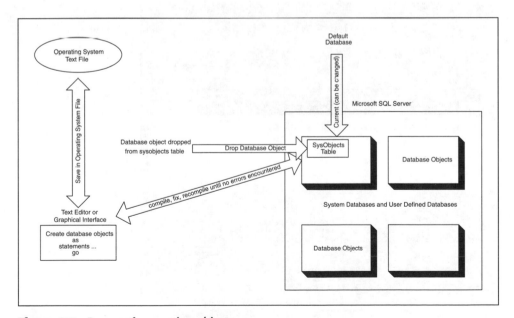

Figure 6.3 Process for creating objects.

Table 6.1 Logical and Physical Environments

FEATURE	DESCRIPTION	RELATED COMMANDS
Application business data	Physical storage of data in the database.	Select, insert, update, delete, truncate
Database objects	Page, extents	Create, alter, drop
Database, transaction logs	Allocation units	Create, alter, drop
Devices (pre-SQL Server 7.x)	There are two types of devices: database devices and dump devices. A device has a logical name that is used with other SQL Server commands.	Disk init Disk resize sp_diskdefault sp_helpdevice sp_dropdevice
Segments	Up to 32 segments/database	
Physical disk drives	The physical storage media	Disk format

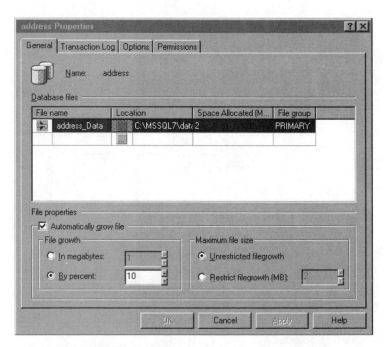

Figure 6.4 Enterprise Manager.

Preparing the Environment for a New Database

Preparing the Windows environment to support SQL Server requires the following basic steps:

1. Determine the version of SQL Server.
2. Locate the devices currently being used.
3. Determine if there is empty physical space on the disk drives.
4. Initialize one or more disks in the physical environment and allocate them to logical names.
5. Allocate databases to the devices.

Preparing the Environment in SQL Server 7

The number of activities required to prepare the SQL Server 7 environment for database creation is greatly reduced from earlier versions of the product. You no longer need to set up devices and segments. Database size estimating only needs to be done to estimate the size of the hard disk that should be configured, not to definitely set the size of the data base itself. The Create Database Wizard leads you through the activities that create a database and the transaction log, and establish the initial database options. The activities for doing this were presented in Chapter 3 and are also discussed in Chapter 8. For SQL Server 7, my suggestion is that you have the following minimum physical environment:

Pentium 133 MHz or higher

64 MB of main memory or higher (a test of a 24 MB system gave sluggish performance)

150–200 MB of free disk space to support the system environment and the user objects.

These are minimum physical configurations. It is recommended that you have 128 MB of RAM or more, especially if there are more than a few concurrent users. The standard desktop configuration at the time of writing consists of a Pentium II 350 to 450 MHz.

Preparing the Environment in SQL Server 6.5

The following example demonstrates the use of system procedures to prepare the SQL Server environment so that databases can be built in the environment in SQL Server 6.5 and earlier:

```
sp_helpdevice
go
```

The following syntax is used to initialize disk space in SQL Server 6.5 in preparation for creating user-defined databases:

```
DISK INIT
     NAME = 'logical_disk_name',
     PHYSNAME = 'path_physical_name',
     VDEVNO = device_number, (must be between 0-255. 0 is used for
master)
     SIZE = 2K_blocks (e.g. divide MB desired by 2)
```

Sample Scripts

The following example creates a 3 MB database device on the hard disk as well as a device for the transaction log. First, the sp_helpdevice is used to display information about the devices already defined in the environment. The sp_helpdevice system procedure displays the following information: device_name, physical_name, description, status, cntrltype, and size. The size allocated to the device is saved in the description column:

```
sp_helpdevice
go

DISK INIT          /* create space for the mobile database */
     NAME = 'mobile',
     PHYSNAME = 'c:\sqltext\mobile',
     VDEVNO = 10,
     SIZE = 5120
go

DISK INIT          /* create space for a transaction log */
     NAME = 'mobllog',
     PHYSNAME = 'c:\sqltext\mobllog',
     VDEVNO = 11,
     size = 1024
go

select * from sysdevices
go
```

To drop a device, it is necessary to drop all databases or transaction logs stored on the device prior to running the sp_dropdevice system procedure. The syntax for the command is as follows:

```
sp_dropdevice device_name
go
```

Following is an example of dropping a device using the sp_dropdevice system procedure:

```
sp_dropdevice mobile
go
```

```
use master
go
select * from sysdevices      /* look at the phyname column */
```

 It is preferable to allocate a database to a single device and the transaction log to another device for performance reasons. Multiple databases and transaction logs can be allocated to the same physical device; however, this approach then bottlenecks several databases and logs on a single I/O thread.

Altering Device Sizes

Device sizes can be altered in either direction (e.g., device shrinkage and device expansion). The basic syntax for resizing a device is the following:

```
DISK RESIZE
    NAME = logical_device,
    SIZE = new_size
```

Transaction Logs

Transaction logs play a critical role in SQL Server in ensuring database recoverability and data integrity. Transactions that are successful but not written to disk can be lost if the system crashes. The transaction log is used to recover from such a situation. SQL Server writes transactions out at a checkpoint (with a few notable exceptions, e.g., fast BCP or the truncate command). Many of the data manipulation activities write data to the transaction log so that it can be used to rebuild a database in the event of an SQL Server problem. Every database has a corresponding transaction log that is physically stored with the database on the same device, or physically separated onto a different device. In SQL Server 7, a database and its transaction log each occupy a different operating system file. Transaction logs also have a critical impact on application performance. Transaction log files contain virtual log files that are allocated or released as a unit. The unused portion of the transaction log is cleared at a checkpoint (assuming that a database option is properly set) or when the log is backed up. Inactive transactions are those than belong to successfully completed transactions that have not yet been written out to disk. Transaction log architecture is shown in Figure 6.5.

Transaction logs should typically be 10 to 25 percent of the size of their associated databases (e.g., if the database is 10 MB in size, the log should be 1–2.5 MB in size). Transaction logs can be expanded after they are created using sp_logdevice or the Enterprise Manager GUI utility.

Transaction logs can easily get filled up in heavily used applications. It is important to monitor transaction log usage and to write completed transactions to disk before the logs are filled up. Some SQL Server data manipulation commands can cause sweeps of large databases, writing records to the log in the process. The difficulty with such commands is their heavy use of transaction log space. In some cases, the queries fill up the

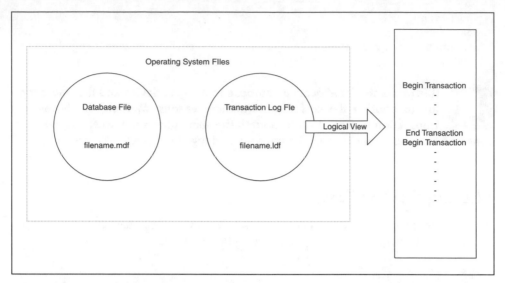

Figure 6.5   Transaction log architecture.

log before they complete, thereby causing a database server error condition. One example of this is the simple command:

```
update large_table
     set purchase_status = 'Done'
go
```

If the large_table has a million rows, this command, or a variation of it, could write a million delete and a million insert records to the transaction log. Depending on the record size, the transaction log space requirement may be too great to support a log of that size.

In development environments with heavy testing, it is useful to use the database option Trunc.Log On Chkpt to drop completed transactions from the transaction log buffers instead of writing them to disk. This is faster and will not fill up the log, but it means that database data will be unrecoverable. This is generally not a problem in development environments, with the exception of stress testing or acceptance testing. In such cases, users will want an accurate reflection of the application performance, so it is better to set the transaction log options to what they would be in production.

Transaction logs are used to ensure database consistency. Transaction logs are created for every database in an SQL Server environment. Transaction logs are saved in separate operating system files and are usually saved on separate physical devices. A sequence of commands is written out to a transaction log. The minimum size for a transaction log file is 512 KB. Transactions are rolled back to undo failed transactions. Transactions are rolled forward when a transaction log is reapplied to a database after a system failure.

Transaction logs are inspected for each database in turn when SQL Server is brought up. If the transaction log contains completed transactions that need to be reapplied to the database, it is done at this time. In fact, depending on the size of the databases being recovered, there can be a fairly long delay between the time the first database is recovered and the last database is recovered. The results of the start-up process are logged to a text file so that they can be audited. Transaction logs grow or shrink automatically in SQL Server. Prior to SQL Server 7, transaction logs could easily get filled up with certain insert/update operations that would write to the transaction log. An example of this is

```
update store Set id = 'new' go
```

If there were enough records, a query like this would fill up the transaction log before the transaction ended and a commit was issued.

A transaction log can contain many transaction chains, some of which can be open at the same time. Active transactions are saved to protect against database failure at a checkpoint. They are a sequential list of modifications that start with a transaction. The checkpoint process initiates writing of database pages and transaction log records to disk. The recovery process, when SQL Server starts up and starts rolling completed transactions forward, starts at the last completed checkpoint.

Performance Impacts

SQL Server has a significant amount of interaction with transaction logs. For this reason, transaction logs have a dramatic effect on application performance. The following list shows some common techniques for preparing transaction logs to provide better performance:

Physically separate transaction logs from database devices. The devices should be on different controllers for better performance.

Checkpoint procedure optimization.

Select commands that do not write to the transaction logs (this should be done wisely and with proper backups before starting).

Large transaction logs to reduce the need for writing out sooner.

Watch runaway commands that write millions of records, such as an update to a large database, without issuing checkpoints. These can be a problem with a fixed size transaction log, and even if the log can grow unchecked, because the storage resources of the database server platform become entirely consumed. Transactions that are not committed or rolled back continue to occupy transaction log space until they are specifically cleared (e.g., the server is restarted).

Clearing Transaction Logs

Two useful commands for monitoring transaction log usage are DBCC CHECKTABLE (syslogs) and DBCC SQLPERF (logspace). DBCC is the database checker utility that is discussed in Chapter 20. Additional commands for monitoring the transaction log size are sp_helpdb database_name, sp_helplog, and sp_spaceused object_name. These are not always as accurate as the DBCC results. Inactive portions of the transaction log are written out to disk at a checkpoint if trunc.log on chkpt sp_dboption has a value of true.

The following example shows one of several methods for clearing completed transactions from transaction logs:

```
DUMP Transaction dbname TO dump_device
     with TRUNCATE_ONLY | NO_LOG | NO_TRUNCATE
```

where

```
     TRUNCATE_ONLY drops the inactive portion of the transaction log.
Backup the database after this option is used.
```

NO_LOG is like setting a database option to truncate the log. This makes the database recoverable only up to the last database backup in the event of a system failure, and thus this option should only be used in development environments. In either case, it is a good idea to back up the associated database after the NO_LOG option is used. For example:

```
DUMP TRANSACTION address WITH TRUNCATE_ONLY
DUMP TRANSACTION address WITH NO_LOG
```

Environment Options

SQL Server supports two types of environment options that play a key role in running SQL Server. These are configuration options and set options. The SQL Server 7 design philosophy is to ensure auto-configuration in most cases. This means that the pre-set parameter values should be your first choice when establishing the environment. However, for situations where these values are inaccurate, it is possible to modify the environment variables. The effects of some of these options are straightforward in terms of optimal effect. However, in other cases, the best value for an environment option must be found through trial and error.

Selecting the optimal environment options requires a significant amount of testing. For this reason, it is imperative that DBAs be available extensively to the project. On some projects, this involvement is only given lip service, as the DBAs assigned to the project may also be responsible for the production environment, which usually keeps them so busy that they are unable to commit to the development effort because of lack of time. This means that they are only able to assume a QA role and this does not help the project.

Configuration Options

The sp_configure system procedure displays the full set of configuration options or variables that are available for tuning the SQL Server environment. SQL Server 7 is constructed to make it less likely that these values need to be adjusted. This is done by establishing defaults that are automatically set by SQL Server at installation time. Another factor that makes this possible is the self-tuning capabilities of SQL Server 7, especially in terms of memory management, index selections, and disk administration. Nevertheless, it is not possible to get away from the need to adjust configuration options indefinitely. This becomes more relevant in development phases that are closer to production. This command displays five pertinent columns of interest:

Name. The name of the environment option.

Minimum. The minimum value that SQL Server allows for the environment variable.

Maximum. The maximum value that SQL Server allows for the environment variable.

config_value. The value requested for the environment variable.

run_value. The value that SQL Server is executing with for the environment variable. A difference between the requested config_value and the actual run_value can be due to physical limitations.

Configuration options can be modified only by the system administrator. Thus it is necessary to be signed on as a system administrator to modify the configuration options. The syntax for modifying a configuration option is as follows:

```
sp_configure 'option_name', value
go
```

This establishes the config_value to the new value that was issued. A reconfigure command can be issued with some of the configuration options to establish the new run_value (e.g., allow updates, free buffers, nested triggers, recovery interval, show advanced option). SQL Server prompts for you to run reconfigure to establish run_values. In other cases, SQL Server must be rebooted after it is brought back up. The new configuration values in SQL Server 7 are cost threshold for parallelism, index create memory, lightweight pooling, max degree of parallelism, max query wait, min memory per query, max server memory, min server memory, query governor cost limit, remote proc trans, scan for startup procs, time slice, unicode comparison style, and unicode local id.

Table 6.2 shows the name of the configuration parameters and their default values as displayed by sp_configure in the Query Analyzer dialogue.

Configuration Values for SQL Server 6.5

Table 6.3 shows the name of the standard configuration options as well as the range of acceptable values and the value they are running with in SQL Server versions earlier than version 7.

Sample Scripts

The following example modifies the default value for the database size from 2 MB to 3 MB using the sp_configure system procedure.

Table 6.2   Default Configuration Values in SQL Server 7

NAME	MINIMUM	MAXIMUM	CONFIG_VALUE	RUN_VALUE
affinity mask	0	2147483647	0	0
allow updates	0	1	0	0
cost threshold for parallelism	0	32767	5	5
cursor threshold	−1	2147483647	−1	−1
default language	0	9999	0	0
default sortorder id	0	255	52	52
extended memory size (MB)	0	2147483647	0	0
fill factor (%)	0	100	0	0
index create memory (KB)	704	1600000	0	0
language in cache	3	100	3	3
lightweight pooling	0	1	0	0
locks	5000	2147483647	0	0
max async IO	1	255	32	32
max degree of parallelism	0	32	0	0
max query wait (s)	0	2147483647	600	600
max server memory (MB)	4	2147483647	2147483647	2147483647
max text repl size (B)	0	2147483647	65536	65536
max worker threads	10	1024	255	255
media retention	0	365	0	0
min memory per query (KB)	512	2147483647	1024	1024
min server memory (MB)	0	2147483647	0	0

Table 6.2 *(Continued)*

NAME	MINIMUM	MAXIMUM	CONFIG_VALUE	RUN_VALUE
nested triggers	0	1	1	1
network packet size (B)	512	65535	4096	4096
open objects	0	2147483647	0	0
priority boost	0	1	0	0
query governor cost limit	0	2147483647	0	0
recovery interval (min)	0	32767	0	0
remote access	0	1	1	1
remote login timeout (s)	0	2147483647	30	30
remote proc trans	0	1	0	0
remote query timeout (s)	0	2147483647	0	0
resource timeout (s)	5	2147483647	10	10
scan for startup procs	0	1	0	0
set working 0 set size	1	0	0	
show advanced options	0	1	1	1
spin counter	1	2147483647	10000	0
time slice (ms)	50	1000	100	100
Unicode comparison style	0	2147483647	196609	196609
Unicode locale id	0	2147483647	1033	1033
user connections	0	32767	0	0
user options	0	4095	0	0

Table 6.3   Default Configuration Values for pre-SQL Server 7

NAME	MINIMUM	MAXIMUM	CONFIG_VALUE	RUN_VALUE
allow updates	0	1	0	0
database size	2	10000	2	2
default language	0	9999	0	0
fill factor	0	100	0	0
language in cache	3	100	3	3
logwrite sleep (ms)	−1	500	0	0
max async IO	1	255	8	8
max text repl size	0	2147483647	65536	65536
max worker threads	10	1024	255	255
nested triggers	0	1	1	1
network packet size	512	32767	4096	4096
open databases	5	32767	20	20
open objects	100	2147483647	500	500
procedure cache	1	99	30	30
RA worker threads	0	255	3	3
recovery flags	0	1	0	0
recovery interval	1	32767	5	5
remote access	0	1	1	1
remote conn timeout	−1	32767	10	10
remote proc trans	0	1	0	0
show advanced options	0	1	0	0
tempdb in ram (MB)	0	2044	0	0
user connections	5	32767	30	30
user options	0	4095	0	0

```
sp_configure
go

sp_configure 'database sizeí, 3
go

reconfigure
go
sp_configure
go
```

The following example modifies the default value for the database size from 2 MB to 4 MB. Also modify the default value for the show advanced options to 1 for true. This will also display additional configuration options. As shown in this example, each instance of the sp_configure 'database option', value is included in a separate batch:

```
sp_configure
go

sp_configure 'database size', 4
go

sp_configure 'show advanced options', 1
go

reconfigure
go

sp_configure
go
```

 The default values for the configuration options should be accepted unless there is a good reason to change them. In most situations, the default values are effective.

Use the SQL Server Service Manager to stop and start SQL Server to use the config_values as the new run_values. The results of this series of batches is shown in Table 6.4. Notice that the list of options has grown because the show advanced options flag is turned on.

Some of the Transact-SQL commands support options that are also covered by the configuration options. The Transact-SQL commands override values specified in the configuration options for that single command whenever there is a difference between the two. The configuration option value is still applicable in other cases.

Table 6.4 List of Advanced Configuration Options

NAME	MINIMUM	MAXIMUM	CONFIG_VALUE	RUN_VALUE
affinity mask	0	2147483647	0	0
allow updates	0	1	0	0
cursor threshold	−1	2147483647	−1	−1
database size	2	10000	4	4
default language	0	9999	0	0
default sortorder id	0	255	52	52
fill factor	0	100	0	0
language in cache	3	100	3	3
locks	5000	2147483647	0	0
logwrite sleep (ms)	−1	500	0	0
max async IO	1	255	8	8
max text repl size	0	2147483647	65536	65536
max worker threads	10	1024	255	255
media retention	0	365	0	0
memory	0	3072	0	0
nested triggers	0	1	1	1
network packet size	512	32767	4096	4096
open databases	5	32767	20	20
open objects	100	2147483647	500	500
priority boost	0	1	0	0
procedure cache	1	99	30	30
RA cache hit limit	1	255	4	4
RA cache miss limit	1	255	3	3

Table 6.4 (*Continued*)

NAME	MINIMUM	MAXIMUM	CONFIG_VALUE	RUN_VALUE
RA delay	0	500	15	15
RA pre-fetches	1	1000	3	3
RA slots per thread	1	255	5	5
RA worker threads	0	255	3	3
recovery flags	0	1	0	0
recovery interval	1	32767	5	5
remote access	0	1	1	1
remote conn timeout	−1	32767	10	10
remote login timeout	0	2147483647	5	5
remote proc trans	0	1	0	0
remote query timeout	0	2147483647	0	0
remote sites	0	256	10	10
resource timeout	5	2147483647	10	10
set working set size	0	1	0	0
show advanced options	0	1	1	1
sort pages	32	511	64	64
spin counter	1	2147483647	10000	0
tempdb in ram (MB)	0	2044	0	0
time slice	50	1000	100	100
user connections	5	32767	30	30
user options	0	4095	0	0

Understanding the Configuration Options

This section explains the objectives of the configuration options that are displayed with the sp_configure system procedure and the units that are used for the value where appropriate.

Affinity mask. This configuration options supports symmetric multiprocessing, in that the mask is used to associate threads with specific processors. The full mask is 0x7ffffff.

Allow updates. A value of 1 is true. If set to true, this variable allows the system catalog to be updated.

Cursor threshold. A value of –1 causes cursors to be built with the open cursor statement with full dedication. A value of 0 establishes another thread to populate data or the cursor. This option is slower than –1, however, it does not dedicate the database server into satisfying a single request. The second option is a better choice for large result sets. Values of 0 and –1 serve as a threshold to determine whether the cursor result set should be built synchronously (e.g., same as a –1 option) or asynchronously (e.g., same as the 0 option).

Database size. This value is the default space amount that is reserved for new databases being created in the SQL Server environment. Because the model database is used as a template for new user databases, this value should be greater than the size of the model database. The units are megabytes.

Default language. This value is the default language ID for the server environment. The default value represents English (United States).

Default sortorder id. It is best to be fairly confident that the sort order selected on installation is the one permanently desired. Changing the sort order after installation requires data unloads, reloads, and rebuilding of clustered indexes so that data is sorted according to the order specified by this variable and the case sensitivity that is indicated. A default value of 52 specifies a dictionary sort order that is not case sensitive.

Fill factor. To understand fill factor, it helps to understand the physical construction of indexes, which are based on pages. This value determines the amount of free space that must be left on each index page. This value affects the overall space requirements in that a low value will leave a lot of empty space but will support better future index growth through index level splits. Until SQL Server introduced row-level locking, the fill factor was an effective method of reducing the number of records stored on an index page and thus reducing user contention because locking was performed at the page level. Low fill factors leave a lot of free space (in percent) on index pages, while a value of 100 means that no free space is left on index pages.

Language in cache. This value specifies the number of languages supported in cache at the same time.

Locks. Locks consume system memory and require processing time. A high number of locks results in contention, but ensures referential integrity. A too high number of locks results in livelocks or performance limitations. This configuration option specifies the number of locks that are allowed at the same time. Each lock requires 32 bytes of memory. With row level locking, the number of locks can easily require a great deal of memory (taking away from memory available to tempdb and the caches).

Logwrite sleep (ms). This configuration variable specifies the time delay in ms units before a transaction log entry is written to disk, if buffer is not full. −1 forces writes continually and will impact performance adversely.

Max async IO. This value establishes the maximum number of asynchronous IO requests extended to hardware. This value is useful for improving performance on systems that support more than half a dozen hardware devices within the database portion of the application.

Max text repl size. This value establishes the maximum size for test replication.

Max worker threads. This value establishes the maximum number of threads that SQL Server can support at one time for different processes and listener devices.

Media retention. This value establishes the number of days that backups should be retained for from the time of the backup.

Memory. The unit of measure for this variable is 2 KB pages (e.g., 1000, 2 KB pages is the minimum size allowed for RAM. In terms of bytes of memory, this is 1000×2000 bytes = 2,000,000 bytes = 2 MB) of RAM that are reserved for SQL Server when the product boots up. It is generally accepted practice to allocate the maximum amount of memory available for SQL Server to operate.

Nested triggers. A value of 0 means this flag is off. This means that only 1 trigger will be fired for a given table data event. A value of 1 supports nested triggers, so that an event from one fired trigger can fire other triggers.

Network packet size. It is not recommended that this value be modified without networking expertise. This value establishes the maximum network packet processed by SQL Server.

Open databases. This value establishes a limit for the number of concurrent open databases in memory.

Open objects. This value establishes a limit on the number of open objects in memory.

Priority boost. A value of 1 forces SQL Server to run at the highest priority relative to other OS-level tasks.

Procedure cache. The value in this variable is represented as a percentage of the total amount of memory available for the total cache. The procedure cache stores the execution plan for running stored procedures. The data cache gets the rest of the memory available to the total cache.

RA cache hit limit. This variable establishes the Read Ahead cache hit limit before SQL Server escalates to direct access to the data page cache.

RA cache miss limit. This variable establishes the Read Ahead cache miss limit before the Read Ahead cache is invoked.

RA delay. This variable establishes a delay in the Read Ahead manager.

RA pre-fetches. This variable establishes the Read Ahead extents.

RA slots per thread. This variable establishes the number of Read Ahead slots per thread reserved by SQL Server for Read Ahead activities.

RA worker threads. This variable establishes the number of Read Ahead worker threads for Windows NT threads.

Recovery flags. This is a diagnostic variable that when turned on (value 1) displays all pending transactions when SQL Server was stopped as well as all subsequent activities to recover the transactions when SQL Server starts up as databases are recovered. A value of 0 limits the diagnostic information to the database being recovered.

Recovery interval. This variable is used by SQL Server to determine when to issue a checkpoint, which writes dirty data pages from the transaction logs to disk. Transactions stored in the transaction logs are applied to databases when SQL Server recovers from a shutdown or crash. The fewer the transactions to recover, the faster the database recovery. This means that as the value for the recovery interval (in minutes) gets larger, the longer the time between checkpoints. This improves online performance. However, recovery will take a longer time.

Remote access. A value of 1 allows remote users to access the current SQL Server engine.

Remote conn timeout. This value specifies the inactive time (in minutes) between two servers, before the connection is disconnected.

Remote login timeout. This value specifies the amount of time before a remote login is timed out and the session is disconnected.

Remote proc trans. A value of 1 specifies DTC transaction protection.

Remote query timeout. This value specifies the wait period (in seconds) for SQL Server before errors are returned to client processes working with remote servers.

Remote sites. The remote site limit.

Resource timeout. This value specifies the amount of time that SQL Server will wait (in seconds) before returning an error to a client process waiting for a server request to respond.

Set working set size. This value forces NT to physically lock memory to SQL Server.

Show advanced options. This value, if set to 1, displays an expanded list of options displayed by sp_configure.

Sort pages. This value specifies the number of pages reserved for each user requiring sort/query activities.

Spin counter. This value limits the number of attempts made for resources from the resource manager.

Tempdb in ram (MB). This value specifies the amount of memory (in megabytes) reserved for the tempdb database. Putting tempdb into main memory can improve the performance of all operations that use this database, including sorts, order by, group by, and temporary tables.

User connections. One of the advantages of SQL Server design from the product's beginning was its low incremental overhead per user connection. This overhead has increased linearly, as 40 KB of main memory is now required for each new user connection. This value specifies the maximum number of concurrent user connections.

User options. This value affects global defaults for users with new sessions under SQL Server.

Configurable Database Options

Configurable database options are used to modify the state of databases to support administrative or high-volume operations against databases. This section examines two methods for modifying a database option: Enterprise Manager and the sp_dboption stored procedure.

Database Option Maintenance Dialogue

Figure 6.6 shows the options that can be established for a database. These are represented in the sp_dboption system procedure as well. These options support making administrative types of changes to databases.

sp_dboption Stored Procedure

The sp_dboption system procedure is the primary mechanism for working with these database options. The syntax for using this system procedure is as follows:

```
sp_dboption database_name, @option_name, @option_value
```

Note the following:

Run the sp_dboption with the master database established as the default database.

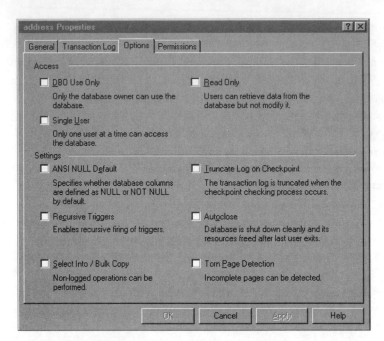

Figure 6.6 Database options maintenance dialogue.

The system administrator should execute the sp_dboption command.

database_name is the name of the database being processed.

@option_name, similar to the processing of sp_configure, is the name of the database option.

@option_value is the new value for the @option_name. As a switch, it takes on the value of true | false.

Run sp_dboption with no parameters to display a list of the database options that can be modified with sp_dboption. sp_dboption should be executed in its own batch.

Use the sp_help system procedure to find out the syntax for other system procedures. The database containing the object of interest should be established as the default database with the use database command or through the pulldown menu of the Query Analyzer GUI utility. In the specific case of the sp_dboption system procedure, it exists in the master database. The commands to locate information about sp_option are then:

```
use master
go
sp_help sp_dboption
go
```

Sample Scripts

The following example displays a set of database options:

```
use master
go

sp_dboption
go
```

The results of this command list are as follows:

```
Settable database options:
--------------------------
ANSI null default
ANSI nulls
ANSI warnings
autoclose
autoshrink
concat null yields null
cursor close on commit
dbo use only
default to local cursor
merge publish
offline
published
quoted identifier
read only
recursive triggers
select into/bulkcopy
single user
subscribed
torn page detection
trunc.log on chkpt
```

The following example displays the database options that are set for a specific database, in this case the pubs database:

```
use master
go

sp_dboption pubs
go
```

The result of this command list, which consists of two batches, is as follows:

```
The following options are set:
trunc.log on chkpt
```

The following example uses a system procedure to display the database options that have been established for the database:

```
use master
go

sp_helpdb
go

sp_helpdb pubs
go
```

 Avoid setting any database options on the master and model databases.

The following example changes the option on a database:

```
sp_dboption "pubs", "autoshrink", true
go

sp_dboption 'pubs'
go
```

The following example renames a database:

```
sp_dboption " Address","single user", "true"  /* this is mandatory */
sp_renamedb " Address", "address"
sp_dboption "address","single user", "false"
sp_databases
```

Understanding the Database Options

This section explains the purpose of each modifiable database option:

ANSI warnings. Displays additional error and warning messages.

ANSI null default. [Default value: off] If true, columns in the create table/alter table commands have null default values. This is compatible with the ANSI database standard.

Autoclose. [Default value: true] Release database resources when there are no more users in the database.

Autoshrink. [Default value: true] A background procedure automatically shrinks data and log files.

dbo use only. [Default value: off] If true, only the database owner can sign onto the database. Current users will not be logged off, but if they leave the database, they cannot get back in as long as the value is true.

No chkpt on recovery. [Default value: false] If true, a checkpoint is initiated after a database/transaction log is recovered.

Offline. [Default value: false] If true, databases are taken offline. This will only be successful if no users have established the database as their default.

Published. [Default value: false] If true, a database transaction log will be monitored for replicable transactions.

Quoted identifier. [Default value: false] Value of true means that double quotes are used for identifiers, single quotes are used for literals.

Read only. [Default value: false] If true, a database becomes read only.

Recursive triggers. [Default value: false] If true, triggers can be engaged recursively.

Select into/bulkcopy. [Default value: false] If true, commands that do not write to the database transaction log can be executed in a database. Fast versions of the bcp (bulk copy) utility must be run with all table indexes dropped and this option set to false.

Single user. [Default value: false] If true, only a single user can log onto the database. Existing users are not logged off, but if they leave the database, they cannot get back in if the value if set to true.

Subscribed. [Default value: false] If true, the database can be used in subscription based replication.

Torn page detection. Uses a flipped bit, when true, to mark pages being written out to disk.

trunc.log on chkpt. [Default value: false] If true, transaction logs for the database are truncated on checkpoint. This involves removing committed transactions at a checkpoint.

 Sybase SQL Server uses databases in much the same way as Microsoft SQL Server. There is significant commonality between them. Both have a master, model, tempdb, and a pubs database. However, the other databases differ. Sybase has moved many of their system procedures to a separate database, while Microsoft has left most of them in the master database.

Set Command

Another method of the database environment is the use of the set command. The set command remains effective for a session or for a batch. Set commands can also be established within the Query Analyzer through the use of the Query-Query-Options pull-down menu and through a wizard. The advantage of using the set command explicitly is that it can be included inside stored procedures:

```
SET variable value
```

Table 6.5 describes the purpose of the variable and provides sample examples modifying the value of the variable.

Table 6.5 Set Commands Variables

VARIABLE	DESCRIPTION
ANSI_NULL_DFLT_OFF/ ANSI_NULL_DFLT_ON	Override the ANSI compatibility status established by the sp_dboption. (e.g., SET ANSI_NULL_DFLT_ON ON)
ARITHABORT	Stops a query that experiences an overflow or division by 0. (e.g., SET ARITHABORT ON; SET ARITHABORT OFF)
ARITHIGNORE	Automatically returns null if a division is by 0 or an overflow occurs in a mathematical operation. (e.g., SET ARITHIGNORE ON)
FMTONLY	Metadata is returned to the client.
FORCEPLAN	Allows a specific index to be specifically used through the select, update, and delete commands.
IDENTITY_INSERT PATH	The path is db_name.owner.table. This overrides an identity value in the table.
NOCOUNT	Shuts off a message that automatically displays the number of rows returned by a select type command.
NOEXEC	A query is parsed and saved, but not executed.
PARSEONLY	A query is only parsed.
QUOTED_IDENTIFIER	Forces distinction between single and double quotes.
SHOWPLAN	Displays the query plan for a query. Toggles on and off.
STATISTICS IO	Displays I/O statistics for a query.
STATISTICS TIME ON/OFF	Displays time for a query.
DATEFIRST	Changes the date format.
DATEFORMAT	Changes the date format.
DEADLOCKPRIORITY LOW/NORMAL	Establishes a deadlock priority.
LANGUAGE	Establishes a default language.
ROWCOUNT:	Limit the number of rows returned by a request. (e.g., SET ROWCOUNT 0, SET ROWCOUNT 15)
TEXTSIZE	Establishes the size for text in the environment.
TRANSACTION ISOLATION	Establishes the transaction isolation error. (e.g. SET TRANSACTION ISOLATION LEVEL REPEATABLE READ).
LEVEL READ	Establish read level.
COMMITTED/READ	Establishes a dirty read/isolation level 0 locking.
UNCOMMITTED/REPEATABLE READ/SERIALIZABLE	Phantom reads are not allowed.

Summary

This chapter focused on the SQL Server physical environment including an examination of configuration options, database options, and set commands. This chapter also reviewed the activities that are required to establish the database environment and prepare it to create new databases. This was done in the context of gaining effective performance, so the structure of transaction logs was also discussed.

Other physical environment activities such as memory utilization, data page manipulation, and physical differences between SQL Server 7 and 6.5 were also discussed in this chapter. This chapter also reviewed some of the other significant physical changes in the SQL Server 7 environment.

Defining and Validating Your Data

Data is the most important part of every information system. The goal is to turn data into meaningful, easily accessible information. It is the reason that database servers exist. Data is stored in database objects, which themselves are stored within databases in the SQL Server environment. Every item of data must have an associated datatype that is used by SQL Server to determine how to store the item of data and how much space to leave for it. Datatypes establish data domains. There are two high level categories of datatypes: system defined and user defined. System-defined datatypes are supported by the engine and are compliant with the ANSI standard in most cases. User-defined datatypes are defined within and across applications using system procedures that are packaged with SQL Server.

Data can be saved in many different locations and formats, including flat files, persistent objects, databases, and even hard coded within application programs. The primary database object that stores data is the user table. Most of the other database objects, such as views, triggers, and stored procedures, manipulate the data contained within user tables. As shown in Figure 7.1, user tables represent entities of interest to the problem domain. User tables are composed of a set of columns, where each column represents one attribute of interest for the entity in the problem domain. A record, or row, is a single instance of the collection of all columns of interest for the entity. Multiple rows represent multiple instances of the columns or attributes. Each column can be provided with the following basic information (note that some fields are marked mandatory):

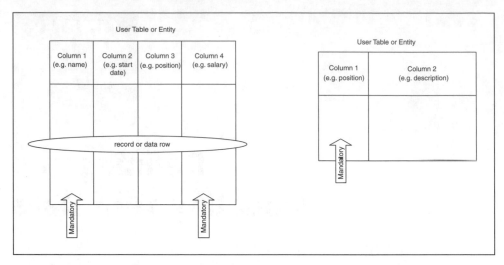

Figure 7.1 Relational tables.

Column name. Alphanumeric value that represents the name of the column. This value must be unique within the same table, but can be nonunique across tables and databases. The value should be descriptive (e.g., street) instead of representative (e.g., x). It is legitimate to connect multiple words with an underscore (_) to form a column name (e.g., street_address). Blanks are not valid characters in the column name. The maximum length for a column name is 128 bytes in SQL Server 7.

Datatype. SQL Server supports datatypes that are more or less consistent with the ANSI/92 standard. The common datatypes are discussed later in this chapter. It is also possible to build user-defined datatypes using system-stored procedures. This is discussed later in this chapter.

Length. Length refers to the amount of storage space required to store a value of a certain datatype. Different datatypes require different amounts of storage. It is generally a good idea to keep the amount of storage to a minimum (e.g., why use an int to store day of the month when a smallint is more than capable of handing the value). Some datatypes, such as real and int occupy a static amount of storage, while others, such as numeric, allow the developer to allocate a specific amount.

Index participation. This is used to indicate that a column or field forms part of an index for the table.

Default value. This value is used to populate nonmandatory table columns with a specific default value in the event that a record is being inserted without specifying a specific value.

Constraints. Constraints are single values, ranges, or groups of values that can be included or excluded for a table column when a record is being inserted or updated. The constraint is applied before a change is written to a table row. Violation of a constraint causes a transaction to roll back with an accompanying error message. Constraints are only applied for records that are inserted or changed after they are created. Records that exist in the table before the constraint was created are not affected by the constraint until the records are changed.

Rules. Rules are similar to but generally more elaborate than constraints. They are also applied to columns to ensure that data row values are consistent with the specified rule. Only one rule can be implemented per column in an SQL Server table. BCP operations are not trapped by column rules. Rules only apply to operations that occur after they are created. Data saved in tables before the rule was established are not filtered through the rule.

Triggers. Triggers are stored procedures that automatically fire when a specified action, such as insert/update/delete occurs on a specific column or table. Triggers are often used to maintain referential data integrity as well as to closely tie activities together.

Built-in Datatypes

Built-in or system-supplied datatypes support the ANSI/92 standard for the most part (but not exactly). This is useful in that it supports some degree of data portability and script portability between different data environments. In SQL Server, the available datatypes are shown in Tables 7.1–7.6 which are organized according to the data category. The tables also provide examples of each datatype as well as the physical space required to store each datatype in the ASCII character set. This information is used for estimating database size.

Table 7.1 represents the binary data datatypes supported by SQL Server.

Table 7.2 represents the character datatypes supported by SQL Server. Character datatypes can store characters, numbers, and special characters.

Table 7.1   Binary Data

DATATYPE	DESCRIPTION	EXAMPLES
binary(n) where n = 1 to x bytes, the fixed byte length x = 255 v6.5 x = 8000 v7 n = 1 is the default	Represents bit patterns, grouped together as two characters for a maximum of 10 groups. Two characters (0xAA, 0xFF) represents 1 bytes. Valid values are 0–9, A–F.	binary (10) binary
varbinary(n) where n = 1 to x bytes x = 255 v6.5 x = 8000 v7	Represents variable-length bit patterns. This is preferable to binary in situations where data size varies greatly from case to case. n is the maximum size and varies with the actual size of each data element being stored. Variable datatypes require additional performance time and can result in more transaction log writes.	varbinary (10)

Table 7.2 Character Data

DATATYPE	DESCRIPTION	EXAMPLES

char(n)
where n = 1 to x
  x = 255 v6.5
  x = 8000 v7
	The physical space required by the char datatype is between 1 and 255 bytes, depending on the size of n and it is fixed. Strings that exceed the defined size are automatically truncated.	char
		char(10)
		char(255)

varchar(n)
where n = 1 to x
  x = 255 v6.5
  x = 8000 v7
	Varchar stores variable-length characters. The declaration establishes the maximum size of the data. The actual physical space required to store the data varies with the size that is actually stored. Varchar should only be used if there is significant variation in the size of the data being stored. It has a negative impact on performance directly, and indirectly through larger record writes to the transaction log.	varchar(255)

Table 7.3 represents the date and time datatypes supported by SQL Server. Date and time datatypes offer the advantage of supporting built in functions that allow useful date and time translations. The datetime datatypes store date and time together. Supported date formats include both alphanumeric and numeric, where use of month signifies an alphanumeric format, while mm signifies a numeric format:

month day, year (e.g., June 14, 1999, Jun 14, 99)

month year day (e.g., June 1999 14)

month year (e.g., June 1999)

day month, year (e.g., 14 June 1999')

day year month (e.g., 14 1999 June')

year month day (e.g., 1999 June 14')

year month (e.g., 1999 June')

mm/dd/yyyy where / can be replaced with - or . (e.g., 06/14/1999, 06-14-99, 06.14.99)

dd/mm/yyyy (e.g., 14/06/1999)

dd/yyyy/mm (e.g., 14/1999/06)

yyyy/mm/dd (e.g., 1999/06/14)

yearmonthday (e.g., 19990225 with no quotes)

The time formats that are supported by SQL Server include those in the following list. Although seconds and milliseconds are included in the internal representation of time, the datetime datatype does not display this information by default. An SQL Server internal function, such as convert, which is discussed later in this chapter, is used to extract this information from the internal format.

Table 7.3 Date and Time Data

DATATYPE	DESCRIPTION	EXAMPLES
Datetime	The disk space required to store datetime fields is 8 bytes. The default date format is month (mmm) day(dd) year (yyyy) hh:mmAM/PM. The datetime range is January 1, 1753, to December 31, 9999. Defaults are January 1, 1900, 2:00:00:000AM. If century is not included, SQL Server assumes that years greater than 50 have a century of 19 while the others have a century of 20.	June 20, 1999 Jun 20, 99 20 June, 1999 1999 June Jun 1999 20
Smalldatetime	The disk space required to store smalldatetime fields is 4 bytes. Both date and time are still stored in this shortened space, however, the range is from 1/1/1900 A.D. to 6/6/2079 A.D.	June 20, 2025 April 30, 2061

hh:mm (e.g., 11:30)

hh:mm:ss:ms (e.g., 11:30:15:04)

hham/pm (e.g., 11 AM)

hhAM/PM (e.g., 8 AM)

hh AM/PM (e.g., 9 AM)

Before rushing to use smalldatetime to save 4 bytes over datetime, remember that the consequences of saving 2 bytes by only using the year has resulted in the year 2000 problem.

Table 7.4 represents the numeric datatypes supported by SQL Server. The p represents precision, which is the total number of digits in the entire number being stored. This can be anywhere from 1 to 28, with 18 being the default limit. The SQL Server environment can be configured for higher precisions on startup or installation. The s represents scale, which is the size of the decimal portion of the number.

Table 7.5 represents the money datatypes supported by SQL Server. Money values are provided to SQL Server with dollar ($) signs but no commas. Money stores both dollars and cents. Rounding of the money datatype is to the cent.

Table 7.6 represents additional datatypes supported by SQL Server. Text and image datatype columns must be initialized with data values before normal use.

The float and real datatypes both support storing numbers that exceed their precision (e.g., 7 for real, 15 for float); however, the numbers beyond the precision limit cannot have guaranteed correctness. Microsoft calls these datatypes approximate because they are not exactly correct due to the rounding. SQL Server rounds up to the next number.

Table 7.4 Numeric Types

DATATYPE	DESCRIPTION	EXAMPLES
decimal (p,s) p = 2 to 18 bytes p is 18 by default s is 0 by default	p is the number of placeholders in the entire number. s is the number of placeholders in the decimal portion of the number (right of the decimal point).	decimal (10,2)
numeric (p,s) p = 2 to 18 bytes p is 18 by default s is 0 by default	p is the number of placeholders in the entire number. s is the number of placeholders in the decimal portion of the number (right of the decimal point).	numeric (10,2)
float (n) n = 8 to 15, 8 by default	Float datatype numbers are stored within 8 bytes of physical storage. n can vary between 1 and 15, so the exact physical storage can vary. Float datatypes can store signed and decimal numbers. Rounding occurs at the precision value that is indicated by n. Float numbers can be between 1.7E–308 and 1.7E+308.	float (8)
real	Real datatype numbers are stored in 4 bytes (4 × 8) of physical storage. Real numbers are hardware dependent so numbers that are close to the outside range of the numbers should be carefully examined during conversions to other environments. The range is 3.4E–38 to 3.4E+38 with a precision of seven digits.	real
int	Int datatype numbers are stored in 4 bytes of physical storage. This represents 4 × 8 bits = 32 bits. Each bit can store a 1 or 0 value. One bit is used to store a positive or negative sign. This means that int can store numbers in the range of -2^{31} to $+2^{31}$ or –2,147,483,648 to 2,147,483,647. None of the integer datatypes can store decimal values.	int
smallint	Smallint datatype numbers are stored in 2 bytes (2 × 8 bits) of physical storage. This represents the range of -2^{15} to $+2^{15}$ or –32768 to +32767.	smallint Useful for employee codes.
tinyint	Tinyint datatype numbers are stored in 1 byte (1 × 8 bits) of physical storage. No sign can be saved with tinyint. This represents numbers in the range of 2^0 to 2^8 or 0 to 255.	tinyint

Table 7.5 Money

DATATYPE	DESCRIPTION	EXAMPLES
Money	Money datatype values require 8 bytes of physical storage space. The values represented are in the range −922,337,203,685,477.5808 to +922,337,203,685,477.5807.	money
Smallmoney	Smallmoney datatype values require 4 bytes of physical storage space. The values represented are in the range −214,748.3648 to +214,748.3647.	smallmoney

Table 7.6 Other Datatypes

DATATYPE	DESCRIPTION	EXAMPLES
Bit	Stores values of 1 or 0. Requires 1 byte of physical space.	
Timestamp	Columns defined with this datatype are automatically maintained by SQL Server in response to maintenance operations against a database table. A maximum of one timestamp column can be included in a table. Not all tables have timestamp columns. Timestamp should be reserved for this purpose. Data is stored in binary(8) format if nulls are allowed for the column, otherwise varbinary(8) is used. Timestamp is a binary value.	timestamp
Text	2 KB data pages linked together containing text information. Capacity is $2^{31}-1$ or 2,147,483,647 bytes.	'this is a very long line of text . . .'
Image	2 K data pages linked together containing image information. Capacity is $2^{31}-1$ or 2,147,483,647 bytes. The ntext, text, and image datatypes now support 2 GB of data. The data is stored in pages outside the normal table data.	0xbinary data
Uniqueidentifier	Supports global GUID	
Unicode (ntext, nchar, nvarchar)	Supports multiple human languages by supporting multiple character sets. Each character is stored using 2 bytes. This can support 65,536 combinations of bit patterns.	

```
DROP TABLE tablename
go

CREATE TABLE  tablename
(
           column1      datatype
)
go

INSERT tablename
(column1) VALUES (.......insert value here .......)
go

SELECT * FROM tablename
go
```

Figure 7.2   Create a datatype test table.

The datatypes that are defined within the ANSI/92 standard include binary varying (n), character(n), char varying (n), character varying (n), dec, double precision, float (n), and integer. Microsoft SQL Server supports many of the ANSI/92 datatypes, but the syntax is slightly different in each case. This has interesting implications in terms of application portability and interoperability. Moving a table creation script to a different database server product will require syntax changes to the script, though most of the changes will be 1 to 1. SQL Server also supports datatypes that are not supported by the standard in a rigid manner. Such extensions are useful for applications; however, their use will require more customization to an application if it is to be moved to a new operating environment.

In this example the SQL Server Enterprise Manager is used to build a table to test the datatypes. One common activity is to insert literals into datatypes with SQL DML commands or by establishing default values with the create/alter table command. Figure 7.2 shows the code to create a table to test the different datatypes.

Creating and Manipulating Datatypes

Datatypes determine the operations that are possible between items of data. For example, does it make sense to add 18 to the letter a. The obvious answer might be no. However, under certain situations this may be the desired result—for example, the requirement may be to determine the value of letter a added to ascii(18), or the require-ment may be to print the text a 18. The rules for datatype manipulation require unam-biguous direction. Some approaches for doing this are discussed in this section.

Binding Defaults to User-Defined Datatypes

A default value is assigned to a user-defined datatype so that inserted records that do not specify a value for an associated field will automatically default to the value speci-fied with the user-defined datatype. Default values can be bound and unbound from user-defined datatypes. The steps to do this are:

1. Create the default.
2. Create the user-defined datatype.
3. Bind the default to the user-defined datatype.

The user-defined datatype can be leveraged wherever other datatypes are leveraged. The sp_unbindefault system procedure is used to unbind a default from a user-defined datatype. This process is explained in the next section.

User-Defined Datatypes

User-defined datatypes are defined by users, often to create subdomains or subsets of data values and to promote data standards within an organization. Another reason to cre-ate user-defined datatypes is that they can be created to comply entirely with the ANSI SQL standard, based on synonyms with the SQL Server datatypes. In the event that an ap-plication needs to be ported, all scripts creating database objects can be recompiled, with code changes being limited to the definition of the user-defined datatypes. One com-mon use for user-defined datatypes is to create default values for specific character field definitions (e.g., SPACE5 is a five-character datatype that defaults to five spaces). Some other common uses for user-defined datatypes are: phone numbers, postal codes, states, provinces, and codes. User-defined datatypes are saved as database objects inside spe-cific databases. A user-defined datatype is only visible inside the database that it is cre-ated in stored procedures. Create a datatype inside the model database if it should be automatically included in all databases created subsequently. It is necessary to manually create the user-defined datatype in existing databases. A script that defaults to the dif-ferent databases is the preferred method of accomplishing this. User-defined datatypes are stored in the systypes system table.

Two system procedures are available to add and drop user-defined databases: sp_add-type and sp_droptype. In order to use these it is also necessary to create defaults and bind them to the user-defined datatypes. This process is shown in Figure 7.3.

Each of the following system procedures will be used in later examples. Note that name_of_type is a valid alphanumeric identifier and sql_server_type is any valid exist-ing SQL Server datatype. One syntax for using the system procedures to create and ma-nipulate user-defined datatypes is as follows:

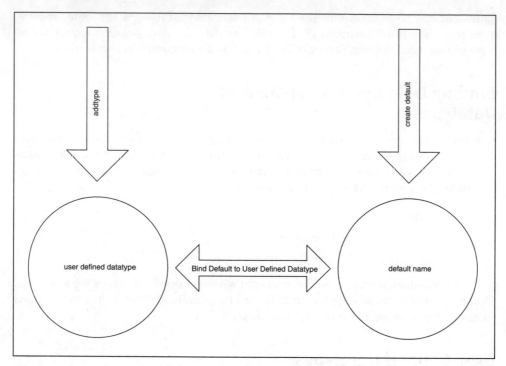

Figure 7.3   Process for leveraging user-defined datatypes.

```
sp_addtype name_of_type, sql_server_type, [NULL/'NOT NULL']
```

The following syntax drops a user-defined datatype:

```
sp_droptype name_of_type
```

The following syntax creates a default and specifies a value for the default:

```
create default default_name as value
```

The following syntax binds a default to a user-defined datatype. Both the user-defined datatype and the default name must be created before this option is possible.

```
sp_bindefault default_name, user_defined_datatype
```

The following syntax displays information about the user-defined datatype:

```
sp_help user_defined_datatype
```

Sample Scripts

The following example creates a user-defined datatype and also creates a default value and binds it to the user-defined datatype :

```
/*create the user defined datatype.
  It can then be used as any other datatype*/

sp_addtype commission, int, 'not null'

    /* create a default value */
    create default comm_default_value as 15
    go      /* the go statement is important, otherwise you will
              receive syntactical errors, as the default as not
              yet been created. */

    sp_bindefault comm_default_value, commission

/* leverage the user defined datatype + default in a table */

if exists (select name from sysobjects where name = "user_test"
             and type = "U")
        drop table user_test
go

create table user_test
(
    sales_agent name      char (50),
    sales_commission      commission
)

insert user_test
(sales_agent_name) values ("bob the agent")

    /* display the results */
select * from user_test
```

This select retrieves the following results and displays them as output:

sales_agent_name	sales_commission
bob the agent	15

The following example drops the commission user defined datatype. You must eliminate occurrences where the datatype is used:

```
sp_droptype commission
```

The following example displays information about the user-defined datatype values:

```
sp_help commission
```

The following example declares a variable and displays its contents based on a user-defined datatype which contains a default value:

```
declare @variable    commission
select '@variable = ', @variable
```

Data Validation

The objectives of data validation are to ensure data integrity and referential data integrity. Data integrity refers to the consistency and quality of data in a single item or an array of item. Quality is based on understanding what values data items should assume, the methods used for trapping exceptions, and on ensuring that only qualifying data is accepted. Figure 7.4 shows a range of data validation methods, including the following:

Type of data. This refers to the type of data stored in an item. This is typically specified by a datatype in a declaration statement. The SQL Server engine automatically ensures that only data that is consistent with that datatype is accepted into the element.

Value of data. The value of data sometimes needs to correspond to a set or domain. This is often enforced through constraints coded into a database table. The basic methods for accomplishing this may include declarative RI, defaults, foreign keys, references, and check constraints.

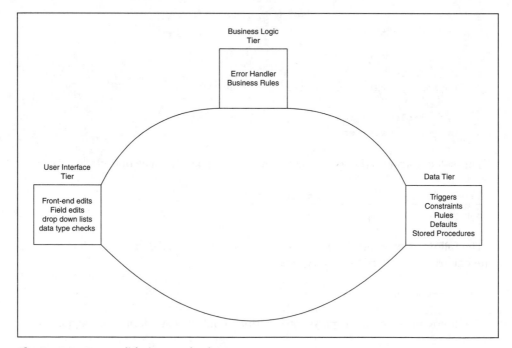

Figure 7.4 Data validation methods.

Business rules. This is similar to the value of data, just more formulistic. Business rules specify more detail about constraints that apply to an element of data. These are often encapsulated into rules.

Applying integrity checks. Integrity checks can be applied at the database level through such things as rules and constraints. They can also be placed in the middle tier through such things as stored procedures and triggers. Or they can be placed in the presentation tier or directly into the user interface. This is useful for value type data consistency checking.

Enforcing data integrity. Integrity is enforced by rejecting data that violates an integrity check. This is usually done with a meaningful message directed at the user or a text log.

Ensuring referential data integrity is more complex. This involves ensuring consistency between fields of data that can cross tables, databases, database servers, and even data formats (e.g., data in SQL Server must be consistent with data in a general ledger). SQL Server provides stored procedures and triggers as convenient ways to identify referential data integrity violations and to correct or reject them. Constraints, such as rules, also allow referential data integrity to be maintained.

Many of the data validation methods discussed in this section involve the creation of database objects that can be examined with the sp_help command. Furthermore, some of the database objects, such as rules, can also be examined with the sp_helptext system procedure, which displays the Transact-SQL commands that comprise the object. Each of these system procedures is followed by one parameter, the name of the object being examined. The object must be in the local or default database. In general, SQL Server accepts multiple data validation objects on the same table or column. There are, however, some restrictions. For example, only one default value can be specified for a column; only one rule can be specified for a column.

Constraints

Constraints are generally applied at the column or table level to ensure data integrity. All constraints involving multiple columns must be established at the table level. Three types of constraints are defined in the ANSI/92 standard: key (primary, PK; and secondary, FK), check, and referential. The following types of constraints are supported: primary key, foreign key, reference, unique, default, and check constraints. PK constraints generate clustered indexes when the table is created [e.g., constraint main_column primary key (field)]. Define the PK constraint at the table level to generate a multicolumn clustered index. Unique key (UK) constraints accept a single null value in the included columns. Check constraints are more efficient than rules. Check constraints can access other columns in the table and can use conditional operators to inspect values. More than one check constraint can be applied to a table column. Referential integrity (RI) constraints are of two types: PK (primary key) and FK (foreign key). FK constraints can be used as code table lookups. RI does not support cascading deletes. Insert operations do not test primary key values. Primary or unique constraints must be defined on referenced table columns. The sp_helpconstraint system procedure provides information about constraints defined on a table.

The syntax for a constraint is as follows:

```
CONSTRAINT    constraint_prefix CONSTRAINT_TYPE (values)
```

Primary Key Constraints

A primary key constraint is used to specify the combination of columns that uniquely identifies a data row in a table. A clustered or nonclustered index is created on this combination of columns. There can only be one primary key constraint in a table. The following example creates a set of user-defined tables, creates primary key constraints, and then displays the constraints using the sp_helpconstraint system procedure:

```
drop table student
drop table subject
drop table advisor
go

create table student
(
    student_id          int    PRIMARY KEY CLUSTERED,
    major_subject       char (10),
    advisor_name        char (10),
    admission_date      datetime,
    previous_gpa        float
)

create table subject
(
    subject_code        char (10),
    description         char (50),
    primary_instructor  char (10)
)

create table advisor
(
    advisor_code        char (10),
    advisor_name        char(50),
    contact_no          char (11)
)
go

sp_helpconstraint student
go
sp_helpconstraint subject
go
sp_helpconstraint advisor
go
```

 It is necessary to drop the tables that reference other tables as a block in a batch.

Foreign Key Constraints

Foreign key constraints are applied to one or more columns in a table. Each table can have more than 1 foreign key constraint. Foreign key constraints are used to enforce referential integrity with other tables in the database. A common use of this constraint is to ensure that code values in one table have matching records in a code table(s). Foreign key constraints are closely tied to Reference constraints. The reference constraint points to another column(s) in another table in the database. A primary key must exist on the reference table referenced fields. If more than one column is being referenced, it is possible to create a concatenated primary key. The syntax of this command is as follows:

```
CONSTRAINT constraint_name foreign key (field_name) references
table_name.
```

In the following example, notice that the tables are rearranged in the sequence that the foreign constraints are being created. The locations of the 'go' statements are important as they end batches that are dependent on other batches:

```
drop table student
drop table subject
drop table advisor
go

create table advisor
(
     advisor_code          char (10) PRIMARY KEY CLUSTERED,
     advisor_name          char(50),
     contact_no            char (11)
)
go

create table subject
(
     subject_code          char (10) PRIMARY KEY CLUSTERED,
     description           char (50),
     primary_instructor    char (10) REFERENCES advisor (advisor_code)
)
go

create table student
(
     student_id            int   PRIMARY KEY CLUSTERED,
     major_subject         char (10) REFERENCES subject(subject_code),
     advisor_name          char (10),
     admission_date        datetime,
     previous_gpa          float

     CONSTRAINT FK_major_advisor_name FOREIGN KEY (advisor_name)
         REFERENCES advisor (advisor_code)
```

```
)
go

sp_helpconstraint student
go
sp_helpconstraint subject
go
sp_helpconstraint advisor
go
```

Referencing Multiple Columns in Constraints

Both primary key and foreign key constraints can reference multiple columns in their tables. This requires a modification to both the foreign key constraint and the primary key constraint in the referenced table. Multiple foreign key constraints can be attached to the table. The referenced table can also reference other tables. The following example demonstrates the use of the primary key constraint and the foreign key constraint:

```
use address
go

drop table car_units
go

drop table automobile_description
go

create table automobile_description
(
 auto_type char(5),
 auto_model char(5),
 description char(40),
 cost money

CONSTRAINT PK_auto_type_model PRIMARY KEY CLUSTERED (auto_type,
auto_model)
)

create table car_units
(
 dealership_no int,
 auto_type char(5),
 auto_model char(5),
 on_hand_qty int,
 total_sold int

CONSTRAINT FK_auto_type_model FOREIGN KEY (auto_type, auto_model)
        REFERENCES auotmobile_description (auto_type, auto_model)
)
go
```

Unique Key Constraints

Unique key constraints are applied to one or more columns in a table to identify uniqueness between data rows in a table. This constraint type differs from primary key constraints in that many unique constraints can be created on a table. The following example creates a unique constraint on a single column in a table:

```
/* drop all three tables, two of which reference the advisor table */
drop table student
drop table subject
drop table advisor
go

create table advisor
(
    advisor_code        char (10) PRIMARY KEY CLUSTERED,
    advisor_name        char(50),
    contact_no          char (11)

CONSTRAINT unique_advisor UNIQUE NONCLUSTERED (advisor_name)
)
go
```

Default Constraints

Default values are used to populate fields with data if data is not provided by the user. This can make sense for nonkey fields and fields that do not require specific information until a later time. Key fields are not good candidates for default values. Default values can apply to both table columns and to user-defined datatypes. The process for working with defaults involves creating a default value and binding it to the field or datatype. Defaults provide values to fields on insert operations. Defaults can be established when a table is created or anytime afterward. Default value type mismatches with table fields are not caught at bind time but at run-time when the default is invoked. This means testing must be thorough to avoid production problems and embarrassment. A default can be manually invoked with the update command by using Set fieldname = DEFAULT. Default values should also match the datatype of a column and comply with column rules and column constraints. By definition, there can be only one default value per column. Default values can also be functions and constants. They are invoked during the execution of the Bulk Copy Program (BCP). The syntax for managing defaults is as follows:

```
Create default defname as value

Where value can correspond to the datatypes shown earlier in this
chapter, such as '     ', 10, 'road'.

sp_bindefault defname, 'tablename.columnname'
sp_bindefault defname, user-defined-datatype
```

Sample Scripts

The following example creates and binds a default value:

```
create default default_name1 as value
sp_bindefault default_name1, 'tablename.fieldname1'
```

Source Listing 7.1 manipulates default values in a number of user-defined tables. The sp_helpconstraint is used to inspect each user-defined table in this example for constraints:

```
drop table student
drop table subject
drop table advisor
go

create table advisor
(
    advisor_code            char (10) PRIMARY KEY CLUSTERED,
    advisor_name            char(50),
    contact_no              char (11)
)
go

create table subject
(
    subject_code            char (10) PRIMARY KEY CLUSTERED,
    description             char (50),
    primary_instructor      char (10) REFERENCES advisor (advisor_code)
)
go

create table student
(
    student_id              int  PRIMARY KEY CLUSTERED,
    major_subject           char (10) REFERENCES subject(subject_code),
    advisor_name            char (10),
    admission_date          datetime  DEFAULT getdate(),
    previous_gpa            float

    CONSTRAINT FK_major_advisor_name FOREIGN KEY (advisor_name)
            REFERENCES advisor (advisor_code)
)
go
sp_helpconstraint student
go
sp_helpconstraint subject
go
sp_helpconstraint advisor
go
```

Source 7.1 Changing default values in user-defined tables.

Check Constraints

Check constraints are a limited method of ensuring data integrity by providing a list of acceptable values for table columns. One check constraint can exist for one column in a table. Every column can have its own check constraint. Another approach is to define a check constraint on the table.

Sample Scripts

The following example defines a check constraint on a user-defined table to enforce a specific data format on a column:

```
CONSTRAINT    CK_fax CHECK (fax LIKE '[4-9][4-9][4-9][4-9][0-9][0-9]
                                     [0-9][0-9][0-9][0-9]')
```

The following example also defines a check constraint at user-defined table level, specifying a fieldname in the statement:

```
CONSTRAINT constraint_hname CHECK (fieldname IN ('value1', 'value2',
'value3', .....)

/* Expand the example to include check constraints */

drop table student
drop table subject
drop table advisor
go

create table advisor
(
     advisor_code          char (10) PRIMARY KEY CLUSTERED,
     advisor_name          char(50),
     contact_no            char (11) CONSTRAINT CK_contact_no CHECK
   (contact_no LIKE '[3-9][0-9][0-9]-[0-9][0-9][0-9]-[0-9][0-9][0-9][0-9]')

CONSTRAINT unique_advisor UNIQUE NONCLUSTERED (advisor_name)
)
go

create table subject
(
     subject_code          char (10) PRIMARY KEY CLUSTERED,
     description           char (50),
     primary_instructor    char (10) REFERENCES advisor (advisor_code)
)
go

create table student
(
     student_id            int  PRIMARY KEY CLUSTERED,
     major_subject         char (10) REFERENCES subject(subject_code),
```

```
        advisor_name          char (10),
        admission_date        datetime  DEFAULT getdate(),
        previous_gpa          float         CHECK (previous_gpa > 0 AND
                                                   previous_gpa <=4.3)

    CONSTRAINT FK_major_advisor_name FOREIGN KEY (advisor_name)
            REFERENCES advisor (advisor_code)
)
go
sp_helpconstraint student
go
sp_helpconstraint subject
go
sp_helpconstraint advisor
go
```

Test the Validation Objects

The previous code creates three tables and establishes the constraints. These can be tested by establishing a series of insert, update, and delete data scripts with a clear idea of which ones will be stopped by the constraints and which ones are consistent with them. This logic is tested in Chapter 18 as part of the testing procedures in a standard life cycle.

Rules

Rules are used to trap inconsistent data and ensure that it is not inserted into a table; they also specifically identify valid data values. Rules are similar to database objects in that a block of Transact-SQL is written for the rule under a rule name. They are like tiny stored procedures or triggers. A bind function is used to attach a rule to a table column. Data that is being updated or inserted into a table passes through the rule and is trapped if it violates the rule. In such an event, the data is rejected with a message. Rules must be created and bound to variables before they are used. Rules that are bound to a column or user-defined datatype do not affect data that is already in the table, even if it violates the rule. However, an update command will invoke the rule when it is issued. The sp_help and sp_helptext system functions can be used to retrieve information about a rule from the system tables.

Rules are dropped in a two-step process. All Bind operations must be Unbind for the rule. The rule can then be dropped where rule_logic consists of the following: search condition commands that are used with the Select clause. The syntax for the first step is

```
create rule rule_name
as rule_logic
go


IN (value1, value2, . . .)
LIKE '%value%'
```

```
Functions
Operators, AND, OR, NOT
Patterns (e.g. _ means any character, [number range separated by a hypen])
sp_bindrule rule_name, table.column | user-defined-datatype
go
```

The syntax for the second step in dropping a rule is

```
sp_unbindrule 'table.column'

drop rule rulename
```

Sample Scripts

The following example creates a rule for car color and identifies the set of allowable colors:

```
CREATE RULE car_color AS @ccolor IN
('Black', 'Red', 'Brown', 'White', 'Blue')
```

The following example creates a rule to enforce that a temperature is within a range of values:

```
CREATE RULE air_temperature
AS @temperature > 0 and temperature < 20
```

Source Listing 7.2 creates a rule and tests it as an example to ensure that the rule was used properly:

```
/* test a rule */
CREATE RULE room_temperature
        AS @temperature > 15 AND @temperature < 30
go

create table rule_test
(
    sequence_no        int  IDENTITY (1,1),
    month              char (3),
    high_temp          int
)
go

sp_bindrule room_temperature, 'rule_test.high_temp'
go

    insert rule_test
    (month, high_temp) values ('Jan',24)
```
(Continues)

Source 7.2 Creating and testing a rule.

```
     go
     /* this insert command is processed successfully */

     insert rule_test
     (month, high_temp) values ('Feb', 40)
     go
     /* this insert command is trapped by the rule. The following
command is displayed:
          A column insert or update conflicts with a rule imposed by a
previous CREATE RULE statement. The statement was aborted. The
conflict occurred in database 'pubs', table 'rule_test', column
'high_temp'. The statement has been aborted.
     */

/* remove and drop the rule */
sp_unbindrule "rule_test.high_temp"
go

drop rule room_temperature
go

drop table rule_test
go
```

Source 7.2 *(Continued)*

Summary

This chapter reviewed two types of datatypes in Microsoft SQL Server: system-defined datatypes and user-defined datatypes. System-defined datatypes, which include money, integer, float, text, image, and bytecode are based on the ANSI/92 standard. User-defined datatypes can be created to modify the domain of a datatype. These are then bound to columns in tables, sometimes with a defined default value.

This chapter also reviewed data validation methods for ensuring referential integrity and data quality. These included working with constraints and rules. Data validation can be programmed directly in the SQL Server engine with declarative referential integrity, can be implemented at the middleware level in n-tier architecture, or can be implemented at the front-end, user interface tier.

Using the Data Definition Language

The ANSI SQL Data Definition Language was envisioned by Dr. E. F. Codd as part of the definition of the relational data model which itself was a product of an IBM research project named System R. This model was based on mathematical set theory, which evolved into the structured English query language (SEQUEL), and was first commercially implemented by Oracle. The relational data model includes the definition of three classes of commands that are nonprocedural in nature: data definition language (DDL), data manipulation language (DML), and data control language (DCL). DDL, the focus of this chapter, defines commands to create, alter, and drop database objects from the database environment. Vendors creating database server products, such as Microsoft, Sybase, and Informix, followed Oracle's lead and leveraged the original nonprocedural DDL command set for their own SQL dialects. DDL commands can be issued interactively through utilities such as the Enterprise Manager, embedded in client applications, and inside stored procedures. Triggers are not generally used to initiate DDL commands.

Building Database Objects with the Data Definition Language

As shown in Figure 8.1, data definition language commands can be used to define databases and database objects. There is a definite procedural hierarchy in the DDL command set. The database definition commands rely on the physical environment to be set up in terms of devices and segments. The database object definition commands require databases to be created before they can be used. The main DDL commands that are covered in this chapter include define object, drop object, and alter object.

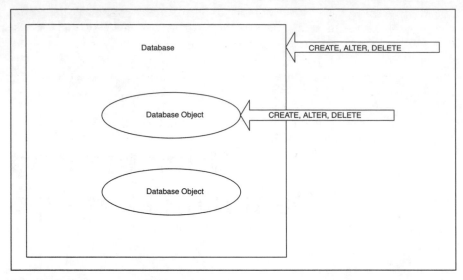

Figure 8.1 DDL command hierarchy.

Creating Databases

One of the differences between Oracle and SQL Server is their use of databases as basic organization mechanisms. Oracle relies on a primary database, within which tables are defined and grouped according to projects. Databases in SQL Server are used to group similar database objects. Databases are also used to separate production, test, and development environments, as well as to create databases for different members of a development team. It is possible to customize the following characteristics of databases being created: size, physical location, database name, database options, and input mechanism.

SQL Server now supports an easy-to-use wizard, Create Database Wizard, that provides an easy-to-follow process for creating a database, a transaction log, and a window into the database options. Chapter 3 provides an example of using this wizard. In general, DDL commands can be executed using a variety of techniques: wizards, Enterprise Manager, profile, and scripts. Each of these methods is discussed in this chapter. Experienced developers or DBAs can still use DDL code in scripts that can be reused to reestablish a database environment at any time. The syntax to create a database in SQL Server 7, as per the Microsoft literature, where x, y, z are the sizes of the components is as follows:

```
CREATE DATABASE database_name
ON PRIMARY
(NAME='database_Primary', FILENAME = 'c:\path\filename. mdf',
SIZE=x, MAXSIZE=y,FILEGROWTH=increment)

LOG ON
(NAME='database_log',
FILENAME='c:\path\filename.ldf',
SIZE=x,
MAXSIZE=y,FILEGROWTH=increment)
```

This is a simpler syntax than earlier versions of this command to create databases. Physical preparation of the environment to create raw partitions and devices is not required. The FILENAME variable accepts a path and filename to hold the database and related transaction log. SIZE is the initial size of the database. MAXSIZE is the maximum size that the file is allowed to grow. FILEGROWTH is the increment with which the file grows when it fills up, but before it has reached the value specified in MAX-SIZE.

The following example creates a database in the primary file and places the transaction log in another file. The units are in megabytes, so in this example, the addr database is created with a size of 5 MB. This will grow 1 MB at a time until the maximum size of 50 MB is reached.

```
CREATE DATABASE addr
ON PRIMARY
(NAME='addr_Primary', FILENAME = 'c:\mssql7\data\addr_prm.mdf',
SIZE=5, MAXSIZE=50,FILEGROWTH=1)

LOG ON
(NAME='addr_log',
FILENAME='c:\mssql7\data\addr.ldf',
SIZE=2,
MAXSIZE=20,FILEGROWTH=1)
```

This command displays the following information messages showing success:

```
The CREATE DATABASE process is allocating 5.00 MB on disk 'addr_Primary'.
The CREATE DATABASE process is allocating 2.00 MB on disk 'addr_log'.
```

The sp_databases system procedure displays useful information about databases. This procedure also accepts a parameter, database_name, to display specific information about a database. The syntax is sp_databases database_name. Another command that displays database information is sp_helpdb.

An example of the results that are displayed by the sp_databases command is the following. The first column displays the name of the database as it is entered in the sysdatabases system table in the master database. The remarks column displays the remarks that are identified by SQL Server for each database.

Database_name	Database_size	Remarks
address	2048	NULL
Database 1	2048	NULL
database	2048	NULL
master	8448	NULL
model	1536	NULL
msdb	8192	NULL
Northwind	8704	NULL
pubs	2104	NULL
tempdb	2560	NULL

The sp_helpdb system procedure shows more detailed information about the databases in the environment. This command produces the following results. The status column shows the dboptions that are set for the corresponding database.

Name	db_size	Owner	dbid	Created	Status
address	2.00 MB	sa	8	Sep 17 1998	No options set
Database 1	2.00 MB	sa	9	Sep 20 1998	No options set
database	2.00 MB	sa	7	Sep 17 1998	No options set
master	8.25 MB	sa	1	Jun 19 1998	trunc. log on chkpt.
model	1.50 MB	sa	3	Aug 9 1998	No options set
msdb	8.00 MB	sa	4	Aug 9 1998	trunc. log on chkpt.
Northwind	8.50 MB	sa	6	Aug 9 1998	Select into/bulkcopy, trunc. log on chkpt.
pubs	2.05 MB	sa	5	Aug 9 1998	trunc. log on chkpt.
tempdb	2.50 MB	sa	2	Jun 19 1998	Select into/bulkcopy

The Enterprise Manager can be used to display similar information. Ensure that SQL Server is running. Start the Enterprise Manager and expand the object hierarchy until the database object is visible. Click on the database object to display Figure 8.2. Clicking on one of the databases in this screen displays information about that database. No-

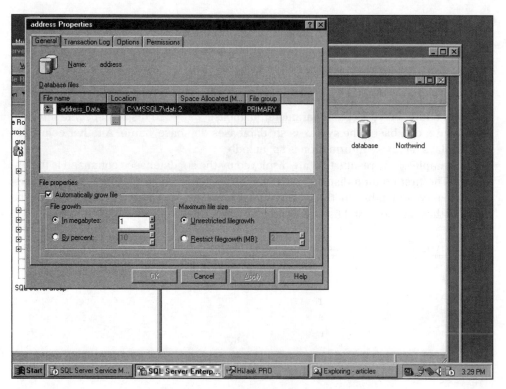

Figure 8.2   Database information through the Enterprise Manager.

tice that the address database is 2 MB in size. Information about the transaction log can be displayed by selecting the transaction log tab.

Dropping Databases

Databases can be dropped if there are no users actively using them. A drop operation on a database requires ownership permissions on that database. Dropping a database also causes all its database objects to be dropped as well. By definition, the drop database operation is destructive and should only be used within tight constraints.

 It is always a good precaution to back up databases before they are dropped in the event that the database is required again. If the database is important, it is also wise to test the recover operation or a slow self-check backup to ensure that the backup is a valid copy.

The basic command syntax for dropping databases using the drop database ANSI data definition language commands is as follows:

```
DROP DATABASE database_name, database_name ...
One example of the syntax for dropping a database is:
DROP DATABASE address
Go
```

Altering Databases

While databases should be created with a size that suits the transaction volumes known about them, it is not unusual to require changes to database sizes after they are built. This method is especially useful for putting limits on the size of databases since they can grow unchecked in the new version of SQL Server and consume all available disk space. Note that this syntax should be used with the sp_logdevice to alter the transaction log. The syntax for altering a database is as follows:

```
ALTER DATABASE database_name
    ON DEFAULT | logical_device = size_in_mb,
                  logical_device = size_in_mb, ...
    FOR LOAD
```

Adding/Removing Databases to SQL Server

Two new system procedures are available in SQL Server to attach or detach database files and their logs to an SQL Server environment. This is a useful option for transferring data between SQL Servers without using BCP or other commands such as Select. These commands are especially useful for databases being created for movable media or for electronic transfer through the Internet, e-mail, or Web sites. This requires a large removable storage unit, such as a writeable CD ROM. SQL Server also creates new transaction log files when attaching to a database file.

Defining Database Objects

Some database objects are extensions to the ANSI/92 standard, in terms of their definition or their implementation. This chapter focuses on tables and indexes, while objects such as views, triggers, and stored procedures are discussed in a separate chapter. The latter are dealt with in the ANSI standard; however, their implementation can vary from database vendor to database vendor. This limits their portability or interoperability support, but they compensate by offering solid benefits to application performance and usability.

Creating Tables

Tables are the physical equivalents of logical entities in the relational data model, and sets in mathematical theory. The following syntax is used to create relational tables in a database. Table_name must be unique within a database, but can be reused in other databases. If the table is to be created outside the default database, the db_name can be used to establish a path to the desired database. "owner" is used to manipulate tables that are created by another owner. Column_name can be a mnemonic string, which cannot contain embedded blanks. This name must be unique within the table, but the same column_name can be used in other tables. Data_type can be a supplied datatype or a user-defined datatype. Constraint can be a primary key, unique, foreign key, default, or check constraint. See Chapter 7 for additional examples of creating and manipulating constraints.

```
CREATE TABLE db_name.owner.table_name
    column_name  data_type constraints
```

The following example shows a script that creates a table, "grade," in the pubs database. A number of the commonly used datatypes are used in this example.

```
CREATE TABLE pubs..grade
(
    student_no        int,
    course_code       char(10),
    grade             float,
    completed         datetime,
    last_mod          timestamp
)
```

The following example inserts a data row into the grade table using an INSERT statement that is discussed in more detail in Chapter 9. This is an example of a data manipulation language (DML) statement. The SELECT statement is used to retrieve information from the GRADE user table in the form of a result set.

```
INSERT pubs..grade

(student_no, course_code, grade, completed)
```

```
values
(105, 'CSC301', 90, 'April 20, 1998')
    go

    SELECT * from pubs..grade
```

The following example drops the grade table from the pubs database. The absence of the owner value in the statement implies that the owner of the table is dropping the table. Conversely, a format similar to drop table pubs.owner.grade could be used to drop a table, assuming the permissions exist, if another owner created the table.

```
drop table pubs..grade
go
```

Altering Tables

The alter table command is used to modify the structure of a table after it is created. This generally consists of adding columns to the tables or constraints to the columns. Note that the nocheck feature overrides any foreign key constraints that are bound to the table. The syntax for this command is as follows:

```
ALTER TABLE dbname.owner.table_name WITH NOCHECK
    ADD col_name column_properties col_contraints . . .
DROP CONSTRAINT constraint_name . . .
```

An example of altering a table is shown in the following script. This example adds a new column, remark, to the existing grade table

```
USE PUBS
GO

ALTER TABLE grade
    ADD remark      char (50)
    GO
```

The following example shows that the remark column has been added to the grade table. A value of NULL is included in the data rows for the remark column, while the previous data values are not changed.

```
select * from grade
go
```

Dropping Tables

Tables must be dropped in order to permanently remove them from the database environment and the system tables. This is done with the drop command, which is different than the delete and truncate commands. The latter two commands remove data from a table but leave the structure intact. The syntax for the drop command is as follows:

```
DROP TABLE database_name.owner.table
```

Sample Scripts

The following example drops the test 1 table from the default database:

```
DROP TABLE test1
go
```

The following example inspects the sysobjects system table in the default database for the existence of the test1 table. The column type has a value of U if the associated data row belongs to a user-defined table. If the table (in this case, test1) exists, it is dropped. If the table does not exist, the overhead related to the drop command is not incurred as the DROP command is skipped. Notice, however, that there is an overhead related to the IF EXISTS statement. This check should be skipped if there is a strong likelihood that the user table exists. If the table is absent, SQL Server displays an error message as a result of attempting to drop a nonexistent user table.

```
IF EXISTS (select name from sysobjects where name = 'test1'
AND type = 'U'
drop table test1
go
```

The following example drops the grade table from the pubs database. This format should be used if the default database does not contain the table being dropped.

```
DROP TABLE pubs..grade
go
```

Using Indexes

Indexes are possibly the single most powerful database object to affect application performance. Optimal index use is both an art and a science. Index use is often expressed using simple adjectives, such as not good and good. Too many indexes can be "not good," and too few indexes can also be "not good." The right combination of indexes based on heavy use or common transactions is "good." By maximizing the good guidelines, the hope is to improve the overall application performance. Indexes allow SQL Server to reduce the overall number of reads to locate a specific item of data or a set of data. Indexes can be based on one or multiple columns. Figure 8.3 shows the common types of indexes used in SQL Server 7.

Here are some general guidelines for index usage based on experiences from a variety of development projects in the last 10 years:

Initiate queries that search for a specific value (e.g., use =) as opposed to those that use range commands or nonspecific values (e.g., between, <=, >=).

Avoid table scans whenever possible. A table scan involves a sequential search of an entire table.

If a table scan is inevitable, attempt to complete all your work in one scan. Avoid multiple passes through the same table.

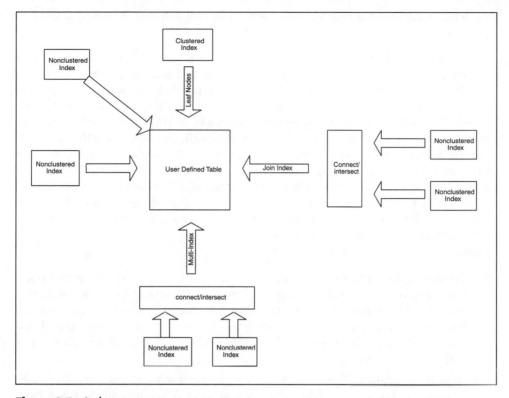

Figure 8.3 Index structures.

Avoid indexing tables that are always involved in table scans.

Avoid indexing tables with less than 500 data rows.

List the where clauses in a Select in the order in which the table is indexed.

Indexed tables should be accessed first in table joins (e.g., be on the left side of the clause).

Avoid retrieving columns that are not required, and be aware that columns read directly from index pages are faster than retrieving them from the data pages due to fewer reads.

Drop indexes in all bulk copy operations, then create them again when the target table is loaded with data.

Keep index keys as small as possible to increase the number of key values that can fit onto one index page. Index key values and record locations are stored on index pages.

Statistics are maintained on the distribution page. This page is used by the optimizer to calculate costs and build plans. Thus the distribution page should match the current data as much as possible. In SQL Server 7, rebuilding the distribution page is done based on a sampling method that provides more accurate statistics. Man-

206 **Building Microsoft SQL Server 7 Applications with COM**

ual rebuilding of this page should be done after high-volume data changes are done to a table.

The distribution statistics page of an index specifies how the key field values are distributed in the index pages. These statistics are used by the query optimizer to build a cost estimate for traversing the index. Every index has a distribution page. Clearly the accuracy of the distribution values determines the accuracy of the cost calculations. The accuracy of distribution values decreases as data is added, updated, or deleted from the table. Large table changes affect this accuracy significantly. At such a time it is necessary to rebuild the statistics page, possibly through a DBCC command, through the SQL Server utilities, or through system procedures. SQL Server 7 contains a new process to update the distribution statistics automatically. However, large table changes should still be followed by a manual recalculation (e.g., through Update statistics). New system procedures are available to suppress the automatic recalculation process (e.g., sp_autostats). Unique keys have a high selectivity.

SQL Server 7 supports a variety of indexes:

Clustered index. The index values match the physical order of the table values. There can be 0 or 1 clustered indexes per table. Having more than one clustered index for the same tape is physically impossible. The lowest level (or leaf node) of the index contains a page that contains the data belonging to a key value. Clustered indexes combine the storage of the data with the storage of the index values in the form of a tree.

Nonclustered index. There can be many nonclustered indexes per table. Nonclustered indexes do not affect the physical order of the data in the table. Each nonclustered index contains a leaf node that points to a data record either in the clustered table or in the table itself (represented as an offset from a specific page). Nonclustered indexes require additional disk space for storage. They are not as efficient as clustered indexes because of the extra read required to locate the actual record data. Nonclustered indexes are supported by a b-tree structure.

Multi-Index. These leverage several table indexes to locate the required data. Multiple tables will leverage a join index. Indexes do not need to be explicitly identified in the commands.

Merge Join. Supports joins that have sorted inputs. These indexes are present on a join key or are ordered on the join key. Merge Join works by processing an outer and inner loop.

Hash join. Supports joins on nonordered input.

Hash aggregation. Builds aggregates on unordered data.

Building Indexes

There are several methods of building indexes on tables:

- With the Create Index set of commands for creating clustered and nonclustered indexes

- Built as a consequence of primary key constraints, foreign key constraints, and unique constraints
- Through the Create Index Wizard, Index Tuning Wizard, and other graphical tools

The syntax for creating an index on a table is

```
CREATE UNIQUE CLUSTERED|NONCLUSTERED INDEX name_of_index
        ON db_name.owner.table column1[, column2, column3Ö]
            WITH FILLFACTOR = x, IGNORE_DUP_KEY, IGNORE_DUP_ROW,
                SORTED_DATA, ALLOW_DUP_ROW
```

The syntax for dropping an index on a table is

```
DROP INDEX db_name.owner.index
```

The syntax for displaying information about an index on a table is

```
sp_helpindex table_name      /* shows the indexes on the table */
```

Sample Scripts

The following example builds a unique clustered index as well as two nonclustered indexes on the employee1 table:

```
USE pubs
GO

CREATE TABLE employee1
(
    employee_no         int,
    last_name           char(30),
    first_name          char(30),
    start_date              datetime,
        salary                  money,
        last_promotion_date     datetime
    )
    go

    CREATE UNIQUE CLUSTERED INDEX emp_employee_no_ndx1 ON
employee1 (employee_no)

    CREATE NONCLUSTERED INDEX emp_name_ndx2 ON
Employee1 (last_name, first_name)

    CREATE NONCLUSTERED INDEX emp_salary_ndx3 ON
                Employee1 (salary)
    GO
```

The following example uses a system procedure to display information about indexes bound to the employee1 table:

```
sp_helpindex        employee1
go
```

This statement syntax produces the following output, showing details about the indexes that are bound to the employee1 user-defined table:

index_name	index_description	index_keys
emp_employee_no_ndx1	clustered located on PRIMARY	employee_no
emp_name_ndx2	nonclustered located on PRIMARY	last_name,
first_name		
emp_salary_ndx3	nonclustered located on PRIMARY	salary

The following example tests the properties of the unique index by attempting to insert a data row containing a duplicate key into the employee1 table:

```
insert employee1
(
        employee_no, last_name, first_name,
start_date, salary, last_promotion_date
)
values
    (
    400, 'Smart', 'Barry', 'June 1 1995', 60000, getdate()
    )


    /* duplicate record */
insert employee1
(
        employee_no, last_name, first_name,
start_date, salary, last_promotion_date
)
values
    (
    400, 'Smart', 'Barry', 'June 1 1995', 60000, getdate()
    )
```

The first INSERT statement is executed successfully. The second INSERT instance violates the unique clustered key, and results in the following message being displayed:

```
Server: Msg 2601, Level 14, State 3
[Microsoft][ODBC SQL Server Driver][SQL Server]Cannot insert duplicate
key row in object 'employee1' with unique index 'emp_employee_no_ndx1'.
The statement has been aborted.
```

The following example drops the indexes from the employee1 table:

```
DROP INDEX emp_employee_no_ndx1
DROP INDEX emp_name_ndx2
DROP INDEX emp_salary_ndx3
go
```

Create Index Wizard

This wizard can be accessed from the SQL Server Enterprise Manager. It is grouped with the database wizards. This tool can be used to create indexes for tables, retrieve index information from the system tables, and choose columns to build the indexes on. A number of screens are presented that allow the selection of options that are equivalent to the Create Index command. As shown in Figure 8.4, several drop-down lists are available to allow the selection of a database and a table within the database. Figure 8.5 shows the dialogue that allows the selection of one or more columns to include in the index. Figure 8.6 allows the selection of several conditions. The index can be designated as a clustered index. If this option is not selected, the index will be nonclustered. The index can also be identified as unique. Not selecting this option means that it will be nonunique. This dialogue also allows Fillfactor to be selected for the index. Fillfactor identifies the amount of free space to leave on an index page. Without row-level locking, which is now included in SQL Server 7, Fillfactor offered an opportunity to spread key values to reduce locking contention. Fillfactor also allows a reduction in the number of page splits required to store data rows with similar key values. Fillfactor can be identified as optimal, which is the default. It is recommended that you accept this option in most situations, as this requires the least intervention from you. Selecting the Fixed option allows a percentage to be entered for Fillfactor. The percentage identifies free space to be left on each index page. For example, 40 percent refers to 40 percent free space.

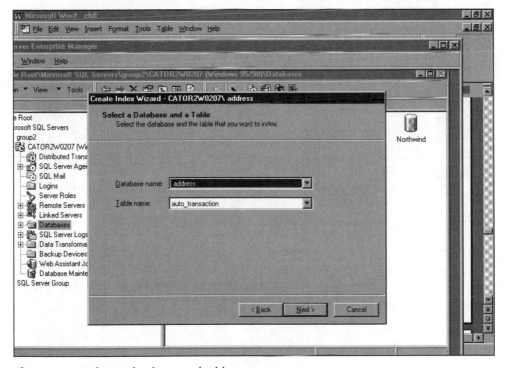

Figure 8.4   Select a database and table.

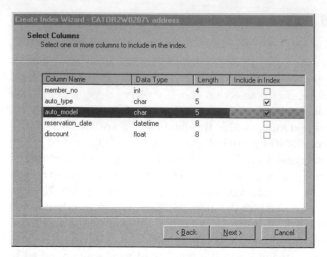

Figure 8.5 Select columns.

Figure 8.7 provides an opportunity to modify the default index name, which is based on the table name as a prefix appended to a suffix of _index_x, where x is a counter starting at 1. The columns selected for inclusion in the index are also summarized on this dialogue. It is possible to change their relative sequence using the MoveUp and MoveDown buttons. The Back button allows you to return to previous dialogues to make changes. The Finish button completes the building of the index. The Cancel button stops the process.

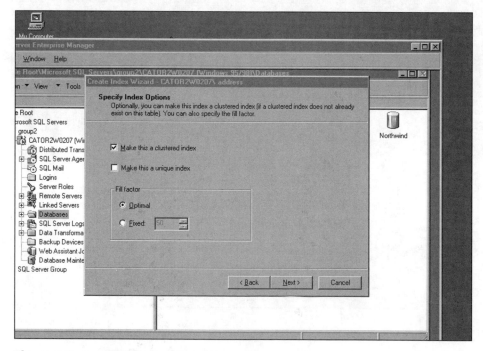

Figure 8.6 Specify index options.

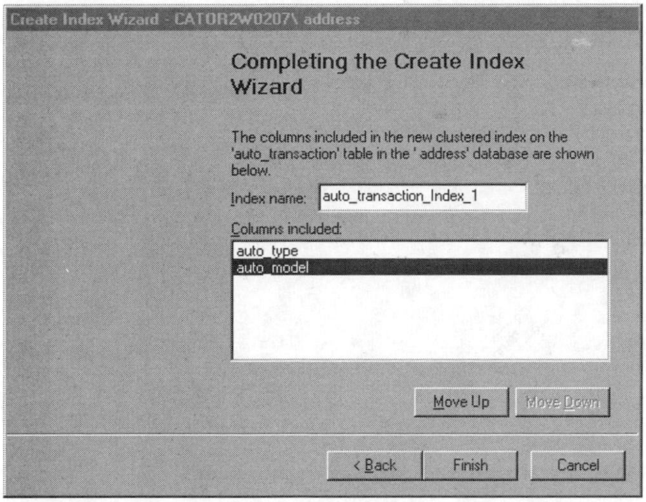

Figure 8.7 Completing the Create Index Wizard.

An sp_helpindex system procedure can be used to inspect the table to ensure that the index was successfully created. For example, sp_helpindex table_name displays the index name, index description, and the index_keys in the index.

Index Tuning Wizard

This tool can be invoked from the Enterprise Manager, Server Profiler, or Query Analyzer. This tool can be used to discover the most likely indexing opportunities. The output of the tool is a recommendation for indexes on a given set of tables and a workload. The workload is the driving force for the calculations. This wizard provides an opportunity to identify areas to tune, recommendations for indexing, workload analysis, and implementation of the recommendations. This is important new functionality in SQL Server 7. This wizard requires the results of SQL Trace to build the recommendations. Details about this wizard are provided in Chapter 19.

Using the Temporary Database

The temporary database (tempdb) is created when SQL Server is installed. As shown in Figure 8.8, this is a common area that is used by SQL Server for intermediate work (e.g., sorting or grouping) and it is used to dynamically allocate space to temporary tables created by users. There are two types of temporary tables that are created in the Temporary database. Both have names that are prefixed with # or ## symbol.

Local. Local tables are created and used in one session. They are automatically dropped when the session ends. The scope for local tables is restricted to the user creating the local table. The name of the temporary table begins with a # sign and is an additional 19 characters in length.

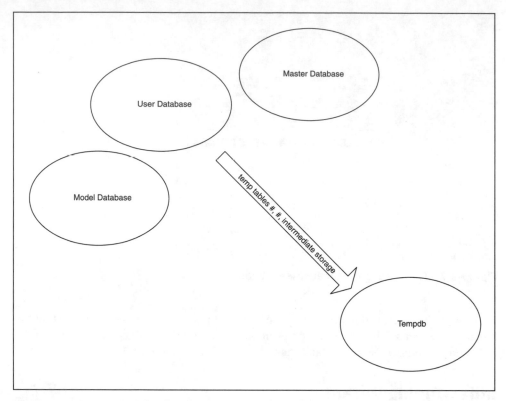

Figure 8.8   Temporary database.

Global. Global tables are created and used in one session. Multiple users can access these tables. Global tables are dropped when all connections to them are dropped.

Tempdb can also be used to store other types of tables; however, my preference is to stay away from doing this. This database is already heavily used by other objects in the SQL Server environment. The configuration variable tempdb in RAM allocates RAM from the operating system to improve system performance. Tempdb can also be moved to a striped disk set to improve performance of functions that use the tempdb. The showplan command shows tempdb use.

The syntax for creating a temporary table in tempdb is

```
CREATE TABLE # | ## table
    (column1 description,
     column2 description,
     column3 description)
```

Sample Scripts

The following example creates a temporary table called ##counter and inserts a series of data rows into it:

```
create table ##counter
(
    employee_no              int,
    comment                  char (50)
)
go

insert ##counter
(employee_no, comment)
values
    (1, 'focusing on suit sales')

insert ##counter
        (employee_no, comment)
values
        (2, 'focusing on leather coats')

insert ##counter
        (employee_no, comment)
values
        (3, 'focus on shirts and ties')

select * from ##counter
```

This syntax produces the following output:

employee_no	comment
1	focusing on suit sales
2	leather coats
3	focus on suits and ties

The following example inserts a new record into the temporary table and also modifies an existing record:

```
insert ##counter
(employee_no, comment)
values
    (4, 'leather coats')
  update ##counter
        set comment = 'front cash register'
            where employee_no = 2

  select * from ##counter
```

This syntax produces the following output:

employee_no	comment
1	focusing on suit sales
2	front cash register
3	focus on shirts and ties
4	leather coats

Summary

This chapter focused on the data definition language (DDL), which is used to generate database objects. Commands to CREATE, DROP, and ALTER databases were examined. SQL Server 7 simplifies the process for creating new databases, and removes the previous size limitations that were placed on the physical environment. SQL Server also provides a powerful wizard to simplify the task of creating databases.

Commands to CREATE, ALTER, and DROP tables and indexes were also examined in this chapter. SQL Server 7 has introduced powerful new indexing strategies that allow multiple indexes to be used in improving data retrieval time. Index manipulation was also discussed. This chapter also showed how to create temporary tables in the TEMP database.

Using the Data
Manipulation Language

The data manipulation language commands (DML) operate at the database object level to manipulate data that is contained within the objects. The primary DML commands that are commonly used in n-tier applications include the following:

Select—is used to retrieve information from database objects (e.g., tables)

Insert—is used to add data to database objects

Update—is used to modify data in database objects

Delete—is used to delete records from a table

These commands can apply to a single table or to multiple tables. They can also be invoked at the SQL Server command prompt, as part of stored procedures, as part of triggers, as embedded commands, and through administration windows.

> ✓ SQL Server is not case sensitive when it comes to parsing the DML command words, but depending on the installation options can be case sensitive with the name of database objects. In terms of command words, upper- and lower-case representation can be freely mixed. INSERT, Insert, insert, INSert are all acceptable syntax. However, for clarity, it is preferable to select a single case and use it consistently.

The Essential DML Commands

The essential data manipulation language (DML) commands that are discussed in this section include select, insert, update, and delete. The basic DML commands share a common syntactical structure that has the following format:

```
DML_command  column_list & functions FROM table_list alternate_names
     WHERE conditions
```

Setting up a Test Environment

This section establishes a test environment to demonstrate the use of these commands. This environment is constructed to demonstrate DML commands, joins, subqueries, stored procedures, and triggers in the context of an application to support sales at a car dealership. Figure 9.1 shows a limited data model that is denormalized for improved performance. The buyer table contains requests from telephone buyers regarding the type of automobile they want to buy. This table is maintained by a telephone salesperson. A sales executive uses the remaining tables to locate a car that matches the buyer's description. Matches that are found are reported back to the prospective buyer.

The schema for the automobile dealership data model is as follows. The entity name is followed by a list of attributes belonging to the entity. The logical view is transformed into a physical view in the next section:

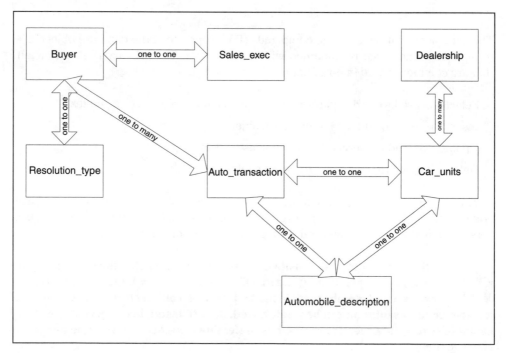

Figure 9.1 Auto dealership data model.

```
Database Name:  Automobile

Buyer (Buyer_no, Last_name, First_name, Phone_no, Fax_no, Email,
    Intersection, Requirement, Request_Date, Budget, Resolution_type,
    Resolution_date, Sales_exec_no, Entry_stamp)

Sales_exec (Sales_exec_no, Last_name, First_name, Sales_target,
Commission)

Resolution_type (Resolution_type, Description)

Auto_transaction (Member_no, auto_type, auto_model, Reservation_date,
    Discount)

Automobile_description (auto_type, auto_model, description, cost)

car_units (dealership_no, auto_type, auto_model, on_hand_qty,
total_sold)

Dealership (Dealership_no, Location, Manager, Phone_no)
```

Create the Database

The automobile database can be quickly created using the Create Database Wizard. Use the standard defaults in the setup dialogues. As shown in Figure 9.2, use the Query Analyzer to ensure that the automobile database has been created successfully. If your ver-

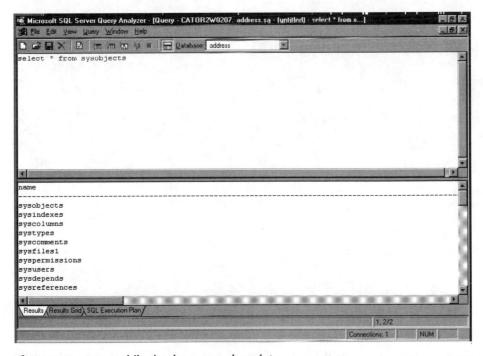

Figure 9.2 Automobile database sample scripts.

sion of SQL Server is adding blanks to the filename, use the sp_renamedb system procedure to rename the database to "automobile" with no embedded blanks, leading blanks, or trailing banks. Recall that the command to do this is as follows:

```
sp_dboption " Automobile","single user", "true"  /* this is mandatory */
sp_renamedb " Automobile", "automobile"
sp_dboption "automobile","single user", "false"
sp_databases
```

Source Listing 9.1 shows a script to create the physical tables based on the logical schema that is shown above. The script creates the tables in a user-defined database called "automobile".

```
/* Filename:        Auto.txt */
/* Database Name:   Automobile */

use automobile
go

drop table buyer
drop table sales_exec
drop table resolution_type
drop table auto_transaction
drop table automobile_description
drop table car_units
drop table dealership
go

/* Buyer table */
Create table buyer
(
Buyer_no          int       Identity,
Last_name         char(30),
First_name        char(30),
Phone_no          char(11),
Fax_no            char(11),
Email             char(20),
Intersection      char(40),
Requirement       char(80),
Request_Date      datetime,
Budget            money,
Resolution_type   char(3),
Resolution_date   datetime,
Sales_exec_no     char(3),
Entry_stamp       timestamp
)


create table sales_exec
```
(Continues)

Source 9.1   Define and build the table creation script.

```
(
sales_exec_no      char(3),
last_name          char(30),
first_name         char(30),
sales_target       money,
commission         float
)


Create Table resolution_type
(
resolution_type    char (3),
description        char (50)
)


Create Table auto_transaction
(
member_no          int,
auto_type          char (5),
auto_model         char (5),
reservation_date   datetime,
discount           float
)


Create table automobile_description
(
auto_type          char(5),
auto_model         char(5),
description        char(40),
cost               money
)


create table car_units
(
dealership_no      int,
auto_type          char(5),
auto_model         char(5),
on_hand_qty        int,
total_sold         int
)


Create table dealership
(
Dealership_no      int,
Location           char(12),
Manager            char(30),
Phone_no           char (11)
)
```

Source 9.1   *(Continued)*

Adding Test Data to the Test Environment

The tables that have been created at this point are empty. Data will be inserted into the tables, with consistent data integrity, throughout this chapter. For this reason, insert is the first command that is examined in this chapter.

Insert

Insert is a basic data manipulation language command that is defined in the ANSI/92 standard. Insert adds one or more data rows to a table or groups of tables. The insert command has a small number of basic formats. The basic syntax for this command can take a variety of forms. The syntax of the first form is the most general and powerful:

```
INSERT [INTO] db_name.owner.table | View
(column_list)
VALUES
(column_list)
WHERE qualifiers
```

The syntax of the second form provides a shortcut by inserting data into the columns in the same physical order as the columns in the table:

```
INSERT table_name1
VALUES
     (column_list)
```

The syntax of the third form creates a table by selecting columns from another table:

```
INSERT table_name1
          (column_list)
SELECT column_list
    FROM table_name2 WHERE conditions
```

The syntax of the fourth form inserts columns into a table in a specific order based on the results of a nested select statement:

```
INSERT INTO price (prod, code, price)
SELECT prod, code, price
    FROM products
                    WHERE price > 20;
```

Sample Scripts

In the following example, a value is provided for every field in the designated table. The order of the values must match the physical order of the fields in the physical table. This command inserts one data row or record to the table:

```
INSERT newtable
        SELECT address_type, description from address_type
            WHERE address_type = ëRí
    Go
```

In the following example, the format of the insert command adds one record or row to the database table identified in table_name. The table can be in the default database. If it is not, then the table_name must be fully qualified as in [[database.user.]tablename]. Specific fields from the table are included within the first parenthesis of the command. There is a one-to-one correspondence to these fields by values contained in the second parenthesis. If fields were identified as NOT NULL in the table creation script, SQL Server will not insert a data row, unless these fields are included in the command and provided with a NOT NULL value. Not all inserts are successful, so it is good programming practice to inspect the results of an INSERT attempt and take an appropriate action in the event that the insert was unsuccessful. Some reasons for this include a referential integrity violation, insufficient space in the database, and insufficient permissions to write to a table.

The sequence of the field names must match the values. For example, value1 will be inserted into fieldname1, value2 will be inserted into fieldname2, and value3 will be inserted into fieldname3. SQL Server will ensure that the datatypes of the values match the datatypes of the fields. The order of the field names in this command does not have to match the physical order of the table. Values can be literals or functions, such as convert(parameters) and getdate():

```
INSERT newtable
(column1, column2, column3, . . .)
Values
      (value1, value2, value3, . . .)
```

In the following example, the format of the command inserts all the matching rows in the select clause associated with table_name2 into table_name1. The rows selected from the second table are inserted/appended into the first table. The number of columns selected from the second table must match the order and the datatypes of the columns in the first table. It is possible to use placeholders for existing columns:

```
INSERT newtable
        SELECT address_type, description from address_type
    go
```

The same insert command can be reexecuted to repeatedly insert the same set of rows so long as the create table command did not specify constraints to limit duplicate rows or keys. The use of INSERT in this example assumes that table_name2 already exists:

```
INSERT newtable
        SELECT address_type, description from address_type
            WHERE address_type = 'R'
    Go


INSERT INTO newtable
        SELECT address_type, NULL from address_type
    go
```

Source Listing 9.2 shows a script that clears user defined tables of data before inserting data rows into them. The DELETE command writes a copy of the deleted record to the transaction log to support rollbacks.

```
/* clear the tables prior to insert data */
delete buyer
delete sales_exec
delete resolution_type
delete auto_transaction
delete automobile_description
delete car_units
delete dealership
go

/* Adding test data to the test database */
insert buyer
(
Last_name,
First_name,
Phone_no,
Fax_no,
Email,
Intersection,
Requirement,
Request_Date,
Budget,
Resolution_type,
Resolution_date,
Sales_exec_no
)
values
(
'Pear',
'Liz',
'231-302-2112',
'231-302-2223',
'lpear@pear.com',
'Bloor & Yonge',
'4 door sports car, North American',
getdate(),
$20000,
'N',
' ',
' '
)
```

(Continues)

Source 9.2   Insert script.

```
insert sales_exec
(
sales_exec_no,
last_name,
first_name,
sales_target,
commission
)
values
(
1,
'Thomas',
'Jones',
$1000000,
20
)

insert resolution_type
(
resolution_type,
description
)
values
(
'N',
'New Request'
)

insert resolution_type
(
resolution_type,
description
)
values
(
'S',
'sold'
)
insert resolution_type
(
resolution_type,
description
)
values
(
'D',
'Request dropped'
)
```

(Continues)

Source 9.2 *(Continued)*

```
insert automobile_description
(
auto_type,
auto_model,
description,
cost
)
values
(
'GM',
'Linc',
'Lincoln Continental 1999',
$40000
)

insert car_units
(
dealership_no,
auto_type,
auto_model,
on_hand_qty,
total_sold
)
values
(
1,
'GM',
'Linc',
10,
2
)

insert car_units
(
dealership_no,
auto_type,
auto_model,
on_hand_qty,
total_sold
)
values
(
2,
'GM',
'Linc',
5,
1
```

(Continues)

Source 9.2   *(Continued)*

```
)

insert car_units
(
dealership_no,
auto_type,
auto_model,
on_hand_qty,
total_sold
)
values
(
1,
'BMW',
'525I',
5,
2
)

insert dealership
(
Dealership_no,
Location,
Manager,
Phone_no
)
values
(
1,
'123 Bay Street off Bloor',
'Terry Box',
'123-456-1234'
)

Insert dealership
(
Dealership_no,
Location,
Manager,
Phone_no
)
values
(
2,
'223 Mississauga Road, Off Derry',
'Sally Adrix',
'545-456-1234'
)
```

Source 9.2   *(Continued)*

Select

The select command is the most commonly used DML command. It can have a deceptively simple context (e.g., SELECT * FROM stores), or be enormously complex consisting of views, subqueries, and multiple WHERE statements. The select statement retrieves and formats information from system and user tables. It can be invoked for objects within the current database, or it can be qualified to retrieve information from objects in another database. The basic syntax for the select statement is as follows:

```
SELECT ALL | DISTINCT    select_list
     INTO    table_name
  FROM [db_name.owner.table_name or view_name    optimizer_hints. . .]
     WHERE
     HAVING
     ORDER BY/GROUP BY
     COMPUTE


/*rename the column name*/
/*multiple views, tables, combinations*/
/*with functions*/
```

This section provides some of the common interpretations of the select statement. The simplest format of the select statement is select * from table_name, for example, select * from dealership. Use of the '*' in this command displays all the columns in the dealership table. No WHERE clause is used so all the data rows are extracted from the table. This section reviews the components of the select command individually:

SELECT. This is a key word that identifies that the SELECT DML statement is being issued.

ALL I DISTINCT. The ALL keyword is used to select all the data rows from the table. The DISTINCT keyword is used to remove duplicate rows from the result set before it is displayed.

select_list. An * selects all the columns in the table. Specific columns from the table are included here, separated by commas. Columns are prefixed by a table alias if one is identified in the table_name command (e.g., alias.column_name). Column names appear in the output result set. These can be renamed in the select list, as follows: select column1 newname1, column2 newname2 . . . . An equals sign (=) can be used to separate the column name and the new column name. Functions can be applied to the columns (e.g., count(*)). SQL Server 7 introduces a new feature to the select statement to limit the number of rows returned in the result set.

INTO Table_name. This keyword is used to create a new table that receives the result set from the select. If the SELECT INTO database option is FALSE, the table being select INTO must already exist. If this value is TRUE, the table is created with the command.

FROM. This is a keyword.

Table_name. This is the table that is processed to satisfy the select command. The table_name is provided without a path (e.g., dealership) if the table is in the current or default database. If the table is in another database, a qualified path needs to be provided in the form database.owner.tablename, for the table to be located. An alias can be provided after the table_name, in the form tablename aliasname. Multiple table names, separated by columns, can be included here. This can also be a view. Optimizer hints can be included to help select an access index path. Optimizer hints can be an index name or ID (e.g., INDEX = index_name), NOLOCK statement, HOLDLOCK statement, UPDLOCK statement, TABLOCK statement, and PAGLOCK statement.

WHERE. WHERE is a keyword.

WHERE clause. This portion of the select statement can be complex. The basic format is WHERE variable1 operator variable2. Variable1 can be an alias.column in one of the tables. Variable2 can be an alias.column or a literal. Functions can be used in the WHERE clause. Joins and subqueries can be used here. The WHERE clause supports multiple conditions with the AND, OR, NOT, BETWEEN, IN (value1, value2, value3, . . .) statements. The WHERE clause supports the use of operators such as =, <>, >=, <=, LIKE "%value%", and NOT. The ORDER BY clause is used to order the output result set. This command uses the tempdb database. The GROUP BY clause is used to collect the result set into a group. This command is useful for reporting purposes. The COMPUTE clause can be used to identify functions that provide summary lines in the row set. The HAVING clause can be used to identify search clauses and replaces the WHERE clause. Use WHERE with AND/OR commands.

Sample Scripts

The following example renames an output column:

```
SELECT 1 first_column, 0 second_column
```

This command displays the following output:

```
first_column second_column
------------ -------------
          0
```

The following example displays the contents of each table in the automobile:

```
use automobile
go

Select * from buyer
Select * from sales_exec
Select * from resolution_type
Select * from auto_transaction
Select * from automobile_description
Select * from car_units
Select * from dealership
go
```

The following example counts the number of data rows in each table:

```
Select 'number of rows in the buyer table', count (*) from buyer
Select 'number of rows in the sales_exec table',
count (*) from sales_exec
Select 'number of rows in the resolution_type table',
count (*) from resolution_type
Select 'number of rows in the auto_transaction table',
count (*) from auto_transaction
Select 'number of rows in the automobile description table',
count (*) from automobile_description
Select 'number of rows in the car_units table',
count (*) from car_units
Select 'number of rows in the dealership table',
count (*) from dealership
go

This command results in the following output:
number of rows in the buyer table 1
number of rows in the sales_exec table 1
number of rows in the resolution_type table 3
number of rows in the auto_transaction table 0
number of rows in the automobile description table 1
number of rows in the car_units table 3
number of rows in the dealership table 2
```

The following example demonstrates different ways of selecting and organizing information from the resolution_type table:

```
Select * from resolution_type where resolution_type = 'D'
Go
Select * from resolution_type where resolution_type <> 'D'
Go
Select resolution_type, description from resolution_type
    ORDER BY resolution_type
```

Update

The update DML command is used to modify existing data rows in tables. The command can affect one or more rows in a table or tables, based on selection criteria. The update command returns a value of zero rows if no records are updated. The performance of the update command is dependent on several factors. This includes the availability of indexes and the type of update being performed, for example, direct updates, which are done immediately, consist of in-place updates, and delete/insert type updates. The direct, in-place update is the fastest type of update as a row is simply updated with minimal transaction log activity. The other type of update is the deferred update, writing changes to a transaction log with a NO-OP flag. Deferred updates are slower as each data row is first written out to the transaction log, then reread and applied to the data rows. The basic syntax for the update command is as follows:

```
UPDATE db_name.owner.table
  [set column_name = value [,]]
      where column_name='value'
```

It is also possible to use the case command within the update command, where clauses of an update statement can contain subqueries and subqueries within the WHERE clause can contain joins:

```
UPDATE tablename
    SET field =
        CASE
            WHEN (condition 1)
                THEN value1
            ELSE value2
        END
```

> ✓ **The insert, update, and delete commands all add information to the transaction log to support database recoverability. A primary objective is to reduce the amount of information added to the transaction log when any of these commands are executed to improve system response time and to reduce the amount of physical space required to store the transaction log.**

Sample Scripts

The following example updates more than one record with an update statement:

```
update car units
        set auto_type = 'GMC'
            where auto_type = 'GM'
        select * from car_units    /* display the results */
```

The following example runs the update again, although it will not find any more data rows satisfying the GM search condition:

```
update car_units
        set auto_type = 'GMC'
            where auto_type = 'GM'
    if @@rowcount = 0 /* validation check */
        print 'no records found to update'
```

The following example updates many columns for one record:

```
Insert dealership
(
Dealership_no,
Location,
Manager,
Phone_no
)
values
```

```
(
2,
'223 Mississauga Road, Off Derry',
'Sally Adrix',
'545-456-1234'
)
```

Delete

The delete command removes data rows from one for more tables or views. This is a dangerous command in that it can delete all the rows in the table. The delete command has the following syntax:

```
DELETE FROM db_name.owner.table
     where column_name = value [, ]

/* multi-table delete */
DELETE from movie, rented
     where movie.subject = rented.subject and rented.subject = 'scifi'
```

The following example creates a new record with the select into command and then deletes all records from the new table:

```
Sp_dboption 'address', 'SELECT INTO', TRUE

drop table testing1
go

select * into testing1
    from sales_exec
  select * from testing1
  delete testing1
  select * from testing1

sp_dboption 'address', 'SELECT INTO'', FALSE

delete dealership
where dealership_no = 100
```

Truncate

The delete command writes the records that are being deleted to the transaction log. A faster command to the delete is the truncate table command which removes records from a table without writing to the transaction log. The truncate command also does not fire triggers. The syntax for this command is as follows:

```
TRUNCATE TABLE_name
Go
```

The following example truncates data from a table:

```
truncate table testing1
```

The following example truncates data from the dealership table:

```
truncate table dealership
```

Summary

This chapter examined data manipulation language (DML) commands that apply to database objects. The list of primary commands that were covered includes different variations of the INSERT, SELECT, DELETE, UPDATE, and TRUNCATE commands. The syntax of these commands can be deceptively simple. The reality is that the commands can be quite complex through the use of nesting and embedding. SQL Server built-in functions can also be used with these commands. Most of the DML commands discussed in this chapter can be used inside stored procedures and triggers.

Each of these statements operate on a table or on specific columns within a table. They can also be combined with WHERE clauses that can sweep the entire table or portions of the table based on selection criteria. The performance of the commands is greatly affected by the indexes that may or may not be in place on the table(s) being manipulated. Indexes in general improve performance, except in cases where the command statements complete table sweeps. This involves reading every record in a table sequentially.

SUMMARY

Using the Data Control Language—Controlling Access to SQL Server

The ANSI standard defines a data control language (DCL) which maps to the user security approach in SQL Server. SQL Server security is partitioned between the Windows NT–SQL Server level, to the SQL Server environment itself, to SQL Server databases, and to database objects. Security is based on a login name (user identification) and a password. The login name determines the role that is allowed within the SQL Server environment. Each role is allocated a different set of activities that can be performed in the SQL Server environment. Login names are also allocated specific permissions within databases and to database objects. SQL Server is installed with a default superuser with a login name of "sa". The default password is blank (type nothing beside the password, just press enter). The password should be changed to some other value in production applications. Figure 10.1 shows the relationship of logins to the database environment and to SQL Server itself. The login name allows access to the SQL Server environment but not the database objects. All database objects are owned by the ID that created them. The owner of a database object grants permissions to other users to access or modify information pertaining to a database object.

The path to a database object is prefaced with the name of the object owner: database_name.db_owner.object_name. The database_name or the db_owner name are optional if the default database is the same as the database_name or the session owner role is the same as the db_owner role. The formats of an object are as follows: addresses; pubs..address; pubs.dbo.address; ..dbo.address; address.

Security is necessary in all environments, including development, and definitely production. There should be a corporate policy regarding security that should act as the

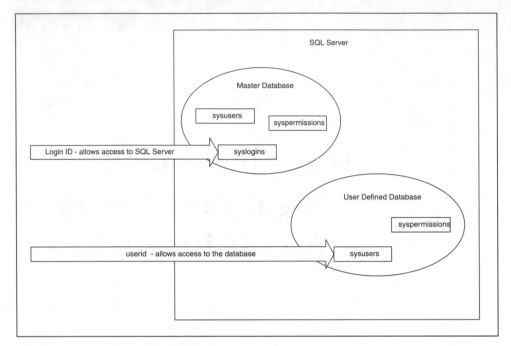

Figure 10.1 Logins and permissions.

blueprint for establishing SQL Server security. Security techniques can be leveraged to restrict access to the SQL Server environment to achieve the following benefits:

- Keep unauthorized users out of the SQL Server environment.
- Restrict user access to specific databases.
- Restrict access and actions on specific database objects.
- Leverage security domains and roles to limit access types.
- Improve the efficiency of workflow by keeping users away from data objects that are not part of their jobs.

Security can also become a bottleneck that impedes development efforts and operational efficiency. Development environments do not require the same level of sophistication that is required in production environments. This does not imply that no safeguards are required in development environments. On the contrary, there is a pressing need to keep unauthorized users out of the development environment to protect against intentional or unintentional damage to source code. There are other factors to consider, as well. Source code must be versioned, test code separated from development code, and a separation of production code from code that is being changed. Many development environments are configured to restrict access to the environment, but to generally allow free access once a user is allowed into the environment. Limits are still placed on tested modules, and certainly on modules waiting to be promoted to production. Some corporations use a similar strategy in production environments to allow users the opportunity to efficiently execute workflow. Severe limitations are placed on entry into the environment. By training users thoroughly, it becomes feasible to include fewer restrictions in the production environment to allow faster workflow. It is always a good policy to ensure that all security strategies are predefined and accepted by corporate auditors before being implemented.

Connection Options

SQL Server supports several types of security connections, including Windows NT authentication and SQL Server authentication. Windows NT authentication must be associated with a trusted SQL Server connection. This requires a trust domain to be established in the Windows environment as well as within SQL Server. The trust relationship means that a user who can log in to NT Server is trusted to log in to SQL Server. Supporting a trust relationship has implications on the types of network protocols that can be leveraged (e.g., named pipes can support trust relationships). In some cases this is quite practical. However, it is often desirable to have an additional level of security by using SQL Server Authentication. This requires another login name to be entered before a user can access SQL Server. SQL Server authentication offers the advantage of allowing users to operate within NT using commonly used applications, such as Microsoft Office, without having the ability to access potentially sensitive information in the database environment.

Roles

Roles are allocated to login names, when the names are created through the Login Wizard. It is not a good idea to select all the roles for every login name that is created. Select the roles that a user account will generally require. In development environments, a commonly used strategy is to create a few specific accounts that are used by the entire team to do things like create more users, add remote servers, conduct backup/recover activities in the environment, and conduct other database activities. The following roles are supported in SQL Server:

System administrators. This role is enabled to manage any activities in the environment.

Security administrators. This role is enabled to manage security information.

Server administrators. This role is enabled for server activities.

Setup administrators. This role is enabled for extended activities.

Process administrators. This role is enabled to manage processes within the environment.

Disk administrators. This role is enabled to administer disk files.

Database creators. This role is enabled for database DDL statements.

Adding Login Name

The login name is the basic security mechanism in SQL Server. A login name should be unique within the SQL Server environment. It is assigned to every user that needs access. Two methods of adding login names are examined in this section: using the Login Wizard and using system procedures.

Using the Login Wizard

This wizard is available through the Database option in the SQL Server Enterprise Manager. It can be used to establish a connection type, manage security roles, and access to databases. The wizard must be used after a database server context is established. Figure 10.2 shows the dialogue that displays if SQL Server authentication is selected as the connection type. Enter a new login ID (e.g., sector), followed by a password (e.g., password). Reenter the password (e.g., password) in the Confirm Password field to ensure that you have not made a spelling mistake, as the password characters appear as asterisks (*).

Click on the Next button to display the dialogue shown in Figure 10.3. Click on the Back button at any time in this wizard process to correct a previous selection. Any number of roles can be selected within this dialogue. You may want to test the capabilities that are enabled by a combination of role types. Click on the squares beside each role that is desired and click on the Next button.

Figure 10.4 allows one or more databases to be selected after the roles dialogue. This list is populated by the database names in the sysdatabases system table in the Master database. Clicking on the Next button displays the dialogue shown in Figure 10.5. This shows the login name, the roles selected, and the databases selected. If the database names are not visible, scroll the list down. You can still select the Back button to return to previous dialogues to make corrections. This is a good idea if you have forgotten the

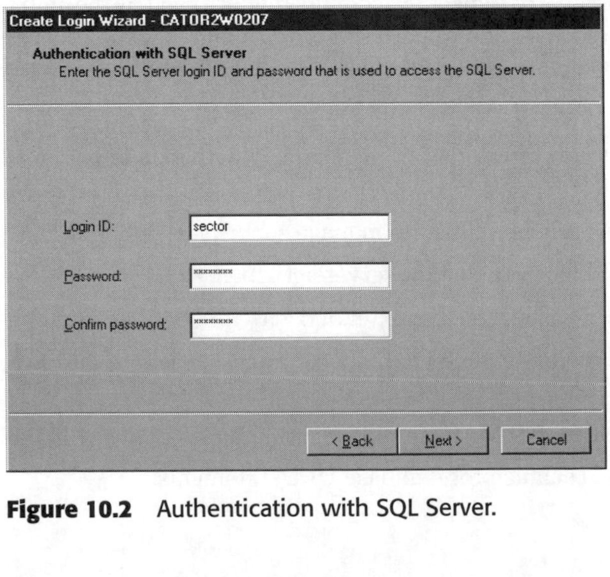

Figure 10.2 Authentication with SQL Server.

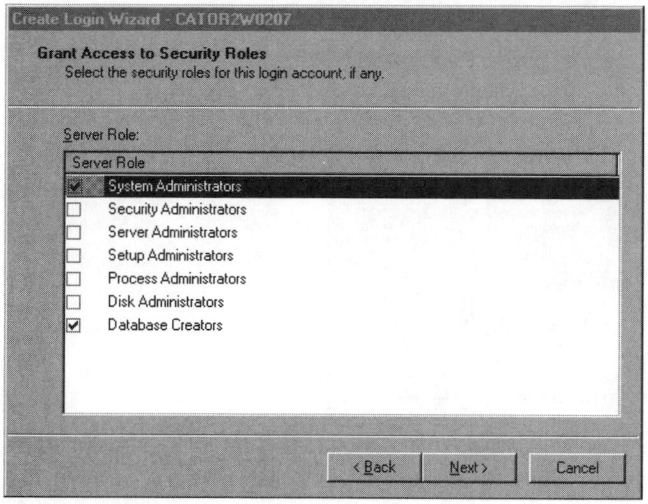

Figure 10.3   Grant access to security roles.

password for the login name being created. Click on the Finish button to finish creating the login name.

The result of a successful execution can be observed by clicking on the Logins folder under the Server group in the Enterprise Manager. The available login names are displayed on the right side of the panel, along with the type of login (e.g., standard), access to the server, the name of the default database, the user type, and the default language. Select the Query Analyzer from the Start menu, which is generally found under Start-Programs-Microsoft SQL Server 7-Query Analyzer, to log on with the name just created. This creates a login name that can access the SQL Server environment. To work with

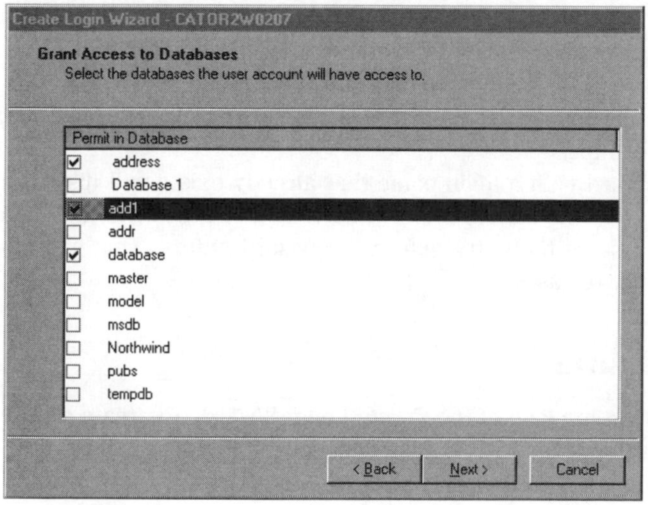

Figure 10.4   Grant access to databases.

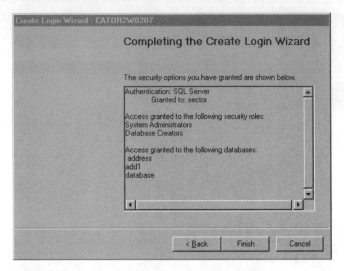

Figure 10.5   Completing the Create Login Wizard.

users and permissions it is still necessary to use system procedures, as will be discussed shortly.

A couple of other events also happen behind the scenes when a login is created using the wizard. Each login name also generates a userid in the databases that were selected with the Grant Access to Databases dialogue. This can be observed by viewing the sysusers system table in the data dictionary of each database in the list that was selected:

```
use pubs
go
select * from sysusers
go
```

Use the wizard again to create another login name with the name Sector1 and a password of password. Do not select any databases with this name, instead leave the Grant Access to Databases dialogue empty.

Using the Create Login Wizard with a login name that already exists will display a message after the databases are selected. The Wizard allows entry of the information in the first few dialogues, but rejects the entry before the wizard enters. This will undoubtedly be modified in future releases.

Using System Procedures

System procedures can be used in place of the Create Login Wizard. To create a login name, use the sp_addlogin system procedure, which has the following syntax:

```
sp_addlogin login_id, password, default_database
```

To see that this command operates similarly to the Create Login Wizard, begin by displaying the contents of the syslogins system table in the system database, as follows:

```
select suid, name, dbname, password, language from syslogins
```

This displays the following reformatted information for my test database:

suid	name	dbname	password	language
1	sa	master	NULL	us_english
7	sector	master	????????	us_english
8	sector1	master	????????	us_english

Add another user login and display the contents of the syslogins table again to examine the format of a login added with the wizard (e.g., sector and sector1). This is done with the following sequence of commands:

```
use master
go
sp_addlogin, 'ryder', 'password', 'pubs'
go

select suid, name, dbname, password, language from syslogins
```

This displays the following reformatted information to be displayed from the database:

suid	name	dbname	password	language
5	ryder	pubs	????????	us_english
1	sa	master	NULL	us_english
7	sector	master	????????	us_english
8	sector1	master	????????	us_english

The results appear equivalent for the fields examined. The select * from syslogins format of the command can be used to compare every column for one login name to another login name. Executing the system procedure with only the first two parameters, without a database name, defaults the database to the current default database. In this sense, the previous example is equivalent to executing the following sequence of commands:

```
use pubs
go
sp_addlogin, 'ryder', 'password', 'pubs'
go
```

A login name can be dropped using another system procedure. This command can be used to drop login names that appear in the master database into the syslogins system table. However, if the login names were added as database users, then it is necessary to drop the userids from each database before dropping the login from the syslogins system table. All login names that were created using the Create Login Wizard and which identified databases for the login name require this additional step. The syntax for dropping a login name from the syslogins table is

```
sp_droplogin login_name
```

The following example drops a login name from the SQL Server environment:

```
sp_droplogin ryder
go
```

Executing these statements displays a Login dropped information message. Ryder was added only to the syslogins system table, so the sp_droplogin system procedure can be executed immediately. The following reformatted information is retrieved from the master database and displayed:

suid	name	dbname	password	language
1	sa	master	NULL	us_english
7	sector	master	????????	us_english
8	sector1	master	????????	us_english

The following example adds another login name:

```
sp_addlogin 'tan', 'password', 'pubs'
go
```

Permissions

Permissions control access to database objects in terms of ability to select, execute, update, add, or delete. Users can be restricted to one or more of these operations. An object owner typically provides a specific type of access to the database object. Allocations are granted or revoked from specific users. Permissions are allocated to users within specific databases. This section examines users and permissions for users.

Managing Users

The sp_adduser system procedure is used to add a user to the current or default database. This function expects two parameters: a logon_name and a user_name within the database. The syntax for this system procedure is

```
sp_adduser logon_name, user_name
```

The following example adds a user to the default database based on a login name:

```
use pubs
go
```

```
sp_adduser 'lll', 'flanders'
go
```

This command sequence displays a message such as "The login 'lll' does not exist." 'lll' is not a valid login name because it was not created earlier. Use a valid login name and display the contents of the sysusers table in the pubs database. Successful execution of the sp_adduser system procedure displays a message such as "Granted database access to 'tan'."

```
use pubs
go
sp_adduser 'tan', 'flanders'
go
select suid, status, name, password from sysusers
go
```

This command displays the contents of the sysusers system table in the pubs database. This example will show that a data row for 'flanders', which is the alias within the database for login name 'tan', is contained in the sysusers table.

User aliases must be dropped from databases before the corresponding login name can be dropped from the syslogins table in the master database. The syntax for dropping users is as follows:

```
sp_dropuser user_name
```

The following example drops a user from a database:

```
use pubs
go

sp_dropuser tan
go
```

This command executes and displays an error message because 'tan' is not a user in the pubs database. 'tan' is a login name that is mapped to a userid of 'flanders'. The following code drops the 'flanders' userid and displays a success message such as "User has been dropped from current database."

```
sp_dropuser flanders
go
```

Since 'tan' is no longer mapped to alias userids in any of the databases, the login name can be dropped as follows. Notice that it is not necessary to change the default database.

```
sp_droplogin tan
go
```

Login names created using the Create Login Wizard and assigning one or more databases can only be dropped after the userids are dropped from each of the databases.

Managing Permissions

Each userid created for a database is allocated permissions to perform actions within the database and to the database objects. These permissions are generally allocated by the owner of the database for each of the following actions: select, insert, update, delete, exec, and ddl. Permissions are allocated to specific userids with the grant command or taken away with the revoke command. Permissions can also be allocated to a public ID that provides access to specific actions to all users active in the database. It is possible to use views and stored procedures to manipulate database objects, while removing permission from all other users. Permissions can be designated to tables, stored procedures, and views. The syntax for the grant and revoke commands is

```
GRANT permissions ON db_object TO users
REVOKE permissions ON db_object FROM users
```

Note that permissions are separated from each other by commas, while users are separated from each other by commas.

Sample Script

The following example adds a login name to the SQL Server environment, provides a password, and establishes a default database for the login name. This login will point to this default database automatically at signon time. The script also creates two test tables and inserts data into the tables. A userid is added to the pubs database based on the login name. Permissions are then granted to the userid for each of the user-defined tables.

```
sp_addlogin 'okiet', 'password', pubs
go

use pubs
go

drop table test_codetable1
drop table test_codetable2
go

create table test_codetable1
(
    code          char(3),
    range         char (20)
)

create table test_codetable2
(
    seq_no        int IDENTITY,
    description   char(50)
)
go
```

```
INSERT test_codetable2
(description) VALUES ('this is the first row')
go


sp_adduser 'okiet', 'userokiet1'
go


GRANT select ON test_codetable1 TO userokiet1
go


GRANT select, insert ON test_codetable2 TO userokiet1


Go
```

Create another instance of the SQL Server Query Analyzer and sign on as login name 'okiet' with the password you saved earlier. Another dialogue of the Query Analyzer is displayed with the login name appearing in the top frame of the window (e.g., (local).pubs.okiet -). If pubs is not the default database, issue a 'use pubs; go' sequence or change the default database using the database dropdown list. It should be possible to select from test_codetable2 using select * from test_codetable2. A single row will display on the screen if this command is entered and executed correctly. It should also be possible to add another data row to the table using the following code, which displays a message of "1 row(s) affected on successful completion." Additional rows can be inserted using the following code fragment:

```
INSERT test_codetable2
(description) VALUES ('this is the second row')
go


SELECT * from test_codetable2
go
```

Deleting or updating a row is not possible because userokiet1 only has select and insert permissions on this table. The following code attempts to update the description in every data row in the table. A message such as "UPDATE permission denied on object 'test_codetable2', database 'pubs', owner 'dbo'" appears in response to the lack of permission to do this action.

```
UPDATE test_codetable2
SET description = 'this row was updated'
go
```

It should be possible to grant update permission to userokiet1 (an alias of login name okiet) for test_codetable2 using another grant statement, such as "GRANT update ON test_codetable2 TO userokiet1." Attempting this command in the window, of course, does not execute properly because the current user cannot give permission to a database object owned by someone else without grant permission. A message such as "Grantor does not have GRANT permission" appears. If another Query Analyzer dialogue is open with a login user that has this permission (e.g., 'sa', the one who created the database and tables above), it is possible to activate that dialogue and try the same code there. Do not forget that you can copy the code into the clipboard, select the 'sa' window, and pass the code into the top half of the dialogue. Select only the lines of code that you want to execute before selecting Query-Execute Query (or selecting the Execute Query button in the toolbar). A message indicating success should appear at this point. Return to the okiet login session and reexecute the update command. A message showing that all the rows in the table have been affected is displayed. The following data rows exist in the test_codetable2 table:

```
seq_no     description
1          this row was updated
2          this row was updated

(2 row(s) affected)
```

Any of the permissions can be revoked by returning to the 'sa' session and entering the following code:

```
REVOKE insert, update ON test_codetable2 FROM userokiet1
go
```

Returning to the okiet login session and repeating the update command displays a permission violation message on the screen. Notice that permissions are cumulative. Every use of the grant command adds another set of permissions that are already given to a userid. This saves the trouble of repeating all permissions in a grant statement. The same is true for revoke. Once a permission has been revoked, it must be granted again to become effective.

Another useful variation of the grant command is the format GRANT ALL ON db_object to PUBLIC. This command grants all permissions on the data object that is designated to all users of the database. This is an especially useful command in a development environment. It is generally a common practice for all object owners in a development environment to include this command after creating the object. Specific permissions can also be revoked from specific users after the GRANT ALL is issued. This command can also be used with stored procedures and views. Another advantage of this command is that it establishes user access to the database objects in advance of the generation of the userids. Thus a userid can be created after the object is created and the userid will be capable of accessing the object. The following example creates a few database objects then grants public access to them with 'sa' signed on:

```
use pubs
go

drop table test_codetable1
go

create table test_codetable1
(
    code        char(3),
    range       char (20)
```

```
)
GRANT ALL ON test_codetable1 TO PUBLIC
REVOKE delete on test_codetable1 FROM PUBLIC
go

insert test_codetable1
     values ('jan', 'Jan 1 to Jan 30')
go
```

Test these permissions by beginning another session with an okiet login name and using the following code. A permission violation message appears in response. The subsequent update command fits within the granted permissions, so it should execute successfully.

```
use pubs
go

delete test_codetable1
     where code = 'jan'
go

update test_codetable1
     set range = 'jan 1 to jan 31'
          where code = 'jan'
```

Create a stored procedure using the 'sa' login name and attempt to execute the stored procedure with the okiet login name. The code that follows drops the stored procedure before creating it. The stored procedure selects all the data rows in the pubs..test _codetable1 table.

```
use pubs
go

drop proc select_codetable
go

create proc select_codetable
AS
     select * from test_codetable1
go

exec select_codetable
```

Signing on with a different session using the okiet login name and attempting to 'exec select_codetable' in that session displays an execute permission denied message. The stored procedure owner can grant this permission directly using any one of the following commands:

GRANT EXEC ON select_codetable TO userokiet1

GRANT ALL ON select_codetable TO userokiet1

GRANT ALL ON select_codetable TO PUBLIC

It is also convenient to include the third choice after the stored procedure is created in a development environment, as follows:

```
create proc select_codetable
AS
      select * from test_codetable1
go
grant all on select_codetable TO PUBLIC
go
```

Summary

This chapter reviewed several security methods that are derived from the NT security methods, including a standard security mode in which SQL Server validates logins to the database. SQL Server also stores information about user accounts in its own environment. This is the default method assigned to SQL Server during installation. NT offers an integrated security mode that relies on a trust relationship being established between NT and SQL Server. Another NT security mode is also available, the mixed security mode. This method supports login validation using either standard security mode or integrated security mode.

This chapter also examined how to use a wizard that is new to SQL Server 7.0 to add login names. Login names establish an account, enabling a user to log in to the SQL Server environment. Login names are complemented by userid aliases that are established for every database within access. Permissions are granted or revoked directly from userids or to all users using the PUBLIC keyword. Permissions consist of the ability to insert, update, select, and execute on database objects. Another keyword, ALL, is available to transfer or revoke all permissions. System procedures were used to demonstrate how to add or drop login names and userids.

An example showing permissions being established for a stored procedure demonstrated a method of restricting user access to specific database objects. The same procedure can be applied to views in order to restrict access to specific columns in a table or to a set of columns in a group of tables.

PART

three

Incorporating Advanced Features

Part Three provides a thorough examination of SQL Server 7 features that support this tool's role in n-tier application development. This involves a detailed view of stored procedures, triggers, views, cursors, joins, and subqueries.

Chapter 11 discusses stored procedures, which support a complex control-of-flow language (e.g., if-else, while, case), DML, DDL, and DCL statements. Stored procedures also support 2-tier, 3-tier, and n-tier architecture. This chapter examines nested procedures, adjusting parameter values in called procedures, and leverages system procedures.

Chapter 12 discusses leveraging SQL functions, which are built-in functions that can be used for date/time manipulation, aggregates, mathematical processing, text processing, and image/text processing. The datatype CONVERT function is discussed in this chapter. System procedures are also discussed in this chapter. This includes help procedures, system table query procedures, and other administrative system procedures.

Chapter 13 discusses triggering events, which are allocated to database tables and are fired as a consequence of specific events, such as insert, delete, and updates against rows in a table. SQL Server 7 enhancements to triggers are also discussed in this chapter.

Chapter 14 discusses using advanced data manipulation techniques, examining the different types of joins, subqueries, views, and server-side cursors. Some very useful examples are developed in this chapter to help readers in their own projects.

Writing Stored Procedures (Transact-SQL Programs)

There are two primary types of stored procedures: user-defined procedures and system procedures, identified by the prefix of sp_. User-defined stored procedures can be sophisticated programs that include sequel commands and a control-of-flow language that provides functionality that is equivalent to that offered by third-generation development languages. System procedures are packaged with the SQL Server software and are used to maintain the SQL Server environment. They were developed as part of the SQL Server environment by Microsoft (and Sybase before that). They provide diverse functionality to do everything from providing user-defined help and displaying and modifying configuration information to establishing security and permissions. Users should not modify system procedures and should learn to use them as they are provided with the product. This chapter examines both types of procedures. Stored procedures can consist of the following types of statements which are a part of Transact-SQL:

Control-of-flow. This is a Transact-SQL extension that provides third-generation language functionality to stored procedures and triggers. Commands such as if-else, while, and case are supported by this extension.

Data definition language. This contains sequel commands that are used to define database objects, such as databases, tables, and views

Data manipulation language. This contains sequel commands to manipulate database objects, such as INSERT, DELETE, UPDATE, and SELECT.

Data control language. This contains sequel commands to define security and permissions on database objects, such as REVOKE and GRANT.

Global variables. Global variables are predefined system variables that provide information about the database environment.

Functions. These are quite extensive and can fall into broad categories such as string functions, mathematical functions, datetime functions, and logic functions.

The Future of Stored Procedures

Stored procedures are an integral part of SQL Server. This has been true since their introduction as part of the 1987 SQL Server product released by Sybase. In a relatively short time, stored procedure functionality was introduced into the database servers of other products such as Oracle and Informix. This was done to compete with SQL Server, and was needed because stored procedures were becoming a key criteria in the selection of database architecture. In the last decade, the initial excitement about stored procedures has cooled and a more balanced set of guidelines is now available. Based on the current direction of SQL Server and Microsoft, it seems likely that the following things will happen to stored procedures in the Microsoft SQL Server product:

Business logic is moving to state-less components that support a more scalable architecture.

Stored procedures are used to interact with the database layer. Stored procedures also communicate with components. They act as middleware between components and the physical database environment.

Transact-SQL will begin to support to support VBA Script to allow more portability between database products.

There will be stronger support for object-oriented and component-based development.

ANSI SQL-3 guidelines will provide greater stored procedure portability between database products from different vendors.

The Benefits Offered by Stored Procedures

Stored procedures provide a variety of benefits to applications that make efficient use of them. These include performance improvements, code encapsulation, thin client support, and code reuse. These benefits are only achieved through effective planning, and haphazard use of stored procedures can have the opposite effect. Stored procedures offer performance improvements over alternative methods of executing Transact-SQL because a set of Transact-SQL statements are precompiled and stored in the SQL Server data dictionary. This reduces the amount of data that is transferred across the network. A cost-based access path is also stored in the data dictionary. This contains instructions for efficient execution of the statements in the stored procedure. Use of this information saves the amount of time required to build it from scratch, as would be the case if the stored procedure needed to be recompiled before every execution.

Concerns about Stored Procedures

Some concerns that have been expressed about stored procedures include a lack of portability between products and the need to have a larger data server to provide the performance for running code for concurrent client platforms invoking the stored procedures. As mentioned in the previous section, bad stored procedure design can have the opposite effect of better performance.

Another issue that has been raised around stored procedures is their lack of support for object-oriented architecture and design. The argument proposed is that both business logic and data are not encapsulated in the same object. Another issue to consider is that business logic and data are virtually in the same tier. System implementations often require compromises to be successful in the real world. An example of this is seen in basic relational theory, where relational tables are denormalized to improve application performance in physical design. Component-based development offers another such compromise. Separating stored procedures into different functions and keeping them distinct, offers a degree of encapsulation.

Stored Procedure Considerations

Stored procedures have received an extensive workout in production business systems in the last 10 years in a variety of industries. Some of the general issues that have emerged regarding the use of stored procedures in client/server systems, n-tier architecture, and network applications include the following:

Change Management

Source code management and version control are both issues in large client/server development projects. Source code management deals with the issue of maintaining copies of the current source code for programs that are in production. Version control refers to managing generations of modified copies of an application. All development projects require a formal, documented process for both of these to ensure that source code is not lost or confused with incorrect versions of the application. Many good tools and processes are available for most of the application components, such as the programming language, classes, and components. However, database objects require additional planning. Since stored procedures are saved inside SQL Server system tables, specifically sysobjects and sysmessages, both source code management and version control, are a challenge to implement consistently. Stored procedures are backed up automatically if SQL Server is backed up; however, this does not provide good source code management and version control because there is no granularity or single-source management capability. Furthermore, versioning occurs only at the application level. Experience shows that it is preferable to maintain scripts for all the stored procedures for an application in the operating system.

Scripts should be put through the change management processes that are required for application components written in outside the database. Good change management tools for a Microsoft development environment (e.g., VC++, VB, NT, Windows 95, and SQL Server) include Microsoft Source Save and PVCS. PVCS offers industrial-strength functionality at the time of writing. MS SourceSave appears to be functional for most development products, and since it is a Microsoft tool, it has good integration with the rest of the development environment. It is also possible to generate scripts directly from the system tables.

Portability and Interoperability

Portability and interoperability refer to the ability to write a stored procedure under one database server product and to seamlessly convert it or execute it under another database vendor product (e.g., Microsoft SQL Server and Oracle). The major database vendors mentioned in the Preface have developed SQL command languages that are based on the ANSI standard. The 1989 standard defined many database constructs in vague or general terms, allowing vendors to comply with the standard and yet be so different that executing a stored procedure in different product environments required extensive rewrites.

✓ **For the purposes of portability and interoperability, the distributed client/ server application model should be viewed as main logical tiers: data, logic, and interface. Portability and interoperability can then be enforced at the level of the tiers. The tiers themselves can be built up as a collection of layers. Ultimately the layers can evolve to a collection of classes or instantiated objects.**

To achieve true portability and interoperability, an application would need to be developed using features that are common across database products. Microsoft's Open Database Connectivity (ODBC) middleware attempts to do this. However, this approach means that many unique features and capabilities offered by different products cannot be used because they are not available elsewhere. For some applications this may be required, but true portability and interoperability is illusive and always comes with a cost. Even database server products that evolved from the same engine, namely Microsoft SQL Server and Sybase SQL Server, have differences in command syntax that require changes to stored procedures that are ported from one environment to another. For most meaningful applications, something less than 100 percent portability and interoperability is possible. The solution is to accept the less than ideal picture, but to develop the application with either of the two goals in mind. The solution will depend on which of the two requirements is dominant. The following guidelines are focused on the database server environment, but they are applicable to the other application tiers as well. In a database server environment, portability and interoperability are integrated with data conversion, index conversion, and datatype conversion.

Application portability is a desired goal by organizations that want to ensure that an application developed under one set of products can be ported without extensive rewrites to operate under another set of products. This need is enhanced by the number of corporate mergers and buyouts that end in a collection of nonstandard IT products that somehow have to be parsed down to a manageable level. It is difficult, if not impossible, to develop complex applications without using features and extensions that are unique to specific products sets. The alternative is to lose functional capabilities or take enormous performance hits. A useful compromise is to develop an application in layers. The database layer can also be developed as sublayers. Each sublayer should attempt to use the common ANSI SQL standards that are rigidly enforced by different vendors. Features that must be implemented using database server extensions can then be isolated in specific sublayers. When the application must be ported, rewrites can essentially be limited to a smaller set of sublayers. Some action steps for porting applications are

Install the new database and configure the database environment.

Convert and modify data.

Load new database tables.

Install new application programming interfaces (APIs) or modify existing APIs.

Modify application code and data scripts.

Recompile and implement ported applications.

Tweak the database environment.

Optimize performance.

 Understand your objectives clearly. Accept less than 100 percent of either layering or localization.

Application interoperability is a desired goal by organizations that want to execute the same application under different operating environments (e.g., a software package). By definition, this is not a one time port of the application into another environment, but rather is a parallel support for different operating environments. The guidelines for achieving interoperability are similar to those for achieving portability. In this method, a layer or component can be replaced to operate in different environments. This is one of the principles behind Windows NT, where a hardware application layer (HAL) is replaced to allow the operating system to support different hardware. Another approach for achieving interoperability is to build additional logic into the application that is invoked by setting application switches.

ANSI SQL Standards

The American National Standards Institute (ANSI) provides standards for a variety of industries, including information technology. The first SQL standard that emerged from ANSI that was adopted by different database vendors was released in 1989 and hence became known as SQL/89. In general, a group of database vendors can all be 100 percent ANSI/89 compliant yet not support application portability or interoperability. This is true for several reasons. The SQL/89 standard was developed after many database vendors had launched their products, so it tried to retrofit many details. This left many details to the interpretation of the vendor including error codes, built-in functions, a limited set of defined datatypes (e.g., varchar is not), interactive SQL that is not entirely covered, an insufficient definition of NULL, and loose naming conventions.

The SQL/92 definition (released in 1992) was far more rigorous than SQL/89. It is still not fully implemented by all major database vendors, and it too suffers from some of the same "loose" definitions and interpretations as the earlier standard. Some of the major additions to SQL/92 include scrollable cursors, standard error messages, and standard system catalogs. Database applications that use the ANSI/92 standard are more likely to be ported or interoperable with fewer changes. Wherever possible, use an ANSI/92 command syntax. ANSI/92 defines the following syntax:

Data definition language: alter domain, alter table, create domain, drop domain, drop table, drop view.

Data manipulation language: delete, insert, update.

Select: all, any, between, exists, having, in, like, group by, order by, unique, with cascaded check option, with check option.

Built-in functions: aggregate: avg, count, group by, max, min, order by, sum; conversion: cast, convert.

Date and time: current_date, current_time, current_timestamp, extract.

Scalar: bit_length, case, cast, character_length (char_length), collate, current_user, position, session_user, system_user.

String: create character set, create collation, drop character set, drop collation, lower, substring, translate, trim, upper.

Datatypes: character(length), char (length), character varying (length), bit (n), bit varying (n), numeric (x,y), decimal (x,y), integer, smallint, float(x), date, time, timestamp.

Indexes: primary key/unique, foreign key.

Joins: A variety of joins are supported by SQL/92, including cross join/Cartesian product, natural, inner, left (outer), right (outer) full (outer), union (except, intersect).

Security and Permissions: grant, revoke.

Transaction: begin transaction, commit, rollback.

Triggers: on delete, on update, no action, cascade, set default, set null.

VARIOUS ORGANIZATIONS DETERMINE STANDARDS

CORBA: Object Management Group's Common Object Request Broker Architecture
COSE: IBM, HP Santa Cruz Operation, Sun Microsystems
IEEE: US Standards body
ISO: International Organization for Standardization
ISOC: Internet standards society
OSF DCE: Open Software Foundation's (OSF) Distributed Computing Environment
POSIX: applications operating with the operating system
SQL Access Group: call-level interface (CLI) and remote database access (RDA)
X/Open: European retailers, vendors, and manufacturers

N-Tier Architecture and Partitioning Decisions

The use of stored procedures does not automatically constitute an n-tier architecture. This requires an additional layer that is supported by a tool such as the MTS. Recall that 3-tier architecture is characterized by the creation of three distinct layers. N-tier architecture is characterized by the creation of n tiers. The use of stored procedures inside database servers still counts as a 2-tier architecture, despite the number of stored procedures that are used.

Partitioning refers to the allocation of modules in a distributed architecture. This refers to questions such as, Should a piece of code run on the client? On the data server? On the file server? The basic rule is to position the partition close to the point where it is being used.

Additional Skill Sets

Developing stored procedures in application development cycles requires knowledge of an additional set of tools, including Transact-SQL, middleware, and debugging utilities. I have seen some development projects try to push the responsibility of building stored procedures onto the DBA or some other resource. The difficulty that can be encountered with this approach is that the developer pushing the development activities onto the dedicated resource must take the time to document the specifications or explain them carefully. This becomes a bottleneck. A preferred approach is to provide just-in-time training for a group of resources to become strong SQL Server developers. It is also useful to retain a strong contract resource to mentor the group on SQL Server programming until the expertise becomes inherent in the group.

Using Stored Procedures

Stored procedures are objects that are created and saved in specific databases under a specific stored procedure name. Stored procedures must be compiled into a data dictionary. A compile procedure applied to a stored procedure ensures that the syntax of the Transact-SQL commands containing stored procedures is correct, the stored procedure code is saved into a number of system tables, and a cost-based execution plan is created and saved in the data dictionary. This compile procedure is not the same as that used in third-generation languages that compile into object code and an executable. Figure 11.1 shows the essential components of a stored procedure. This includes the name of the stored procedure, input parameters, local variables, control-of-flow statements, DML statements, DDL statements, global variables, and the return statement.

Stored procedures can be written inside or outside the SQL Server environment, but they are stored directly in SQL Server system tables, including sysobjects and sysmessages. Stored procedures themselves are a combination of SQL data manipulation language, data definition language, data control language, and Transact-SQL. SQL by itself does not support repetitive program flows and conditional structures. Transact-SQL

```
IF EXISTS (SELECT * FROM sysobjects WHERE name = "procedure_name2")
        DROP PROC procedure_name2
go
IF EXISTS (SELECT * FROM sysobjects WHERE name = "procedure_name1")
        DROP PROC procedure_name1
go

CREATE PROC procedure_name2
(       @called_varaible2   datatype,
        @called_variable1   datatype  output)
AS
        DECLARE @return_code        int
        /* ------ insert statements */

        print 'procedure_name2 called'
        select @called_variable1 = 5
        select @return_code = 0

        RETURN @return_code
go


/*******************************************************************/
CREATE PROCEDURE procedure_name1
(       @parameter1         datatype  output,
        @parameter2         datatype)
AS
        DECLARE   @local_variable1 datatype,
                  @local_variable2   datatype,
                  @return_code       int
        /* initialize variables */
        SELECT @local_variable1 = value

        print 'procedure 1 called'
        select '@local_variable1 = ', @local_variable1
        select @return_code = 0

        /* ---- Insert DDL commands ----           ---- Insert DML commands ---- */

        /* issue a nested stored procedure call  - NOTE: @called_variable1 is declared as
           a parameter in the called procedure */
        EXEC   procedure_name2 @local_variable2,
                       @called_variable1 = @local_variable1  output

        select   'after procedure_call', '@local_variable1=', @local_variable1
        RETURN   @return_code
go

EXEC procedure_name1 100, 200
```

Figure 11.1 Parts of a stored procedure.

provides this enhancement to the SQL language. The combination of all these command structures enable stored procedures to write programs that are as sophisticated and complex as 3GL and 4GL languages.

A stored procedure can be written using a text editor in the operating system environment or directly into the SQL Server system tables using the SQL Server Query Analyzer (previously SQL/w) dictionary or the SQL Server Enterprise Manager. These are the most common methods of writing stored procedures. Other methods also exist. For example, a stored procedure can be written using a third-generation language (e.g., C programming language) with embedded SQL Server. However, this latter method has performance implications that make it less desirable than the other methods. This method also creates a "fat" client and a "thin" server, which creates a high network load for client/server applications. In the case where a stored procedure is written into an operating system file using a text editor, the stored procedure must be parsed into an SQL Server database using ISQL or one of the other methods of invoking SQL commands in the SQL environment. The parse procedure is sometimes called a compile procedure, but this is not a true compile in the 3GL sense in that object code is not created. Rather, the parse procedure interprets the code in the stored procedure and returns error messages if there are syntactical or some types of logical errors (e.g., a reference to a database object that does not exist). If the stored procedure commands are successfully interpreted, the entire code belonging to that stored procedure is saved into the default database system tables. When the stored procedure is executed, it is compiled by SQL Server. An execution plan is also created for the stored procedure which identifies the most cost-effective manner to satisfy the query. This will vary depending on the amount of data in the table, the amount of data required by the query, and the number and types of indexes available. Parameters in a WHERE clause can have a dramatic impact on the contacts of the execution plan.

Stored procedures are generally executed on the server platform after they are invoked by client-side processes. It is not unusual for a particular portion of functionality that could be developed on a client platform (e.g., with Visual Basic or VC++) to be developed on the server platform through a stored procedure instead. This allows all calling client platforms to invoke the same block of code.

Putting functionality on the client platform leads to a fat client. At one time this was actually the preferred direction in the marketplace that was supported by many software vendors (e.g., SAP, Peoplesoft). The reason for this was that applications could be developed in a third or fourth generation language using the database as a commodity. The database was only used to store the application data. All the business processing was done outside the database environment. This allowed the vendor to package their application with a variety of databases by avoiding the use of the database extensions.

Stored Procedure Syntax

The stored procedure contents consist of all the code between the CREATE statement and the go that ends the batch. This is the code that is compiled and executed under the name of the stored procedure. Since stored procedures are created and stored as database objects, it is necessary to drop them before they are created. The syntax for creating a stored procedure is as follows:

```
CREATE PROCedure [owner.] name
[@input_parm_list   dtype   =default      OUTput]
[options]
AS
     Transact SQL Statements
GO
```

This syntax works where options = FOR REPLICATION | WITH RECOMPILE, EN-CRYPTION, OUTput = is used to allow a passed parameter to be updated, and RECOM-PILE is used to automatically generate a query plan when the stored procedure is executed, taking additional time, but by providing an optimal query plan. This is not required in SQL Server 7.

The Transact SQL Statements that are supported within stored procedures is a comprehensive list that consists of SQL commands and built-in functions. Stored procedures can also call nested stored procedures or call themselves recursively. Stored procedures are dropped from a database using the following syntax:

```
DROP PROCEDURE proc_name
go
```

Stored procedures that are successfully compiled into the database system tables can be executed using the following command syntax:

```
EXECUTE proc_name [parameters]
go
```

Steps for Working with Stored Procedures

The following steps provide a process for creating, debugging, compiling, and running stored procedures. Two approaches are presented: the wizard approach and the text editor approach. The wizard approach should be restricted to stored procedures that insert, delete, and update into single tables. Furthermore, minimal customization should be performed on the stored procedures that are generated by the wizards. The other method that is discussed can be selected for any type of stored procedure regardless of complexity.

Understand the business requirements of the stored procedure.

Select a text editor or a wizard approach to create the stored procedure.

If a wizard approach is selected for creating stored procedures:

Start an SQL Server session.

Start an Enterprise Manager session.

Select a database in the Enterprise Manager.

Select the Create Stored Procedures Wizard.

Select the tables and the types of stored procedures that are required.

Edit the generated stored procedures and change the default names according to your standards.

Complete the generation of the stored procedure.

Start a Query Analyzer session.

Select the database that contains the stored procedure.

Type in the command EXEC stored_procedure_name parameter_list.

Test the stored procedure.

Export the stored procedure into an external text file if any changes are to be made at this time. The Transact-SQL code belonging to the stored procedure can be extracted from the system dictionary using the command sp_helptext sp_who. Follow the instructions for the text editor approach. Be careful to realize that future generations of the stored procedure through the wizard will not contain the customized code.

If a text editor approach is selected to develop stored procedures:

Use the template shown in Chapter 3 to build a stored procedure.

Save the contents in an operating system file and exit the text editor.

Start an SQL Server session.

Start an active Query Analyzer session.

Open the operating system file in the Query Analyzer.

Execute the stored procedure.

Fix any bugs that are identified in the code within the Query Analyzer.

Save the changes to the operating system file.

Repeat the test-fix bug cycle until the stored procedure compiles successfully.

Type in the code EXEC stored_ procedure_name parameter_list.

Highlight the EXEC command and execute it.

Test-enhance the stored procedure until you are satisfied with its functionality.

The text files containing the stored procedure code should be put through the normal version control and backup procedures that are established within your organization. Future changes to the stored procedure should follow the text editor process.

Some Stored Procedure Examples

This section demonstrates how to create and execute a few straightforward stored procedures using both scripts and the Create Stored Procedures Wizard. These examples show the full life cycle of working with stored procedures, including a view of the relevant system tables and helpful system procedures that provide information about stored procedures without complicating the picture with detailed commands. Figure 11.2 shows two methods of achieving this objective. One is to use an external set of

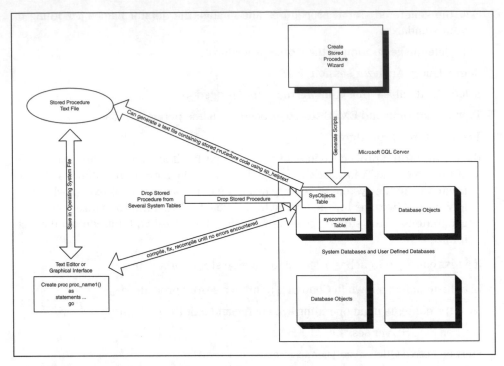

Figure 11.2 Maintaining stored procedures.

tools, such as a text editor like Microsoft Quick C editor, to write the stored procedure and save the code into a text file with a specific operating system file name. A file can contain many stored procedures.

Using Scripts to Create Stored Procedures

The business requirement is to create a stored procedure that accepts an input and displays a friendly message along with the current date and time. This stored procedure will be built iteratively. The first pass builds the infrastructure for the stored procedure then compiles and tests it in the Query Analyzer:

```
/* filename: test11a.txt */
drop procedure example11a
go

create proc example11a
(
    @name        char(40)
)
AS
    select 'How are you today', @name, ' '
```

```
        return 0
go


exec example11a 'Joe'
go
```

After testing and fixing the code from pass one, enhance the stored procedure by inserting functions to display the current date and time in the second pass:

```
/* filename: test11a.txt */
drop procedure example11a
go

create proc example11a
(
    @name           char(40)
)
AS
    select 'How are you today', @name, ' '
    select getdate()
    return 0
go

exec example11a 'Joe'
go
```

> It is convenient to cut or copy pieces of code into the clipboard and to paste it into the Query Analyzer window to test it. This approach saves you the time of having to save and open text files. However, it is important to be careful that changes are not lost if you follow this approach. Be sure to save the changes you make. If the pulldown menu options are not available you can still use the keyboard. Ctrl-X copies highlighted text to the clipboard. Ctrl-V pastes the text in the clipboard to the location of the cursor.

Using Wizards to Create Stored Procedures

The Create Stored Procedures Wizard is a quick way to build three basic types of stored procedures for tables. Invoking this wizard allows you to select a default database. As shown in Figure 11.3, a list of user table objects is shown in the wizard dialogue. Options to build stored procedures to insert, update, and delete data into the user tables of the default database are presented. You are free to select as many procedures as desired.

Clicking on the Next button displays the dialogue shown in Figure 11.4. The name of the stored procedure defaults by the following formula: sp_ + operation + table_name + _+ sequential counter. Selecting an option to build an insert stored procedure on the authors table generates a name of sp_insert_authors_1 the first time it is selected and processed. The name generated on the second generation is sp_insert_authors_2. It is also possible to edit the details of the stored procedure by clicking on the Edit button.

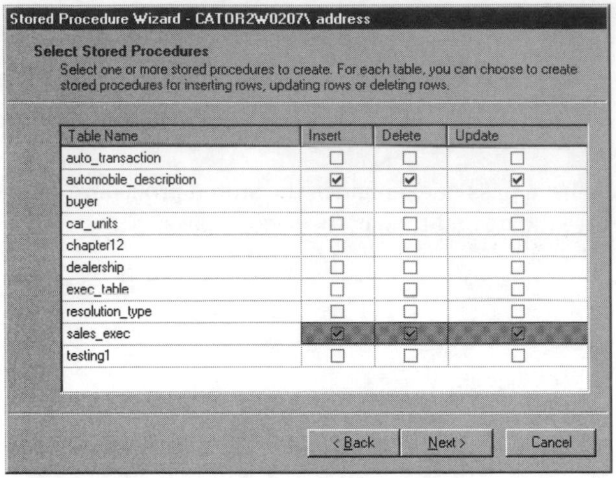

Figure 11.3 Create Stored Procedures Wizard.

Selecting the Edit button displays the dialogue shown in Figure 11.5. It is possible to change the name of the stored procedure in this dialogue, remove specific columns included in the code, and potentially to edit the SQL. It is possible to interactively observe the effect of including or excluding columns from the operation. Exclude most of the table columns and select the Edit SQL function. You will notice that the SQL statements no longer reference the excluded columns. Click on the Cancel button, include a field, and click the Edit SQL button to observe that SQL statements are generated to access the selected column. If you decide to edit the SQL statements that are automatically generated by the wizard, you have in effect customized the application code. This will require you to make the same customization every time you generate this stored procedure. This requires an additional level of work on your part. My preference is to use the

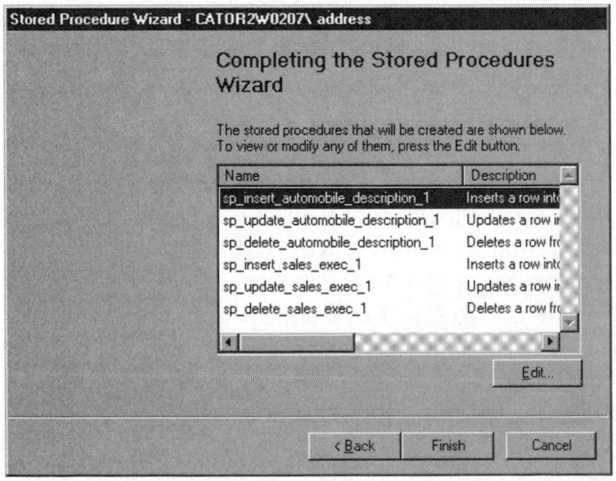

Figure 11.4 Completing the Stored Procedures Wizard.

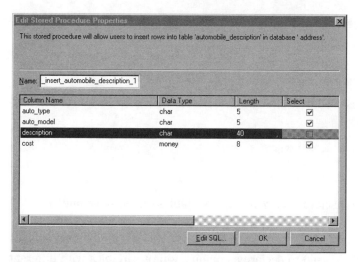

Figure 11.5 Edit stored procedure properties.

wizard to generate a set of required stored procedures for every table and to export the stored procedure scripts to text files outside the database. These text files can then be customized, enhanced, and included in version control.

Clicking the OK button and the FINISH button generates the stored procedure if there are no problems encountered by the wizard.

 The Create Stored Procedures Wizard only displays user-defined tables, not system tables.

Variable Declarations and Manipulation

SQL Server supports user-defined local, user-defined global, and system supplied global variables. SQL Server requires user-defined variables to be explicitly declared before they are used. Not doing so results in syntactical errors.

User-Defined Variables

User-defined variables must be declared before they are used. They are generally used in stored procedures and triggers. The declare command is used to declare a variable and it is assigned a datatype. The datatypes that are supported by SQL Server can be assigned to declared variables. User-defined variables are dropped at the end of a session or when an object is released (e.g., when the stored procedure ends). User-defined variables have an @ prefix. The following syntax is used to declare one variable:

```
declare @variable      datatype
```

The following syntax is used to declare three variables separated by commas:

```
declare @variable1       datatype,
        @variable2       datatype,
        @variable3       datatype
```

The following syntax is used to declare three variables with their own declare statements:

```
declare @variable1       datatype
declare @variable2       datatype
declare @variable3       datatype
```

The following syntax is used to declare multiple variables on the same line:

```
declare @variable1     datatype, @variable2     datatype
```

The following example is used to declare a combination of variables with different datatypes:

```
declare @last_name       char(30),
        @first_name      char(30),
        @age             int,
        @birthdate       datetime
```

The following example is used to declare variables on the same line:

```
declare @last_name     char(30), @first_name     char(30)
```

Variables can be used interactively or inside database objects. For example, the contents of a variable can be displayed using the following code:

```
print 'variable is ', @variable
select @variable
```

Global Variables

Global variables contain information about the system environment. You can display these values with the select command or the print command. The values can also be inspected with control-of-flow statements, such as IF-ELSE and WHILE. Global variables can be accessed interactively in the Query Analyzer and within database objects such as stored procedures and triggers.

> The value of the global variables can change as a result of many environmental conditions or actions. If relying on the value of these variables for decisions, ensure that the value is inspected at the right time, before another event changes the value. An example of this is the @@ERROR variable that contains the last error number generated by SQL Server. Clearly this value can change as a result of a sequence of events that the user may not be aware of. For this reason, inspect a global variable immediately after an event.

Table 11.1 contains a list of useful global variables that will benefit development efforts. The value of the variables can be inspected as follows: select @@VERSION or print @@VERSION.

Table 11.1   Global Variables

GLOBAL VARIABLE	DESCRIPTION
@@CONNECTIONS	Number of active connections.
@@DBTS	DBTS value.
@@ERROR	The last error number trapped in the environment.
@@FETCH_STATUS	Status of the last fetch statement in a cursor operation.
@@IDENTITY	Identity constraint value.
@@IDLE	Amount of idle time.
@@IO_BUSY	IO busy value.
@@LANGID	The ID of the language that is installed.
@@LANGUAGE	The language that is installed.
@@MAX_CONNECTIONS	The maximum number of connections that are allowed.
@@MAX_PRECISION	The maximum number of digits in a number.
@@NESTLEVEL	The current level of transaction nesting.
@@PACK_RECEIVED	Number of packets received.
@@PACKET_ERRORS	Packets in error.
@@PROCID	ID of the current/last procedure.
@@ROWCOUNT	The number of rows returned by the last DML command.
@@SERVERNAME	The name of the SQL Server.
@@SERVICENAME	Name of the current/last service.
@@SPID	SPID value.
@@TEXTSIZE	Size of the text manipulated in the last statement.
@@TIMETICKS	Time increments.
@@TOTAL_ERRORS	Total errors encountered.
@@TOTAL_READ	Total read operations.
@@TOTAL_WRITE	Total write operations.
@@TRANCOUNT	Transaction count.
@@VERSION	Contains the version number of the SQL Server engine.

The following code displays the contents of the global variables. The format of the select displays the mnemonic name of the information being displayed. Not including this information will display several screens of numbers that are difficult to read:

```
select "connections", @@CONNECTIONS
select "dbts", @@DBTS
select "error", @@ERROR
select "fetch_status", @@FETCH_STATUS
select "identity", @@IDENTITY
select "idle", @@IDLE
select "io_busy", @@IO_BUSY
select "langid", @@LANGID
select "language", @@LANGUAGE
select "max_connections", @@MAX_CONNECTIONS
select "max_precision", @@MAX_PRECISION
select "nestlevel", @@NESTLEVEL
select "pack_received", @@PACK_RECEIVED
select "packet_errors", @@PACKET_ERRORS
select "proc_id", @@PROCID
select "rowcount", @@ROWCOUNT
select "servername", @@SERVERNAME
select "servicename", @@SERVICENAME
select "spid", @@SPID
select "textsize", @@TEXTSIZE
select "timeticks", @@TIMETICKS
select "total_errors", @@TOTAL_ERRORS
select "total_read", @@TOTAL_READ
select "total_write", @@TOTAL_WRITE
select "trancount", @@TRANCOUNT
select "version", @@VERSION
```

This syntax produces the following output:

```
connections          13
dbts                 0x00000000000001F4
error                0
fetch_status         0
identity             NULL
idle                 0
io_busy              0
langid               0
language             us_english
max_connections      32767
max_precision        28
nestlevel            0
pack_received        49
packet_errors        0
proc_id              0
rowcount             1
servername           CATOR2W207
servicename          MSSQLServer
```

```
spid                 8
textsize             64512
timeticks            31250
total_errors         0
total_read           386
total_write          90
trancount            0
version

          Microsoft SQL Server 7.00 - 7.00.517 (Intel X86)
          Jun 19 1998 17:06:54
          Copyright (c) 1988-1998 Microsoft Corporation
          Enterprise version on Windows
```

Control-of-Flow Commands

The control-of-flow extensions that are available to build sophisticated stored procedures include the following statements: BEGIN..END, IF..ELSE, IF EXISTS, CASE ..END, WAITFOR, GOTO LABEL [label:], COMPUTE, WHILE, CONTINUE, BREAK, and RETURN. These are discussed in this section. Stored procedures using these control-of-flow commands are presented later in this chapter.

BEGIN..END

This command block is used to surround multiple Transact-SQL statements in stored procedures. They are used to surround multiple statements so that they appear as one. Some of the other control-of-flow statements only accept a single statement. Surrounding multiple statements in this construct makes them appear as a single statement. The IF..ELSE block is an example of this. Processing of the statements within this construct is unconditional. The syntax for this command is

```
BEGIN
Statements
Statements
Statements
END
```

IF..ELSE

The IF..ELSE command block is the classical third-generation if-else construct. If the condition belonging to the IF is true, the statement immediately following the IF is executed. The statement belonging to the ELSE is skipped. If the condition belonging to the IF is false, then the statement corresponding to the ELSE is executed. Multiple statements surrounded by the BEGIN..END block count as a single statement. IF..ELSE constructs can also be nested.

The following syntax reflects the basic IF-ELSE block that is supported in the Control-of-Flow language. When "condition" is evaluated to be TRUE, the statements between the IF and the ELSE are executed. If the "condition" is evaluated to be FALSE, the statements after the ELSE are executed. The ELSE block is optional. There must be an IF statement corresponding to the ELSE block.

```
IF condition
Statements
ELSE
Statements
```

In the following syntax, statement represents a single command. As shown, it can be replaced by a BEGIN...END statement block:

```
IF condition
BEGIN
Statements
Statements
Statements
END
    ELSE
        Statements
```

The following syntax shows chaining of additional ELSE statements to the basic IF-ELSE block. The statements belonging to an IF are evaluated for the first IF condition that evaluates to TRUE. The final, unconditional ELSE statement is optional. When it exists, the statements belonging to it are executed.

```
IF Condition
    Statements
ELSE
IF Condition
    Statements
ELSE
IF condition
    Statements
ELSE
    Statements
```

The following syntax shows an example of a nested IF statement. The Condition 2 is only evaluated if Condition 1 evaluates to TRUE. Then, the statements belonging to Condition 2 are only executed if this condition also evaluates to TRUE. It is possible to continue nesting and chaining additional IF-ELSE statement blocks.

```
IF Condition 1
   IF Condition 2
         Statements
       ELSE
      Statements
ELSE
IF Condition 3
     Statements
ELSE
```

```
IF condition 4
     Statements
ELSE
     Statements
```

IF EXISTS

The IF EXISTS test is used to determine if a certain object exists. The statement following the IF EXISTS is executed if the object does in fact exist. A common use of this statement is to inspect the sysobjects table for an object name before dropping it. This avoids the problem of trying to drop an object that does not exist, which generates an error message. The IF EXISTS statement causes a read of the sysobjects table and then another read to drop the object if it is found. This can have an impact on performance.

The following syntax shows a basic IF EXISTS command block. The condition inside the brackets is evaluated. If the SELECT evaluates to TRUE, meaning that the object exists, the corresponding statements are executed. The IF EXISTS statement, in itself, does not result in any work.

```
IF EXISTS (select name from sysobjects where name = 'value_of_name'
        AND type = 'INITIAL'
drop table table_name
go
```

CASE..END

The CASE..END block is similar to the IF..ELSE block. A condition is evaluated at the start of the block and a branch that matches the condition is found and executed. The other statements in the block are skipped. Control is passed to the statement immediately following the CASE..END block after the statement is executed. The syntax for this command is the following

```
CASE condition
     WHEN condition THEN statements
     WHEN condition THEN statements
     WHEN condition THEN statements
     ELSE statements
END
```

GOTO LABEL [label:]

This statement has two components. The first component consists of the GOTO LABEL code that causes an unconditional branch to the LABEL. The second component of this construct is a label: that marks a spot somewhere in the same stored procedure batch. This is where program control is passed. Use of a GOTO is always controversial. It should always be used consistently and clearly to avoid countless branches. The syntax for this command is

```
GOTO label_name
label_name:
```

WAITFOR

The WAITFOR statement pauses active processing until a given statement is true. This command is generally used in conjunction with a timer that stops the processing for a specified time increment before continuing. The syntax for this command is

```
WAITFOR DELAY 'time_meter' | TIME 'specific_time'
```

COMPUTE

The COMPUTE statement is used to calculate results and save them in a declared variable. Following is an example of the COMPUTE statement:

```
COMPUTE BY will print totals with the select command as in:
    SELECT * FROM store
        Order by
        Compute . . . . By . . .
```

WHILE

The WHILE statement is used to repeatedly execute a set of statements until a condition is met. The condition can be a compound statement that combines multiple conditions using AND and OR. The syntax for this command is the following

```
WHILE condition
Statements
```

CONTINUE

The CONTINUE statement is used to pass control to the start of a WHILE statement where the condition is evaluated. This syntax for this command is the word itself: CONTINUE.

BREAK

The BREAK statement is used to immediately and unconditionally exit a WHILE command block. Program control is passed to the statement immediately following the WHILE block. The syntax for this command is the word itself: BREAK.

Capturing Select Column Data in Variables

It is common to capture data row values using select statements inside stored procedures. This allows the variables to be used in the stored procedure. The syntax for this is as follows:

```
SELECT @variable1 = column1, @variable2 = column2,
       @variable3 = column3, @variable4 = column4
```

```
    FROM TABLE
            WHERE columnx = 'value'

SELECT @variable1, @variable2, @variable3, @variable4
```

RETURN

The RETURN statement is used to send a status back to the calling program and exit from the current program. The following values and their interpretations are defined in the Microsoft manuals. Negative numbers mean that an error has occurred and been intercepted:

```
  0 a successful return
 -1 indicates a missing object
 -2 indicates that a datatype error occurred
 -3 the process was the victim of a deadlock competition
 -4 a permission error occurred
 -5 a syntax error occurred
 -6 a miscellaneous user error occurred
 -7 a resource error occurred
 -9 a system limit was surpassed
-12 bad table or index encountered
-13 bad database encountered
-14 hardware encountered
```

Generating Errors with Raiserror

The following examples demonstrate how raiserror is used to raise errors in stored procedures or triggers:

raiserror 60100 'test of raiserror', 2

select @@error

sp_addmessage message_id, severity, 'message text'

sp_dropmessage

sp_addmessage 60100, 11, 'message'

raiserror (60100, 11, 1)

Arithmetic Operators

SQL Server supports the common arithmetic operators that most other development languages do, including those shown in Table 11.2. These mathematical operators can be used in conjunction with other Transact-SQL commands. They can also be combined into complex calculations and can be nested.

Boolean Operators

SQL Server supports the common Boolean and comparison operators that most other development languages do, including those shown in Table 11.3.

Table 11.2 Mathematical Operators

OPERATOR	DESCRIPTION	EXAMPLES
+	Addition	Compute x = y + z
–	Subtraction	Compute x = y – z
/	Division	Compute x = y/z
*	Multiplication	Computer x = y * z
%	Modulo	Compute x = y % z

Table 11.3 Boolean Operators

OPERATOR	DESCRIPTION	EXAMPLES
>	Greater than	If a > b AND b > c statements
<	Less than	If a < b OR b < c statements
>=	Greater than or equal to	If a >= b AND b>= c statements
<=	Less than or equal to	If a <= b OR b<= c statements
<>	Not equal to	If a <> b Statements
=	Equal to	If (a = b AND b = c) OR c = d statements

✓ When working with stored procedures, two names are relevant. The first name is the operating system file name that contains the script for the stored procedure. The second name is the stored procedure name that is saved in the sysobjects table. In the example 1, the operating system file name is stexple1.sql. The stored procedure name is stexample1.

Stored Procedure Examples

This section demonstrates the use of the control-of-flow commands discussed previously and the mathematical operators. These stored procedures also demonstrate common functionality that is expected of stored procedures. The examples include both single table and multiple database table applications.

✓ The stored procedure examples in this section require a set of primary enhancements to prepare them to support mission critical, high data volume, transactional production environments: transactional controls, data validation, error processing, and reuse. These enhancements will be made to the stored procedures throughout this book. The stored procedures, as they exist, can be used in non-mission-critical environments.

Sample Scripts

The following example creates a stored procedure in the default database under the object name stexample1.

```
/*———————————————————————————*/
/*———- Code below this line is saved into memch11a.sql ———*/
/*———————————————————————————*/

/* Filename: memch11a.sql */

/* drop the stored procedure */
DROP PROC stexample1
go     /* test this procedure without the go statement. Does it still
work without it? */

CREATE PROC stexample1
AS
     SELECT 'this is a stored procedure'
     RETURN 0   /* return a 0 code to the calling routine */
go

/*———————————————————————————*/
/*———- Code above this line is saved into memch11a.sql ———*/
/*———————————————————————————*/
```

Execute the stored procedure by entering the following commands in the MS SQL Server Query Analyzer, a batch file, or through an ISQL session:

```
stexample1
go
```

 Stored procedures (and other objects like views and triggers) are compiled into several system tables within the default database. The text is stored in syscomments under an ID. Several system procedures, discussed later in this chapter, can be used to retrieve the code for a stored procedure and to save it in an ASCII operating system file. Sysobjects contain header information for all objects including stored procedures.

The Basic Database Model

The following script creates the database tables that are accessed by the stored procedures in this section. This is based on a common real world example that consists of a member table. The member belongs to a specific category, identified by the member_code table. The address table contains 0 or more address codes belonging to a member. This can capture relationships, such as mailing address, shipping address, and billing address:

```
drop table member_code
drop table member
```

```
drop table address
go

create table member_code
(
        member_code             char (1),
        description             char (30)
)

create table member
(
          member_no             int,
        last_name               char(30),
        middle_initial          char(1),
        first_name              char(30),
        home_phone              char(15),
        business_phone          char(15),
        fax                     char(15),
        email                   char(25),
        preference              char(80),
        member_on               datetime,
        member_code             char(1)
)

create table address
(
        member_no               int,
        address_code            char(1),
        streeta                 char(30),
        streetb                 char(30),
        city_name               char(20),
        state                   char(20),
        country                 char(20),
        zip                     char(10)
)
go
```

This script can be compiled into one of the databases that you have created in the environment. If there are no user-defined databases in the environment, use the "pubs" databases to support the examples contained in this chapter.

Scripts for the MEMBER_CODE Table

It is a common application design practice to have four basic stored procedures for every relational table in the system. These stored procedures, described here, are developed for the member_code table:

Insert table. Insert a full data row into a table, accepting parameters for every non-Identity column.

Update table. Update a data row based on a combination of key fields. Parameters must include the new values for each column that can be updated. Performance is impacted by the types of indexes that are available to support the operation. It may be necessary to support more than one update script for a table.

Delete table. Delete a data row based on a combination of key fields.

Select table. Select all the columns in a table.

The following stored procedure inserts one data row record into the member_code table:

```
/* Filename: memch11b.sql */

/* drop the stored procedure if it exists in the database. */
IF EXISTS (select name from sysobjects where name = 'insert_member_code')
BEGIN
      select 'stored procedure found'
      DROP PROC insert_member_code
END
go

CREATE PROC insert_member_code
(
   @member_code      char (1),
   @description      char (30)
)
AS
      /**********************************************************/
      /* include data validation tests here for input parameters */
      /**********************************************************/

      INSERT INTO member_code
      (
          member_code,
          description
      )
      VALUES
      (
          @member_code,
          @description
      )

      /**********************************************************/
      /* test for an insert error and take appropriate action  */
      /* if it occurred.                                       */
      /**********************************************************/

      RETURN 0   /* return a 0 code to the calling routine */
go
```

The following example inserts a member_code data row into the member_code table:

```
insert_member_code 'Y', 'Yearly renewal'go
```

The following example inserts a member_code data row into the
member_code table:insert_member_code 'M', 'Monthly renewal' /* insert
another member_code */

SQL Server reports a successful INSERT operation when a record is successfully inserted in a table. The following command retrieves all the data rows in the member_code table, and displays them.

```
select * from member_code /*display the contents of the member_code table*/
go
```

Attempting to execute the stored procedure without the sufficient number of parameters or the correct datatypes for each parameter displays meaningful error messages to report that the insert was not completed successfully. In fact, SQL Server displays meaning information to identify the missing parameters in the execute command

The following sample script updates the description column for an existing member_code:

```
/* Filename: memch11b.sql */

/* drop the stored procedure from the data dictionary if it exists.*/
IF EXISTS (select name from sysobjects where name = 'update_member_code')
   DROP PROC update_member_code
go

CREATE PROC update_member_code
(
  @member_code      char (1),
  @description      char (30)
)
AS
    /************************************************************/
    /* include data validation tests here for the input parameters */
    /************************************************************/
    /************************************/
    UPDATE member_code
    SET description = @description
        where member_code = @member_code

    if @@rowcount < 1    /* no rows were affected by the UPDATE */
        print 'no record found to update'   /* raiserror code here */
    else
        print 'record was updated'

    RETURN 0   /* return a 0 code to the calling routine */
go
```

The following example updates the description for a data value in the member_code table:

```
update_member_code 'Y', 'Bi-Yearly' go
```

The following statement displays the contents of the member_code table:

```
select * from member_code
go
```

The following example deletes a record from the member_code table based on the value contained in a member_code variable :

```
/* Filename: memch11c.sql */

/* Drop the stored procedure if it exists. */
IF EXISTS (select name from sysobjects where name =
'delete_member_code')
DROP PROC delete_member_code
go

CREATE PROC delete_member_code
(
  @member_code      char (1)
)
AS
     DELETE member_code
         WHERE member_code = @member_code

     /***********************************************/
     /* Trap and process INSERT errors. */
     /*****************************************************/
     if @@rowcount < 1    /* no rows were affected */
         print 'No record found to be deleted'  /*raiserror statements
                                                              here*/

     else
         print 'record is deleted'

     RETURN 0   /* return a 0 code to thc calling module  */
go
```

The following example deletes a member from the member_code table:

```
delete_member_code 'Y' '
go
```

Scripts for the MEMBER and ADDRESS Tables

This section creates INSERT, UPDATE, DELETE, and SELECT scripts for both the member and the address tables. An insert operation adds one member record and an address record. The insert_address script can be executed a number of times to insert more than one address. An update operation can update the columns in either the member or the address tables. The sample script updates the column for all the data rows related to a member record. The delete_address script deletes all the related address records in the address tables before deleting the member record in the member table. The select_address script can be as simple as individual select that use a wildcard to return all the columns in a table. This approach, though simple to program, is easily broken if a change is made to the structure of a table. It is preferable to select specific columns into local variables and then to return the local variables in a specific order. This limits the automatic propagation of structure changes, and may keep an application functioning during volatile times.

Source Listing 11.1 inserts two records into the address database, one into each of the customer and address tables. This example demonstrates how to issue a nested procedure call.

```
/* Filename: memch11d */

/* Drop the stored procedure if it exists in the database. */
IF EXISTS (select name from sysobjects where name = 'insert_member')
    DROP PROC insert_member
go

/* Drop the stored procedure if it exists in the database. */
IF EXISTS (select name from sysobjects where name = 'insert_address')
    DROP PROC insert_address
go

/*******************************************************/
/* Create the insert_member stored procedure */
/*******************************************************/
CREATE PROC insert_member
(
    @member_no          int,
    @last_name          char(30),
    @middle_initial     char(1),
    @first_name         char(30),
    @home_phone         char(15),
    @business_phone     char(15),
    @fax                char(15),
    @email              char(25),
    @preference         char(80),
    @member_on          datetime,
    @member_code        character(1),
    @address_code       char(1),
    @streeta            char(30),
    @streetb            char(30),
    @city_name          char(20),
    @state              char(20),
    @country            char(20),
    @zip                char(10)
)
AS
    DECLARE
    @return_code        int   /* variable names must begin with @ */
```
(Continues)

Source 11.1   Insert records into the address table.

```
/****************************************/
/* Insert data validation tests here */
/****************************************/

INSERT member
(
    member_no,
    last_name,
    middle_initial,
    first_name,
    home_phone,
    business_phone,
    fax,
    email,
    preference,
    member_on,
    member_code
)
VALUES
(
    @member_no,
    @last_name,
    @middle_initial,
    @first_name,
    @home_phone,
    @business_phone,
    @fax,
    @email,
    @preference,
    @member_on,
    @member_code
)

/********************************************************/
/* Process insert errors that are returned. */
/********************************************************/

/* Call stored procedure to insert an address record */
EXECUTE @return_code = insert_address @member_no,
            @address_code, @streeta, @streetb,
       @city_name, @state, @country, @zip

/****************************************************************/
/* Inspect return_code and process any errors that are detected */
/****************************************************************/

RETURN 0    /* return a 0 code to the calling routine */
go
```

(Continues)

Source 11.1 *(Continued)*

```
/*********************************************/
/* Create insert_address stored procedure */
/*********************************************/

CREATE PROC insert_address
(
    @member_no          int,
    @address_code       char(1),
    @streeta            char(30),
    @streetb            char(30),
    @city_name              char(20),
    @state      char(20),
    @country            char(20),
    @zip            char(10)
)
AS
    /*************************************/
    /* insert data validation statements  here */
    /*************************************/
    INSERT address
    (
     member_no,
     address_code,
     streeta,
     streetb,
     city_name,
     state,
     country,
     zip
     )
    VALUES
    (
        @member_no,
     @address_code,
     @streeta,
     @streetb,
     @city_name,
     @state,
     @country,
     @zip
     )

    /*****************************************************/
    /* Process insert errors received from the INSERT statement */
    /*****************************************************/

    RETURN 0    /* return a 0 code to the calling routine */
go
```

Source 11.1 *(Continued)*

The following example executes the insert_member stored procedure:

```
insert_member 200, 'Sector', 'S', 'Bill', '9999888888',
        '9899899999', '9999998888',
        'msector@asgirus.com', 'Billiards', 'Oct 1994', '2',
        'Y', '123 Sig Blvd', ' ', 'LA', 'California', 'US', '20202'
go
```

The following statements display the results saved in the two tables:

```
select * from member
select * from address
go
```

It is also possible to insert additional address records by directly executing the insert_address procedure. The following example adds another address record for the previous member:

```
insert_address 200, 'B', '23 Consec Rd', ' ', 'San Jose', 'California',
'US', '20203'
go
```

Source Listing 11.2 updates records in the address database inside the member and address tables. This example also demonstrates a nested procedure call.

```
/* Filename: memch11e.sql */

/* drop the stored procedure if it exists in the database. */
IF EXISTS (select name from sysobjects where name = 'update_member')
    DROP PROC update_member
go

/* drop the stored procedure if it exists in the database. */
IF EXISTS (select name from sysobjects where name = 'update_address')
    DROP PROC update_address go

/********************************************/
/* Create the update_member stored procedure */
/********************************************/
CREATE PROC update_member
(
    @member_no          int,
    @last_name          char(30),
    @middle_initial     char(1),
    @first_name         char(30),
    @home_phone         char(15),
    @business_phone     char(15),
    @fax                char(15),
    @email              char(25),
```

(Continues)

Source 11.2 Updating two tables.

```
      @preference          char(80),
      @member_on           datetime,
      @member_code         character(1),
      @address_code        char(1),
      @streeta             char(30),
      @streetb             char(30),
      @city_name           char(20),
      @state               char(20),
      @country             char(15),
      @zip                 char(10)
)
AS
   DECLARE
   @return_code         int   /* variable names must begin with @ */


   /***************************************/
   /* Insert data validation tests here */
   /***************************************/
   UPDATE member
     SET
        last_name         = @last_name,
        middle_initial    = @middle_initial,
        first_name        = @first_name,
        home_phone        = @home_phone,
        business_phone    = @business_phone,
        fax               = @fax,
        email             = @email,
        preference        = @preference,
        member_on         = @member_on,
        member_code       = @member_code
     WHERE
          member_no = @member_no


   /********************************************************/
   /* Process update errors */
   /********************************************************/


   /* Call stored procedure to update address record */
EXECUTE @return_code = update_address @member_no,
             @address_code, @streeta, @streetb,
       @city_name, @state, @country, @zip


   /*****************************************************************/
   /* Inspect return_code, test for error and take appropriate action */
   /*****************************************************************/


   RETURN 0   /* return a 0 code to the calling routine */
go
```
(Continues)

Source 11.2   *(Continued)*

```
/***********************************************/
/* Create the update_address stored procedure */
/***********************************************/

CREATE PROC update_address
(
    @member_no          int,
    @address_code       char(1),
    @streeta            char(30),
    @streetb            char(30),
    @city_name               char(20),
    @state      char(20),
    @country            char(15),
    @zip            char(10)
)
AS

    /*****************************************/
    /* insert data validation tests here */
    /*****************************************/
    UPDATE address
      SET
        address_code        = @address_code,
        streeta             = @streeta,
        streetb             = @streetb,
        city_name               = @city_name,
        state       = @state,
        country             = @country,
        zip             = @zip
      WHERE
member_no = @member_no

    /***********************************************************/
    /* process update errors */
    /***********************************************************/

    RETURN 0   /* return a 0 code to the calling routine */
go
```

Source 11.2 *(Continued)*

The following example updates the member and address records:

```
update_member 200, 'Sector','S', 'Sam', '9999888888',
        '9899899999', '9999998899',
      'msector@asgirus.com', 'Golfing', 'Oct 1994', '2',
      'Y', '123 Siggr Blvd', ' ', 'LA', 'California', 'US',
        '20202'
go
```

The following statements display the results saved in the two tables:

```
select * from member
select * from address
go
```

Source Listing 11.3 deletes a logical member record. This requires that the customer and address tables be processed for the deletion.

The following example deletes a member record and the related address records based on a member_code number:

```
exec delete_member 200
go
```

```
/* Filename: memch11f.sql */

/* drop the stored procedure if it exists in the database. */
IF EXISTS (select name from sysobjects where name = 'delete_member')
    DROP PROC delete_member
go

/**********************************************/
/* Create the delete_member stored procedure */
/**********************************************/
CREATE PROC delete_member
(
    @member_no          int
)
AS
    DECLARE
    @return_code          int    /* variable names must begin with @ */

    /**************************************/
    /* Insert data validation tests here */
    /**************************************/

    /* delete all qualifying data rows in the address table */
    DELETE address
      WHERE member_no = @member_no

    /*********************************************************************/
    /* process errors reported by return_code */
    /*********************************************************************/

    /* delete the member data row */
    DELETE member
      WHERE member_no =@member_no

    /*********************************************************************/
    /* process errors reported by return_code */
    /*********************************************************************/

    RETURN 0    /* return a 0 code to the calling routine */
go
```

Source 11.3 Deleting a member.

The SELECT example in this section retrieves a logical member record based on a member_code. This is a common requirement for applications running on a client platform. There are two methods worth considering for satisfying this requirement.

The first method performs a join on the two tables and returns all the rows. The results are returned in a batch, so there can be many qualifying records in the batch. Each record will contain the same information belonging to the member portion of the logical record. The address portion of the record will change for each qualifying record in the address table.

The first method suffers from two primary drawbacks. The duplication of the member portion of the logical record sends unneeded data across the network, requiring both higher bandwidth and more processing power. Another drawback is that the selected data cannot be modified before being sent to the client platform. The second method for doing this is to retrieve all the records from the master table into local variables, perform the work required, and then to SELECT the local variables to the client platform. The qualifying records in the child table are then retrieved into local variables in a WHILE loop, manipulated, and also sent back to the client platform.

The following script provides a solution to the first method. A solution to the second method is described in Chapter 16.

```
/* Filename: memch11g.sql */

/* drop the stored procedure if it exists in the database. */
IF EXISTS (select name from sysobjects where name =
'selecta_member')
    DROP PROC selecta_member
go

/*******************************************/
/* Create the selecta_member stored procedure */
/*******************************************/
CREATE PROC selecta_member
(
   @member_no          int
)
AS
select a.member_no, a.last_name, b.address_code,
b.streeta, b.state
   from member a, address b
     where a.member_no = b.member_no and
           a.member_no = @member_no
RETURN 0   /* return a 0 code to the calling routine */
go
```

The following example retrieves a logical member record:

```
EXEC selecta_member 200
```

Recursive Stored Procedure Calls

In the following example, a method of recursive execution of the same stored procedure is demonstrated:

```
IF EXISTS (select name from sysobjects where name = 'recmember')
drop proc 'recmember'
go

create proc recmember
(
    @count          int
)
AS
    select * from member_code
    select @count = @count + 1

    if @count > 1000    /* set a maximum limit before the script ends */
        return 0

    select "@count = ", @count

    exec recmember @count   /* try removing the EXEC-does it still work? */
    return 0
go
```

The following example executes the recmember stored procedure. Notice that it ends when the maximum nested procedure limit is reached. By default, this is 32.

```
EXEC recmember 1
```

Summary

This chapter examined how to create, drop, and modify user-defined stored procedures. Stored procedures are one of the defining features that popularized SQL Server in the early 1990s. They both contain business logic and interact directly with the database. Stored procedures can be used to implement an n-tier application. This chapter reviewed experiences from numerous development projects. Stored procedures support sophisticated language constructs including a detailed control-of-flow language, DDL, DML, DCL, global variables, and functions.

Stored procedures are stored directly inside the SQL Server data dictionary and are specific to the database that holds their precompiled code. The code can be written using a common text-editor and then compiled all at once into SQL Server using an interactive utility or ISQL.

N-tier applications generally require small stored procedures that individually INSERT, DELETE, UPDATE, and SELECT information from relational tables. These stored procedures communicate to a middle layer which communicates with the user interface.

Despite alternative methods of doing the work of stored procedures, these continue to be powerful and popular extensions to the database standard for improving application performance and satisfying detailed application requirements.

Leveraging SQL Server Functions

SQL Server supports an extensive range and depth of functions that can be used in stored procedures, triggers, and as part of DML commands. The major areas that are discussed in this chapter include string functions, date/time functions, mathematical functions, and the convert function. Although the functions have the same behavior in SQL Server 7 as they did in earlier versions of the product, adjustments have been made for them to better support the current release. An example of this is the ability of the functions to support the larger column size in SQL Server 7. Functions return results based on input parameters. The results do not go anywhere unless they are captured in a variable, stored, or displayed using a command like select or print.

Creating a Test Environment

The examples in this section are based on a simple table that is created and populated here to demonstrate the use of the functions. The table can be refined by adding more fields, specifically to separate the manager and the message text. The table contains three columns. The first column contains the name of the manager on duty at a health club. Any special instructions can be appended to the name of the manager. The second column contains a count of the members who attended the club during the day. The third column contains the amount of money collected during that day. The following syntax creates a test environment with a couple of tables and some data:

```
/* Filename: chapter12.txt    */
use pubs
go

drop table chapter12a
go

create table chapter12a
(
      manager_name_message      char (80),
      attendance_count          int,
      daily_sales               money
)
go

insert chapter12a
values ('Joan Saily',5, $599)
go

insert chapter12a
values ('Rebecca Manny',10, $600)
go

insert chapter12a
values ('Bob Jones',15, $400)
go

insert chapter12a
values ('Tom Jaas',20, $300)
go


insert chapter12a
values (Karen Bouston,25, $200)
go

insert chapter12a
values (Karen Bouston,30, $100)
go

select 'count=', count(*), '  avg membership=', avg attendance_count),
 ' total sales = ', sum(daily_sales) from chapter12a

select manager_name_message, attendance_count, daily_sales from chapter12a
      WHERE manager_name_message != "end"
ORDER BY manager_name_message, attendance_count
COMPUTE AVG (attendance_count) by manager_name_message
go
```

Here is a reformatted view of the information that is displayed in response to a successful compilation and execution of these statements:

```
count= 6            avg membership= 17          total sales= 2199.0000
```

```
manager_name_message          attendance_count          daily_sales
Bob Jones                            15                    400.0000
avg
___
15
```

```
manager_name_message          attendance_count          daily_sales
Joan Saily                            5                    599.0000
avg
___
5
```

```
manager_name_message          attendance_count          daily_sales
Karen Bouston                        25                    200.0000
Karen Bouston                        30                    100.0000
avg
___
27
```

```
manager_name_message          attendance_count          daily_sales
Rebecca Manny                        10                    600.0000
avg
___
10
```

```
manager_name_message          attendance_count          daily_sales
Tom Jaas                             20                    300.0000
avg
___
20
```

 Functions support complex nesting in expressions, statements, and data manipulation language.

String Functions

A string is a set of letters, numbers, and special characters. String functions perform operations against variables declared as text or characters. These functions, described in Table 12.1, can be used as filters to display information or to make changes to text or character information permanently. For example, to reformat string information, a generic format is the following: select string_function (string), and select string_function (column_name) from table. To make a permanent change to a string format, use the following generic format: select @variable1 = string_function (@variable2), and select

Table 12.1   String Functions

FUNCTION NAME	DESCRIPTION	EXAMPLES
ASCII	Returns the ASCII value of the first letter in the parameter.	ASCII (parameter_value) Select ASCII ('Z')
CHAR	Returns the CHAR value of the ASCII parameter.	CHAR (parameter_value) Select char (90)
SOUNDEX	Returns a numeric value for a string based on the way it sounds. Use two SOUNDEX functions to generate two numeric expressions. Compare the numeric expressions to establish how closely they sound.	SOUNDEX (parameter1) Select soundex ('c') Select soundex ('see') Select soundex ('sea') /* notice that 'see' and 'sea' produce the same value */
DIFFERENCE	Returns an integer value up to 4 based on the differences between two strings. A value of 0 means the least similarity.	DIFFERENCE (param1, param2) Select difference ('c', 'sea') Select difference ('see', 'sea') /* a value of 4 shows a high degree of similarity in the sound */
LOWER	Returns the lowercase representation of the parameter.	LOWER (parameter_value) Select LOWER ('CONVERT TO LOWER CASE')
UPPER	Returns the uppercase representation of the parameter.	UPPER (parameter_value) Select UPPER ('convert to upper case') Select upper (manager_name_message) from chapter12a
RTRIM	Removes blank characters from the right side of a string.	RTRIM (parameter_value) Select RTRIM ('get ') + ' ' + 'Started'
LTRIM	Removes blank characters from the beginning of the string.	LTRIM (parameter_value) Select 'Started'+' '+LTRIM ('get ')
CHARINDEX	Returns the position of 'key' in the parameter_value. The position offset is from the left side of the string starting with 1.	CHARINDEX ('key', parameter_value) Select Charindex ('f', 'abcdefghijklm')
PATINDEX	Returns the first occurrence of a string in the parameter_value string, 0 otherwise. The position offset is from the left side of the string starting with 1.	PATINDEX ('%value%', parameter_value) Select Patindex ("%as%", "the tree is as a leaf")

Table 12.1 (*Continued*)

FUNCTION NAME	DESCRIPTION	EXAMPLES
REPLICATE	Replicates a character string a specified number of times and returns the full expanded string.	REPLICATE (parameter_value, number) Select Replicate ("aeiou-", 7)
REVERSE	Returns the string contained in parameter_value in reverse format.	REVERSE (parameter_value) Select REVERSE ('loop')
RIGHT	Returns a string that is extracted from the parameter_value starting with an offset from the right of the parameter_value string.	RIGHT (parameter_value, offset) Select right ("1234567890", 4)
SPACE	Returns a blank character string of a specified size.	SPACE (number_of_spaces) Select space (79)
STR	Returns a character value converted from a numeric value.	STR (parameter1, size, precision) Select str (100, 7, 2)
STUFF	Replaces a string expression by another string expression in a parameter_value string starting at a specific offset.	STUFF (parameter_value, offset, size, char_to_insert) Select stuff ("1234567890", 4,2,"BTB")

string_function. The first example captures the value returned from the function and saves it in a variable for subsequent use. The second example displays the value that is returned by the function. String expressions can be concatenated with the "+" sign.

Another important string function is SUBSTRING, with the following syntax. This function uses the offset as a position within the parameter_value string and returns a string of size number_of_characters. Parameter_value can be a string expression, a table column, or a variable. SUBSTRING can also be used with text and image data. Following is the syntax for the SUBSTRING function:

```
SUBSTRING (parameter_value, offset, size)
```

The following example extracts a subset of characters from the string 'this is a sentence', with a length of 5 characters from an offset of 2.

```
select substring ('this is a sentence', 2, 5)
go

declare @fragment    char (50)
select @fragment = ('this is a sentence', 2, 5)
go

declare @fragment    char (50)
select @fragment = ('this is a sentence', 2, 1000)
go
```

```
select substring ('this is a sentence', -2, 5)
go
```

Aggregate Functions

The aggregate functions that are available in Transact-SQL are shown in Table 12.2. The basic syntax for using aggregate functions is the following: function SWITCHES parameter_values. Switches can have a value of ALL or DISTINCT. Since ALL is the default it normally does not need to be specified. The Distinct switch is applied to the parameter_values to produce a list of unique numbers that are then passed to the function. Parameter_values can be a number list, table_column, or variable_list.

Mathematical Functions

The mathematical functions available in Transact-SQL are shown in Table 12.3.

Table 12.2 Aggregate Functions

FUNCTION NAME	DESCRIPTION	EXAMPLES
AVG	Computes the average of the parameter_values.	AVG (parameter_value) Select avg (attendance_count) from chapter12a
COUNT	Returns a count of the number of entries in the parameter_values.	COUNT(parameter_value) Select count (*) from chapter12a
MAX	Returns the maximum value in the parameter_values.	MAX (parameter_value) Select max (daily_sales) from chapter12a
MIN	Returns the minimum value in the parameter_values.	MIN (parameter_value) Select min (daily_sales) from chapter12a
SUM	Returns a sum of all the parameter_values.	SUM (parameter_value) Select sum(daily_sales) from chapter12a
SIGN	Returns the sign of the parameter value.	SIGN (parameter_value) Select sign (-12) Select sign (12)
DISTINCT	Removes duplicates from the parameter_values and returns unique numbers.	DISTINCT (parameter_list) Select distinct (manager_name_message) from chapter12a

Table 12.3   Mathematical Functions

FUNCTION NAME	DESCRIPTION	EXAMPLES
ACOS	Returns an ACOS value.	ACOS(parameter_value) Select acos (0)
ASIN	Returns the ASIN value.	ASIN(parameter_value) Select asin (0)
ATAN	Returns the ATAN value.	ATAN(parameter_value) Select atan (0)
COS	Returns the COS value.	COS(parameter_value) Select cos (0)
COT	Returns the COT value.	COT(parameter_value) Select cot (90)
SIN	Returns the SIN value.	SIN(parameter_value) Select sin (0)
TAN	Returns the TAN value.	TAN(parameter_value) Select tan (0)
RADIANS	Converts degrees to radians.	RADIANS (parameter_value) Select radians (90)
DEGREES	Converts radians to degrees.	DEGREES (parameter_value) Select degrees (90)
CEILING	Rounds the integer to the next integer value. Useful when estimating resources.	CEILING (parameter_value) Select ceiling (15.1243)
FLOOR	Returns the integer portion of the number.	FLOOR (parameter_value) Select floor (15.1243)
EXP	Returns an exponential value.	EXP (parameter_value) Select exp(2)
LOG	Returns a log value.	LOG (parameter_value) Select log (1)
LOG10	Returns a log value to a base 10.	LOG10 (parameter_value) Select log10 (1)
PI	Returns the value of pi.	PI () Select pi()
POWER	Returns the value of a number to its power (a to the power of b).	POWER (a, b) Select power (2,4)
SQRT	Returns the square root of the parameter_value.	SQRT (parameter_value) Select sqrt (9)
ABS	Returns the absolute value of the parameter.	ABS(parameter_value) Select abs(−9)
RAND	Returns a random number between 0 and 1, based on the parameter.	RAND (seed_number) Select rand (.3)
ROUND	Returns the rounded value of the parameter to the precision that is specified.	ROUND (param_value, precision) Select round (pi (), 2)

Table 12.4 Date/Time Functions

FUNCTION NAME	DESCRIPTION	EXAMPLES
GETDATE()	Returns the current date and time.	GETDATE() Select 'Today is:', getdate()
DATEADD	Adds two dates together and returns the value specified in the date_component (e.g., days, months, years).	DATEADD (date_component, number, date) Select dateadd (dy, 7, getdate()) /* date next week */
DATEDIFF	Returns the difference between two date fields in the units specified in date_component (e.g., days, months, years).	DATEDIFF (date_component, d1, d2) Select datediff (dy, getdate(), dateadd (dy, 7, getdate()))
DATENAME	Returns the name of the date component identified in the syntax.	DATENAME (date_component, d1) Select datename (dy, getdate()) Select datename (dd, getdate()) Select datename (dw, getdate())
DATEPART	Returns the value of the date component that is identified in the syntax in a numeric format.	DATEPART (date_component, d1) Select datename (dy, getdate()) Select datename (dd, getdate()) Select datename (dw, getdate())

Date/Time Functions

SQL Server supports an extensive list of data/time formats and functions that are examined in Table 12.4. A full date in SQL Server is of the format Oct 1 1999 23:59:45. The components of the date in this example are divided into the date portion and the time portion. The date portion has the following components: yy, year; qq, quarter; mm, month; dy, a value from 1 to 366; dd, a value from 1 to 31; wk, week; dw, a value from 1 to 7. The time portion has the following components: hh, hour; mi, minute; ss, second; ms, millisecond.

Convert

This important function is used to convert one datatype value to another database value. This function is needed in cases such as when trying to add two datatypes together, they must be compatible. This is true even with string variables. SQL Server handles some conversions automatically. Convert is required in the cases where this is not done. The Microsoft Transact-SQL manual contains a matrix that shows implicit/

explicit conversion requirements. In general, datatypes that are obvious mismatches, such as money to char, require a conversion. Datatypes like float to int require a conversion. The syntax for this function is the following:

```
CONVERT (datatype length, expr. , style)
```

Sample Scripts

The following example demonstrates a common problem that is encountered when trying to display a concatenated string. This can occur if you want to display a message preceding the value of a variable that is printed. Suppose you want to display the contents of a float variable @temperature, but want to display a meaningful tag line. Using the following syntax displays the results in an unformatted string:

```
Declare @temperature  float
select @temperature = 25.0
Select 'The current temperature is ', @temperature
Go
```

The display format can be improved by concatenating the values together using the "+" operator, as in: select 'The current temperature is ' + @temperature. However, this results in a datatype mismatch error that can be corrected with the convert command, as follows:

```
Declare @temperature  float
select @temperature = 25.0
Select 'The current temperature is ' + convert (char (3), @temperature)
Go
```

The following example results in an improved format:

```
The current temperature is 25
```

The following example returns the first 10 characters of the data from the left side:

```
Select convert (char(10), getdate())
```

The following example converts a decimal number to an integer:

```
Select convert (int, 82.2918338)
```

System Functions

The values in the system functions can be inspected using the select command with the code SELECT FUNCTION_NAME (parameter_list). An example of this syntax is SELECT HOST_NAME(). Table 12.5 describes the system function names with examples of their use.

Table 12.5   System Functions

SYSTEM FUNCTION NAME	DESCRIPTION	EXAMPLES
HOST_NAME	Returns the number of the client.	HOST_NAME() Select host_name()
SUSER_ID	Returns the login ID number based on a login name.	SUSER_ID('login') Select suser_id ('sa')
SUSER_NAME	Returns the login ID name . based on an ID	SUSER_NAME(id#) Select suser_name (suser_id ('sa'))
USER_ID	Returns the login ID based on a login name at the database level.	USER_ID('user') Select user_id ('sa')
USER_NAME	Returns the login ID name based on an ID at the database level.	USER_NAME(id#) Select user_name ( )
DB_NAME	Returns a database name given a database ID.	DB_NAME(db_id) Select db_name (db_id('master'))
DB_ID	Contains a database identification number.	DB_ID('db_name') Select db_id ('master')
GETANSINULL	Returns a 1 if a database has ANSI NULLIBILITY.	GETANSINULL(db_name) Select getansinull ('model')
OBJECT_ID	Returns an object's ID number based on an object name.	OBJECT_ID ('name') Select object_id ('pubs')
OBJECT_NAME	Returns an object's name based on an ID number.	OBJECT_NAME (id#) Select object_name(object_id ('pubs'))
INDEX_COL	Returns the name of an indexed column.	INDEX_COL ('table', indexid, keyid)
COL_LENGTH	Returns the length of a column given a table name and a column name.	COL_LENGTH ('table', 'column') Select col_length ('sysobjects', 'type')
COL_NAME	Returns the name of a column based on a table ID and a column ID.	COL_NAME (tableid, col_id)
DATALENGTH	Returns the length of the data in a variable.	DATALENGTH ('param1')
IDENT_INCR	Returns the increment value for the table's only IDENTITY column.	IDENT_INCR ('table')
IDENT_SEED	Returns the seed value for a table's only IDENTITY column.	IDENT_SEED ('table')
STATS_DATE	Returns the last date that statistics were updated for the index that is identified in the parameter.	STATS_DATE (table, index)
ISNULL	Used to replace NULL values.	ISNULL (parameter_value, replace_by)
APP_NAME	Displays the name of the current application (e.g., MS SQL Query Analyzer)	APP_NAME() Select app_name()

Table 12.6   User Related System Functions

SYSTEM FUNCTION NAME	DESCRIPTION	EXAMPLES
USER	Contains the role of the user.	Select user
CURRENT_USER	Contains the role of the current user.	Select current_user
SESSION_USER	Contains the role of the session user.	Select session_user
SYSTEM_USER	Contains the username of the system user.	Select system_user

The variables listed in Table 12.6 can be inspected with the select statement as follows: SELECT VARIABLE. An example of this command statement is SELECT USER.

System Procedures

System procedures are really stored procedures that are already built for you to administer and interact with the SQL Server environment. System procedures are prefaced by an sp_. The bulk of the system procedures are stored in the master database. It is recommended that all user-defined stored procedures avoid using this prefix. It is also recommended that you never modify the system procedures yourself. The following code displays the system procedures in the master database. A value of 'P' in the type field means that the entry is a stored procedure. A value of 'X' identifies the extended system procedures. Extended system procedures also have a prefix of xp_. The Transact-SQL code belonging to a stored procedure can be displayed with the statement sp_helptext sp_who.

```
use master
go

select name, type from sysobjects
     where type = 'P' OR type = 'X'
go
```

This command produces a list of 797 rows for my version of SQL Server 7. A selection of the useful system procedures are included in this section. To display information about system procedures, especially the number of input parameters that are expected by the procedure, use the following code:

```
sp_help system_procedure_name
e.g. sp_help sp_who
```

This displays the following reformatted information. Notice that the sp_who system procedure accepts one parameter of length 256 characters:

```
Name              Owner      Type              Created_datetime
sp_who            dbo        stored procedure  1998-06-19 00:25:58.870


Parameter_name    Type       Length            Prec   Scale   Param_order
@loginame         sysname    256               128    NULL    1
```

Help Functions

The following system procedures inspect the system tables and environment and provide help:

sp_help. This is the most basic help command. It reports information about database objects. The syntax for using this command is sp_help parameter_name. Parameter_name can be blank or the name of an existing object. A blank parameter displays the contents of sysobjects and is similar to using the select * from sysobjects statement.

sp_helptext. This command can be used to construct the Transact-SQL code for database objects. This code is saved in the syscomments system table. The syntax for using this command is sp_helptext object_name.

sp_helpdb. This command provides information about the database objects recorded in the sysdatabases system table in the master database. The syntax for using this command is sp_helpdb db_name. A blank parameter displays information about all the databases. db_name is the name of a database. An example of using this command is sp_helpdb address.

sp_helpstartup. This command provides information about automatic startup procedures. The syntax for using this command is sp_helpstartup.

sp_helpgroup. This command provides information on groups in the environment. The syntax for using this command is sp_helpgroup group_name.

sp_helplog. This command provides information about transaction logs. The syntax for using this command is sp_helplog.

sp_helpconstraint. This command is used to report information about constraints that are created for a table. The syntax for using this command is sp_helpconstraint name_of_table. An example of using this command is sp_helpconstraint address_type.

sp_helpdevice. This command was used in previous versions of SQL Server to display information about devices. The syntax for using this command is sp_helpdevice.

sp_helpfile. This command is used to map the current database to the external physical files and the filegroups. The information shows the fully named operating system files that are used to store the current database. The syntax for using this command is sp_helpfile.

sp_helplogins. This command displays information about logins across the environment. The syntax for using this command is sp_helplogins login.

sp_helpindex. This command provides information on the indexes on tables. The syntax for using this command is sp_helpindex tablename.

sp_helptrigger. This command provides information about triggers on tables. The syntax for using this command is sp_helptrigger table_name.

sp_helpuser. This command operates at the local database level and displays the users that can access the database. The syntax for using this command is sp_helpuser user_name.

sp_helpremotelogin. This command provides information about remote server logins. The syntax for using this command is sp_helpremotelogin remote_server, remote_name.

sp_helpsort. This command provides information about sort orders. The syntax for using this command is sp_helpsort.

sp_helpserver. This command provides information about remote servers. The syntax for using this command is sp_helpserver server.

sp_help_index. This command displays information about table indexes. The syntax for using this command is sp_helpindex table.

sp_helprolemember. This command displays information about the roles and owners in a database. The syntax for using this command is sp_helprolemember.

sp_helpsql. This command can be used to display syntactical information about statements. The syntax for using this command is sp_helpsql search_category.

sp_helprole. This command displays information about the roles in the current environment. The syntax for using this command is sp_helprole role_id.

sp_helplanguage. This command reports information about the languages supported by SQL Server. The syntax for using this command is sp_helplanguage lang_name.

sp_helpextendedproc. This command displays information about extended stored procedures, also identifying the defining DLL. The syntax for using this command is sp_helpextendedproc module.

sp_helprotect. This commands displays permission information for objects. The syntax for using this command is sp_helprotect object_name, u_name.

The syntax of these system procedures generally follows the format shown here:

```
sp_system_procedure [optional_parameter]
```

Entering the name of the system procedure with no parameter displays a list of the objects. Entering the system procedure with a parameter displays information about that specific object.

Environment Information Functions

Environment information functions retrieve information from system tables:

sp_who. This command displays information about who is using the current environment. The syntax for using this command is sp_who login | process_id.

sp_who2. This command displays an expanded version of who is using the current environment. The syntax for using this command is sp_who2.

sp_stored_procedures. This command displays information about stored procedures. The syntax for using this command is sp_stored_procedures proc_name.

sp_spaceused. This command displays information about the space used by objects. The syntax for using this command is sp_spaceused object_name.

sp_depends. This command provides information about object dependencies. The syntax for using this command is sp_depends object_name.

sp_processinfo. This command provides information about processes. The syntax for using this command is sp_processinfo.

sp_catalogs. This command provides information about system catalogs in a database server. The syntax for using this command is sp_catalogs.

sp_columns. This command displays information about columns in tables. The syntax for using this command is sp_columns object, column_name.

sp_tables. This command displays information about database objects. The syntax for using this command is sp_tables table.

sp_databases. This command displays information databases in the environment. The syntax for using this command is sp_databases db_name.

Administrative Functions

The following administrative functions perform administrative tasks and generally update system tables:

sp_dboption. This command is used to modify database options. The syntax for using this command is sp_dboption database_name, option_name, TRUE I FALSE.

sp_renamedb. This command is used to rename a database. The syntax for using this command is sp_renamedb old_database_name new_database_name.

sp_rename. This command is used to rename a database object. The syntax for using this command is sp_rename old_object_name, new_object_name, COLUMN, INDEX.

sp_attach_db. This new SQL Server 7 command is used to attach an external database file to the database server environment.

sp_detach_db. This new SQL Server 7 command is used to detach a database file from the database server environment.

sp_db_upgrade. This command is used to upgrade a previous database version to SQL Server 7. The syntax for using this command is sp_db_upgrade db_name.

sp_dbremove. This command is used to remove a database from the environment. The syntax for using this command is sp_dbremove database.

sp_remove_tempdb_file. This command is used to remove tempdb files from the environment.

sp_changeobjectowner. This command is used to change an object's owner.

sp_changedbowner. This command is used to modify the identity of the database owner. The syntax for using this command is sp_changedbowner login, true.

sp_addextendedproc. This command is used to add an extended stored procedure to the environment. The syntax for using this command is sp_addextendedproc stored_procedure.

sp_dropextendedproc. This command is used to remove an extended stored procedure. The syntax for using this command is sp_dropextendedproc store_procedure.

sp_create_removable. This command is used to build a removable database (e.g., on a writeable CD ROM). The syntax for using this command is sp_create_removable database_name, physical information.

sp_dropserver. This command is used to drop a server from the environment. The syntax for using this command is sp_dropserver server.

sp_addserver. This command is used to identify a remote server. The syntax for using this command is sp_addserver servername, LOCAL.

sp_datatype_info. This command is used to display information about datatypes.

sp_objectfilegroup. This command is used to manage objects, files, and groups.

sp_tempdbspace. This command is used to manage tempdbspace.

Object Maintenance Functions

The following system functions create constraints, rules, and cursors:

sp_unbindefault. This command is used to unbind defaults from a datatype or table column. The syntax for using this command is sp_unbindefault object_name.

sp_unbindrule. This command is used to unbind a rule from a datatype or rule. The syntax for using this command is sp_unbindrule object_name.

sp_bindefault. This command is used to bind defaults to datatypes or columns. The syntax for using this command is sp_bindefault default_name, object_name.

sp_bindrule. This command is used to bind a rule to a datatype or column. The syntax for using this command is sp_bindrule rule_name, object_name.

sp_addalias. This command is used to create an alias so that a user can appear as another in a database. The syntax for using this command is sp_addalias login, user_name.

sp_dropalias. This command drops an alias from a database. The syntax for using this command is sp_dropalias login.

sp_addtype. This command is used to define a user-defined database. The syntax for using this command is sp_addtype type_name, phsyical_type.

sp_droptype. This command is use to drop a datatype from the environment. The syntax for using this command is sp_droptype datatype.

sp_addmessage. This command adds an error message to the sysmessages system tables which makes it accessible to the raiserror message. The syntax for using this command is sp_addmessage message_id, severity, "message", language, WITH_LOG, REPLACE.

sp_dropmessage. This command is used to drop a error message. The syntax for using this command is sp_dropmessage message_id.

sp_altermessage. This command is used to modify the state of an existing error message. The syntax for using this command is sp_altermessage messageid, WITH_LOG, TRUE | FALSE.

sp_addgroup. This command creates a group that consists of a set of users that can be administered together. The syntax for using this command is sp_addgroup group_name.

sp_dropgroup. This command drops a group from the environment. The syntax for using this command is sp_dropgroup group_name.

sp_changegroup. This command transfers a user from one group to another. The syntax for using this command is sp_changegroup group_name, user_name.

Indexes and Keys

The following functions manage indexes and keys in the environment:

sp_primarykeys. This command displays a primary key for an object.

sp_foreignkeys. This command displays the foreign key for an object.

sp_fkeys. This command displays foreign key information. The syntax for using this command is sp_fkeys table_primarykey, table_foreignkey.

sp_fixindex. This command attempts to fix a corrupted index without having to re-build it from scratch.

sp_indexes. This command shows the indexes allocated to a table.

sp_pkeys. This command displays information about primary keys. The syntax for using this command is sp_pkeys table.

sp_indexoption. This command adjusts index options.

sp_table_privileges. This command displays privilege information about tables. The syntax for using this command is sp_table_privileges table.

Roles, Users, Security, and Permission Functions

The following functions manage roles, users, security, and permissions in the environment:

sp_addrole. This command adds a role to the environment.

sp_droprole. This command drops a role from the environment.

sp_addlogin. This command is used to add a new user to the SQL Server environment. The syntax for using this command is sp_addlogin login, password, default_database, default_language.

sp_droplogin. This command is used to drop login IDs from the default database. The syntax for using this command is sp_droplogin login.

sp_grantlogin. This command is used to grant login privileges to a login.

sp_revokelogin. This command is used to remove login privileges from a login.

sp_adduser. This command is used to add a user to a database. This is a companion command to the sp_addlogin, and generally is executed after it. The syntax for using this command is sp_adduser login, user_name, groupname.

sp_dropuser. This command drops a user from the default database. The syntax for using this command is sp_dropuser user.

sp_dropremotelogin. This command is used to drop a remove login. The syntax for using this command is sp_dropremotelogin server, login.

sp_addremotelogin. This command is used to create a remote login ID. The syntax for using this command is sp_addremotelogin remote_server, login, remotename.

sp_grantdbaccess. This command is used to grant database access to a user.

sp_revokedbaccess. This command is used to revoke database access from a user.

sp_password. This command is used to modify passwords for a login ID. The syntax for using this command is sp_password old_password, new_password, loginid.

sp_column_privileges. This command displays information about privileges at the table column level. The syntax for using this command is sp_column_privileges table.

Changing Defaults and Options

The following functions change defaults and options in the environment:

sp_configure. This command is used to modify configuration values. The values generally become effective after a reconfigure command is issued. The syntax for using this command is sp_configure configuration_variable_name, new_value.

sp_defaultdb. This command is used to change a user ID's default database. The syntax for using this command is sp_defaultdb login, default_database.

sp_defaultlanguage. This command is used to modify the default language for a user. The syntax for using this command is sp_defaultlanguage login, language.

sp_tableoption. This command is used to adjust the table options.

sp_remoteoption. This command is used to update remote login information. The syntax for using this command is sp_remoteoption server, login, remote_name, Option_name, TRUE | FALSE.

sp_diskdefault. This command is used to modify the default disk.

sp_serveroption. This command is used to establish server options. The syntax for using this command is sp_serveroption name, option_name, true | false. The option_name can be dist, dput, pub, rpc, or sub.

sp_makestartup. This command is used to identify stored procedures that are automatically executed when SQL Server is started. The syntax for using this command is sp_makestartup stored_procedure. The syntax for removing the startup status is sp_unmakestartup name.

Statistics Functions

The following functions manage statistics in the SQL Server environment:

sp_statistics. This command displays information about table indexes. The syntax for using this command is sp_statistics table.

sp_estimate. This command is used to estimate space requirements.

sp_autostats. This command is used to display information about the auto-statistics status of a table. The syntax for using this command is sp_autostats tablename.

sp_updatestats. This command is used to update statistics on an object.

sp_createstats. This command is used to create statistics for an object.

Performance Functions

The following functions manage and monitor performance:

sp_monitor. This command displays statistical information about the environment, including total_reads, total_writes, and number of connections. The syntax for using this command is sp_monitor.

sp_recompile. This command is used to identify a user table in the default database so that all stored procedures and triggers that access that table will be recompiled for optimization before their next execution. The syntax for using this command is sp_recompile table_name.

sp_lock. This command displays information about locks in the environment. The syntax for using this command is sp_lock processid1, processid2.

sp_lockinfo. This command is used to display information about locks in the environment. The syntax for using this command is sp_lockinfo.

Summary

This chapter focused on built-in functions and system procedures. SQL Server supports a broad range of built-in functions that can be classified as string functions, date/time functions, mathematical functions, and the convert function. Functions can be used interactively, within stored procedures, and within triggers. When used within applications, functions return values that can be saved in local or global variables and subsequently manipulated within applications.

System procedures are stored procedures that are packaged and installed with SQL Server. This chapter provided definitions for some of the commonly used system procedures. System procedures inspect or manipulate information that is stored in system tables. System procedures often accept parameters and return additional information about the parameter. The procedures belonging to the HELP class are particularly useful.

CHAPTER 13

Triggering Events

Triggers are stored procedures that are created and related to specific database table events including table insert events, table delete events, and table update events. Triggers also have a similarity to constraints in that both can be used to maintain data and referential integrity. Triggers, however, are able to handle more complex code than constraints. Triggers can also be programmed to communicate outside the database. Whenever these operations are applied against a table, the associated trigger fires and executes the code belonging to the trigger. Since triggers are stored procedures, they support most of the Transact-SQL commands that regular stored procedures support. Some exceptions are discussed later in this chapter. Figure 13.1 shows the components of a trigger and how triggers are fired. The operation of triggers is simple, but their effect is powerful in terms of data validation, referential integrity, and table synchronization. They can be used to roll back a transaction or insert records in other tables. They can also be used in cascading operations (inserts/deletes), code reuse, transaction rollbacks, and simplified development, and to insert datatypes into type tables.

SQL Server 7 not only continues to support triggers, but it includes some useful enhancements that improve the flexibility that they offer:

Multiple triggers for the same event can be allocated to database tables.

Triggers can be fired recursively.

Triggers can fire other triggers.

This is direct recursion (e.g., trigger1-trigger2-trigger1-trigger2). Trigger recursion is activated through the sp_dboption feature.

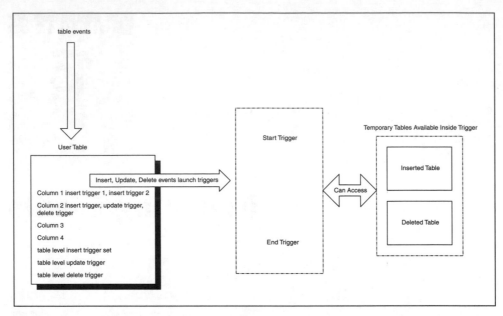

Figure 13.1 Trigger components and operations.

Trigger Syntax

Triggers are stored procedures, but not all stored procedures are triggers. Consequently they can be written in the same way that stored procedures are written. Triggers are compiled and stored in the data dictionary belonging to a specific database. A record is saved into the sysobjects table for every trigger and can be identified with the following code:

```
Select * from sysobjects where type = 'TR'.
```

Triggers are fired by specific events that occur on a table or a table column. Triggers can access two intermediate tables—inserted and deleted—which are available until the trigger completes. Insert operations use the inserted trigger table. Delete operations use the deleted trigger table. Update operations use both the inserted and deleted trigger tables. Reference these two tables using the specific spelling in inserted and deleted for the inserted and deleted tables, respectively. These tables contain columns to match the data rows being processed.

While triggers are created using a process that is similar to stored procedures, they are executed differently. Stored procedures are executed explicitly using the EXEC command, while triggers are executed implicitly due to specific events occurring against a table. The syntax for creating triggers is as follows:

```
CREATE TRIGGER [owner].trigger_name
    ON owner.table_name
```

```
            FOR [INSERT/UPDATE/DELETE]/[INSERT/UPDATE]
    AS

            [IF UPDATE (column_field) [AND/OR column_field(s)]]
            commands
```

 The sp_configure system procedure can be used to set nested triggers to change the default nested level value.

The syntax for dropping triggers is as follows:

```
DROP TRIGGER [owner].trigger
```

 Environment variable values are also changed during the trigger. When inspecting an environment variable, do so before the variables are modified by commands that are executed inside the trigger. The values of the environment variable are local to the trigger.

Sample Scripts

The following example creates a trigger that fires when an employee record is deleted so a warning and reminder to the user to resave the record is displayed. Use the employee1 table that was created in Chapter 8.

```
use pubs
go

drop trigger trdelete_employee
go

drop table employee1
    go

    CREATE TABLE employee1
(
    employee_no int, last_name   char(30), first_name   char(30),
 start_date datetime, salary money, last_promotion_date datetime
)
go
    CREATE UNIQUE CLUSTERED INDEX emp_employee_no_ndx1 ON
employee1 (employee_no)
    Go

CREATE TRIGGER trdelete_employee
ON employee1
FOR DELETE
AS
          IF @@rowcount <= 0 /* no records found */
    PRINT ('Employee not found. No records deleted')
```

```
ELSE
PRINT ('Employee Deleted. Save screen image to undelete employee.')
go
```

Ensure that the trigger was parsed successfully into the database by inspecting several system tables, including sysobjects and syscomments. This can be accomplished as follows. The first select confirms that a trigger with the given name has been inserted into the sysobjects system table belonging to the current database. The sp_helptext system procedure retrieves the statements belonging to the trigger from the syscomments table, where they are stored:

```
select * from sysobjects where name = 'trdelete_employee'
go


sp_helptext trdelete_employee
go
```

The row associated with the table that fires the trigger is updated in the sysobjects table. The following SQL command displays the modified column containing the ID of the delete trigger that was created above. Notice that the SQL code also displays the columns for other triggers (e.g., insert, update) that could be created for the table as well. The deltrig column in the sysobjects system table contains the ID of the trigger selected by the join with the syscomments table:

```
select name, id, deltrig, instrig, updtrig, seltrig
    from sysobjects where name = "customer"
```

A join command can be used to retrieve the trigger text from the syscomments table. The name of the trigger is contained in the sysobjects table. The join finds this reference and then joins to the child records in the syscomments table. There are multiple data rows for every trigger that is represented in that table:

```
SELECT a.type, b.text
    FROM sysobjects a, syscomments b
        WHERE a.name = 'trdelete_employee' AND
            a.id = b.id
go
```

This join command displays the following results in the Results tab of the Microsoft SQL Server Query Analyzer:

```
type    text
--      ----------------------------------------
TR    create trigger trdelete_employee
ON employee1
FOR DELETE
AS
  IF @@rowcount < 1
    PRINT ('Employee not found. No records employee.')
```

```
    ELSE
        PRINT ("Employee Deleted. Save screen image to undelete employee.")
```

The following example tests the trdelete_employee trigger by creating a table that was used in Chapter 8, creating and inserting test data, and then deleting a record from that table:

```
insert employee1
(
    employee_no, last_name, first_name,
 start_date, salary, last_promotion_date
)
values
    (
     1, 'Sector', 'Sam', 'Jan 1 1995', 100000, getdate()
    )

insert employee1
(
    employee_no, last_name, first_name,
 start_date, salary, last_promotion_date
)
values
    (
     2, 'Flanders', 'Marsha', 'Feb 1 1996', 200000, getdate()
    )

insert employee1
(
    employee_no, last_name, first_name,
 start_date, salary, last_promotion_date
)
values
    (
     3, 'Ryder', 'Steve', 'Mar 1 1995', 50000, getdate()
    )

/* display the data rows in the employee1 table */
select * from employee1

delete employee1                    /* test the delete trigger */
    where employee_no = 2
go

/* Successfully displays the following message: Employee Deleted. Save
screen image to undelete employee. The row with employee_no = 2 is deleted */
```

The following example displays all of the dependencies on the employee1 table:

```
sp_depends employee1
go
```

Maintaining Referential Integrity

The insert trigger is useful for inserting information into related tables to ensure referential integrity. For example, suppose that a record is being inserted into one table that references another table. Instead of appending, a trigger can be built to create an audit record and to insert a placeholder into the referenced table The trigger declares a local variable that is used to determine if an advisor exists for a subject. If the advisor does not exist, the trigger logs the need to do this. The example developed in this section uses several passes to complete the process to better illustrate an iterative method of developing the complete trigger. The example is designed to clear the data and drop the tables before building them so that the batches can be rerun without constraints.

 Triggers must be included in their own batches. A batch includes all statements between two go statements.

Sample Script

Source Listing 13.1 is the first phase of the example. It creates a series of batches, the tables, an insert trigger and then inserts data into the primary table.

```
use pubs
go

drop trigger tradd_subject1
drop table subject1
drop table tracking1
drop table advisor1
go

create table subject1
(subject_code char(10), description char(50), instructor_code char(10))

create table advisor1
(advisor_code char(10), advisor_name char(50), contact_no char(11))

create table tracking1
(event_time datetime, event_type    char(20), caller char(20),
                                              description char(80) )
go

/* create a trigger */
CREATE TRIGGER tradd_subject1
   ON SUBJECT1 FOR INSERT
   AS
```
(Continues)

Source 13.1 Phase 1: Creating an Insert Trigger.

```
      DECLARE
            @advisor_code      char(10)

      /* display some information messages */
            /* notice that the columns in the INSERTED table match the
columns in the data row initiating the trigger. The same is true for
the DELETED table. */

            Print 'inserting a subject record'
      Select 'about to display the contents of the INSERTED trigger table'
      Select * from inserted
      Select 'about to display the contents of the deleted trigger table'
      Select * from deleted

      /* display the fields in the inserted table */
      SELECT subject_code, description, instructor_code
            FROM INSERTED

   Go
/* attempt to insert a subject1 data row */
insert subject1
(subject_code, description, instructor_code)
values
('sci101', 'science 101', 'davis')
go

Print '——- here are the table contents ——'
select * from subject1
select * from advisor1
select * from tracking1
```

Source 13.1 *(Continued)*

Source Listing 13.2 shows the second phase of the example. This modifies the insert trigger to examine the reference table and take appropriate action if a reference data row is not found. The information messages are removed from the trigger in this phase.

```
use pubs
go

drop trigger tradd_subject1
drop table subject1
drop table tracking1
drop table advisor1
go
```
(Continues)

Source 13.2 Phase 2: Enhancing the trigger script.

```
create table subject1
(subject_code char(10), description char(50), instructor_code char(10))

create table advisor1
(advisor_code char(10), advisor_name char(50), contact_no char(11))

create table tracking1
(event_time datetime, event_type   char(20), caller char(20),
                                              description char(80) )
go

/* create a trigger */
CREATE TRIGGER tradd_subject1
   ON SUBJECT1 FOR INSERT
   AS
      DECLARE @advisor_code      char(10)

      select @advisor_code = instructor_code
             from INSERTED

      select '@advisor_code = ', @advisor_code

      IF EXISTS (select advisor_code from advisor1 where
                              advisor_code = @advisor_code)
      BEGIN
              Select 'record is already there'
      END
      ELSE
      BEGIN
              Select 'record is not there'
              INSERT advisor1
                    (advisor_code, advisor_name, contact_no)
              VALUES
                    (@advisor_code, 'place holder',
                        convert (char(11), getdate()))

              INSERT tracking1
                    (event_time, event_type, caller, description)
              VALUES
                    (convert(char(20), getdate()), 'INSERT',
                     'TRADD_SUBJECT1', 'advisor not on file ' +
                                              @advisor_code)

      END

      /* display the fields in the inserted table */
      SELECT subject_code, description, instructor_code
             FROM INSERTED
   Go
```

(Continues)

Source 13.2 *(Continued)*

```
/* insert a data row into the subject1 table */
insert subject1
(subject_code, description, instructor_code)
values
('sci101', 'science 101', 'davis')
go

Print '—— here are the table contents ——'
select * from subject1
select * from advisor1
select * from tracking1
```

Source 13.2 *(Continued)*

Source Listing 13.3 is the third phase. This removes the intermediate message statements and finalizes the formatting of the batches.

```
use pubs
go

drop trigger tradd_subject1
drop table subject1
drop table tracking1
drop table advisor1
go

create table subject1
(subject_code char(10), description char(50), instructor_code char(10))

create table advisor1
(advisor_code char(10), advisor_name char(50), contact_no char(11))

create table tracking1
(event_time datetime, event_type   char(20), caller char(20),
                                            description char(80) )
go

/* create a trigger */
CREATE TRIGGER tradd_subject1
   ON SUBJECT1 FOR INSERT
   AS
      DECLARE @advisor_code    char(10)

      select @advisor_code = instructor_code from INSERTED
```
(Continues)

Source 13.3 Phase 3: Enhancing the trigger script.

```
        IF EXISTS (select advisor_code from advisor1 where
                             advisor_code = @advisor_code)
(Continues)
        BEGIN
                return
        END
        ELSE
        BEGIN
                INSERT advisor1
                        (advisor_code, advisor_name, contact_no)
                VALUES
                        (@advisor_code, 'place holder',
                            convert (char(11), getdate()))

                INSERT tracking1
                        (event_time, event_type, caller, description)
                VALUES
                        (convert(char(20), getdate()), 'INSERT',
                         'TRADD_SUBJECT1', 'advisor not on file  ' +
                                                    @advisor_code)
        END
GO

/* insert a data row into the subject1 table */
insert subject1
(subject_code, description, instructor_code)
values
('sci101', 'science 101', 'davis')
go

/* insert another data row into the subject1 table */
insert subject1
(subject_code, description, instructor_code)
values
('his101', 'history 101', 'davis')
go

/* insert a data row into the subject1 table */
insert subject1
(subject_code, description, instructor_code)
values
('geo101', 'geography 101', 'davis')
go

Print '—— displaying the table contents ——'
select * from subject1
select * from advisor1
select * from tracking1
```

Source 13.3 *(Continued)*

The reformatted output results of this syntax are as follows:

```
—— displaying the table contents ——
subject_code description                              instructor_code
———— ———————————————— ————                            ————

sci101      science 101                               davis
his101      history 101                               davis
geo101      geography 101                             davis


advisor_code advisor_name                             contact_no
———— ———————————————— ————                            ————

davis        place holder                             Sep 25 1998


event_time                  event_type  caller        description
——————————— ———— ———— ————

1998-09-25 01:34:00.000 INSERT    TRADD_SUBJECT1 advisor not on file  Davis
```

Raiserror

The raiserror command is used to trap errors and raise error messages. The business rule for the previous example was to add a stub into the advisor1 table when a reference key record was missing. Instead the following example rolls back a transaction and raises an error using the raiserror command:

```
use pubs
go

drop trigger tradd_subject2
drop table subject1
drop table advisor1
go

create table subject1
(subject_code char(10), description char(50), instructor_code char(10))

create table advisor1
(advisor_code char(10), advisor_name char(50), contact_no char(11))
go

/* create a trigger */
CREATE TRIGGER tradd_subject2
   ON SUBJECT1 FOR INSERT
   AS
      DECLARE @advisor_code      char(10),
              @error_message   char(80)

      select @advisor_code = instructor_code from INSERTED

      IF EXISTS (select advisor_code from advisor1 where
                          advisor_code = @advisor_code)
```

```
              return
       ELSE
       BEGIN
              /* build an error message and display it using raiserror */
              Select @error_message = 'advisor not on file  ' + @advisor_code
raiserror (@error_message, 11, 1)
       END
GO

/* insert a data row into the subject1 table */
insert subject1
(subject_code, description, instructor_code)
values
('sci101', 'science 101', 'davis')
go

Print '——- displaying the table contents ——'
select * from subject1
select * from advisor1
```

Attempting to insert a data row into the subject1 table causes the error message to be displayed if there is no reference data row in the advisor1 table. This message is expected. However, notice that the insert command succeeds in the insert operation against the subject1 table. This results in a referential integrity error. The subject data row has no reference data row and so the two tables are no longer consistent. Without proceeding to the tracking1 table process that was described in the previous example, it would be appropriate to roll back the entire transaction. One example of this is shown in the next section.

The output for this syntax is as follows:

```
Server: Msg 50000, Level 11, State 1, Procedure tradd_subject2, Line 18
[Microsoft][ODBC SQL Server Driver][SQL Server]advisor not on file
davis

——- displaying the table contents ——
subject_code description                              instructor_code
——— ———————— ————
sci101       science 101                              davis

advisor_code advisor_name                             contact_no
——— ———————— ———
```

Including Rollbacks in Triggers

Triggers are used to roll back during inconsistent transactions. When a rollback transaction command is issued in a trigger, work is rolled back to the start of the transaction or until the last save point was issued. The previous example is modified to roll back the entire transaction, including the insert into the subject1 table, using the statement

ROLLBACK TRANSACTION. The modified code batches to include this are shown in Source Listing 13.4:

```
use pubs
go

drop trigger tradd_subject2
drop table subject1
drop table advisor1
go

create table subject1
(subject_code char(10), description char(50), instructor_code char(10))

create table advisor1
(advisor_code char(10), advisor_name char(50), contact_no char(11))
go

/* create a trigger */
CREATE TRIGGER tradd_subject2
   ON SUBJECT1 FOR INSERT
   AS
      DECLARE @advisor_code        char(10),
                @error_message      char(80)

      select @advisor_code = instructor_code from INSERTED

      IF EXISTS (select advisor_code from advisor1 where
                             advisor_code = @advisor_code)
              return
      ELSE
      BEGIN
ROLLBACK TRANSACTION
         /* build an error message and display it using raiserror */
         Select @error_message = 'advisor not on file  ' +
@advisor_code
raiserror (@error_message, 11, 1)
      END
GO

/* insert a data row into the subject1 table */
insert subject1
(subject_code, description, instructor_code)
values
('sci101', 'science 101', 'davis')
go

Print '——- displaying the table contents ——'
select * from subject1
select * from advisor1
```

Source 13.4 Including a rollback in a trigger.

Delete Trigger

A delete trigger can be used to ensure that codes are not removed from a type table, if they are being referenced by another table. Source Listing 13.5 demonstrates how this can be done:

```
use pubs
go

drop trigger trdelete_advisor1
drop table subject1
drop table advisor1
go

create table subject1
(subject_code char(10), description char(50), instructor_code char(10))

create table advisor1
(advisor_code char(10), advisor_name char(50), contact_no char(11))
go

/* setup data */
insert subject1
values ('csc401','advanced data structures', 'bobsad')

insert advisor1
values ('bobsad', 'Bob Saderson', '121-231-2121')

insert advisor1
values ('suejoe', 'Sue Joelly', '213-313-4231')
go

/* create a trigger */
CREATE TRIGGER trdelete_advisor1
    ON ADVISOR1 FOR DELETE
    AS
        DECLARE @advisor_code         char(10),
                @error_message        char(80)

        select @advisor_code = advisor_code
                    FROM deleted

        Select '@advisor_code = ', @advisor_code

        IF EXISTS (SELECT instructor_code FROM subject1
                        WHERE instructor_code = @advisor_code)
```

(Continues)

Source 13.5 Delete trigger.

```
      BEGIN
              ROLLBACK TRANSACTION

        Select @error_message =
@advisor_code + ' is being used in the subject table'
raiserror (@error_message, 12, 1)
      END
      ELSE
              return
GO

/* attempt to delete data rows from the advisor1 table based on keys */
delete advisor1
      where advisor_code = 'bobsad'
```

Source 13.5 (*Continued*)

The delete trigger traps an attempt to delete a record that will leave a referential integrity problem between the subject1 table and the advisor1 table. The following message displays in response to this delete attempt:

```
Server: Msg 50000, Level 12, State 1, Procedure trdelete_advisor1, Line
20
[Microsoft][ODBC SQL Server Driver][SQL Server]bobsad     is being used
in the subject table
```

Deleting an advisor1 data row that does not have any relationships to the data rows in the subject1 table will not create a referential integrity problem. The following example deletes the data row successfully from the advisor1 table, as shown by the last two selects in the following batch:

```
delete advisor1
      where advisor_code = 'suejoe'

Print '——- displaying the table contents ——'
select * from subject1
select * from advisor1
```

Trigger Limitations

Stored procedures support more commands than triggers. The following commands cannot be used in triggers: many DDL commands, such as create/alter objects and drop objects; many DCL commands, such as grant, revoke, update statistics, truncate table, reconfigure, disk commands, select into, and load commands. Triggers have a performance overhead that can slow down the performance of the application. My recommendation is to use triggers after attempting to use declarative referential integrity (e.g., constraints), rules, and stored procedures. Overutilization of triggers can have a negative impact on performance.

There are some limitations on triggers. These limitations include that they can apply to a single table as specified in the syntax, they can be nested to 16 levels, and they cannot contain certain types of commands, such as drop, alter, permissions, update statistics, create, and load.

SQL Server has several features to stop trigger infinite loops (e.g., a trigger inserting a record into a table firing an update trigger on the same table firing the update on the same table and so on). The first is the nested-level limit and the second is that a trigger does not fire itself. This prevents the example given earlier from occurring.

It is important to realize that triggers have had a performance overhead since SQL Server first emerged in the marketplace. This overhead performance has been reduced with faster CPU chips and streamlined with SQL Server releases in the future. Before designing a large number of triggers it is important to benchmark the use of a few triggers to ensure that the application response time is sufficient to meet requirements. Triggers cannot be created on views.

Summary

This chapter examined triggers from a variety of perspectives. Triggers are used to maintain referential integrity and to complete work that would otherwise need to be done using more complicated programming. Triggers are created and tied to insert, update, and delete events against specific columns or tables. Data rows undergoing any of these events automatically fire the trigger. This chapter demonstrated how a trigger could be created, compiled, and executed. System procedures for retrieving trigger code from system tables was also shown. Triggers have access to two intermediate tables: inserted and deleted. SQL Server 7 has introduced several important enhancements to triggers. A significant one of these is that each of the three events can now support more than one trigger. This supports n-tier architecture by allowing business logic to be encapsulated in a number of triggers, all of which will be stateless, and all of which can be called from a multitude of tables and table/column combinations.

CHAPTER

14

Using Advanced Data Manipulation Techniques

This chapter examines the different types of joins, subqueries, views, and cursors that are supported in SQL Server. Examples of manipulating relational tables and data using each of these techniques or data objects are provided. These four methods of data manipulation also have interrelationships with each other. For example, views are database objects that often include two or more table joins. Subqueries can also operate on views as easily as they work on relational tables. Figure 14.1 shows the relationship and components of these four methods:

Joins. The process of a join combines data rows in multiple relational tables based on the values in the primary key columns or the foreign key columns. The result of a join is a new virtual or logical table that combines columns from a variety of physical tables. A variety of joins will be examined in more detail in this chapter. The results of these are strikingly different.

Subqueries. Subqueries and joins produce similar results; however, their implementation is different. A subquery is typically used to process multiple relational tables, first by focusing on one table to produce a result set, then using that result set to locate compliant data rows in other tables in the database. Choosing between joins and subqueries requires three considerations: your personal preference, performance for the specific type of implementation, and the intuitive solution to satisfy a specific requirement.

Views. Views can be thought of as logical relational tables built on top of physical relational tables. While the physical relational tables are implemented for perfor-

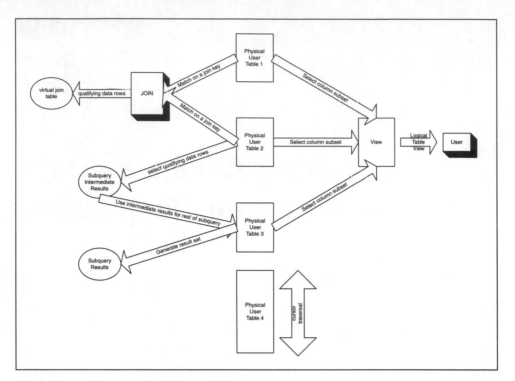

Figure 14.1 Data manipulation techniques.

mance, views are built to satisfy user interface requirements. A view combines specific columns from multiple tables under a common view name. Instead of combining the tables manually, a user can use the single view name for access. This is far easier for most users to do. Views are generally tailored to the requirements of individual end users. View names can also be used instead of table names in most Transact-SQL commands. Views are database objects that are stored within each database. There is one row in the sysobjects table for every view available in the database.

Cursors. The objective of a cursor is to browse through the data rows in a result set one record at a time. Sophisticated cursor processing provides the ability to locate a specific row within a result set, establish a pointer to a specific row, move forward one or more records, or move backward one or more records at a time. There are basically two types of cursors: client-side cursors and server-side cursors. Client-side cursors have been implemented since 1990 through middleware such as DBLibrary, and to a lesser extent through embedded SQL. Client-side cursors have also been built using arrays and multidimensional arrays. Client-side cursors are discussed in Chapter 16. Server-side cursors were not included in the initial releases of SQL Server but have been implemented in the last few releases. They are used inside stored procedures and triggers to process one or more tables simultaneously.

Setting Up the Test Database and Test Data

The examples in this chapter are based on the automobile application tables defined in Chapter 9. The script to create this database, consisting of nine tables, is reformatted below with slight alternations to demonstrate the examples in this chapter. The relationships between the tables in the data model are shown in Figure 14.2. Indexes are also created for the relevant tables.

```
use automobile
go

drop table buyer
drop table sales_exec
drop table sales_exec_type_description
drop table resolution_type
drop table auto_transaction
drop table automobile_description
drop table car_units
drop table dealership
drop table auto_type_description
go
```

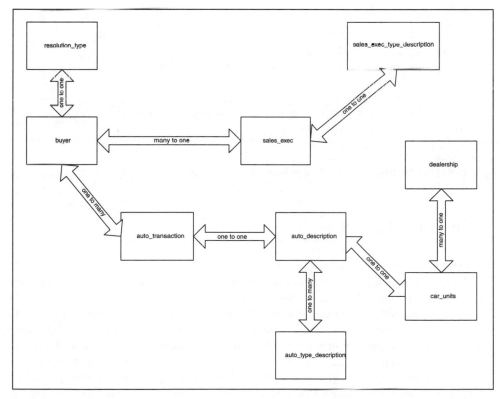

Figure 14.2 Enhanced automobile application data model.

```
create table buyer
(Buyer_no int, Last_name char(30), First_name char(30),
 Phone_no char(11), Fax_no     char(11), Email char(20),
 Intersection char(40), Requirement char(80), Request_Date datetime,
 Budget money, Resolution_type char(3), Resolution_date datetime,
 Sales_exec_no char(3), Entry_stamp timestamp)

create table sales_exec
(sales_exec_no char(3), sales_exec_type char(5), last_name char(30),
first_name char(30), sales_target money, commission float)

create table sales_exec_type_description
(sales_exec_type char(5), description char(30), salary_range char(30),
 reports_to_type char(5))

create table resolution_type
(resolution_type    char (3), description    char (50))

create table auto_transaction
(member_no int, auto_type char(5), auto_model char(5),
 reservation_date datetime, discount float)

create table automobile_description
(auto_type char(5), auto_model char(5), description char(40), cost
money)

create table auto_type_description
(auto_type char(5), auto_type_description char(40))

create table car_units
(dealership_no int, auto_type char(5), auto_model char(5),
 on_hand_qty int, total_sold int)

create table dealership
(Dealership_no int, location char(12), Manager char(30), Phone_no
char(11))
```

Join Operations

Each table in a relational database can be viewed as a mathematical set. This means that mathematical operations can be used to manipulate the data in the sets to produce other sets. The join is the most commonly used mathematical operation applied to relational database sets (also called tables). The join operation, at its most basic, is only possible if there are common key columns between relational tables. The join takes place on one or more columns in table A, with one or more columns in table B, and one or more columns in table C. This can continue to grow. The result of a join operation is the creation of another temporary or virtual table consisting of the columns specified in the join statements. As shown in Figure 14.3, several types of joins are discussed in this chapter, including the following:

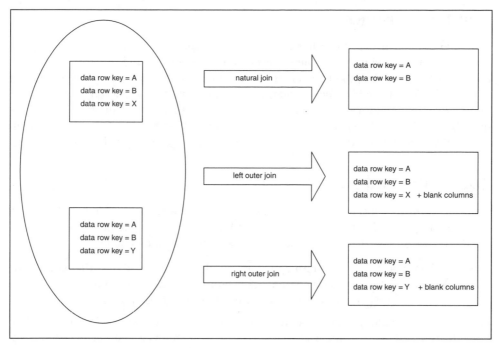

Figure 14.3   Types of joins.

Equi-join/natural join. This is arguably the most common type of join. It consists of joining two or more tables based on the same number and types of columns between the tables. The columns are not required to have the same names. This join combines data rows from one table with matching data rows in the tables being joined. The result is a temporary result set that combines specific columns from all the tables involved in the join.

Outer join. There is an interesting side effect of the natural join. Only data rows that have matching columns in all the tables involved in the join are retrieved. Data rows with no matching rows in the other tables are not selected by the operation. In some cases this is entirely undesirable. For example, suppose there are two relational tables. The first table contains a list of bank customers. A second table contains a list of accounts. A natural join between these two tables will only retrieve bank customers that have accounts. Customers who have loans, bonds, security boxes, or RRSPs will not be picked up. In some cases this situation is not desirable. The outer join picks up all the records in one of the tables involved in the join, regardless of whether there are matching records in the other table. There are two types of outer joins, the left-outer join (*=) and the right-outer join (=*). The left-outer join retrieves all the records in the table on the left side of the join command. The right-outer join retrieves all the records in the table on the right side of the join command.

Join Performance

Joins have a performance overhead that must be minimized during the testing cycle. Some considerations for improving their performance include the order of the join tables, index positioning, the number of records in the inner table, and the number of records in the outer table. Poorly constructed joins have the potential to lock up SQL Server resources and make the server virtually inaccessible to production users. Frequently used join tables should be placed into separate filegroups that are placed on different physical devices to improve performance by leveraging parallel processing.

Equi-Joins and Natural Joins

Natural joins are equivalent to the Cartesian products between tables. There is generally no WHERE clause. Equi-joins generally have WHERE clauses that select a portion of the data rows in the tables. Some common uses of an equi-join include

Join two tables, one containing a code for a employee's role and the other containing the employee's name and personal information. Joining these two tables displays the employee's personal information and actual role description.

Involve three tables in a join. The first two tables consist of the ones described earlier, the third table contains a list of addresses for the employee. Joining these tables together produces a combined result set from columns coming from three tables.

The syntax for performing an equi-join on any number of tables is as follows:

```
SELECT [alias.]column_list
FROM table1 alias1, table2 alias2 ....
    WHERE selection_clause
```

Sample Scripts

The following example joins a customer table with a member code table:

```
SELECT a.last_name, a.first_name, b.description
    FROM customer a, member_code b
    WHERE a.member_code = b.member_code
go
```

The following example forms a three-table join:

```
SELECT cs.first_name, cs.last_name, mt.description,
        ad.address_type, ad.street1, ad.city
    FROM customer cs, member_type mt, address ad
    WHERE cs.member_type = mt.member_type AND
        cs.customer_no = ad.customer_no
go
```

Source Listing 14.1 uses two tables in the test database to build an equi-join. Begin by adding test data to the two tables.

```
drop index sales_exec.sales_exec_ndx2
go

drop index sales_exec_type_description.sales_exec_type_ndx1
go

create index sales_exec_ndx2 on sales_exec (sales_exec_type)

create unique clustered index sales_exec_type_ndx1 on
     sales_exec_type_description (sales_exec_type)

/* clear the tables */
delete sales_exec
delete sales_exec_type_description
go

/* setup data in the sales_exec table */
Insert sales_exec
(sales_exec_no, sales_exec_type, last_name, first_name,
 sales_target, commission)
values
(100, 'man01', 'Trus', 'Joe', 300000, 15)

Insert sales_exec
(sales_exec_no, sales_exec_type, last_name, first_name,
 sales_target, commission)
values
(110, 'man02', 'Svensun', 'Jo-anne', 400400, 12)

Insert sales_exec
(sales_exec_no, sales_exec_type, last_name, first_name,
 sales_target, commission)
values
(1, 'presi', 'Scot', 'Amanda', 200500, 20)

    /* insert data into the sales_exec_type_description */

    Insert sales_exec_type_description
    (sales_exec_type, description, salary_range, reports_to_type)
    values
    ('man01', 'manager level 1', '$100,000 - $200,000', 'man02')

    Insert sales_exec_type_description
    (sales_exec_type, description, salary_range, reports_to_type)
    values
    ('man02', 'manager level 2', '$150,000 - $210,000', 'man03')
```

(Continues)

Source 14.1   Equi-Join.

```
Insert sales_exec_type_description
(sales_exec_type, description, salary_range, reports_to_type)
values
('man03', 'manager level 3', '$200,000 - $220,000', 'vp01')

Insert sales_exec_type_description
(sales_exec_type, description, salary_range, reports_to_type)
values
('vp01', 'Vice President level 1', '$250,000 - $270,000', 'presi')

Insert sales_exec_type_description
(sales_exec_type, description, salary_range, reports_to_type)
values
('presi', 'President', '$350,000 - $400,000', ' ')

select * from sales_exec
select * from sales_exec_type_description
```

Source 14.1   *(Continued)*

The output for Source Listing 14.1 is as follows:

```
The clustered index has been dropped.
```

sales_exec_no	sales_exec_type	last_name	first_name	sales_target	commission
100	man01	Trus	Joe	300000.0000	15.0
110	man02	Svensun	Jo-anne	400400.0000	12.0
1	presi	Scot	Amanda	200500.0000	20.0

sales_exec_type	description	salary_range	reports_to_type
man01	manager level 1	$100,000-$200,000	man02
man02	manager level 2	$150,000-$210,000	man03
man03	manager level 3	$200,000-$220,000	vp01
presi	President	$350,000-$400,000	
vp01	Vice President level 1	$250,000-$270,000	presi

The following example builds an equi-join between the sales_exec and the sales_exec_type_description:

```
SELECT a.last_name, a.first_name, b.description TITLE,
a.sales_target,     b.salary_range
        FROM sales_exec a, sales_exec_type_description b
            WHERE a.sales_exec_type = b.sales_exec_type
```

The output for this command is as follows:

last_name	first_name	TITLE	sales_target	salary_range
Trus	Joe	manager level 1	300000.0000	$100,000-$200,000
Svensun	Jo-anne	manager level 2	400400.0000	$150,000-$210,000
Scot	Amanda	President	200500.0000	$350,000-$400,000

The following example uses a right-outer join to retrieve job titles that have not yet been filled. These are identified by NULL in the fields that are not available:

```
SELECT a.last_name, a.first_name, b.description TITLE,
a.sales_target,     b.salary_range
        FROM sales_exec a, sales_exec_type_description b
            WHERE a.sales_exec_type =* b.sales_exec_type
```

The output for this command is as follows:

last_name	first_name	TITLE	sales_target	salary_range
Trus	Joe	manager level 1	300000.0000	$100,000-$200,000
Svensun	Jo-anne	manager level 2	400400.0000	$150,000-$210,000
NULL	NULL	manager level 3	NULL	$200,000-$220,000
Scot	Amanda	President	200500.0000	$350,000-$400,000
NULL	NULL	Vice President level 1	NULL	$250,000-$270,000

The following example shows how a left-outer join can also be used to build a result set. The results of this left-outer join are equivalent to the equi-join:

```
SELECT a.last_name, a.first_name, b.description TITLE,
a.sales_target,     b.salary_range
        FROM sales_exec a, sales_exec_type_description b
            WHERE a.sales_exec_type *= b.sales_exec_type
```

The following example shows how a left-outer join can be used to produce the equivalent of the right-outer join in example 4:

```
SELECT a.last_name, a.first_name, b.description TITLE,
a.sales_target,     b.salary_range
        FROM sales_exec_type_description b, sales_exec a
            WHERE b.sales_exec_type *= a.sales_exec_type
```

The following example uses self-joins and involves a multitable join where a table has a relationship with itself:

```
select b.employee_name
    from employee a,employee b
    where a.role = b.role
        AND a.employeeno <> b.employeeno
```

Subqueries

Both subqueries and joins access two or more relational tables to produce result tests with specific columns from each table. Subqueries are characterized by nesting queries into other queries. Subqueries start with a table to produce a result set that is then used to process other tables. The process is like using a cursor behind the scenes. Entirely equivalent results can be produced using either a subquery or a join.

Subqueries are frequently nested within the WHERE or HAVING clauses of DML statements such as select, update, insert, and delete. This section focuses on some common subquery verbs including ANY, ALL, and IN. These are used with operators such as = and <; for example, > ANY, >ALL.

Subqueries involve both inner and outer queries. Processing starts with the inner query, which is generally surrounded by parenthesis. Inner queries can return one or more data rows to the outer query, or a true/false condition. The syntax for using this command is as follows:

```
SELECT column_fields FROM table_list
  WHERE [EXISTS/IN] (selection_clause)
```

Sample Scripts

The easiest subquery to formulate involves using the keyword EXISTS. In the following example, the subquery returns a true/false to the WHERE clause when customer_no exists in the address table and has an address_type of 'R':

```
        SELECT first_name, last_name, home_phone
    FROM customer
        WHERE EXISTS (SELECT * from address
                        WHERE customer_no = customer.customer_no
AND address_type = 'R')
    go
```

In the following example, the IN command word can be used to select from a list:

```
SELECT last_name, first_name, sales_target
    FROM sales_exec a
    WHERE a.sales_exec_type IN (SELECT b.sales_exec_type from address b)
    go
```

Views

Views are database objects that are created to provide a logical table that consists of specific columns from one or more physical tables. Views are created to provide custom access to specific physical tables. For example, an employee table and an address table are normalized into two tables. However, it may be more convenient to build a logical physical view that accesses both tables with one name. This is easier for many users to leverage and removes the need for understanding the physical data architecture. Some view considerations are included in the following list:

Using views to simply SQL queries of a database is not free. Someone needs to be charged with building and maintaining views for users to access. Since this can often become a full-time job, the activities for view management may require a full-time database resource. The caretaker of the views must understand the business application.

Views do not support database triggers.

Simplify user access to relational data by providing nontechnical users.

Combine columns from multiple tables under a common database object name.

Restrict user access to a subset of columns in a single table.

Implement security on views to restrict user access to specific columns only.

Views are created, maintained, and dropped using Transact-SQL commands, similar to the way that relational tables are managed. Views must be dropped before another view with the same name can be created within a database. The syntax to create a view is as follows:

```
CREATE VIEW owner.view_name [column_list] AS select_clause
```

An alternate syntax to create a view is

```
DROP VIEW owner.view_name
```

Use the following syntax to execute a view:

```
SELECT [*/column_names] from view_name where search_clause
```

 View objects are created in the default database only.

Sample Scripts

The following example creates a view for a user that needs access to a subset of the columns in the sales_exec table:

```
DROP VIEW sales_exec_list
go

CREATE VIEW sales_exec_list
AS
      SELECT last_name, first_name, sales_exec_type FROM sales_exec
go

SELECT * FROM sales_exec_list
go

SELECT sales_exec_type from sales_exec_list
go
```

The output for this example is

last_name	first_name	sales_exec_type
Trus	Joe	man01
Svensun	Jo-anne	man02
Scot	Amanda	presi

```
sales_exec_type
man01
man02
presi
```

The following example updates the view to retrieve data rows for managers only:

```
DROP VIEW sales_exec_list1
go

CREATE VIEW sales_exec_list1
AS
        SELECT last_name, first_name, sales_exec_type FROM sales_exec
            where sales_exec_type like ëman%í
go

SELECT * FROM sales_exec_list1
go

SELECT sales_exec_type from sales_exec_list1
go
```

The output for this example is

last_name	first_name	sales_exec_type
Trus	Joe	man01
Svensun	Jo-anne	man02

```
sales_exec_type
man01
man02
```

The following example creates a view that joins the sales_exec and the sales_exec_type_description tables:

```
DROP VIEW sales_exec_list2
go

CREATE VIEW sales_exec_list2
AS
    SELECT a.last_name, a.first_name, b.description Title
        FROM sales_exec a, sales_exec_type_description b
            Where a.sales_exec_type = b.sales_exec_type
go

SELECT * FROM sales_exec_list2
go
```

The following example displays the control information saved in the database system tables for these views:

```
        sp_depends sales_exec_list1
        go
        sp_depends sales_exec_list2
        go

sp_helptext sales_exec_list1
        go
        sp_helptext sales_exec_list2
        go
```

The following example creates a view and then uses it to select information from a table:

```
DROP VIEW sales_exec_list3
go

CREATE VIEW sales_exec_list3
AS
        SELECT a.last_name, a.first_name, b.description Title,
             b.reports_to_type
           FROM sales_exec a, sales_exec_type_description b
                Where a.sales_exec_type = b.sales_exec_type
go

SELECT * FROM sales_exec_list3
go
```

Create View Wizard

SQL Server has a Create View Wizard that can be used to create select type views. This is a good place to start if your objective is to create a set of views to select one or more columns in one or more tables. Figure 14.4 shows the dialogue that is used to select the

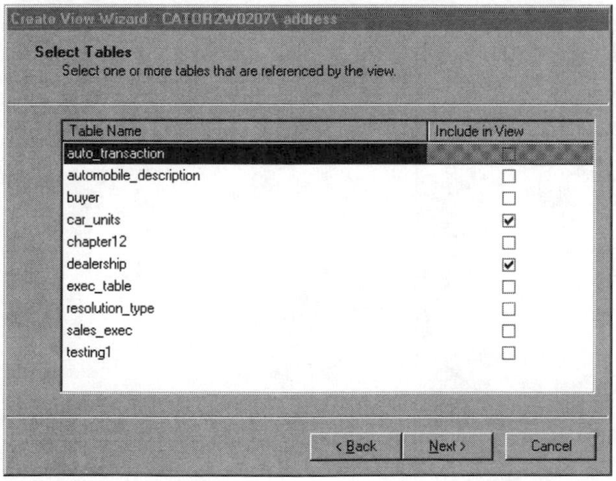

Figure 14.4 Select tables.

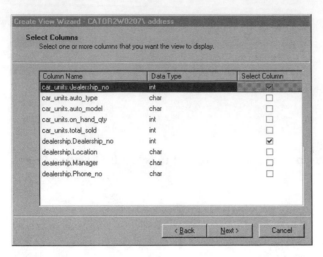

Figure 14.5 Select columns.

tables within a database to be included in the view. The dialogue allows you to select one or more tables. Figure 14.5 shows the dialogue that is used to select columns to be included in the view from each table. The names are presented in the form [table_name].[column_name]. At least one column must be selected. The dialogue allows the selection of the same key columns in the tables; however, the wizard will not generate the view with duplicate columns. The dialogue allows you to use the Back button to modify the columns selected in the view. The wizard also presents a dialogue that accepts restrictions coded in a WHERE clause. Figure 14.6 shows the Transact-SQL code that is generated by the wizard for the columns and tables that were identified in the previous steps. The wizard allows the view name and the generated code to be manually adjusted before the view is saved.

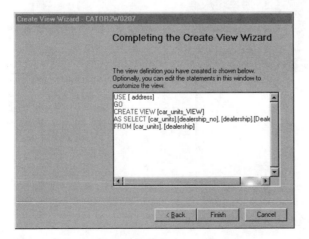

Figure 14.6 View Transact-SQL code.

The following activities are used to create views with the Create View Wizard:

Select a database.

Select tables to include in the view.

Select columns to include in the view from each table that was identified.

Include restrictions on the view using a WHERE clause.

Accept or modify the view name.

Accept or modify the generated view code.

Make any final adjustments to the view.

Generate the view.

 As with most tools that allow the customization of generated code, once this is done it becomes the developer's responsibility to maintain the customization in future generations of the code.

Server-Side Cursors

Server-side cursors support row-by-row processing of a result set. Cursors are generally included within stored procedures. Multiple cursors can be included in the same stored procedure. Each is identified by a unique cursor name. As shown in Figure 14.7, a cursor builds a result set from a base table in a database and then accepts commands to position a pointer at specific rows in the result set. The relevant activities for cursor processing include the following:

Declare the cursor.

Open the cursor.

Fetch the result set and process rows.

Close and deallocate the cursor.

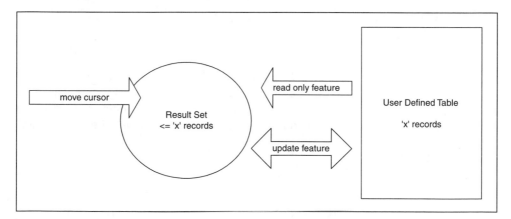

Figure 14.7 Server-side cursor processing.

The open cursor operation selects information from a base data table and builds a result set that is processed by the user. The data included in the result set is a mirror to the actual data in the database table. This raises several referential integrity possibilities. For example, changes can be made to data in the result set. Changes can also be made to data in the base table. In both of these situations, a key decision is whether to couple the changes between the result set and the base table. There are a variety of possibilities in linking these two images together. There is flexibility in the type of integration that exists between the result set and the base table while the fetch operation is in effect. The trade-offs here are the timeliness of the fetched data and the amount of contention experienced on the base table. Following are five activities to define and use cursors to manipulate data rows on a row by row basis. The syntax for declaring the cursor_name is as follows:

```
DECLARE cursor_name INSENSITIVE SCROLL CURSOR
FOR statements FOR   READ ONLY | UPDATE OF columns
```

Following are definitions for the terms used in this syntax:

INSENSITIVE. This option creates a copy of the result set based on the base table. This results in reduced contention on the underlying base table. The result set is then used for the fetch command. The main drawback with this option is that data in the base table and the result set can be out of sync. This feature should be used when results do not need to be exact or in real time.

SCROLL. This option closely ties the table and the result set. This provides timely and accurate information to the cursor process. Changes to the base table are propagated to the actual result set.

READ ONLY. This option prevents cursor data from being updated.

UPDATE. This option is used to identify columns that can be updated in the column list. All columns will be updated if none are identified.

STATEMENTS. This option consists of a select statement. The order of the columns in the select statement must match the order of the columns in the fetch statement.

The syntax for opening the cursor_name is as follows:

```
OPEN cursor_name
```

This command modifies the global variable @@CURSOR_ROWS with the number of data rows that are fetched into the result set. If a negative number is returned, then an asynchronous load of the result set will occur. A positive number reflects the number of data rows that were returned in the result set. The syntax for fetching the cursor_name is as follows:

```
FETCH operation FROM cursor_name
INTO @variable_list
```

The operations are used to position the cursor. These can be next, prior, first, last, absolute n, and relative n.

The order of the @variable_list must match the column order in the select statement. The @@FETCH_STATUS global variable is used to track the results of the fetch operation. A 0 reflects a successful completion. A –1 indicates that data was not returned by the fetch. A –2 is returned if a previously fetched row is deleted in the base table.

The syntax for closing the cursor_name is as follows:

```
CLOSE cursor
```

The syntax for deallocating the cursor_name is as follows:

```
DEALLOCATE cursor
```

Sample Scripts

Source Listing 14.2 builds a cursor to walk through the sales_exec_type_description.

```
DROP PROC test_cursor
go

CREATE PROC test_cursor
AS
    DECLARE      /* local variables are used to hold cursor rows */
@sales_exec_type    char(5),
@description        char(30),
@salary_range       char(30),
@reports_to_type    char(5)


    DECLARE cursor_sales_exec_type INSENSITIVE CURSOR
        FOR SELECT sales_exec_type, description,
            salary_range, reports_to_type
                FROM sales_exec_type_description
    ORDER BY sales_exec_type

    OPEN cursor_sales_exec_type

    /* Cursor Processing */

    /* get first data row */
FETCH FROM cursor_sales_exec_type
INTO
@sales_exec_type,
@description,
@salary_range,
@reports_to_type

    select 'About to display the fetched columns from the result set:'
                                                        (Continues)
```

Source 14.2 Cursor for sales_exec_type_description.

```
        /* loop through the cursor result set. The following WHILE
            statement executes only if the @@FETCH_STATUS returns a 0 */

        WHILE @@FETCH_STATUS = 0
        BEGIN

        print @sales_exec_type + '     ' +
            @description      + '    ' +
            @salary_range     + '    ' +
            @reports_to_type

            /* INCLUDE MORE PROCESSING STATEMENTS BEFORE FETCHING
    THE NEXT ROW */

            /* fetch the next data row */
FETCH FROM cursor_sales_exec_type
INTO
@sales_exec_type,
@description,
@salary_range,
@reports_to_type
        END

        CLOSE cursor_sales_exec_type

        DEALLOCATE cursor_sales_exec_type

go

/* execute the stored procedure and the cursor */
exec test_cursor
go
```

Source 14.2   *(Continued)*

The output for Source Listing 14.2 is as follows:

```
About to display the fetched columns from the result set:

man01    manager level 1        $100,000-$200,000      man02
man02    manager level 2        $150,000-$210,000      man03
man03    manager level 3        $200,000-$220,000      vp01
presi    President              $350,000-$400,000
vp01     Vice President level 1 $250,000-$270,000      presi
```

Source Listing 14.3 builds a cursor that uses the scroll command so that the fetch row positioning operations are enabled. This allows the use of the next, prior, first, last, absolute n, and the relative n commands.

```
DROP PROC test_cursor1
go

CREATE PROC test_cursor1
AS
    DECLARE        /* local variables are used to hold cursor rows */
@sales_exec_type      char(5),
@description          char(30),
@salary_range         char(30),
@reports_to_type      char(5)

    DECLARE cursor_sales_exec_type1 SCROLL CURSOR
        FOR SELECT sales_exec_type, description,
              salary_range, reports_to_type
                FROM sales_exec_type_description
    ORDER BY sales_exec_type

    OPEN cursor_sales_exec_type1

    /* Cursor Processing */

    /* get first data row */
FETCH FIRST FROM cursor_sales_exec_type1
INTO
@sales_exec_type,
@description,
@salary_range,
@reports_to_type

print     'FIRST ROW ' + @sales_exec_type + '     ' + @description
  + '     ' +  @salary_range + '     ' + @reports_to_type

FETCH LAST FROM cursor_sales_exec_type1
INTO
@sales_exec_type,
@description,
@salary_range,
@reports_to_type

print     'LAST ROW ' + @sales_exec_type + '     ' + @description
  + '     ' +  @salary_range + '     ' + @reports_to_type


    CLOSE cursor_sales_exec_type1

    DEALLOCATE cursor_sales_exec_type1

go

/* execute the stored procedure and the cursor */
exec test_cursor1
go
```

Source 14.3 Cursor for scoll command.

Summary

This chapter focused on advanced uses of the different types of joins, subqueries, views, and server-side cursors. Joins and subqueries can often produce the same results despite their different methods of approaching the requirement. Their purpose is to link one or more columns in two or more tables to produce a new virtual table. The new table consists of columns from all the tables involved in the operation.

Views can be used on one or more tables to restrict access, and operations, on a set of specific columns. Views are used to implement security and to simplify logical access to data by hiding the physical details. Views must be maintained as separate objects in the database. If underlying table structures are modified, the corresponding views must also be updated to reflect the new structure. It is not uncommon to allocate a dedicated DBA resource to maintain the set of views for a project or group of projects.

Server-side cursors are used to process data in relational tables on a row-by-row basis. The standard DML and DDL commands operate on a set of data, rather than individual data rows. An alternative to server-side cursors is to use client-side cursors. The latter are often simpler to implement; however, they may require substantial data to be transferred across the network.

Build Advanced Applications Using COM, Internet/Intranet, Visual Basic, and MTS

Part Four focuses on providing examples for building COM, MTS, and n-tier architecture-based applications using Visual Basic. Connecting SQL Server to the Internet/Intranet and ASP are also discussed in this section of the book.

Chapter 15 demonstrates the process of building a logical data model and object model and leveraging this for constructing an n-tier distributed application using the Microsoft Transaction Server and Visual Basic.

Chapter 16 examines principles that affect user interface usability and performance in n-tier applications. This includes locking and transaction management, both of which have been greatly enhanced in SQL Server 7.

Chapter 17 demonstrates how to build applications that leverage Internet/intranet technology in conjunction with COM, SQL Server, and Active Server Pages. This chapter also examines the use of JavaBeans for building n-tier applications.

Building a COM-Based, N-Tier Application

This chapter examines how to build a COM-based application using Visual Basic in an SQL Server environment. The initial sections describe the components of a multitiered application and the fundamental development challenges that are encountered while implementing a multitiered approach. These examples build a 3-tiered application and deploy the business-tier components using MTS. This chapter also contains practical tips and other technical pointers from actual large-scale systems implementation projects using this fundamental architecture.

Building 3-Tiered Distributed Applications

In a 3-tiered architecture, an application is divided into three tiers or layers: the presentation or user tier, the business tier, and the data access tier. As mentioned in other chapters of this book, the major benefits derived from 3-tiered architecture include a higher degree of reusability, scalability, flexibility, and reduced maintenance costs. Table 15.1 summarizes the names, objectives, characteristics, and responsibilities of these three application tiers.

Distributed 3-Tiered Architecture

3-tiered application architecture offers a powerful approach for designing applications. It provides a tremendous amount of reuse of common business components. Tradition-

Table 15.1 3-Tier Architecture

TIER NAME	OTHER NAMES	TYPE OF SERVICE	CHARACTERISTICS	RESPONSIBILITY
Presentation	Client, user, front-end	Client applications	GUI interface	Presentation, navigation, and handling user input
Business	Middle	Business servers	Business components	Business rules, security and interbusiness component, communication, and navigation
Data	Persistence, back-end	Data servers	Data-based managers	Managing integrity and persistence of data

ally the multitiered components are local to a given physical system. The only remote tier in most cases is the database. The database may contain stored procedures that are used on a shared basis. The other common components, like the business components, are usually part of dynamic linked libraries (DLLs) that reside on individual desktops. This architecture provides a lot of benefits but still has problems in terms of maintenance and administration. Modified common components need to be copied or installed on every affected desktop system. They also need to be installed because these DLLs need to be registered in the systems registry.

A better situation is to reuse common components residing on different physical systems—the client tier of the application can call remote functions without knowing where the functions physically reside. This opens up the possibilities of having features such as enhanced scalability, load balancing, fault tolerance, and good component administration. This architecture suggests that the client application be little more than a plain GUI with very little logic. The main function of the client tier, and sometimes its only function, is to display information received from remote application servers, accept user input, and send it to the remote systems. This approach is similar to the now-popular Internet or web-based applications. The browser is used to display information received from the Internet server and also to send user responses and requests to the server. Building distributed multitiered applications opens up the possibility of server components being accessed by systems that have native operating systems and design tools on a given platform and also platform-independent browsers. This is really what we want, access to our applications from systems that are independent of the hardware, operating system, and specific tools. This is a major advantage of the distributed application architecture. Others include

- Effective use of front-end and back-end services
- Shared business rules and policies built into business components
- Increased flexibility in deployment and administration
- High reusability system and code base
- Support for a thin client architecture

N-Tier Architecture Challenges

This section examines the common challenges that are faced by project teams who are working with n-tier, distributed applications. This list is intended to be representative, but not exhaustive. Recommended solutions are described following the list of challenges.

Connection to Remote Servers

Since the business and data service components reside on remote servers, how do client applications access them? These are not just files or devices connected to remote servers, but applications. Therefore traditional file server and print server networking technology cannot provide the level of interaction that is needed.

Proper Redirection of Function Calls

Functions residing in an in-process DLL are executed in the same address space as the calling application. Functions residing in out-of-process servers run in different address spaces. These servers can reside on local or remote computers. A mechanism to address this issue and provide integration with the application is required.

Handling Return Data

Passing data from one server to another and back again is a complex operation, especially through an application being built in-house using standard application development tools. Network performance issues become important. Passing data by reference or passing objects prove to be expensive operations, and sometimes are not possible at all. These requirements need to be addressed before proceeding with development efforts.

Error Handling

The occurrence of errors is commonplace and is an accepted fact in all walks of life. Software systems are not devoid of errors. Errors occur due to various reasons: Some are human errors, some are data errors, and some are due to bugs in the application software. The last reason for error is handled by debugging the code. The first two instances of errors are mostly observed during runtime. These errors can be classified further as system errors and business errors. Mechanisms have to be put into place to detect these errors and handle them appropriately. Distributed systems require a little more in this area than monolithic systems.

Performance Issues for Remote Function Calls

Applications need to make function calls to carry out the tasks required of them. In nondistributed applications method calls can be made to carry out functions such as setting object properties and executing functionality built into these objects. Therefore, if there are ten properties that need to be set, then ten calls can be made to set them. This is not a big issue as all of this is done on the local machine. In distributed applications, functions reside on remote servers. These functions, which may be part of remote components, reside in objects as exposed methods. To make calls to set or get every property of an object will require making as many calls. This causes an increase in network traffic which could result in performance degradation.

Reporting and Printing Functions

Applications, besides providing transaction-related functionality, arc also used as decision support systems (DSSs). A DSS provides query and reporting facilities. Report generators and tools built into the application development tools provide support for reporting functions . These tools require direct access to tables in the databases. The distributed architecture model does not provide direct access to tables in the database from the presentation layer. Hence third-party tools cannot be directly used to provide reporting facilities.

Reporting systems traditionally provide page-formatting features for reports. Since the reporting tools cannot be directly used, printing mechanism issues need to be addressed.

Scalability and Security

The number of client applications supported by a given component tier configuration for a fixed amount of system resources determines the scalability of a system. Systems that can support a large number of clients with a small number of component tier machines are said to be scalable. Efficient sharing and management of components in a 3-tiered distributed architecture is the key for building scalable systems.

Vitally important to an organization is protecting and maintaining the integrity of its business information. Security management plays an important role in business applications. Many systems have been designed to provide virtually none or, in some cases, too much security. A balanced approach is required. In the multitiered environment, it is very important to identify where and how security is implemented.

The Solution

This section describes some common approaches for dealing with the challenges faced in a distributed n-tier environment. Some issues may be more pressing than others in a given setting and therefore would need more attention. The keys in addressing these issues are maintaining balance and adapting to a specific environment.

Connection to Remote Servers

The connection to applications residing on remote servers is, at the very lowest level, handled by the use of remote procedure calls (RPCs). Both operating systems and network operating systems provide this mechanism. The application developer is not required to understand the details of RPC implementations, but should be able to use the tools and technologies that support these mechanisms. Microsoft's COM provides a single programming model for accessing components regardless of where they are located. Distributed COM (DCOM) provides an extension of the COM programming model beyond the boundaries of one physical machine.

Proper Redirection of Function Calls

Function calls on remote components can be issued using the proxy-stub mechanism provided by DCOM. When a function call is made to a remote server, a proxy in the client's address space is used in place of the server object that resides in a different address space on a local or remote system. The proxy forwards all client requests to a stub residing on the server. The proxy packages all parameters that are needed to invoke a particular method, a process called marshaling. The stub receives requests from the proxy and unmarshalls any parameters before invoking any function on the server. This is how functions are executed on the server from a client machine. This does not have to be programmed by the Visual Basic developer. The client and business components, when developed, reside on the same system. The client is programmed as an executable program and the remote business object can be developed as an out-of-process server.

The business object is installed and registered on the remote system. A similar registration is done on the client side. A DCOM configuration utility is then run to register information about the server where the remote component is installed. This process can get complicated and is difficult to manage. A simplified approach is available through the use of MTS. In order to install business components in MTS, the components have to be built as ActiveX DLLs and not as ActiveX Servers.

Handling Return Data

It is recommended that data between the client and server platforms in a Visual Basic environment be transferred using the ByVal keyword. Object references can be expensive in terms of causing network chatter, resulting in added network traffic.

Variant arrays can be used to transfer data from the server side to the client side and vice versa. The business component or the data service component can be programmed to handle the object to array conversion on the server side. The client application must convert object attributes to an array before sending the information to the server and must convert the return array to object attributes before using it on the client side. Following is a code snippet of a SetAttributes method exposed in an object. The method takes a predefined and previously agreed upon array structure as an argument and uses it to set attributes within the object. The code following the SetAttributes method shows how this method is called from the application.

```
Public Sub SetAttributes(vCustomer As Variant)
    'Populate array from private member variables.
    m_oCustomerID = vCustomer(m_iCUSTOMER_ATTR_CUSTOMERID)
    m_sFirstName = vCustomer(m_iCUSTOMER_ATTR_FIRSTNAME)
    m_sLastName = vCustomer(m_iCUSTOMER_ATTR_LASTNAME)
    m_sMiddleInitial = vCustomer(m_iCUSTOMER_ATTR_MIDDLEINITIAL)
```

```
End Sub
        .

        .

        .
'Declare the object
    Dim oCustomer as CCustomerBus

'Instantiate the object.
Set oCustomer = New CCustomerBus

'Set the Attributes for the object
OCustomer.SetAttributes(vCustomerArray)
```

The previous method showed how attributes could be set. It is also necessary to receive this data in an array format. This is achieved by building another method for the object which does the total opposite of the SetAttributes method. This method is the GetAttributes method and is shown here.

```
Public Function GetAttributes() As Variant
    'Declare local variables for current procedure.
    Dim aCustomer(m_iCUSTOMER_ATTR_MIDDLEINITIAL) As Variant

    'Populate array from private member variables.
    aCustomer(m_iCUSTOMER_ATTR_CUSTOMERID) = m_oCustomerID
    aCustomer(m_iCUSTOMER_ATTR_FIRSTNAME) = m_sFirstName
    aCustomer(m_iCUSTOMER_ATTR_LASTNAME) = m_sLastName
    aCustomer(m_iCUSTOMER_ATTR_MIDDLEINITIAL) = m_sMiddleInitial

    'Format function return value.
    GetAttributes = aCustomer

End Function
```

Another technology that is proving to be the answer to the "how to transfer data across. . ." question is the use of the Extensible Markup Language (XML). This technology is gaining popularity and is used to transfer self-defining data. One of the problems with the variant array approach is that both the packager and the receiver must know the array index definitions and therefore changes to the data formatting on the packaging side also require changes to the receiving side. This then brings up other issues such as modifying code, recompiling, and testing which can increase the possibility of introducing defects. With XML the data is defined within the structure and therefore clients can just pull out only the data that is applicable to their application.

Error Handling

A server- and client-side error object can be used to provide custom error handling support. Mechanisms such as maintaining a collection of context information in the error objects can be useful to provide call history.

This is similar to the above approach of handling return data. The difference is that the error object does not contain attributes related to the business but is specialized in that it contains information collected through the course of its travel from one function to another. The error object is passed from one function to another and collects context information. In case of an error, the error is handled by the error handler and functions within the error object are called which are responsible for logging the error in some sort of error log and displaying relevant messages to the user.

Context information collected from the server side can be passed to the client side using the variant array or XML transfer mechanism. The error object used for the error-handling mechanism may be built to handle only fatal errors such as those caused by invalid data connections, invalid server, and the inability to create a remote object. The error object may be further tweaked to handle business error messages such as Total exceeds 100%, or Age is invalid. The other way to handle this is to create separate mechanisms to handle generic errors and business errors.

Performance Issues for Remote Function Calls

The number of function calls made across the network must be reduced in a distributed application environment. In order for this to happen business component classes must be designed to get required data into a single call rather than allowing the client to issue individual property function calls to get or set attributes a repeated number of times. Methods with fine granularity must be replaced by those offering coarser granularity. This means that a method must do more than setting or getting one attribute value. This does not mean that single property get and set methods should be done away with. These methods should continue to exist. What is required is additional methods within these classes that will locally call the individual get and set property methods. An example of this is to support a method that inserts an address into a database through an array that contains information on the street name, suite number, city, province, and postal code rather than calling the set street name method, then the set suite number method, and so on for all the rows of data. The bottom line is to reduce the number of calls across the network to a minimum in order to improve performance.

Reporting Functions

Business components can be developed to provide information in either the variant array or the XML format to the client tier. The client tier, depending on whether it is browser based or not, can then take available approaches such as converting the returned data to HTML or populating visual controls. Thus displaying the data is not a complicated issue, but printing the data is, depending on the type of client tier that is being supported. If the client is browser based, then printing can be done using the print command. On non-browser-based clients such as Visual Basic or C++, printing reports must follow one of two options. The first option is to use third-party reporting controls that accept variant array or XML-based data and then call the print method to produce a hardcopy of the report. The second option is to create report templates with embedded bookmarks using a word processor such as Microsoft Word and then to use the methods in the Word Object model to insert relevant data into the template to produce a printout.

Building a 3-Tiered Application

Armed with all the information in the preceding sections of this chapter we can now move to the final round of actually building a 3-tiered distributed application. This application is built using Microsoft Visual Basic 5 and the business components are deployed in the MTS environment. Let's now move to the first phase of identifying what is going to be built. Throughout this section code snippets will be provided to demonstrate important concepts.

Business Requirements

The application that will be built through the course of this chapter will be a customer management system. This system will maintain customer information such as names and addresses. This is part of a bigger project and therefore it is required that interfaces and entry points for other applications are properly designed from the beginning of the project.

Application Functions

The following customer management functions must be supported by the system being developed in this example:

Inserting new customer information (names and addresses)

Modifying existing client information (names and addresses)

Deleting customer information (names and addresses)

Searching for a customer based on account ID and last name

Application Data

The company requires access to the customer information that is shown in Table 15.2.
Table 15.3 identifies the address information that is required by the company and which must be maintained by the application.

Table 15.2   Information Type Table

INFORMATION TYPE	DESCRIPTION	COMMENTS
CustomerID	A unique customer identifier	Unique, mandatory
First name	Customer's first name	Mandatory
Last name	Customer's last name	Mandatory
Middle initial	Customer's middle initials	Optional

Table 15.3 Address Information

INFORMATION TYPE	DESCRIPTION	COMMENTS
CustomerID	The Customer ID	Mandatory
Address Type	This will classify the address as home or work address	Mandatory
Street Address	The street address	Mandatory
Apartment Number	The Apartment number	Optional
City	Name of the city	Optional
Province	Name of Province	Optional
Postal Code	Postal Code	Optional
Country	Name of the Country	Optional
Telephone Number	Telephone number	Optional
Email	Email Address	Optional

Business Rules

Table 15.4 contains business rules that are applicable to the customer information management functions. The rules are not listed in any order of precedence.

Table 15.5 contains business rules that are applicable to the address management functions.

Table 15.4 Customer Information Business Rules

RULE NUMBER	DESCRIPTION
C1	All mandatory information must be entered before customer information can be inserted or updated.
C2	All addresses belonging to the customer must be deleted when the customer is deleted.

Table 15.5 Address Business Rules

RULE NUMBER	DESCRIPTION
A1	All mandatory information must be entered before address information can be inserted or updated.
A2	A maximum of two addresses can be stored for a given customer – one home and one work address

Business Object Model

This object model is an abstraction of the business model for the above requirements. It illustrates the various classes that are involved and their relationships. Figure 15.1 is constructed using the Unified Modeling Language (UML)–based tool from Rational Rose.

The following observations can be made about the business model. This model is not an implementation model. The implementation model contains implementation classes that are based on the design approach:

- A customer is an entity that is related to addresses
- One Customer can have a maximum of two addresses

The methods listed in the classes in the business model are typical operations to load, insert, delete, and update customer name and address information.

Application Layers

Based on the above business model and the application architecture, various components and the classes contained within them are identified. These classes are then placed in the appropriate tiers: presentation, business, or data services. Figure 15.2 shows the classes in the appropriate tiers for a 3-tiered application and their relationships.

Figure 15.3 contains the forms and the client side classes. The dialog boxes interact with the client side classes which interact with the business services layer. The CustomersClass is the collection that holds the Customer objects which are returned after a search criteria. These Customer objects are then used to create address information.

Figure 15.4 contains the MTS, component services, and business objects. The business services objects are usually installed on a remote system. The MTS read and write classes are gatekeeper classes and allow access to the interface services. The interface

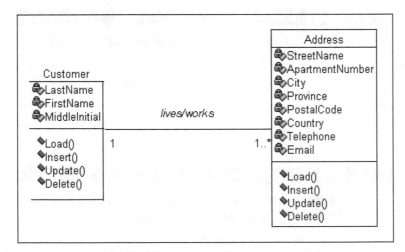

Figure 15.1 Business object model.

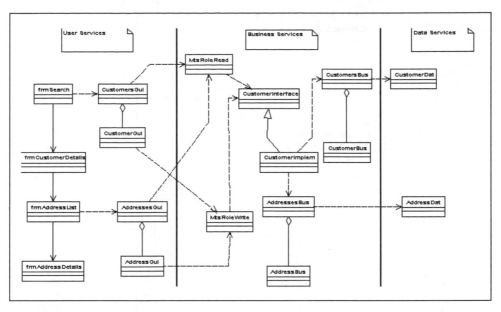

Figure 15.2 Application layers.

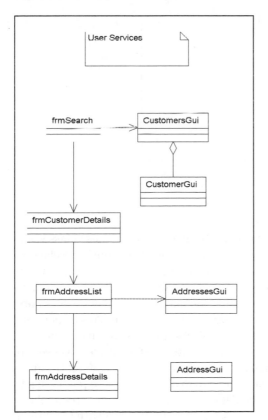

Figure 15.3 User, client, or client tier model.

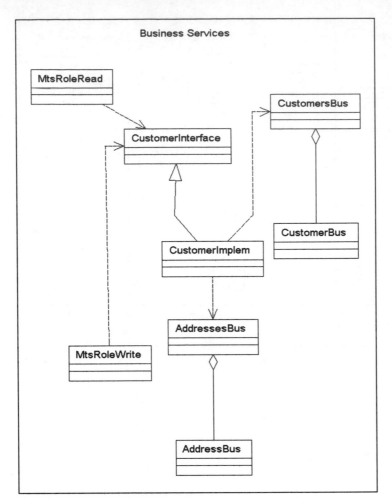

Figure 15.4   Business tier.

classes contain methods that interact with the actual business classes. These classes expose methods which are then implemented by controller classes or the business classes.

Figure 15.5 contains the data services classes for this project. These classes contain methods that implement the insert, delete, update, and load methods. These classes are the only ones that are aware of the storage mechanism and devices. The business objects just request the data service classes to load, insert, or delete them. This is then carried out by the data service. Designing the system in this fashion provides independence in terms of the mechanism, type, and location of the datastore. If a flat file was used to store data in the past, a change to a relational or object database will not affect the business side of the application. The diagram shows one data class for each type of object. It is normal for a database table to map to one data class for simple data entry applications, but for complex business applications one data class may interact with more than one table in the database.

```
┌──────────────────────────────────┐
│           Data Services          │
│                                  │
│                                  │
│   ┌──────────────┐               │
│   │ CustomerDat  │               │
│   ├──────────────┤               │
│   │              │               │
│   └──────────────┘               │
│            ┌──────────────┐      │
│            │ AddressDat   │      │
│            ├──────────────┤      │
│            │              │      │
│            └──────────────┘      │
└──────────────────────────────────┘
```

Figure 15.5   Data tier.

The Data Model

Figure 15.6 shows the data model that is derived for this project. The create table, index, and database object DDL commands were discussed in earlier chapters of this book. The data model contains the tables required to satisfy the business requirements for the application. The data model may require change depending upon other requirements that may come up in the future. One of the requirements could have included two cus-

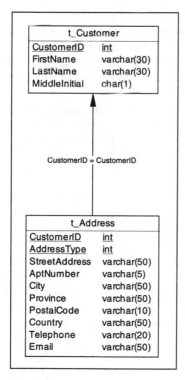

Figure 15.6   Data model.

tomer entries will be considered duplicates if the firstname, lastname, and the middle initials are the same. Since the customerid is the primary key, this may not enforce the above mentioned duplication rule. A way around is to have the firstname, lastname, and the middle initial as the primary key, letting the application generate a unique customerid. This may not be necessary if the chances for two customers to have the same firstname, lastname, and middle initials are low. Please note that the database structure for this application is very basic and was not intended to handle complex scenarios.

Application Framework

In an earlier part of this chapter mention was made about the challenges that are faced when building distributed applications and their solutions. Some of those solutions were techniques that needed to be applied in every application that was built. A few of them were to be built as application service frameworks that would be used across all applications. This chapter does not include code for these application service framework components, but this section briefly explains some common components that must be part of this framework.

Code Decode Component

Most applications require information such as province and city that is usually populated in list boxes on the client GUI screen. This information is very static and is usually used by more than one application. Instead of building code within applications to load the province code from the database, decoding it when needed in the list box, and then coding it when saving it in the database, a code-decode component can be created which can be used across all applications. This component provides interfaces with GUI controls such as list boxes, combo boxes, and radio buttons while providing code-decode functions as required.

A basic code decode component will hold a collection of code decode types such as Province, City, and others. These objects will then contain collections of objects which will have attributes such as code and decode and methods such as GetCode and GetDecode.

Fatal Error-Handling Component

There must be a standard way to handle fatal errors across all applications. Visual Basic and other applications provide excellent ways to trap and raise errors but some changes are required in the error handling strategy in distributed applications. Objects cannot be passed by reference from one system to another in a distributed computing environment. COM provides marshaling for standard data types. Custom marshaling is required for user-defined datatypes. This means that error objects that are passed from the client must be dehydrated and then rehydrated on the server. In our architecture, error objects were sent as byVal function parameters and therefore could not be returned to the client side. The handling of errors on the client and server sides of the architecture is also different. On the server side, errors need to be logged but not displayed in a dialog box. On the client side it is important for errors to be displayed in a dialog box. Therefore, two error components, one for the server side and the other for the client side, with similar data structures in terms of attributes, but with different methods, were built as part of the fatal error-handling component.

Data Service Component

These components can be referenced by the data layer components. This data service component provides a standard method to access databases; in this case, relational databases. There are many methods to connect to relational databases depending on the type of database used. Some of the data access methods are data access objects (DAO), remote data objects (RDO), and ActiveX data objects (ADO). Each of these access methods has its own distinct object models and changing from one access method to another becomes difficult if the data layer components use code specific to a given data access method. Building a data service component prevents making changes in the data layer component of the application because the interface to the data service component is unchanged when a new data access method is employed. The implementation change in the data service component to conform to the new data access method does not have any impact on the rest of the applications. Therefore building a data service component to provide this isolation or decoupling in the application framework is important for ease of maintenance.

Business Error Component

The fatal error-handling component mentioned earlier was meant to handle exception handling only. Applications must have the capability to handle business rule violation errors. It is also a good idea to keep these methods separate. The fatal error-handling component for fatal or hard errors and the business error components to respond to business errors are useful approaches. As mentioned earlier in the chapter, both the fatal error and the business message components are specialized versions of the basic object and collection classes.

Common Components

Other common components may be required across all applications and these may be wrappers around components that are already available. These wrappers provide some custom features. Examples of such components are calendar, calculator, and tables.

Getting Started

This section provides information on how to create a project and the steps required to build applications using Visual Basic 5.

Creating a Project

The first screen displayed on executing VB contains three tabs : New, Existing and Recent. These tabs make it easy to locate projects. The recent tab contains a list of projects that were recently created or modified. The existing tab allows you to access a directory and locate a project. The new folder has options to create different types of projects. For the application we are building we will need two of the project types: Standard EXE and ActiveX DLL. The standard EXE project will reside on the client side during application execution. The ActiveX DLL projects will reside on the remote servers. The DLLs will be inserted into the MTS environment. The process for doing this is explained in detail in a later section of this chapter. Figure 15.7 shows the options that are available to create the executables.

While developing a project it is advisable to create a group and have all the other projects added to this group. This helps in debugging and is a ready reference tool. It also helps in making changes to other projects easier. This project contains five projects in the group, namely the client exe and four DLLs. This includes the MTS gatekeeper DLL, the business DLLs for each business component, and DLLs for the data services. There is no hard and fast rule for packaging the DLLs. The business components DLL may be packaged such that the data classes are included along with the business classes.

Adding a Class to a Project

Figure 15.8 lists the steps that are required to add a class to a given project from the pull-down menu. This displays the "Add Class Module" dialogue that contains two tabs, NEW and EXISTING.

Setting Project References

This project has various components, namely, the GUI components, the MTS components, the interface, business, and the data service components. The classes within

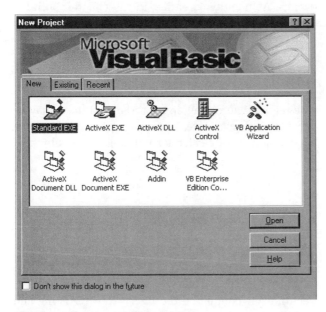

Figure 15.7 New project folder.

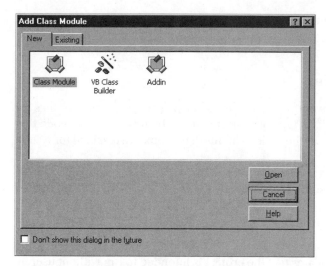

Figure 15.8   Adding a class.

these components need to access methods exposed by other classes in local and remote projects. The mechanism used to make this possible is setting project references. Setting a project reference allows the classes in the one project to access classes in the referenced project.

Figure 15.9 shows the project references screen in Visual Basic 5.0. Clicking on Project-References on the menu bar will get you to this screen. The following references are needed to be set:

The client .exe needs no reference.

The MTS components need to refer to the interface components.

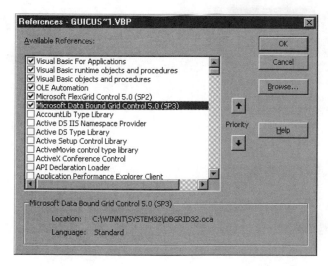

Figure 15.9   Project references.

The interface components need to refer to the business components.

The business components need to refer to the data services components.

Setting Project Properties

Figure 15.10 shows the contents of the General tab of the project properties settings for a standard executable project. This type of project ends up being executable code that runs on the client system. Some of the options in this dialog box are disabled for a standard .exe project.

Figure 15.11 shows the General tab of the project properties dialog screen for an ActiveX DLL project. Notice that some of the options that were disabled for the standard .exe type of project are enabled for the ActiveX DLL project.

The following is a brief explanation of the various options seen in the General tab of the project properties dialog box:

Unattended execution indicates that the project is intended to run without user interaction. Unattended projects have no interface elements. Any run-time functions such as messages that normally result in user interaction are written to an event log.

Thread per object indicates that each instance of a class marked as multiuse in the Instancing property will be created on a new and distinct thread. Each thread has a unique copy of all global variables and objects, and will not interfere with any other thread.

Thread pool indicates that each instance of a class marked as multiuse in the instancing property will be created on a thread from the thread pool. The choice of thread is determined in a round-robin fashion. Each thread has a unique copy of all

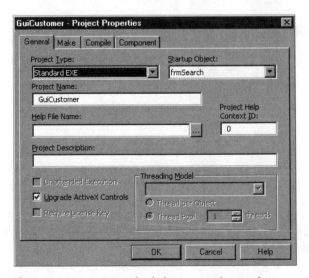

Figure 15.10   General tab for properties settings.

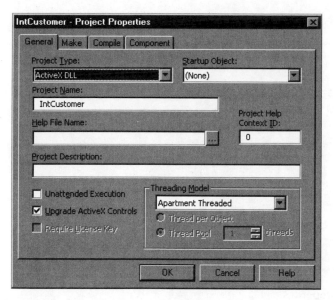

Figure 15.11   ActiveX project properties.

global variables, but multiple instances reside on a given thread and can potentially interfere with each other.

Number of threads determines the maximum number of threads created for the
thread pool. When a multiuse class is instantiated, threads are created as needed
up to the number set here. After the maximum number is reached, Visual Basic begins assigning new instances to existing threads.

The component tab is an important tab for ActiveX DLL projects. The part that is very
important is the version compatibility section. Version compatibility allows you to set
the level of version compatibility. There are three possible settings, which are explained
briefly below:

No compatibility means that compatibility is not enforced.

Project compatibility. If checked, the location box becomes active and allows you
to search for the file with which this project is to be compatible. If cleared, the location box is not available. For all ActiveX project types, project compatibility is
checked by default.

Binary compatibility is useful for maintaining compatibility among projects that
have been compiled using your component. The file location box displays the
name and location of the file with the project it is compatible with. You can type a
name and location or can use the Browse button to display the Compatible ActiveX Server dialog box where you can locate the file, as shown in Figure 15.12.

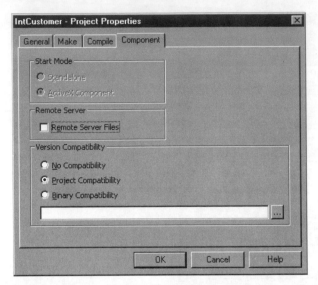

Figure 15.12 Component properties.

The GUI Forms and GUI Classes

This project produces the executable that runs on the client system. It contains all the GUI-based forms and the GUI classes. What are GUI classes? They are classes that store state information of objects retrieved from the server.

Figure 15.13 allows the user to search for a customer based on any combination of customer ID, and last name. When the Search button is clicked the following sequence of events takes place:

1. The CustomersGui class is instantiated. This class contains a collection of customer objects.

2. The load method in the CustomersGui class is called and the two parameters are passed.

3. The load method instantiates the MTS Customer component CRoleReadclass on MTS and calls the LoadCustomer method.

4. The LoadCustomer method instantiates the interface component and calls the load method.

5. The load method in the implementation class instantiates and calls the load method on the server-side customer business component, CustomersBus.

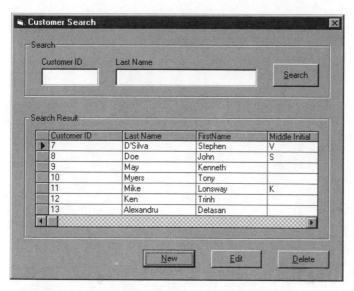

Figure 15.13 Search function.

6. The load method in the CustomersBus then instantiates the data service object, CustomerDat, and calls the load method on it, passing itself as the parameter.

7. The data services object then formats an SQL select statement and executes it. This returns a result set that contains zero or more rows depending on the contents of the WHERE clause.

8. The data in the result set has to be populated in the customer object. This is done by looping through the result set. Within the loop the CreateNewobject in the CustomersBus class is called which provides a new instance of the CustomerBus object. This object is then populated.

9. Since an object or a collection of objects cannot be passed across servers as previously explained, the GetArray method is used to create a variant array of the collection of objects. This variant array is then sent through to the client side. The load method in the CustomersGui class then proceeds to populate the objects from the returned variant array.

10. The final step is to populate controls on the form. In this case it is the Microsoft DBGrid control.

The exact sequence of events is also used to load addresses on the GUI side. Source Listing 15.1 gives code segments from within the CustomersGui class.

```
This method loads the customer information based on the customerid and
                                                     the lastname.
Public Sub Load(oError As CError, Optional vCustomerID As Variant, _
            Optional vLastName As Variant)

    'Declare local variables for current procedure.
    Dim oServer As Object

    'Add current procedure name to error object.
    oError.AddProcedure "CCustomersGui.Load"

    'Set error handler for current procedure.
    On Error GoTo HandleError

    'Create new instance of server object
    Set oServer = CreateObject("MtsCustomer.CRoleRead")

    'Load records into server-side collection and populate it into a
                                                collection object.
    SetArray vCustomers:=oServer.LoadCustomers(oError.LogInfo,
                                        vCustomerID, vLastName)

    'Destroy server object.
    Set oServer = Nothing

    'Remove current procedure name from error object.
    oError.RemoveProcedure

Exit Sub

HandleError:

    'Call error handler to process fatal error condition.
    oError.HandleError Err.Number, _
                    Err.Description, _
                    Err.Source

    'Destroy server object.
    Set oServer = Nothing

    'Raise error condition to calling procedure.
    oError.RaiseError
```

(Continues)

Source 15.1 CustomerGui code segments.

```
End Sub
'This method takes an array and populates multiple objects
Public Sub SetArray(vCustomers As Variant)
    'Declare local variables for current procedure.
    Dim oCustomer As CCustomerGui
    Dim lIndex As Long

    'Loop through array structure to populate collection.
    If Not IsNull(vCustomers) Then
        For lIndex = 0 To UBound(vCustomers)
            Set oCustomer = New CCustomerGui
            oCustomer.SetAttributes vCustomers(lIndex)
            m_colCustomers.Add oCustomer
        Next
    End If

    'Destroys the local gui object
    Set oCustomer = Nothing

End Sub

'The getarray method creates a multidimensional array from a collection
                                                        of objects.
Public Function GetArray()

    'Declare local variables for current procedure.
    Dim aCustomersGui() As Variant
    Dim lIndex As Long

    'Populate return array from private collection
    If (Me.Count >= 1) Then
        ReDim aCustomersGui(Me.Count - 1)
        For lIndex = 0 To (Me.Count - 1)
            aCustomersGui(lIndex) = Me.Item(lIndex + 1).GetAttributes()
        Next
        GetArray = aCustomersGui
    Else
        GetArray = Null
    End If

End Function
```

Source 15.1 *(Continued)*

Why GUI Classes?

You might be wondering about the continued mention of GUI classes, and their use in this example. Since we are working in a distributed environment and because we want our applications to be scalable, there are some design decisions that must be made early in the process. First of all, we cannot hold on to resources like it was done in the old days. Resources are very precious and we need to return them to the pool the moment we are done with them. Other users can then use these. This means that we have no reference to the objects once they are returned to the pool. Also, we do not want to go to the server for every request that is issued. This would be too costly. The object states must be preserved somewhere. This then brings us to the "how." There are many possibilities. Storing data in a variant array is one option. This option is good, but managing the data itself becomes a problem. Objects and collections of objects are good structures to store data returned by the server. These are also very manageable. Unlike variant arrays, objects can contain methods to process data in addition to storing data. Some client-side validations can also be done using methods within these objects. These are only a few reasons why it makes sense to use client-side objects. One important thing that must be noted is that client-side objects are data-holding structures with some client-side methods. They are not related to server-side objects. They may have similar structures but that is all.

The MTS-Specific Component

This is the component that is installed in the MTS environment using the MTS explorer. All other server-side components function as in-process DLLs to this component.

This component is application specific and is closely tied to the GUI classes of the presentation layer. It can be viewed as a gatekeeper, as it provides role-based security access to server components. The MTS components are packaged in one DLL.

In this project we have two MTS components. One is a read component and the other is a write component. The read component contains methods that read information such as LoadCustomer, LoadAddresses, and so on. The write MTS component contains methods that eventually write to the database such as InsertCustomer, UpdateAddress, and so on.

There is no need to have two components—all of the methods can be put into one component. The reason for doing this is because many times, clients require applications that allow some users to only view data and some to read and write data. By keeping the two functions separate, we can then use the role settings within MTS to set read-only and read-write user settings.

The MTS components are simple components. They are application specific and are closely linked to the client layer of the application. This component is not meant to be reused.

Source Listing 15.2 contains code from the MTS component.

```
This method is called by the GUI collection class. It instantiates the
customer interface and calls methods exposed by the interface.
Public Function LoadCustomers(ByVal vLogInfo As Variant, _
                    Optional vCustomerID As Variant, _
                    Optional vLastname As Variant) As Variant


    'Declare local variables for current procedure.
    Dim oDatabase As CConnection
    Dim oError As CError

    'Declare private Customer Interface object.
    Dim m_oCustomerInt As CCustomerInt

    'Initialize error object for current procedure.
    Set oError = New CError
    oError.LogInfo = vLogInfo

    'Add current procedure name to error object.
    oError.AddProcedure "CRoleRead.LoadCustomers"

    'Set error handling to for current procedure.
    On Error GoTo HandleError

    'Instantiate new database connection.
    Set oDatabase = New CConnection
    oDatabase.Initialize oError


    'Instantiate interface
    Set m_oCustomerInt = New CCustomerImp

    'Load Customer objects from database.
    LoadCustomers = m_oCustomerInt.Load(oError, oDatabase, vCustomerID,
                                                        vLastname)

    'Destroy database connection.
    Set oDatabase = Nothing
    Set m_oCustomerInt = Nothing

    'Remove current procedure name from error object.
    oError.RemoveProcedure

Exit Function

HandleError:
```

(Continues)

Source 15.2 MTS component code.

```
                'Call error handler to process fatal error condition.
                oError.HandleError Err.Number, _
                                    Err.Description, _
                                    Err.Source


                'Destroy database connection.
                Set oDatabase = Nothing
                Set m_oCustomerInt = Nothing


                'Raise error condition to calling procedure.
                oError.RaiseError

         End Function



         Public Function InsertAddress(ByVal vLogInfo As Variant, ByVal vCustomer
                                                            As Variant) As Variant

                'Declare local variables for current procedure.
                Dim oDatabase As CConnection
                Dim oError As CError

                'Declare private Customer interface object.
                Dim m_oCustomerInt As CCustomerInt

                'Initialize error object for current procedure.
                Set oError = New CError
                oError.LogInfo = vLogInfo

                'Add current procedure name to error object.
                oError.AddProcedure "CRoleWrite.InsertAddress"

                'Set error handling to for current procedure.
                On Error GoTo HandleError

                'Instantiate new objects
                Set oDatabase = New CConnection
                oDatabase.Initialize oError
                Set m_oCustomerInt = New CCustomerImp

                'Insert Customer properties into database.
                InsertAddress = m_oCustomerInt.InsertAddress(oError, oDatabase,
                                                              vCustomer)
```

(Continues)

Source 15.2 *(Continued)*

```
        'Destroy objects.
        Set oDatabase = Nothing
        Set m_oCustomerInt = Nothing

        'Remove current procedure name from error object.
        oError.RemoveProcedure

Exit Function

HandleError:

        'Call error handler to process fatal error condition.
        oError.HandleError Err.Number, _
                        Err.Description, _
                        Err.Source

        'Destroy objects.
        Set oDatabase = Nothing
        Set m_oCustomerInt = Nothing

        'Release server resources (with database rollback).
        SetAbort oError

        'Raise error condition to calling procedure.
        oError.RaiseError

End Function

Public Function UpdateCustomer(ByVal vLogInfo As Variant, ByVal
                                        vCustomer As Variant) As Variant

        'Declare local variables for current procedure.
        Dim oDatabase As CConnection
        Dim oError As CError

        'Declare private Customer interface object.
        Dim m_oCustomerInt As CCustomerInt

        'Initialize error object for current procedure.
        Set oError = New CError
        oError.LogInfo = vLogInfo

        'Add current procedure name to error object.
        oError.AddProcedure "CRoleWrite.UpdateCustomer"
```

(Continues)

Source 15.2 *(Continued)*

```
    'Set error handling to for current procedure.
    On Error GoTo HandleError

    'Instantiate new objects
    Set oDatabase = New CConnection
    oDatabase.Initialize oError
    Set m_oCustomerInt = New CCustomerImp

    'Update Customer properties into database.
    UpdateCustomer = m_oCustomerInt.Update(oError, oDatabase, vCustomer)

    'Destroy database connection.
    Set oDatabase = Nothing
    Set m_oCustomerInt = Nothing

    'Remove current procedure name from error object.
    oError.RemoveProcedure

Exit Function

HandleError:

    'Call error handler to process fatal error condition.
    oError.HandleError Err.Number, _
                       Err.Description, _
                       Err.Source

    'Destroy database connection.
    Set oDatabase = Nothing
    Set m_oCustomerInt = Nothing

    'Release server resources (with database rollback).
    SetAbort oError

    'Raise error condition to calling procedure.
    oError.RaiseError

End Function

Public Function UpdateAddress(ByVal vLogInfo As Variant, ByVal vCustomer _
                                                As Variant) As Variant

    'Declare local variables for current procedure.
    Dim oDatabase As CConnection
    Dim oError As CError

    'Declare private Customer interface object.
    Dim m_oCustomerInt As CCustomerInt
```

(Continues)

Source 15.2   *(Continued)*

```
        'Initialize error object for current procedure.
        Set oError = New CError
        oError.LogInfo = vLogInfo

        'Add current procedure name to error object.
        oError.AddProcedure "CRoleWrite.UpdateAddress"

        'Set error handling to for current procedure.
        On Error GoTo HandleError

        'Instantiate new objects
        Set oDatabase = New CConnection
        oDatabase.Initialize oError
        Set m_oCustomerInt = New CCustomerImp

        'Update Customer properties into database.
        UpdateAddress = m_oCustomerInt.UpdateAddress(oError, oDatabase, _
                                                        vCustomer)

        'Destroy database connection.
        Set oDatabase = Nothing
        Set m_oCustomerInt = Nothing

        'Remove current procedure name from error object.
        oError.RemoveProcedure

Exit Function

HandleError:

        'Call error handler to process fatal error condition.
        oError.HandleError Err.Number, _
                        Err.Description, _
                        Err.Source

        'Destroy database connection.
        Set oDatabase = Nothing
        Set m_oCustomerInt = Nothing

        'Release server resources (with database rollback).
        SetAbort oError

        'Raise error condition to calling procedure.
        oError.RaiseError

End Function
```

(Continues)

Source 15.2 *(Continued)*

```
Public Sub DeleteCustomer(ByVal vLogInfo As Variant, ByVal vCustomer As
                                                                    Variant)

    'Declare local variables for current procedure.
    Dim oDatabase As CConnection
    Dim oError As CError

    'Declare private Customer interface object.
    Dim m_oCustomerInt As CCustomerInt

    'Initialize error object for current procedure.
    Set oError = New CError
    oError.LogInfo = vLogInfo

    'Add current procedure name to error object.
    oError.AddProcedure "CRoleWrite.DeleteCustomer"

    'Set error handling to for current procedure.
    On Error GoTo HandleError

    'Instantiate new objects
    Set oDatabase = New CConnection
    oDatabase.Initialize oError
    Set m_oCustomerInt = New CCustomerImp

    'Delete Customer properties into database.
    m_oCustomerInt.Delete oError, oDatabase, vCustomer

    'Destroy objects.
    Set oDatabase = Nothing
    Set m_oCustomerInt = Nothing

    'Remove current procedure name from error object.
    oError.RemoveProcedure

Exit Sub

HandleError:

    'Call error handler to process fatal error condition.
    oError.HandleError Err.Number, _
                       Err.Description, _
                       Err.Source

    'Destroy objects.
    Set oDatabase = Nothing
    Set m_oCustomerInt = Nothing
```

(Continues)

Source 15.2 *(Continued)*

```
        'Release server resources (with database rollback).
        SetAbort oError

        'Raise error condition to calling procedure.
        oError.RaiseError

End Sub



Public Sub SetComplete(ByVal vLogInfo As Variant)

        'Declare local variables for current procedure.
        Dim oObjectContext As CObjectContext
        Dim oError As CError

        'Initialize error object for current procedure.
        Set oError = New CError
        oError.LogInfo = vLogInfo

        'Add current procedure name to error object.
        oError.AddProcedure "CCustomerRoleRead.SetComplete"

        'Set error handling to for current procedure.
        On Error GoTo HandleError

        'Obtain reference to transaction server context.
        Set oObjectContext = New CObjectContext

        'Call method of transaction server context.
        oObjectContext.SetComplete

        'Destroy reference to transaction server context.
        Set oObjectContext = Nothing

        'Remove current procedure name from error object.
        oError.RemoveProcedure

HandleError:

        'Call error handler to process fatal error condition.
        oError.HandleError Err.Number, _
                        Err.Description, _
                        Err.Source

        'Destroy reference to transaction server context.
        Set oObjectContext = Nothing
```

(Continues)

Source 15.2 *(Continued)*

```
    'Raise error condition to calling procedure.
    oError.RaiseError

End Sub


Private Sub SetAbort(oError As CError)

    'Declare local variables for current procedure.
    Dim oObjectContext As CObjectContext

    'Add current procedure name to error object.
    oError.AddProcedure "CRoleRead.SetAbort"

    'Set error handling to for current procedure.
    On Error GoTo HandleError

    'Obtain reference to transaction server context.
    Set oObjectContext = New CObjectContext

    'Call method of transaction server context.
    oObjectContext.SetAbort

    'Destroy reference to transaction server context.
    Set oObjectContext = Nothing

    'Remove current procedure name from error object.
    oError.RemoveProcedure

Exit Sub

HandleError:

    'Call error handler to process fatal error condition.
    oError.HandleError Err.Number, _
                       Err.Description, _
                       Err.Source

    'Destroy reference to transaction server context.
    Set oObjectContext = Nothing

    'Raise error condition to calling procedure.
    oError.RaiseError

End Sub
```

Source 15.2 *(Continued)*

The SetComplete and SetAbort methods are part of the MTS APIs and are used to indicate to MTS that we have finished what we wanted to do and want to release the resources. The SetComplete method tells MTS that we have successfully completed the task and therefore the transaction can be committed and resources released. The SetAbort method informs MTS that the task was not successful and therefore the transaction must be rolled back and resources returned to the pool.

The Business Components

These are the components that are called by the MTS components and they fulfill business tasks. For a given application they are broken down into two primary DLLs. The first one contains the interface and the implementation for a controller component. These components are exposed to the outside world and may be broken into multiple DLLs based on subject areas. In our project one interface is exposed which contains methods for querying and manipulating customer name and address information. This interface is then implemented by the implementation class. In large projects it is advisable to have them separated based on subject areas for reasons such as keeping the size small, reducing the impact of making changes, and the amount of regression testing. These controller component DLLs have classes that expose interfaces and classes that implement the interfaces. These controller classes then call the actual business objects such as customer, address , etc., and manage interaction between various business components.

In our project the IntCustomer component is the controller component. These are COM components with an interface and implementation. As projects evolve and changes are made, new interfaces can be created thereby not affecting older client applications. Also the business classes are encapsulated and there is no need for other business classes to know and depend on the internals of our business classes whose implementations are guaranteed to change. This approach also reduces dependencies on business classes within the same subject area.

The following syntax is the source for the interface class. The interface class contains the method declarations. This Instancing property for this class is set as Public Not Createable. The class that implements this interface is set to multiuse. The implementation class, however, has methods that are declared as private. This means that even though the implementation class can be instantiated, the methods that can be used by the user are those that are specified in the interface class:

```
Public Function Load(oError As CError, oDatabase As CConnection, _
                Optional vCustomerID As Variant, _
                Optional vLastname As Variant) As Variant

End Function

Public Function Insert(oError As CError, oDatabase As CConnection, _
                vCustomer As Variant) As Variant

End Function
```

```
Public Function Update(oError As CError, oDatabase As CConnection, _
                vCustomer As Variant) As Variant

End Function

Public Sub Delete(oError As CError, oDatabase As CConnection, _
                vCustomer As Variant)

End Sub

Public Function LoadAddress(oError As CError, oDatabase As CConnection, _
                    Optional vCustomerID As Variant) As Variant

End Function

Public Function InsertAddress(oError As CError, oDatabase As CConnection, _
                    vAddress As Variant) As Variant

End Function

Public Function UpdateAddress(oError As CError, oDatabase As CConnection, _
                    vAddress As Variant) As Variant

End Function

Public Sub DeleteAddress(oError As CError, oDatabase As CConnection, _
                    vAddress As Variant)

End Sub
```

Source Listing 15.3 contains code from the implementation class. The implements keyword is the key to this class. An implementation class can implement the methods within multiple interface classes. However, all methods in an interface class have to be implemented.

```
'Set environment option to require explicit variable declaration.
Option Explicit

'Implementation for Customer Interface class
Implements CCustomerInt


Private Sub CCustomerInt_Delete(oError As CError, oDatabase As
CConnection, vCustomer As Variant)

    'Declare local variables
    Dim m_oCustomerBus As CCustomerBus
```

(Continues)

Source 15.3 Implementation class code.

```
Dim m_oAddressesBus As CAddressesBus
Dim lCount As Long
Dim lCounter As Long


'Add current procedure name to error object.
oError.AddProcedure "CCustomerImp.CCustomerInt_Delete"

'Set error handling to for current procedure.
On Error GoTo HandleError


'Instantiate address object
Set m_oAddressesBus = New CAddressesBus


'Instantiate  object
Set m_oCustomerBus = New CCustomerBus

'Delete Customer object from database.
With m_oCustomerBus
    .SetAttributes vCustomer
End With

'Load Addresses
m_oAddressesBus.Load oError, oDatabase, m_oCustomerBus.CustomerID

lCount = m_oAddressesBus.Count

'Delete all addresses for the customer
If lCount > 1 Then

    For lCounter - 1 To lCount

        m_oAddressesBus.Item(lCounter).Delete oError, oDatabase

    Next

End If

'Delete Customer object
m_oCustomerBus.Delete oError, oDatabase


'Destroy object
Set m_oCustomerBus = Nothing
```
(Continues)

Source 15.3 *(Continued)*

```
        'Remove current procedure name from error object.
        oError.RemoveProcedure

Exit Sub

HandleError:

    'Destroy object
    Set m_oCustomerBus = Nothing

    'Call error handler to process fatal error condition.
    oError.HandleError Err.Number, _
                    Err.Description, _
                    Err.Source

    'Raise error condition to calling procedure.
    oError.RaiseError

End Sub

Private Sub CCustomerInt_DeleteAddress(oError As CError, oDatabase As
CConnection, vAddress As Variant)

    'Declare local variables
    Dim m_oAddressBus As CAddressBus

    'Add current procedure name to error object.
    oError.AddProcedure "CCustomerImp.CCustomerInt_DeleteAddress"

    'Set error handling to for current procedure.
    On Error GoTo HandleError

    'Instantiate  object
    Set m_oAddressBus = New CAddressBus

    'Delete Customer object from database.
    With m_oAddressBus
        .SetAttributes vAddress
        .Delete oError, oDatabase
    End With


    'Destroy object
    Set m_oAddressBus = Nothing


    'Remove current procedure name from error object.
    oError.RemoveProcedure
```

(Continues)

Source 15.3   *(Continued)*

```
    Exit Sub

HandleError:

    'Destroy object
    Set m_oAddressBus = Nothing


    'Call error handler to process fatal error condition.
    oError.HandleError Err.Number, _
                       Err.Description, _
                       Err.Source

    'Raise error condition to calling procedure.
    oError.RaiseError


End Sub

Private Function CCustomerInt_Insert(oError As CError, oDatabase As
CConnection, vCustomer As Variant) As Variant

    'Declare local variables
    Dim m_oCustomerBus As CCustomerBus


    'Add current procedure name to error object.
    oError.AddProcedure "CCustomerImp.CCustomerInt_Insert"

    'Set error handling to for current procedure.
    On Error GoTo HandleError

    'Instantiate  object
    Set m_oCustomerBus = New CCustomerBus

    'Insert Customer properties into database.
    With m_oCustomerBus
        .SetAttributes vCustomer
        .Insert oError, oDatabase
        CCustomerInt_Insert = .GetAttributes
    End With

    'Destroy object
    Set m_oCustomerBus = Nothing

    'Remove current procedure name from error object.
    oError.RemoveProcedure
```

(Continues)

Source 15.3 *(Continued)*

```
Exit Function


HandleError:

    'Destroy object
    Set m_oCustomerBus = Nothing

    'Call error handler to process fatal error condition.
    oError.HandleError Err.Number, _
                       Err.Description, _
                       Err.Source

    'Raise error condition to calling procedure.
    oError.RaiseError

End Function

Private Function CCustomerInt_InsertAddress(oError As CError, oDatabase
As CConnection, vAddress As Variant) As Variant

   'Declare local variables
   Dim m_oAddressBus As CAddressBus

    'Add current procedure name to error object.
    oError.AddProcedure "CCustomerImp.CCustomerInt_InsertAddress"

    'Set error handling to for current procedure.
    On Error GoTo HandleError

    'Instantiate  object
    Set m_oAddressBus = New CAddressBus

    'Insert  properties into database.
    With m_oAddressBus
        .SetAttributes vAddress
        .Insert oError, oDatabase
        CCustomerInt_InsertAddress = .GetAttributes
    End With

    'Destroy object
    Set m_oAddressBus = Nothing



    'Remove current procedure name from error object.
    oError.RemoveProcedure

Exit Function
```

(Continues)

Source 15.3 *(Continued)*

```
HandleError:

    'Destroy object
    Set m_oAddressBus = Nothing


    'Call error handler to process fatal error condition.
    oError.HandleError Err.Number, _
                       Err.Description, _
                       Err.Source

    'Raise error condition to calling procedure.
    oError.RaiseError

End Function

Private Function CCustomerInt_Load(oError As CError, oDatabase As
CConnection, Optional vCustomerID As Variant, Optional vLastname As
Variant) As Variant

    'Declare local variables
    Dim m_oCustomersBus As CCustomersBus

    'Add current procedure name to error object.
    oError.AddProcedure "CCustomerImp.CCustomerInt_Load"

    'Set error handling to for current procedure.
    On Error GoTo HandleError

    'Instantiate Customers collection
    Set m_oCustomersBus = New CCustomersBus

    'Load Customer objects from database.
    m_oCustomersBus.Load oError, oDatabase, vCustomerID, vLastname

    'set return array
    CCustomerInt_Load = m_oCustomersBus.GetArray

    'Destroy object
    Set m_oCustomersBus = Nothing

    'Remove current procedure name from error object.
    oError.RemoveProcedure


Exit Function

HandleError:
```

(Continues)

Source 15.3 *(Continued)*

```
        'Destroy object
        Set m_oCustomersBus = Nothing


        'Call error handler to process fatal error condition.
        oError.HandleError Err.Number, _
                           Err.Description, _
                           Err.Source


        'Raise error condition to calling procedure.
        oError.RaiseError

End Function

Private Function CCustomerInt_LoadAddress(oError As CError, oDatabase As
CConnection, Optional vCustomerID As Variant) As Variant

    'Declare local variables
    Dim m_oAddressesBus As CAddressesBus

    'Add current procedure name to error object.
    oError.AddProcedure "CCustomerImp.CCustomerInt_LoadAddress"

    'Set error handling to for current procedure.
    On Error GoTo HandleError

    'Instantiate  collection
    Set m_oAddressesBus = New CAddressesBus

    'Load  objects from database.
    m_oAddressesBus.Load oError, oDatabase, vCustomerID

    'set return array
    CCustomerInt_LoadAddress = m_oAddressesBus.GetArray

    'Destroy object
    Set m_oAddressesBus = Nothing

    'Remove current procedure name from error object.
    oError.RemoveProcedure


Exit Function

HandleError:
```

(Continues)

Source 15.3 *(Continued)*

```
        'Destroy object
        Set m_oAddressesBus = Nothing


        'Call error handler to process fatal error condition.
        oError.HandleError Err.Number, _
                           Err.Description, _
                           Err.Source


        'Raise error condition to calling procedure.
        oError.RaiseError

End Function

Private Function CCustomerInt_Update(oError As CError, oDatabase As
CConnection, vCustomer As Variant) As Variant

        'Declare local variables
    Dim m_oCustomerBus As CCustomerBus

    'Add current procedure name to error object.
    oError.AddProcedure "CCustomerImp.CCustomerInt_Update"

    'Set error handling to for current procedure.
    On Error GoTo HandleError

    'Instantiate  object
    Set m_oCustomerBus = New CCustomerBus

    'Update Customer properties into database.
    With m_oCustomerBus
        .SetAttributes vCustomer
        .Update oError, oDatabase
        CCustomerInt_Update = .GetAttributes
    End With

    'Destroy object
    Set m_oCustomerBus = Nothing

    'Remove current procedure name from error object.
    oError.RemoveProcedure

Exit Function

HandleError:
```

(Continues)

Source 15.3 *(Continued)*

```
    'Destroy object
    Set m_oCustomerBus = Nothing

    'Call error handler to process fatal error condition.
    oError.HandleError Err.Number, _
                       Err.Description, _
                       Err.Source

    'Raise error condition to calling procedure.
    oError.RaiseError
End Function

Private Function CCustomerInt_UpdateAddress(oError As CError, oDatabase
As CConnection, vAddress As Variant) As Variant

    'Declare local variables
    Dim m_oAddressBus As CAddressBus

   'Add current procedure name to error object.
    oError.AddProcedure "CCustomerImp.CCustomerInt_UpdateAddress"

    'Set error handling to for current procedure.
    On Error GoTo HandleError


    'Instantiate  object
    Set m_oAddressBus = New CAddressBus

    'Update properties into database.
    With m_oAddressBus
        .SetAttributes vAddress
        .Update oError, oDatabase
        CCustomerInt_UpdateAddress = .GetAttributes
    End With

    'Destroy object
    Set m_oAddressBus = Nothing


    'Remove current procedure name from error object.
    oError.RemoveProcedure

Exit Function

HandleError:

    'Destroy object

    Set m_oAddressBus = Nothing
```
(Continues)

Source 15.3 *(Continued)*

```
        'Call error handler to process fatal error condition.
        oError.HandleError Err.Number, _
                        Err.Description, _
                        Err.Source

        'Raise error condition to calling procedure.
        oError.RaiseError


End Function
```

Source 15.3   *(Continued)*

The Data Components

The data components are built in one project as an ActiveX DLL. They contain SQL code and code and methods that are used to retrieve, insert, delete, and update data. The data components also contain code to generate primary key data and also have methods to handle concurrency.

Source Listing 15.4 contains code for the load method, which loads information from the database into the proper objects. The contents of the code were explained earlier in the GUI section of this chapter.

```
This method loads address information from the database

Public Sub Load(oError As CError, oDatabase As CConnection, _
                oAddressesBus As Object, Optional vCustomerID As Variant)

    'Declare local variables for current procedure.
    Dim rsAddress As CRecordset
    Dim oAddressBus As Object
    Dim sSql As String

    'Add current procedure name to error object.
    oError.AddProcedure "CAddressDat.Load"

    'Set error handler for current procedure.
    On Error GoTo HandleError

    'Create sql string for database select.
    sSql = "SELECT "
    sSql = sSql & "CustomerID, "
    sSql = sSql & "AddressType, "
    sSql = sSql & "StreetAddress, "
                                                      (Continues)
```

Source 15.4   Load method code.

```
      sSql = sSql & "AptNumber, "
      sSql = sSql & "City, "
      sSql = sSql & "Province, "
      sSql = sSql & "PostalCode, "
      sSql = sSql & "Country, "
      sSql = sSql & "Telephone, "
      sSql = sSql & "Email"
      sSql = sSql & " FROM t_Address "

      If Not IsMissing(vCustomerID) Then
          sSql = sSql & "WHERE CustomerID = " & vCustomerID
      End If

      'Open recordset for requested Address rows.
      Set rsAddress = oDatabase.OpenRecordset(oError, sSql, _
  dboUnlimitedRows)

      'Loop through recordset to populate collection.
      Do Until rsAddress.EOF
          Set oAddressBus = oAddressesBus.CreateNewObject
          With oAddressBus
              .Initialize rsAddress("CustomerID"), _
                          rsAddress("AddressType")
              .StreetAddress = rsAddress("StreetAddress")
              .AptNumber = rsAddress("AptNumber")
              .City = rsAddress("City")
              .Province = rsAddress("Province")
              .PostalCode = rsAddress("PostalCode")
              .Country = rsAddress("Country")
              .Telephone = rsAddress("Telephone")
              .Email = rsAddress("Email")
          End With
          oAddressesBus.Add oAddressBus
          rsAddress.MoveNext
      Loop

      'Destroy recordset object.
      Set rsAddress = Nothing

      'Remove current procedure name from error object.
      oError.RemoveProcedure

  Exit Sub

  HandleError:

      'Call error handler to process fatal error condition.
```

(Continues)

Source 15.4 *(Continued)*

```
        oError.HandleError Err.Number, _
                            Err.Description, _
                            Err.Source

        'Destroy recordset object.
        Set rsAddress = Nothing

        'Raise error condition to calling procedure.
        oError.RaiseError

    End Sub
```

Source 15.4 *(Continued)*

The update method is basically a method that contains the SQL update statement. There is some additional code that requires more attention. First, this method does not modify primary keys. In a distributed disconnected system there is always a possibility for concurrency problems. For example data is loaded and modified at the client side and before this data is updated another client may have deleted or updated the data. This means that the first clients data is not valid for an update. This is the concurrency problem. This is handled by using an additional column in each of the tables that will maintain a time stamp. When the data is first loaded using the load method, the modify-date field from the database is also brought to the client side. After making the changes, the changed data is sent along with the modifydate attribute. In the data services the checkconcurrency method could check if a row with the modifydate is still present in the database. If a row is present, the modifydate attribute is changed to the current date and the time and the whole record is updated in the database. This is a simple technique to check concurrency. If no row is returned in the checkconcurrency method, then up-date is not called. The logic is that someone else may have changed the data after the data was loaded but prior to sending the update method. This technique is also used in the delete method.

Source Listing 15.5 contains several methods for manipulating data.

```
'This method inserts a Customer record into the database
Public Sub Insert(oError As CError, oDatabase As CConnection,
oCustomerBus As Object)

    'Declare local variables for current procedure.
    Dim sSql As String
    Dim rsCustomer As CRecordset

    'Add current procedure name to error object.
    oError.AddProcedure "CCustomerDat.Insert"
```
                                                            (Continues)

Source 15.5 Method code.

```
    'Set error handler for current procedure.
    On Error GoTo HandleError

    'Create sql string for database insert.
    sSql = "INSERT INTO t_Customer ( "
    sSql = sSql & "FirstName, "
    sSql = sSql & "LastName, "
    sSql = sSql & "MiddleInitial"
    sSql = sSql & ") "

    sSql = sSql & "VALUES ("
    sSql = sSql & SqlFormat(oCustomerBus.FirstName) & ", "
    sSql = sSql & SqlFormat(oCustomerBus.LastName) & ", "
    sSql = sSql & SqlFormat(oCustomerBus.MiddleInitial)
    sSql = sSql & ")"

    'Execute query to insert record into database.
    oDatabase.Execute oError, sSql

    'Create sql string for database select.
    sSql = "SELECT MAX(customerid) AS customerid FROM t_customer"

    'Get current maximum primary key.
    Set rsCustomer = oDatabase.OpenRecordset(oError, sSql, dboSingleRow)

    'Save next avalailable key.
    If Not IsNull(rsCustomer("customerid")) Then
        oCustomerBus.Initialize Int(rsCustomer("customerid"))
    Else
        oCustomerBus.Initialize 1
    End If



    'Remove current procedure name from error object.
    oError.RemoveProcedure

Exit Sub

HandleError:

    'Call error handler to process fatal error condition.
    oError.HandleError Err.Number, _
                       Err.Description, _
                       Err.Source

    'Raise error condition to calling procedure.
    oError.RaiseError
                                                    (Continues)
```

Source 15.5   *(Continued)*

```
End Sub

'This method updates customer information

Public Sub Update(oError As CError, oDatabase As CConnection,
oCustomerBus As Object)

    'Declare local variables for current procedure.
    Dim sSql As String

    'Add current procedure name to error object.
    oError.AddProcedure "CCustomerDat.Update"

    'Set error handler for current procedure.
    On Error GoTo HandleError


    'Create sql string for database update.
    sSql = "UPDATE t_Customer SET "
    sSql = sSql & "FirstName = " & SqlFormat(oCustomerBus.FirstName) & ", "
    sSql = sSql & "LastName = " & SqlFormat(oCustomerBus.LastName) & ", "
    sSql = sSql & "MiddleInitial = " & SqlFormat(oCustomerBus.MiddleInitial)
    sSql = sSql & " WHERE "
    sSql = sSql & "CustomerID = " & SqlFormat(oCustomerBus.CustomerID)

    'Execute query to update record in database.
    oDatabase.Execute oError, sSql

    'Remove current procedure name from error object.
    oError.RemoveProcedure

Exit Sub

HandleError:

    'Call error handler to process fatal error condition.
    oError.HandleError Err.Number, _
                       Err.Description, _
                       Err.Source

    'Raise error condition to calling procedure.
    oError.RaiseError

End Sub

'This method deleted a customer record
Public Sub Delete(oError As CError, oDatabase As CConnection,
oCustomerBus As Object)
```

(Continues)

Source 15.5 *(Continued)*

```
    'Declare local variables for current procedure.
    Dim sSql As String

    'Add current procedure name to error object.
    oError.AddProcedure "CCustomerBus.Delete"

    'Set error handler for current procedure.
    On Error GoTo HandleError


    'Create sql string for database delete.
    sSql = "DELETE FROM t_Customer "
    sSql = sSql & "WHERE "
    sSql = sSql & "CustomerID = " & SqlFormat(oCustomerBus.CustomerID)

    'Execute query to delete record from database.
    oDatabase.Execute oError, sSql

    'Remove current procedure name from error object.
    oError.RemoveProcedure

Exit Sub

HandleError:

    'Call error handler to process fatal error condition.
    oError.HandleError Err.Number, _
                    Err.Description, _
                    Err.Source

    'Raise error condition to calling procedure.
    oError.RaiseError

End Sub
```

Source 15.5   *(Continued)*

Validation on the Client or the Server?

Application systems are systems and they imply operations based on rules. In a previous section we listed the rules that apply to this application. There were rules that applied to the order management system and different rules that applied to the customer management system.

Data that is entered into the system has to be validated against the stated business rules. These rules are normally handled by the business components. Information has to be passed over the network for validation. This can be costly for some types of validation. For example, if a date is entered in the wrong format it is best that this is checked at the client GUI end rather than the server end. Generally speaking it is best to do syntactic validation on the client side and let the server components handle the semantic validations.

Some validations do not have to be explicitly coded in the business components because these can be implemented in the database. Validations such as checking if a product ID is valid should not be coded because these can be handled by designing the databases for referential integrity. Another way to avoid having to code validations is to provide a list of available options rather than letting the users type data into the input fields.

There are other advanced validation techniques that are beyond the scope of this chapter. These are used in large scale distributed projects and may be an overkill for small to medium size projects.

MTS Application Packaging and Security

This section explains how the MTS components are added using the MTS Explorer and also the required settings for security and transactions.

As shown in Figure 15.14, the MTS includes the Transaction Server Explorer, a graphical management tool that makes it easier to deploy and manage solutions across a network. Transaction Server Explorer provides developers and administrators with a complete view of all the components deployed within a solution.

The MTS Explorer includes point and click wizards for assembling and configuring a solution from prebuilt packages and components. Using the File-New option on the menu bar, a package can be created. Figure 15.15 appears in response to this request. Click on create an empty package to create a package.

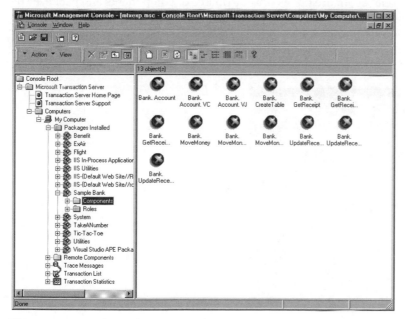

Figure 15.14   Microsoft Server Explorer.

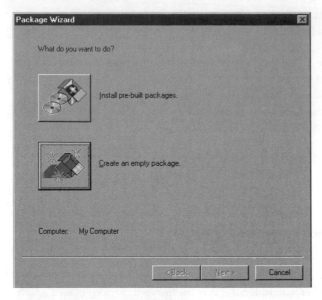

Figure 15.15 Package Wizard.

As shown in Figure 15.16, Transaction Server includes a wizard to add components to a package. The wizard either lists all components already registered in the system or enables the administrator to install new components.

Administrators and developers can set the transactional properties of components deployed within a package by using the dialogue shown in Figure 15.17.

Administrators can configure the security attributes of components and packages by creating roles and then assigning users to those roles. As shown in Figure 15.18, MTS Explorer includes a GUI utility for monitoring transaction status and tracking transaction performance. Administrators can intervene and resolve transaction outcome.

Figure 15.16 Component Wizard.

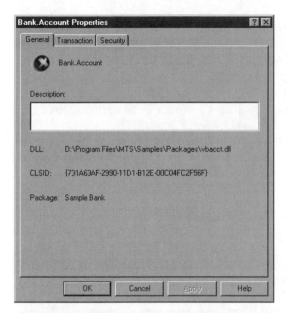

Figure 15.17   Component properties.

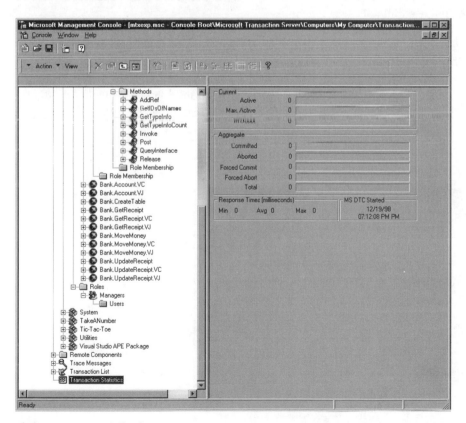

Figure 15.18   Monitoring status.

The Application

The completed application opens with the dialogue shown in Figure 15.19, to search for customers, create new customers, or edit or delete existing customers.

Once a customer is selected from the search results grid, double-clicking on the selected row or clicking on the Edit button opens the Customer Details screen. Here customer names can be modified and updated, as shown in Figure 15.20.

Figure 15.21 shows the screen that allows a user to view the addresses for a selected customer. The user can then create a new address or modify or delete existing addresses, as shown in Figure 15.22.

How the Application Gets Connected to the SQL Server Database

In the non-distributed environment every user is connected to a database and consumes a minimum of one connection. Each user then needs to be setup to access the database. Database object rights must be granted and revoked all adding up to a lot of administrative tasks. Developing applications the way we have done in this chapter and then deploying it on MTS simplifies a whole lot of database administration tasks. It also allows for efficient use of database connections.

In MTS, the application, rather than users accessing the application, has access to the database, which, in this case is SQL Server. Users access the client portion of the application from their local workstation or server. So far there is no database accesss. When the user accesses a component on MTS, the MTS components access a connection pool to pick up connections to the database. Also, since a pool is maintained, the time required to start up a connection is further reduced. This improves application performance.

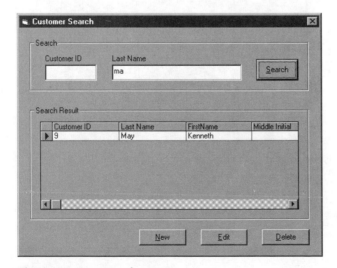

Figure 15.19   Search screen.

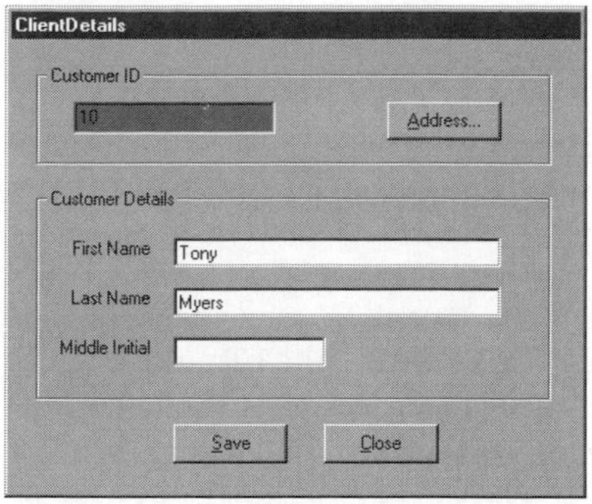

Figure 15.20   Customer information screen.

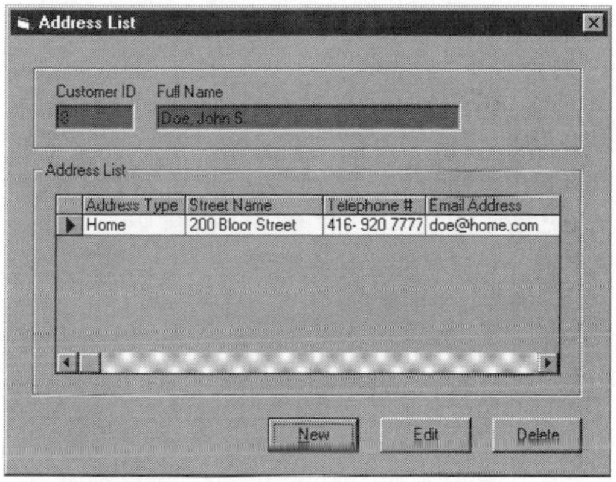

Figure 15.21   Address list.

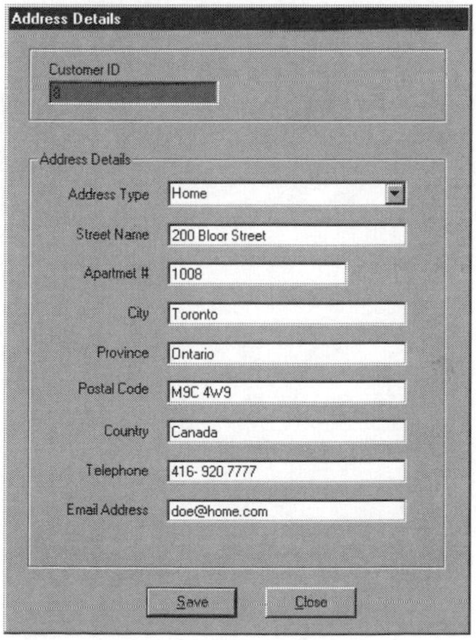

Figure 15.22   Address details.

The actual connection to the database is fairly straightforward. An ODBC configuration setting is created for the database on MTS. Next an NT account is created for the package. The next step is to access the package property and set the userid and password after selecting the "This User" option in the Identity tab. Finally check the "Enable Authorization checking" checkbox in the Security tab and the application is set. This is shown in Figure 15.23.

The other important aspect of any transactional application is "transactions." MTS comes to the aid to manage components that are transactional. No longer is there need to write code to handle transactions. MTS along with the Distributed Transaction Coordinator (DTC) does the job for us. The thing to remember is to set the components properly using the following dialog and to properly use the two API functions setcomplete() and setabort(). SetComplete is used to indicate to MTS that your work with the component is finished and your transactions were successfully completed. SetAbort is used to signal MTS to rollback your transactions. This is shown in Figure 15.24.

Move to the Web

The application described previously contained four distinct parts: the Client GUI, the MTS component, the business component, and the data layer component. The difference between a typical client server application and an application that runs on the Web is that the client on the Web uses a browser to connect to the server. The client in a client server environment has an executable application running, typically in a Microsoft Windows environment. Users in both environments need the same business and data services. Only the client layer is different. Here the application has been designed and built in such a way that both Web and non-Web users can use it. The client part for

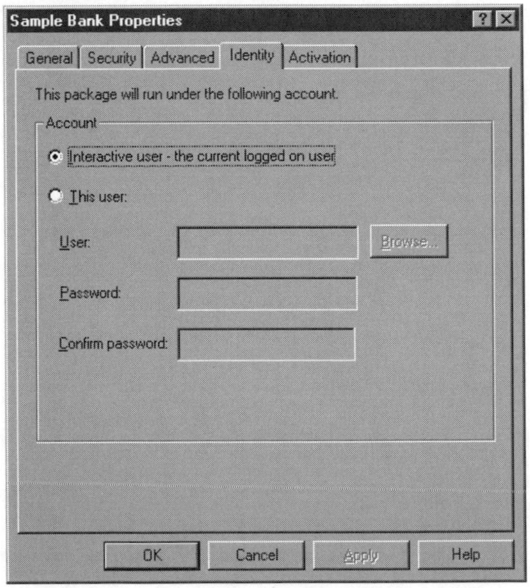

Figure 15.23 Package properties.

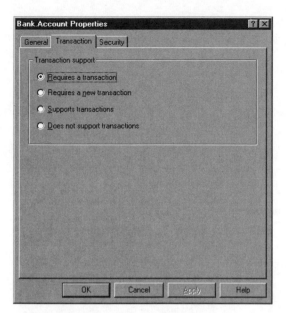

Figure 15.24   Handling transactions.

the Web user will be different. The browser understands HTML and therefore all our information from the server side will have to be converted to HTML, and passed on to the client-side browser. This can be done by building server side Active Server Pages (ASP). Active server pages use JavaScript or VBScript and can access server-side components. The data returned can be converted to HTML within the ASP code and then sent across. The quality of the graphics is not as good as the Visual Basic client application. This can be improved using client-side controls. Using client-side controls means that the users will have to run their browser on the Windows operating system, and in some cases they will work only when using Internet Explorer.

Summary

This chapter provided an object model that was supported by three tiers and a data model. An application to maintain customer information was developed using Visual Basic 5.0 and distributed using Microsoft Transaction Server. The application was built on top of COM and processed information ultimately managed in an SQL Server database.

The application was built from first principles, beginning with business requirements. The requirements were used to generate a business model, object model, and a data model. This allowed objects to be defined and built for the different tiers in the n-tier architecture. This chapter also discussed opportunities for building generic components that could be reused across applications.

Developing the User Interface

The user interface is often the only portion of an application that users see. The user interface therefore plays a large role in the acceptance of an application. What do users look for in an interface? Some common features include usability, appearance, and consistency. Users also want strong performance from their applications, protection from other users, and consistent operation. This chapter divides client platform development into three sections: interface development, data locking, and transaction control. It examines concepts and approaches for each of these.

User Interface Development

Developing the user interface requires several important activities. At a high level, these include defining the architecture, designing the user interface, building the process, and interacting with data. These are described in more detail in this section.

Defining Architecture

The architecture consists of both the technical and the application architecture. The technical architecture is the selection of different product groups in the client, the server, and in-between all the other tiers involved in the system. The application architecture consists of the placement of the application components in the system.

SQL Server 7 interacts with the user interface through middleware, supporting 2-tier, 3-tier, and n-tier applications. In n-tier architecture, the user interface represents a tier that generally resides on a client platform. This is usually a personal computer, but other options include Network Computers (NC), workstations, and server platforms. Client platforms are not required to be on the high-end machines, especially since much of the heavier processes in n-tier architecture are shifted to other tiers, which are generally on other platforms. These tend to be on the high-end of the performance side.

The user interface on the client platform is an application that communicates to the other tiers through a middleware product like an Application Programmer Interface (API). The other tiers can be applications, databases servers, and increasingly transaction monitors like products such as MTS. Visual Basic is becoming a standard user interface for SQL Server n-tier applications.

Visual Basic applications communicate with the database server through a range of techniques or open APIs. These include ActiveX Data Objects (ADO), Data Access Objects (DAO), Open Database Connectivity Application Program Interface (ODBC API), OLE Database (OLE DB), Open Database Connectivity Direct (ODBCDirect), and jet database. Remote Data Objects (RDO) and Data Access Objects (DAO) are object APIs built over ODBC. The jet database engine uses data controls and data bound controls to access Jet databases, ISAM databases, and ODBC compliant databases such as SQL Server. ODBCDirect supports Office 97 developers and supports DAO. VB libraries are also used to access MSQL. Another API that has a publicly defined specification is Embedded SQL for "C" language (ESQL). ODBCDirect provides a connection to SQL Server through ODBC data sources without going through the JetDBengine. The more common of these open APIs are discussed in Chapter 17.

Legacy or proprietary APIs are developed to be used with specific database servers. SQL Server has historically been supported by DB-Library for C and DB-Library for Visual Basic. This API consists of two components. A DB component connects to the database. A network component connects the application to the network or network operating system. DAO and ESQL are also considered to be legacy-type APIs.

The selection of the API or the data access method determines the types of commands that are available for applications to interact with either the middle tier or to the database server. It also determines the performance of the connection. Proprietary APIs tend to have faster performance than non-proprietary ones, such as ODBC. Other considerations for selecting an API include the stability of the API, cost, language support (e.g., C++, VB), functionality, and flexibility.

A major consideration of application architecture is partitioning. This deals with where components of the application are positioned throughout the application architecture. It should be stated up front that the answer to this question is not an exact science. Component placement, whether in-process or out-process, will affect things such as reusability, performance, maintenance, and support for other applications. Historically, component logic can also be positioned in the database server or in the user interface. In n-tier architecture, components should be as simplified as possible to support stateless operation. Each component should address a single business rule. Components should be in-process for faster performance. Business logic or business rules should also be moved closer to the location where the business rule is being collected. It is necessary to test the application partitioning for performance and ease of use, and to change it as needed before the application is deployed.

Designing the User Interface

The objective of the user interface is to present and collect information in an efficient and usable manner. Usability is both measurable and testable. Usability means that the user interface should be intuitive, easy to learn, and easy to use. The metaphor should be natural and applicable to the business solution. For example, if the application is used to rent motor vehicles, an interface that contains bitmaps of vehicles is appropriate. The interface should also be consistent. Once the user expects a certain action to produce a specific result, the interface should always produce that result. For example, if a change to a data field causes a confirmation message to appear before exiting the dialogue happens once, it should be done throughout the other dialogues as well. A usable interface also provides immediate feedback. Every user event should provide a response so that the user always knows what the application is doing. Messages, error or for information, should be meaningful, clear, and precise. The interface should minimize keystrokes and also mouse gestures. Required precision of movement should also be carefully thought out so that users are not frustrated trying to locate the cursor on a tiny spot anywhere on the screen. The user interface should not treat the user in a condescending manner, but neither should it expect that the user will always provide the correct input.

User interfaces in an organization should have the same look and feel. This can be done by adopting a set of user interface standards for specific categories. A significant amount of time can be spent defining standards; however, the simpler and easier they are to use, the more likely the standards are to be used. User interface standards must be straightforward and easy to implement. User interface standards can be borrowed from product vendors or built from specific projects within the organization. Standards can be built from one project and passed to another. There should not be great resistance to making changes or adjustments to existing standards if there are compelling arguments to do so. Table 16.1 shows a list of categories that should be considered when building user interface standards in an organization.

Building the Process

The process logic in the user interface in n-tier architecture generally does not include business rules. This means that the application process is restricted to gathering data, displaying data, and interacting with another tier, which can be either a component or a database server. Some types of edit checks or data validation is also handled in the user interface. This can be implemented through options available in the object properties on the screen or through components or procedural logic attached to specific user events, such as entering data into a field on a dialogue. Data validation can also be performed against local flat files or against remote database servers.

The user interface can also interact directly with a database server or with a component. In the case of a database server, dialogues can interact with it in two ways. The first method is to rely on object properties and their ability to add, delete, or update relational tables with information entered into the dialogue. The other method is to override some of the control properties with code to interact with the objects in the dialogue and with components that interact with other components or with the database server.

Table 16.1 User Interface Standards

FEATURE	DESCRIPTION
Background Color and Foreground Color	Should be used to distinguish between areas on the screen, enterable versus nonenterable fields.
Controls	Data aware controls include the check box, image, label, picture box, text box, list box, radio boxes, group boxes, combo box, OLE controls.
Help Screens	The appearance, context and location of help screens. The buttons and function keys that display the help functions.
Message Areas and Contents	The wording, location, and dialogue boxes used to display error or status messages.
Fonts	The type and size of fonts for titles, labels, and other data on the screen.
Menus	Consider the placement, functions, and actions on the menus throughout the application. Menus can also be supplemented with command buttons (e.g. icons) for rapid access.
Action Buttons	The types and functions of buttons on each dialogue. Examples include <OK>, <CANCEL>, <HELP>.
Text	The wording of the text, usage of verbs and nouns, usage of abbreviations, codes and content.
Titles	Titles are used to identify dialogues, controls, menus, and other areas in the dialogue.

Interacting with Data

The user interface can communicate with the database server through a variety of methods. These can be moved into components, which themselves can communicate with the database server using similar methods. A common method is to send a message that invokes a stored procedure. The logic in the stored procedure interacts with the database server. The message can also collect parameters from the interface objects and pass them to the server. The following example shows a basic message to a stored procedure in psuedo-language:

```
BEGIN_SQL
Return_code = "exec server_name.dbname.stored_procedure_name
parameter_list"
    EXECUTE_SQL
```

In this example, return_code captures the error_level returned by SQL Server. The stored_procedure_name corresponds to a name in the sysobjects system table for the path specificied in the command, or the default database. Parameter_list contains a row of delimited local variables that match the parameter_list of the stored procedure being executed. If the variables do not match in terms of number of data type, an unexpected error will occur and may be difficult to trap. It is worth paying special attention in testing that these variables match and are consistent. The BEGIN_SQL and EXECUTE_SQL are functions that are defined in the API being used. They generically surround the code that is being passed to the SQL Server parser.

An alternative to stored procedures is to use embedded SQL. Embedded SQL is supported by specific APIs and defines DML and DDL statements based on the ANSI '92 standard. The following example shows a psuedo language for representing an embedded SQL batch:

```
BEGIN_SQL
    Return_code = "use address"
    PREPARE_SQL
    Return_code = "set rowcount 5"
    PREPARE SQL
    Return_code = "select * from employee"
    PREPARE SQL
    EXECUTE_SQL
```

The embedded SQL example does not require that a stored procedure be prebuilt. However, it is clearly transferring more data across the network. It also will require that each statement be compiled and optimized. Furthermore, these actions are repeated whenever the component is reinvoked. All of this takes additional time, which stored procedures may save.

The user interface must also process data that is returned by SQL Server. SQL Server returns data using the SELECT command or other built-in functions. Data received by the user interface can take one of the following forms:

A "no more data message." This value should be captured in a local variable and processed with a conditional control statement.

An error message. This value should be captured in a local variable or string variable and passed to a message dialogue.

A data row in the result set. The number of columns in the data row should be identified. Each column in the data row should be bound to a local variable. The local variables are then processed.

Several data rows in the result set. The same processing for a single data row in the result set should be repeated inside a "while" loop. Each data row is then processed until there are no more data rows in the result set. This is an example of a client-side server.

A combination of data rows of different sizes. The same processing for a single data row in the result set should be repeated inside a "while" loop; however, the number of columns in each data row should be reexamined and rebound if there is a change in the number of columns in the previous data set.

Before interaction with a database server can begin, it is necessary to open a connection with SQL Server using command statements similar to the following example:

```
Dim FirstSQLServer As Connection
Set FirstSQLServer = OpenConnection _
        ("New", dbReturn, false, _
"ODBC; DATABASE=address; UID=joe; PWD=where;
DSN=SqlServer1")
```

The following example provides pseudo-code to manage processing information from a relational table in the address database:

```
Private Sub Form_load()
    Set dbMydb = OpenDatabase ("C:\sqlserv\data\address.mdb")
    Set recDealer = dbMydb.OpenRecordset
                            ("dealers", dbOpenTable, dbReadWrite)
    If recDealer.BOF or recDealer.EOF Then
        MsgBox Err.Description
    Else
    Do
            Bind to columns()
            set_local variables()
            Process variables()
    Loop Until EOF (filehandle)
    End If
End Sub


Sub_BindFields()
    Local_variable.Text = SQL_column.xxx
    For all variables
End_Sub

Sub set_local_variable ()
    Local_variable.Text = SQL_column.xxx
    For all variables
End Sub

Sub Process_variables ()
    Process_all variables
End Sub
```

From a performance perspective, it is necessary to keep the amount of data sent over the network to a minimum. Invoking stored procedures is an effective method of sending a request to SQL Server from the user interface. The following example demonstrates how a stored procedure can reduce the volume of information that is returned to the user interface. This is based on the address and member tables defined in Chapter 11:

```
/* Filename: memch16a.sql */

/* drop the stored procedure if it exists in the database. */
IF EXISTS (select name from sysobjects where name =
'select16a_member')
    DROP PROC select16a_member
go
```

```
/**************************************************/
/* Create the select16a_member stored procedure */
/**************************************************/
CREATE PROC selecta_member
(
    @member_no          int
)
AS
DECLARE @last_name      char(30),
        @first_name     char(30)

/* save header information in local parameters */
select @last_name = last_name, @first_name = first_name
        from member where member_no = @member_no

/* return the header information */
select @member_no, @last_name, @first_name

/* return the qualifying columns from the address table */
select address_code, streeta, state
        from address where member_no = @member_no

RETURN 0    /* return a 0 code to the calling routine */
go
```

The following example executes the stored procedure:

```
exec select16a_member 200
go
```

This displays the following information. Notice that there are two
batches in the result set. The first batch consists of a single row with
three columns, that serves as the header information. The second batch
contains multiple records that have three columns, but with different
datatypes from the columns in the first batch.

```
----- ---------------   ---------
200    Sector            Bill
```

address code	streeta	state
Y	123 Sig Blvd	California
B	23 Consec Rd	California

Notice that the second batch displays column headings because of the format of the
SELECT statement. These headings can be suppressed by renaming the columns in the
SELECT statement using the following syntax:

```
declare @member_no      int
        select @member_no = 200
        select address_code ' ', streeta ' ', state ' '
                from address where member_no = @member_no

        go
```

Locking

Locking, or data locking, plays an important role in any systems that support concurrent users. The purpose of locking is to ensure data integrity while users are simultaneously accessing the same relational data tables or records. Locking also affects application performance and locking contention. These factors usually work against each other. Low levels of locking contention can decrease data integrity or at least result in a large number of transaction roll backs. Application architecture should be optimized to protect data integrity, which is nonnegotiable in any meaningful application, while accepting trade-offs to improve system performance. Figure 16.1 shows several trade-offs that must be considered when designing a locking strategy. The key factors to consider with locking trade-offs include the amount of data that is held by a lock, the length of time the lock is in place, the number of locks that are active at any given time, and the amount of CPU processing required to manage the active locks. A high number of locks applied at low levels of data records reduce data contention by only locking a minimum amount of data as it is needed by application sessions. However, this increases the amount of processing and memory required to manage the locks, and this in turn can negatively impact performance.

Locking Levels

Historically SQL Server supported page-level locking. This meant that the lowest level that locks could be applied at was SQL Server's definition of a "page." A page was roughly equal to 2 KB, which meant that many data records could be held on a single page. A transaction requiring a specific record would lock all the records on the same

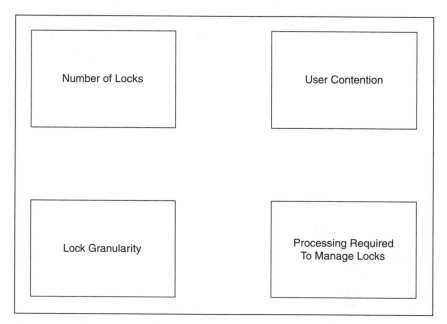

Figure 16.1 Locking trade-offs.

physical page during some operations. This created contention in high transaction volume environments. Other competing products have supported row-level locking. This difference has provided a large competitive advantage to competing products in their support for ERP applications. SQL Server now supports row-level locking, functionality that has played a large role in the relatively recent support of row-level locking by ERP applications like SAP and PeopleSoft. Row-level locking locks data rows individually, thus the other records held in the same physical table page are not effected.

Figure 16.2 shows some of the commonly used types of locks that are now supported by SQL Server. These include row-level, page-level, and table-level locking. SQL Server supports lock escalation as a key feature of its database optimizers. There is a supported procedure for lock escalation based on a cost-based calculation. Lock escalation consists of promoting row-level locks, then page-level locks, and then table-level locks. At some point a table lock becomes more efficient than managing multiple page locks. The optimizer makes this decision. Full row-level locking is supported for data index rows. A lock manager is supported for improved management of locks. The lock manager selects escalation strategies. SQL Server supports dynamic locking by leveraging both the query processor, storage engine, schemas, and queries. SQL Server locks include RID, key, page extent, table, and database. Locks cannot be applied to specific columns in a data row.

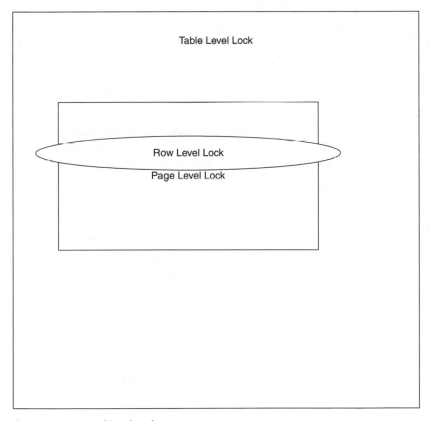

Figure 16.2 Locking levels.

Isolation Levels and Locking Modes

Without implementing an appropriate locking architecture, OLTP applications can suffer from several common problems. These are based on two concurrent transactions—transaction A and transaction B—running at virtually the same time. These problems include the following:

Dirty read. This involves transaction A reading data that is being modified by transaction B. The data that is read by transaction A is obsolete as soon as it is read because the original copy is being modified by transaction B.

Phantom read. This involves data that disappears or appears for a transaction on a second read.

Nonrepeatable reads. This involves having modified data values returned to a transaction on successive reads.

The Set Transaction Isolation Level command is available to control the type of isolation level for the environment. To avoid these common problems, SQL Server supports the following types of locking modes:

The shared mode does not modify data. It supports concurrent read access from concurrent user sessions, while providing no update access.

The update mode is used to update data. It reserves an object for update by a single session, but allows multiple users to access the same object for read-only purpose.

The exclusive mode is used in conjunction with update, insert, and delete operations. It reserves access to a data object to a single user. Other users are not allowed access, even for read-only purposes.

The intent mode is used to signal a future intent to issue a lock. This mode is used to allow other users an opportunity to work with a data object, but it communicates an intent so that other users cannot lock out a pending transaction.

The schema mode is used with DDL commands.

Manipulating Locks

While the SQL Server optimizer supports implicit locking, making decisions based on a cost-based calculation, a set of keywords are available to explicitly issue data locks with the DML commands. The basic syntax uses the keyword as an optimizer hint:

```
SELECT * FROM table_name LOCKNAME_HINT where_clause
```

The LOCKNAME can consist of the verbs NOLOCK, HOLDLOCK, UPDLOCK, TABLOCK, PAGLOCK, TABLE_OCKX, and ROWLEVELLOCK.

The following example shows how to issue an UPDLOCK with the SELECT statement:

```
SELECT * FROM TABLE HOLDLOCK
```

The sp_lock system procedure is used by the locks that exist in the SQL Server environment to display information. It is executed on its own command line in the Query Analyzer or in batch mode, as shown in the following syntax:

```
sp_lock
go
```

This command results in the following output:

spid	dbid	ObjId	IndId	Type	Resource	Mode	Status
1	1	0	0	DB	S		GRANT
6	1	0	0	DB	S		GRANT
7	1	0	0	DB	S		GRANT
7	2	0	0	DB	S		GRANT
7	2	0	0	DB	S		GRANT
7	8	0	0	DB	S		GRANT
7	1	117575457	0	TAB	IS		GRANT

The spid column uniquely identifies the process-id of the session. This column has a relationship with the spid column in the output of the sp_who system procedure. Joining these two tables allows a login_name to be identified for a particular lock instance. The type column shows the type of lock that is being supported by the spid. Valid type values can be DB for database, IDX for index, FIL for file, PG for page, TAB for table, EXT for extent, KEY for key field, and RID for row identifier. The mode column shows the mode type of the lock being supported by the spid. The dbid column identifies a database number. The ObjId column identifies an object ID. The IndId identifies an index ID. The resource column identifies a lock resource type. The lock status column can contain values of GRANT, WAIT, and CNVRT (for converted).

The spid can also is used by the Kill command to remove sessions that may be locking other sessions, as shown in the following example:

```
Kill spid
```

Locking information about a specific spid can be retrieved using the following syntax:

```
sp_lock spid
go
```

Understanding Deadlocks

A deadlock situation occurs when two transactions are both waiting for resources that the other is waiting for before proceeding. Because both transactions are waiting on the other they are deadlocked. Another way to understand this is to consider that transaction A is waiting for record B while locking record A. At the same time, transaction B is waiting for record A while locking record B. SQL Server detects this situation and selects the transaction with the least amount of waiting/running time and stops it. The other transaction should be restarted after an application module pause of a few moments.

Pessimistic versus Optimistic Locking

As was discussed earlier, the locking approach plays a powerful role in application performance, from a user contention perspective and due to the work required to maintain locks. Two approaches, commonly referred to as pessimistic versus optimistic locking, are available. The pessimistic approach assumes that data being modified by one process will usually be modified by another process before the first process is complete. For this reason the pessimistic approach issues locks for a longer period of time. The optimistic approach assumes that data being modified by one process is unlikely to be modified by another process. This approach resists issuing locks until the end. The optimistic approach compares values (e.g., timestamp columns) and rolls back a transaction if data has changed. Codes that are returned can include the following:

3260 reports that a record is locked so no update occurs

3186 reports that a records is locked so data is not saved

3197 reports that data has changed

Clearly this latter approach can become an expensive alternative if the optimism is unfounded. Set LockEdits to TRUE for the pessimistic approach; Set LockEdits to FALSE for the optimistic approach.

Transactions

Transactions are used to maintain referential integrity in local or distributed data. A transaction is an all or nothing proposition. This means that all statements in a set are processed together or their results are rolled back together. Transaction results must always be consistent, no matter when or how the transaction is executed.

Explicit transactions can be described using a single transaction format or a nested transaction format. The following syntax shows the basic format for defining explicit transactions:

```
Begin Transaction
statements
if condition
   Rollback transaction
else
   Commit Transaction
```

The following syntax shows a more advanced format that nests transactions inside other named transactions:

```
Begin Transaction 1
    Begin Transaction 2
    statements
 if condition
       rollback Transaction 2
     else
       commit transaction 2
```

```
     statements
     if condition
        rollback transaction 1
     else
        commit transaction 1
```

The @@TRANCOUNT global variable keeps track of the current nested transaction level. This variable is automatically incremented as you move into deeper nesting of the transaction level. It is decremented as transaction levels are committed or rolled back. A value of 1 means that you are inside a transaction. The global variable can be inspected with the SELECT command, as follows:

```
SELECT @@TRANCOUNT
```

The following example demonstrates the use of transactions, beginning with setting up two test tables. One table contains an employee record. The other table contains the daily sales made by the employee sorted by date and employee_no. There is also an index on date, employee_no. The syntax to create the tables in the pubs database is as follows:

```
use pubs
drop table employee
go

drop table sales
go

create table employee
(
     employee_no          int,
     last_name       char(30),
     first_name      char(30),
     commission      float,
     title           char(20),
     date_hired      datetime
)

create table sales
(
   employee_no      int,
   date_of_sale     datetime,
   amount_of_sale   money,
   item_sku         char(30)
)
```

The following syntax inserts test data rows into the employee table:

```
Insert employee
VALUES (100, 'Sector', 'Sam', .15, 'Salesperson', 'Jan 1 1990')

Insert employee VALUES
(101, 'Tan', 'Victoria', 20, 'Supervisor', 'Dec 15, 1989')
go
```

The following syntax inserts data into the sales table. This is done through a transaction so that if it is later discovered that there is no employee table, the transaction is rolled back:

```
begin transaction
declare @emp_no        int,
        @current_date  datetime,
        @sale_value    money,
        @sku           char(30)

select @emp_no = 101
select @current_date = getdate()
select @sale_value = 101.15
select @sku = '10104213'

select 'nested transaction level =', @@trancount
insert sales VALUES
  (@emp_no, @current_date, @sale_value, @sku)

if NOT exists (select * from employee where employee_no = @emp_no)
begin
  select 'rolling back transaction'
  Rollback transaction
end
else
begin
  select 'committing transaction'
  commit transaction
end
select * from sales
select 'nested transaction level =', @@trancount
```

Many of the DDL commands cannot be used inside transactions. This includes alter, create, disk init, drop, dump, grant, invoke, load, reconfigure, select into, truncate, and update statistics.

Summary

This chapter reviewed considerations for developing the user interface. This involved an examination of technical architectures, application architecture, user interface design, building the process logic at the user interface level, and options for interacting with the database.

This chapter also reviewed concepts relevant to build client applications, including building the user interface, building locking strategies, and leveraging transactions for data integrity. Locking strategies include balancing factors such as the scope of the lock, length of time, and the type of lock being applied. Transactions are used to ensure data integrity by completing a set of statements as a single unit or by rolling them back as a single unit.

Connecting SQL Server to the Internet

This chapter examines methods of connecting SQL Server to the Web using primarily ASP and ADO. This chapter also illustrates some of the other tools and techniques available to do this, including Java Server Pages and Servlets.

Microsoft's Way of Data Access

To understand Microsoft's current approach for retrieving data from data sources, it is necessary to examine the recent history and definition of common Microsoft data access methods and techniques, especially as they pertain to accessing SQL Server data from client applications. This includes an examination of VBSQL, ODBC, DAO, RDO, OLE DB, and ADO.

VBSQL

VBSQL is an API-interface to Microsoft SQL Server built around the C-based DBLibrary interface. This is a historical interface that preceded many of Microsoft's other methods for accessing SQL Server data from client applications. This method is only used to access SQL Server data and is no longer recommended as an active data access method.

ODBC

ODBC is the standard data access interface designed to access relational databases that have an ODBC driver. All code specific to a database is placed in the ODBC driver. The ODBC layer requires the programmer to work at a fairly low level, consequently it is difficult, and certainly time consuming, to write code that is capable of accessing heterogeneous databases.

DAO

DAO is an object-based interface that used the Microsoft Jet database engine to access native Jet databases, a number of popular ISAM databases, and ODBC data sources. DAO was next after VBSQL and ODBC and enjoyed widespread popularity in the marketplace. DAO organizes tables, queries, fields, and other database objects into a hierarchy of objects.

Database tables are represented by a collection. Tables are objects, each of which support a collection of fields and optional indexes. DAO provides a full complement of methods to access data, to open tables, to execute queries, and to locate or modify records.

RDO

RDO is an object-based data access interface that provides a lightweight ODBC wrapper. RDO acts as a thin wrapper on the ODBC application programming interface. It is performance tuned for SQL Server 6.x and Oracle 7 database servers. The ODBC-based RDO offers server-specific features. RDO requires a very small memory footprint. It also exposes the underlying ODBC, allowing developers access to features not available while using RDO.

OLE DB

This new low-level, object-based interface introduces a common data access interface that is used for any data source. A data source can be a Jet database, a relational database, a mainframe ISAM or VSAM database, hierarchical databases such as IMS, text, graphics, geographical data, and business objects. OLE DB is designed to handle any data with a common set of semantics regardless of the data's format or storage method. OLE DB is essentially a set of COM interfaces. Microsoft is positioning it as a universal approach for accessing data. OLE DB is to data what ODBC is to relational databases. Microsoft's recommendation is to use ADO, unless it is necessary to work at a low level of detail. Some common OLE DB terms include the following:

OLE DB provider. An OLE DB provider is any software component that exposes an OLE DB interface. OLE DB providers are expected to support a specific data storage mechanism.

OLE DB interfaces. This is a CLI (call-level interface) or API for the OLE DB COM environment.

OLE DB consumer. Any application software that calls and uses the OLE DB API.

ADO

ADO is the name Microsoft has given its API wrapping of OLE DB for use in languages such as Microsoft Visual Basic, Visual Basic for Applications, Active Server Pages, and Microsoft Internet Explorer Visual Basic Scripting. ADO is supposed to be the bridge between your application and OLE DB. ADO has objects, properties, methods, and events; the basic infrastructure of the object world. As mentioned before, this is the interface recommended for client applications. ADO's primary benefits are ease of use, high speed, low memory overhead, and a small disk footprint. ADO also supports essential features for building client/server and Web-based applications.

ADO features remote data service (RDS), by which you can move data from a server to a client application or Web page, make needed changes to the data on the client, and return updates to the server in a single trip. Previously released as Microsoft Remote Data Service 1.5, RDS has been combined with ADO to simplify client-side data access. The newly release ADO version 2.0 implements a superset of both RDO and DAO.

RDS

Remote Data Services (RDS) provides a straightforward interface for three-tiered systems. RDS was designed to work with ActiveX enabled browsers such as Microsoft Internet Explorer. RDS is a framework that allows clients to connect easily to data sources, especially if they have an ODBC driver or use the ADO interface. RDS also allows client-side caching of data results, easy updates to data, and support for data-aware ActiveX controls. Visual Basic developers will find the object model quite familiar.

RDS can work in several ways:

It can use the middle tier as nothing more than a subordinate process. In this case it specifies the program that should be called on the server. That program could be a simple, default program that satisfies the RDS.DataSpace requirement. In return the client application gets a proxy. The client then sends the connection and command parameters to this program via the proxy. The program then fetches the data and returns it to the client. Notice in this model, the middle-tier contains no business rules.

RDS could follow a true three-tiered model and have the client call a server program, the RDS.DataSpace that hosts the business rules.

A middle option exists where you can extend the default RDS.DataSpace program on the server using ADO 2.0. To effect changes in the data source, in our case the SQL Server database, the client will update the RecordSet and send it back to the server.

The simple way to use RDS is to use the RDS.DataControl. It tries to allow visual controls to use the RecordSet object returned by a query. To do that we would associate a Visual Control with the RDS.DataControl (this is called binding). We can have many visual controls bound to many RDS.DataControls on a single Web page.

RDS.DataControl can automatically invoke two underlying elements of RDS, the RDS.DataSpace and the RDS.DataFactory. By setting the command and connection properties of the RDS.DataControl, it will automatically use the RDS.Data-

Space to create a reference to the RDSServer.DataFactory, that is, the server program. The RDSServer.DataFactory in turn uses the connection property to connect to the data source and the command property to obtain a RecordSet from the data source and return that object to the RDS.DataControl.

The RDS.DataSpace object contains a single method, which is used to send a proxy to the server program.

The RDSServer.DataFactory object represents the server program. The server program is a proxy, an enhanced proxy, or a custom program (which could also use portions of the default proxy behavior). The server program is called a business object by Microsoft and is responsible for retrieving and updating data from data sources.

Getting SQL Server Data to the Internet Options

There are many methods for displaying data on the Internet and specifically on a Web page. These include the following:

CGI. The first attempt to deliver something on the Web that was not just a static page used CGI. Unfortunately CGI was designed to support a few hits per day. When a Web server receives a CGI request, it begins an entirely new session; if the request needs to have data from a database, then an entirely new database connection is established. This is far too expensive on system resources. Web vendors created several proprietary high-performance plug-ins to address these problems, but these solutions require additional programming skill and are not portable.

HTML and ASPs. Microsoft tools offer two basic modes of generating HTML code on the server. Both use ASP scripting. ASP can use all scripting or use script to hand off control to code, usually a C++ class, a COM component, or a Java class. For truly scalable applications, you will not use the all-scripting approach.

Web page directly to the database. We can use a Web page with data-aware controls or a Java applet that binds controls directly to the database (similar to what is often done in quick, throwaway programming applications with Visual Basic on the Windows platform). Many vendors and JavaBean component developers offer solutions with this capability.

Publishing data using Visual Basic or Java applications on Internet servers. Visual Basic applications can be built as automation servers and deployed on an intranet or Internet server; even the Microsoft JVM can function as an automation server, providing database services to Web browser-based clients. For example, your intranet Web page can contain an application written in VBScript that connects to IIS. IIS in turn hands off control to your automation server that connects to a data source, which could include SQL Server. Your application retrieves the data, processes it in some way, and then returns the processed information to your browser.

High-Performance Remote Data Access

Remote data control, available in the Visual Basic Enterprise Edition, is designed for high-performance remote data access from SQL Server 6, Oracle 7 database servers, or any other ODBC-compliant database servers and is used to populate controls with data from a remote database.

Publishing Data on the Web Using ASP

Active Server Pages, which was shipped in December 1996, is discussed in this section.

Technology Architecture

The normal HTML page has text on it to be displayed, including HTML tags. The tags tell the browser how to format the text. A Web page with ASP will also contain ASP statements that tell the Web server how to create parts of the Web page.

Active Server Pages is a standard allowing server-side scripting, which is transparent to the client. ASP is executed on the server. With ASP you mix the normal HTML tags with <% %>. <% %> are tags which contain your script. There are many script language options, but the server script language in the Microsoft world tends to be VBScript. The server runs VBScript, converts its output to HTML, updates the Web page, then sends it to the browser. The browser never sees anything but HTML.

Software Requirements

The example in this section was developed using the following software resources:

- SQL Server
- Active Server Pages
- Windows 95 or NT
- Internet Explorer 4.0
- Web page tool or text editor
- A web server that can host Active Server Pages

Active Server Pages 2.0 and the IIS Web server are freely available in the NT 4.0 option pack.

Building the Application

To begin this example, it is first necessary to launch the IIS. From the start menu, choose Programs-Windows NT 4.0 Option Pack-Microsoft Internet Information Server-Internet Service Manager (HTML). Modify the address to http://localhost/default.asp. If you do not have an appropriate hosts file on your system, replace localhost with

127.0.0.1. This page is located in the C:\INetPub\WWWRoot\ subdirectory. It may be necessary to modify the Internet settings in your browser to bypass a proxy server if there is one. The browser should be pointed to the address http://localhost/default.asp.

Creating an ASP Page

Following is the syntax for creating an ASP page with any text editor (e.g., WordPad):

```
<HTML>
<HEAD>
     <TITLE>Hello World</TITLE>
</HEAD>
<BODY>
<P>This is our First ASP page. </P>
<P>Today's date is <% = Date%>.</P>
</BODY>
</HTML>
```

This code should be saved in the file C:\INetPub\WWWRoot\ourFirstPage.asp. Point the browser to http://localhost/ourFirstPage.asp, and you will see the screen shown in Figure 17.1. Notice that the code following <P> appears as text on the screen. The variable <% = Date%> is replaced by the current date so the actual date that appears on the screen reflects the system clock of the platform running the application.

Note the Window title. If you choose to view the HTML source, the following code is displayed:

```
<HTML>
<HEAD>
     <TITLE>Hello World</TITLE>
</HEAD>
<BODY>
<P>This is our First ASP page. </P>
<P>Today's date is 10/14/98.</P>
```

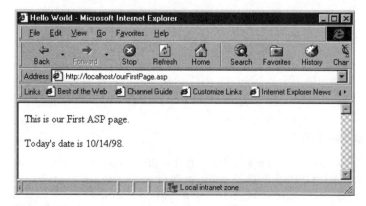

Figure 17.1   First ASP page.

Figure 17.2   ODBC data source.

```
</BODY>
</HTML>
```

The date is displayed as plain HTML and there is no evidence that a VBScript is executed to display the actual date. If you change the extension to .htm you will not receive an error message, but the VBScript code will not be executed.

Using ASP to Publish Database Information

To publish database information using ASP, it is useful to begin by creating test data in SQL Server. The data will be stored in a database and a table named Member. Figure 17.2 shows the screen that is used to open an ODBC connection with SQL Server.

Figure 17.3 shows the columns in the member table and the corresponding datatypes and lengths. Creating user tables was discussed extensively in earlier chapters of this book.

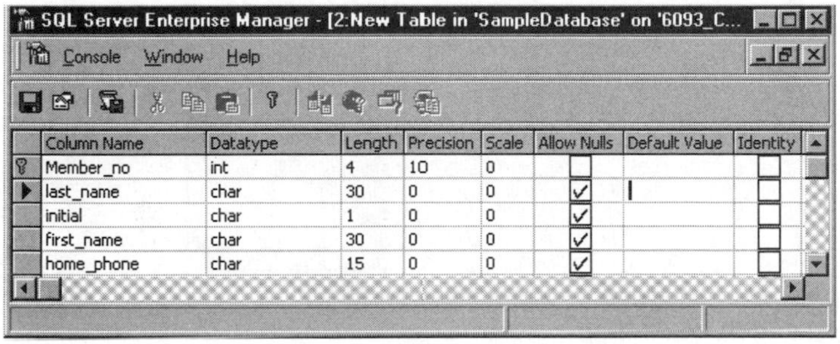

Figure 17.3   Adding a new table.

An ASP page can be used to add some data rows to this table and then to browse them. There are more powerful tools, such as NetObjects ScriptBuilder (which has strong support for several script languages including server-side scripting) and includes sample ASP VBscript files, VisualInterDev, and others.

The following example was built using a combination of tools mainly to demonstrate the wide variety that is available. The form was initially built as an .html file using Symantec's VisualPage. The extension was then modified to .asp and opened using Net-Objects ScriptBuilder. (See Figures 17.4 and 17.5.) Using one of the standard asp files available in NetObjects, a procedure to read a table in the database and create a form was imported, then a few minor cosmetic changes were made. The finished application consists of an initial .asp page that displays an input form and the records currently in the database. If a new member's information is entered into the form and the Submit button is pressed, the data is added to SQL Server. When we return to the Sample-Form.asp page, the database is displayed and the change is evident.

Please note, the sample does not have any error checking nor is it designed to demonstrate highly tuned architecture. This is a minimal example designed to show how data can go from a client's browser to the database and back.

Apart from painting the screen in the tool of choice, we also need to modify it to be a good program (i.e., meaningful fieldnames) and the html POST command which passes all form input in the HTTP request must be directed to the URL that we created, SimpleDatabase.asp.

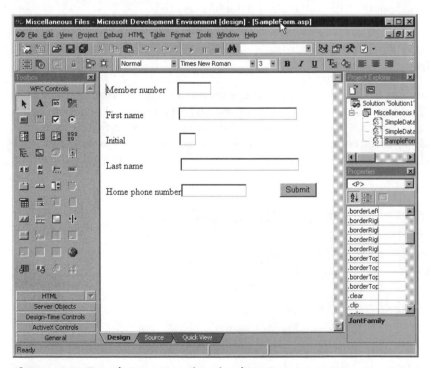

Figure 17.4 SampleForm.asp using VisualInterDev 6.0.

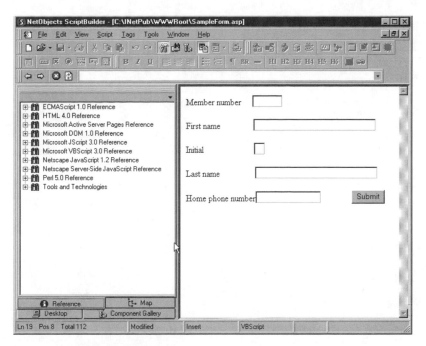

Figure 17.5   SampleForm.asp using NetObjects ScriptBuilder 3.0.

Source Listing 17.1 shows the code for SampleForm.asp. Any text editor can also be used to create this code:

```
<!DOCTYPE HTML PUBLIC "-//W3C//DTD HTML 3.2//EN">
<HTML>
<HEAD>
    <META HTTP-EQUIV="Content-Type" CONTENT="text/html;CHARSET=iso-8859-1">
    <META NAME="GENERATOR" Content="Visual Page 1.1a for Windows">
    <TITLE>Main Entry Page </TITLE>
</HEAD>
<BODY>
<FORM ACTION="SimpleDatabase.asp" METHOD="post" >
<P>Member number     <INPUT
NAME="member_noField" SIZE="6" MAXLENGTH="6" ></P>
<P>First
name           &n
bsp;   <INPUT NAME="firstNameField" SIZE="30"
MAXLENGTH="30" ></P>
<P>Initial          &n
bsp;           &n
bsp;<INPUT NAME="initialField" SIZE="1" MAXLENGTH="1" status =
"ini"></P>
<P>Last
```

Source 17.1   SampleForm.asp.

```
name           &nb
sp;    <INPUT NAME="lastNameField" SIZE="30"
                                              MAXLENGTH="30" ></P>
<P>Home phone number<INPUT NAME="homePhoneNumberField" SIZE="15"
                                              MAXLENGTH="15"
>            
                        ;  <INPUT TYPE="submit" NAME="Submit"
 VALUE="Submit"></P>
</FORM>
</BODY>
</HTML>
<%
Dim objConnection
Dim objCommand
Dim objRecord
Dim member_noField
Dim firstNameField
Dim initialField
Dim lastNameField
Dim homePhoneNumberField
Dim rs
Dim str

Set objConnection  = Server.CreateObject ("ADODB.Connection")
Set objCommand     = Server.CreateObject ("ADODB.Command")
Set objRecord       = Server.CreateObject ("ADODB.RecordSet")

strConnect          = "DSN=SQL7_test;UID=sa;PWD=tttt"
objConnection.Open strConnect

'Fill in the command object, that is
objCommand.ActiveConnection = objConnection

Call ShowSQLTable(objConnection, "Select * from Member", 4, 1, 4, 3)

'Finally clean up
Set objCommand = Nothing

'===================================================================
' PROCEDURE:      ShowSQLTable
' INPUT:          db (object)        - an opened database connection
object
'               sql (string)       - the SQL query string used to open the
'                          record set
'               tblborder (number)    - the HTML table border value
'               tblwidth (string)    - the HTML table width value
'               cellpadding (number)   - the HTML table cellpadding value
'               cellspacing (number)   - the HTML table cellspacing value
' DESC:            This procedure performs a SELECT SQL query and
'                          displays the result set in an HTML table
```

(Continues)

Source 17.1 *(Continued)*

```
'==================================================================
Sub ShowSQLTable(db, sql, tblborder, tblwidth, cellpadding, cellspacing)
    Dim rs, align, numfields, i, str
    Set rs = db.Execute(sql)

    If Not rs.EOF Then
        numfields = rs.Fields.Count

        ' Begin table
        str = "<table border=" & Chr(34) & tblborder  & Chr(34) & "
                                                cellpadding=" & Chr(34)
        str = str & cellpadding & Chr(34) & " cellspacing=" & Chr(34) &
                                                cellspacing & Chr(34)
        str = str & " width=" & Chr(34) & tblwidth & Chr(34) & "><tr>"
        Response.Write str

        ' Display the field names as column headers. Align column
        ' headers with numeric field values to the right and all
            ' others to the left.
        For i = 0 to numfields - 1
            If IsNumeric(rs.Fields(i).Value) Then
                align = "right"
            Else
                align = "left"
            End If
            str = "<td align=" & Chr(34) & align & Chr(34) & "><strong>"
            str = str & rs.Fields(i).Name & "</strong></td>"
            Response.Write str

        Next

        Response.Write "</tr>"

        ' Display all field values aligning numeric values to the
        ' right and all others to the left.
        Do Until rs.EOF
            Response.Write "<tr>"
            For i = 0 to numfields - 1
                If IsNumeric(rs.Fields(i).Value) Then
                    align = "right"
                Else
                    align = "left"
                End If
                str = "<td align=" & Chr(34) & align & Chr(34) & ">"
                str = str & rs.Fields(i).Value & "</td>"
                Response.Write str
            Next
            Response.Write "</tr>"
            rs.MoveNext
        Loop
    End If
```

(Continues)

Source 17.1   *(Continued)*

```
        rs.Close
    Set rs = Nothing
    ' End table
    Response.Write "</table>"
End Sub ' End of ShowSQLTable
%>
```

Source 17.1 *(Continued)*

Following is the code for SimpleDatabase.asp:

```
<!DOCTYPE HTML PUBLIC "-//W3C//DTD HTML 3.2//EN">
<HTML>
<HEAD>
    <META HTTP-EQUIV="Content-Type" CONTENT="text/html;CHARSET=iso-8859-1">
    <META NAME="GENERATOR" Content="Visual Page 1.1a for Windows">
    <TITLE>Process data entered</TITLE>
</HEAD>
<BODY>
<H1>Your data has been processed. </H1>
<H1>Return to main entry page to view results.</H1>
<P>
<FORM ACTION="http://localhost/SampleForm.asp"  FORM
<>
<INPUT TYPE="submit" NAME="Submit" VALUE="Return to Main entry
page"></P>
<H1>Thank you.</H1>
</FORM>
</BODY>
</HTML>
<%
Dim objConnection
Dim objCommand
Dim objRecord
Dim member_noField
Dim firstNameField
Dim initialField
Dim lastNameField
Dim homePhoneNumberField

Set objConnection  = Server.CreateObject ("ADODB.Connection")
Set objCommand     = Server.CreateObject ("ADODB.Command")
Set objRecord      = Server.CreateObject ("ADODB.RecordSet")

strConnect = "DSN=SQL7_test;UID=sa;PWD=tttt"
objConnection.Open strConnect

'Fill in the command object
objCommand.ActiveConnection = objConnection

'Extract all of the information entered into the form on the main entry page
'Assign the values to the variables defined at the top of the page

Set member_noField          = Request.Form("member_noField")
Set firstNameField          = Request.Form("firstNameField")
```

```
Set initialField              = Request.Form("initialField")
Set lastNameField           = Request.Form("lastNameField")
Set homePhoneNumberField    = Request.Form("homePhoneNumberField")

'Setup the SQL command
objCommand.CommandText = "Insert into Member (member_no, first_name,
initial,last_name,  home_phone) values ('" & member_noField & "', '" &
firstNameField & "','" &initialField    & "','" & lastNameField  & "','
                                          " & homePhoneNumberField & "')"
'Execute the SQL
objCommand.Execute
'Finally clean up
Set objCommand = Nothing
Response.Write "Database activity concluded"
%>
```

To test this application, first we ensure that SQL Server and IIS are running. Then we can point our browser to http://localhost/SampleForm.asp. We can fill in the fields as shown in Figure 17.6.

We then press the submit button. Control passes to the SimpleDatabase.asp. The data is extracted from the form and inserted into the database. Please note that the client is unable to see anything except html; all of the asp activity occurs on the server.

If everything works correctly you will see the screen shown in Figure 17.7.

If we press the "Return to Main Entry page" button, the displayed data from the database is refreshed and the addition is evident. (See Figure 17.8.)

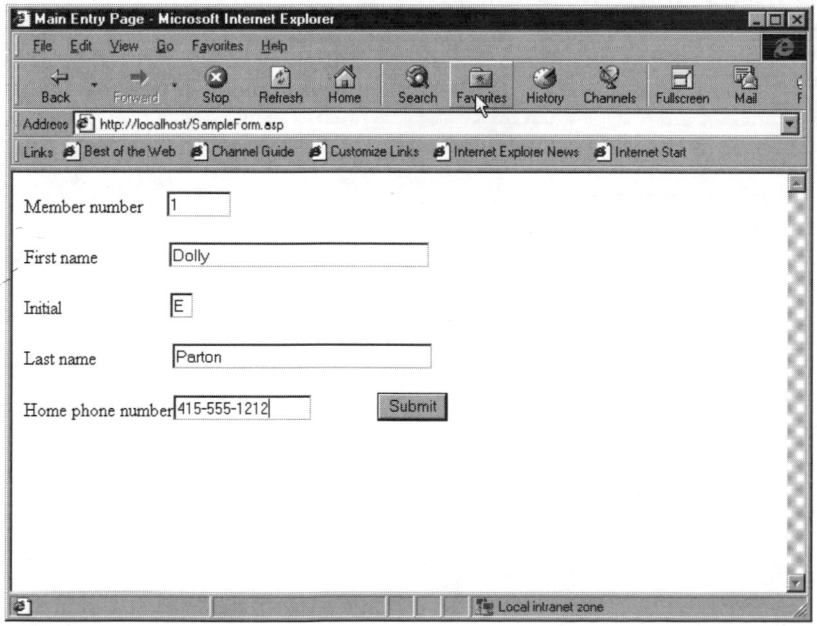

Figure 17.6   Main entry page.

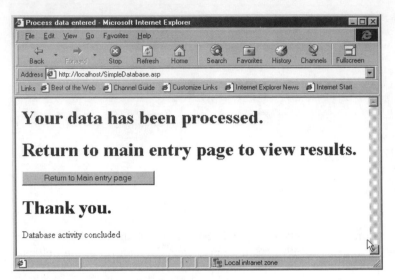

Figure 17.7 Process data entered.

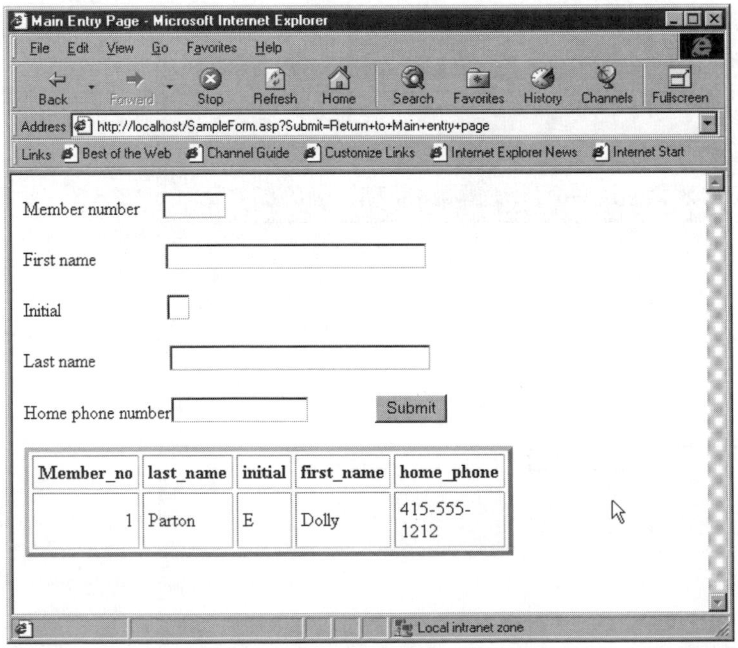

Figure 17.8 Table with record displayed.

HTML with Java Server Pages and Java Servlets

Applets enhance the user interface within a browser and are able to execute client-side logic. Servlets generate HTML pages (just like ASP), and they are written in Java, consequently they can do anything a Java program is able to, such as accessing databases or performing other server-side tasks. Using tools such as IBM's VisualAge for Java, you can set breakpoints in your servlet code and debug your program. Java servlets are a standard JDK 1.2 extension to the JDK 1.1.x JavaServlet API. Servlets are also a subset of the Java Server API.

According to JavaSoft, servlets can be viewed as applets without a user interface for servers. Servlets are a good replacement for CGI. Java servlets are used because of the following features:

- Dynamic behavior on the Web.
- Platform independence.
- Performance. (Reuse of database connection/s gives servlets a major advantage over CGI.)
- Compiled.
- Easy integration with applets.
- Java code is easier to write and maintain than the script languages.

Java Server Pages use the servlet mechanism under the cover. When the Web server receives a file with a .jhtml extension, a servlet is created. Servlets require Web servers to be servlet-enabled before they can be used. There are many ways to add servlet support to standard Web servers, including Microsoft's IIS. One way is to use JavaSoft's Java Servlet Developers Kit. IBM has released a tool called WebSphere Application Server (formerly called Servlet Express). The WebSphere application server allows Web servers that do not have Java to run servlets. Microsoft is a proponent of servlet development using Visual J++. JavaSoft is another vendor that provides servlet adapters that plug into Netscape, Microsoft, and Apache Web servers.

Figure 17.9 shows one of the screens generated by the wizard that can be used to install Jrun and connect to varying Web servers. Jrun is another popular way of implementing the servlet API.

SQL Server Web Assistant Wizard

To start the SQL Server Web Assistant Wizard, launch the SQL Server Enterprise Manager (from the menus choose Microsoft SQL Server 7/Enterprise Manager, shown in Figure 17.10), then navigate further down the hierarchy to your databases in the hierarchy. Should you see No items under your SQL Server group (Figure 17.11), you need to register your server. Highlight SQL Server Group, then right mouse click, select Register SQL Server from the popup menu, and the Register SQL Server appears (see Figure 17.12). Press Next, and you are then asked to select a SQL Server (see Figure 17.13). Choose a server or type in the desired server name (you can use the alt+tab keyboard

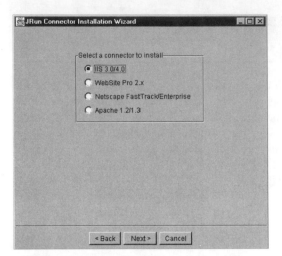

Figure 17.9   Jrun installation.

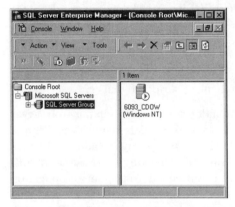

Figure 17.10   SQL Server Enterprise Manager.

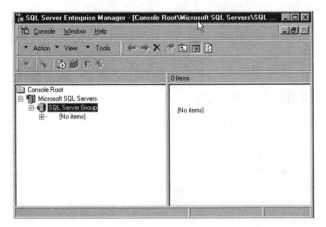

Figure 17.11   [No items].

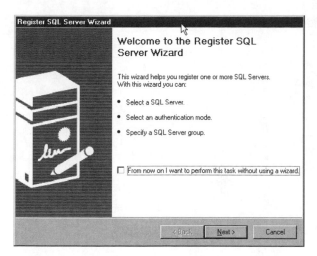

Figure 17.12   Register SQL Server Wizard.

combination to view the SQL Server Service Manager window, which has a dropdown with all servers, should you need help to remember the correct server).

You are then asked to choose an authentication mode; see Figure 17.14. Note: It is very important for the example that follows to choose the lower radio button "The SQL Server login information that was assigned to me by the System Administrator. (SQL Server authentication)." Then press Next; on the next window, choose the lower radio button "Prompt for the SQL Server information when connecting", see Figure 17.15. On the following window, you are asked to select a SQL Server Group; choose the one you desire. You should then see Figure 17.16. Press the Finish button. You should then see Figure 17.17; press the Close button.

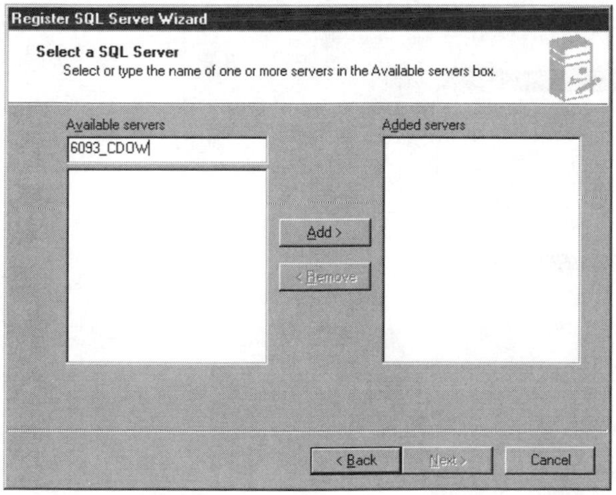

Figure 17.13   Select a SQL Server.

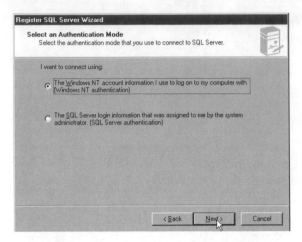

Figure 17.14 Select an Authentication Mode.

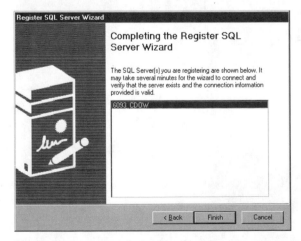

Figure 17.15 Select Connection Option.

Figure 17.16 Completing the Register SQL Server Wizard.

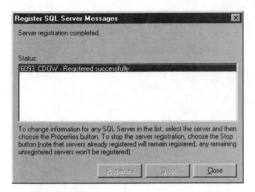

Figure 17.17   Register SQL Server Messages.

Navigate to your database of choice. In this exercise, we will use the SampleData-base: Highlight it and choose Tools/Wizards (see Figure 17.18.) Press the + sign to expand the Management (Wizards). You will then see the wizard menu shown in Figure 17.19: This figure shows the wizards that are available in the management section. A shortcut for displaying the wizard menu is to press the magic wand on the toolbar.

Choose the Web Assistant Wizard. Figure 17.20 shows the start of the Web creation process for publishing data on the Web.

Press the Next button. Figure 17.21 is used to select the database that contains the tables which will provide data to the Web. Highlight the SampleDatabase and press the Next button. We can use the default name and option that is provided, then press the Next button.

The next window shows all available tables in the drop down box. The lower panels allows one or more columns to be selected from the table of choice, in this case Table Member. Go ahead and select all the fields and press the Add button so that your win-

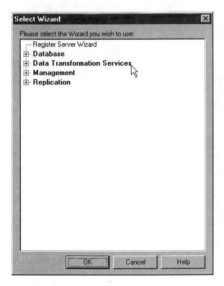

Figure 17.18   Select Wizard.

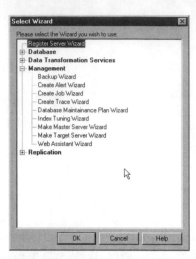

Figure 17.19 Select a Management Wizard.

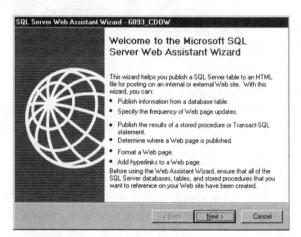

Figure 17.20 Web Assistant Wizard.

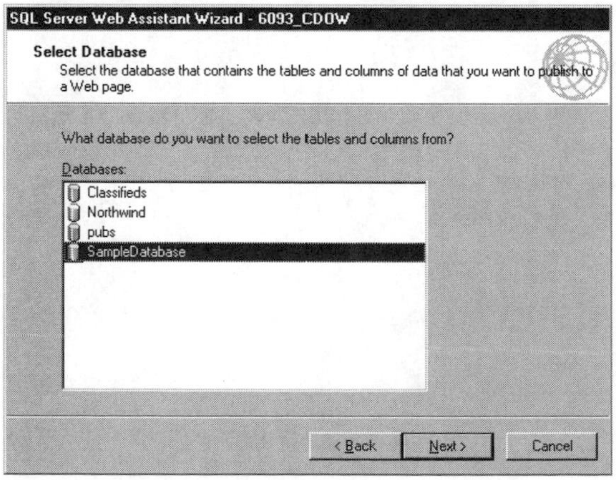

Figure 17.21 Select Database.

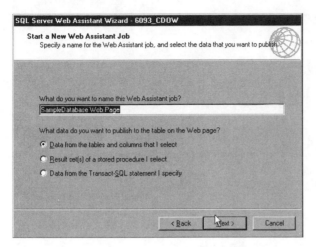

Figure 17.22 Start a new Web Assistant job.

dow looks like Figure 17.23. It is also possible to remove columns once they have been selected by pressing the <<Remove button. Press the Next button.

Figure 17.24 shows the window that is used to either select all the rows in the selected tables, or to specify criteria for selecting subsets of the data. Press Next.

Figure 17.25 is used to schedule a job for generating and updating the Web page. The options available include immediately after the wizard is completed, on demand, once at a specific time, when data changes in the database, or at regularly scheduled intervals. Choose the options as shown in Figure 17.25 and press the Next button.

Figure 17.26 shows a window that can be used to establish monitoring requests for a table and columns in a table. Press the AddAll button, then press the Next button.

Figure 17.27 shows the window that is used to publish the Web page. The filename for the Web page can be modified. Note the default location; on my machine it is d:\MSSQL7\HTML\WebPage1.htm. Press the Next button.

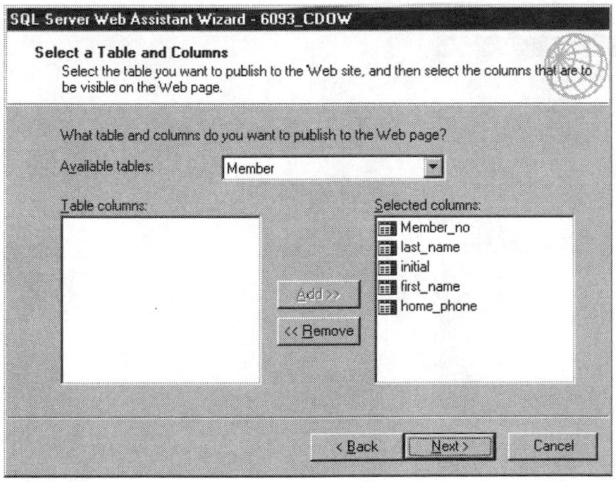

Figure 17.23 Select tables and columns.

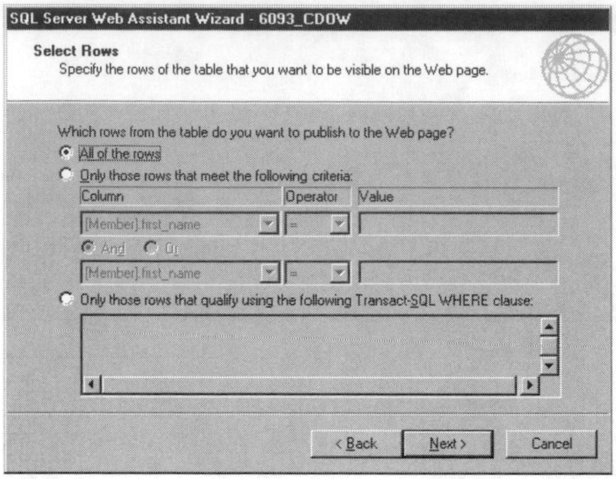

Figure 17.24 Select rows.

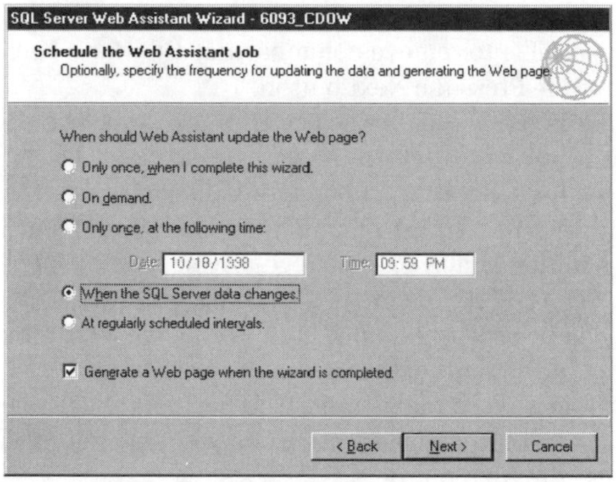

Figure 17.25 Schedule the Web Assistant job.

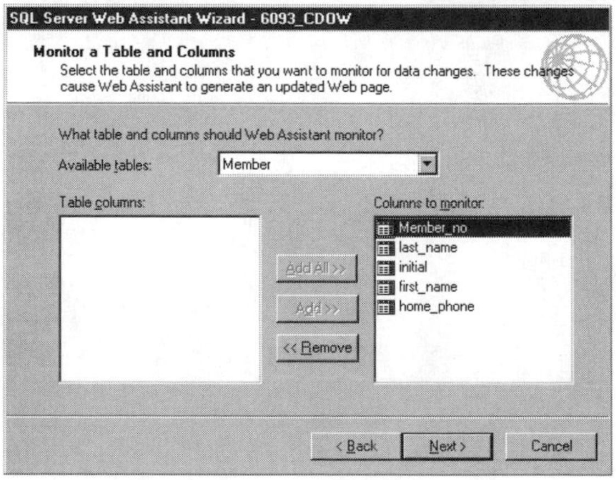

Figure 17.26 Monitor tables and columns.

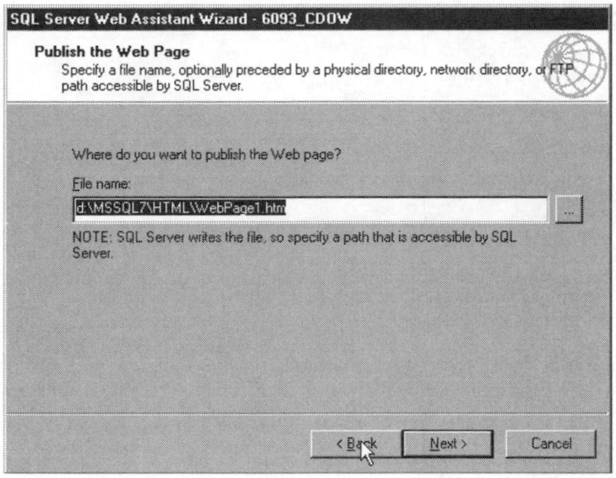

Figure 17.27   Publish the Web page.

Figure 17.28 shows that a Web page can be formatted manually or input from a template file. Leave the default Yes, help me format the web page, and press the Next button.

Figure 17.29 shows the window that is used to format the title of the Web page. Make the changes so that yours looks like the figure.

Figure 17.30 shows a window that can be used to display table column names with the data, or to display the data only. The latter option is useful if text is displayed on the Web page through other means. Leave the defaults and press the Next button.

Figure 17.31 shows several options for adding hyperlinks to a Web page. This includes suppressing all hyperlinks, specifying one hyperlink, and specifying a list of hyperlinks saved in an SQL Server table. Leave the defaults and press the Next button.

Figure 17.32 shows the window that is used to specify the number of data rows that are allowed in the result set returned to the Web page and displayed on the Web page.

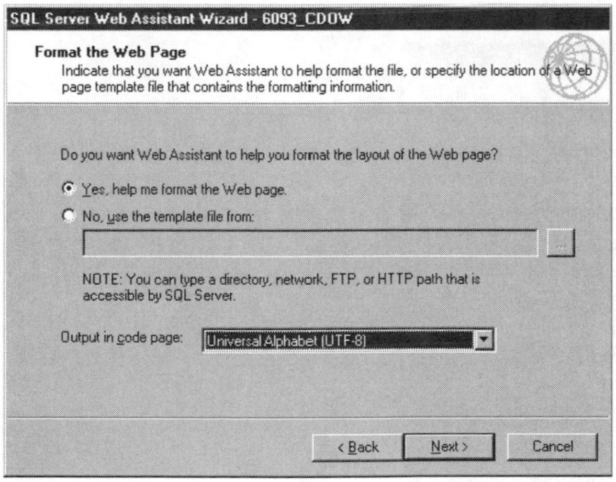

Figure 17.28   Format the Web page.

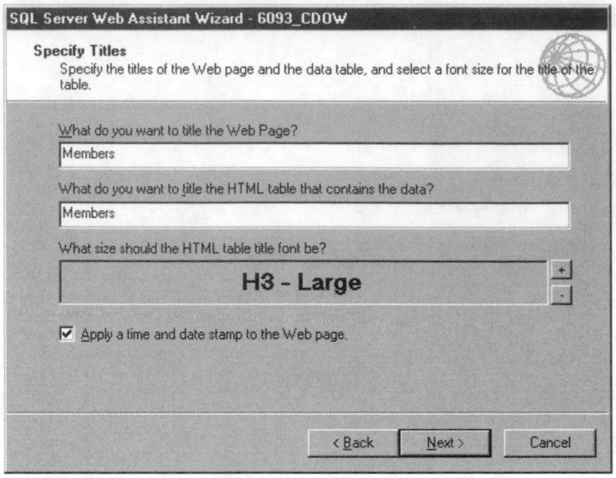

Figure 17.29 Specifying titles.

The options are divided into two parts on the screen. The top set of options is used to control the data rows that are returned by SQL Server. All the qualifying rows can be returned, or only a specific number from the top of the result set. The second set of options controls the number of data rows displayed on the Web page, and how they are connected.

Make the needed changes so that your options are similar to Figure 17.32, then press the Next button.

Figure 17.33 shows the conditions that were selected in the other windows of this wizard process. It is still possible to return to a previous window to make an adjustment by pressing the Back button. As shown in Figure 17.33, the Transact-SQL code can be written and browsed into a file. Press the Finish button.

You should then get a popup shown in Figure 17.34 indicating that the Web Assistant has successfully completed the task.

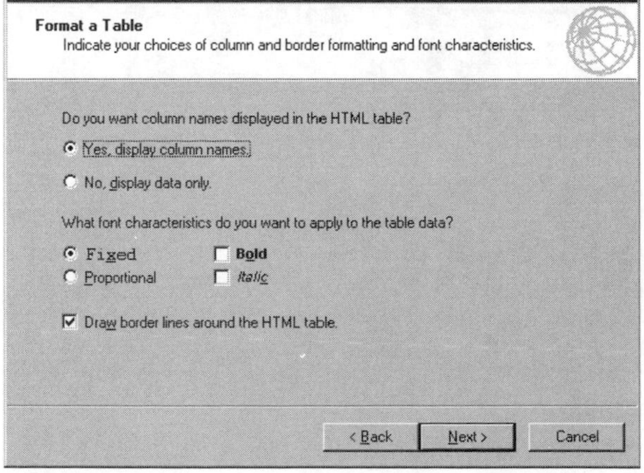

Figure 17.30 Table formatting.

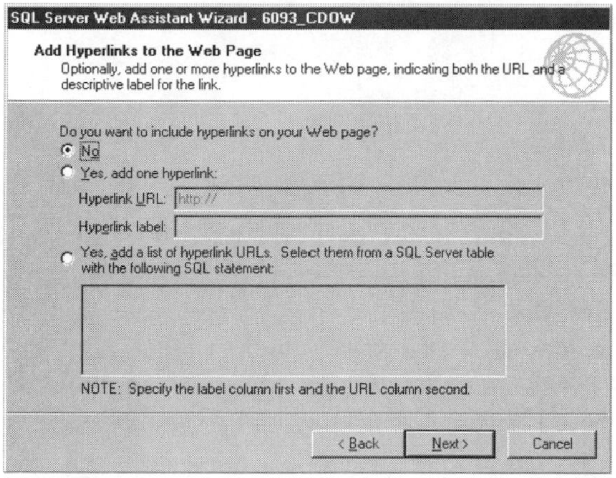

Figure 17.31 Adding hyperlinks.

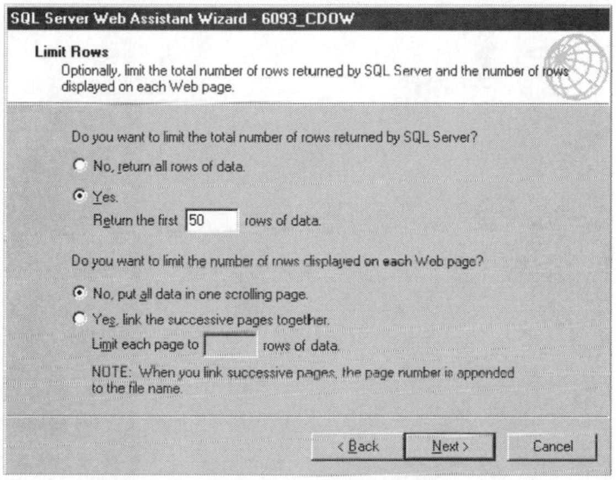

Figure 17.32 Limiting the size of result sets.

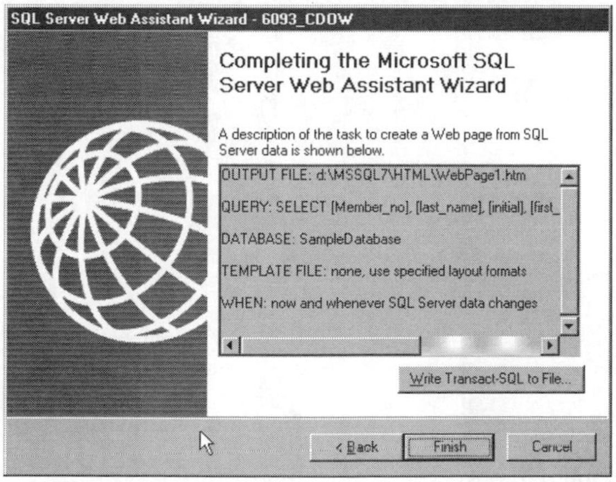

Figure 17.33 Completing the Web Assistant Wizard.

Figure 17.34 Saving the Transact SQL file.

Now navigate to the file that we generated (in my case, d:\MSSQL7\HTML\Web-Page1.htm), and double-click. Assuming that your file associations are set correctly, you should see your data appear, as in Figure 17.35.

You can experiment with changing the data in SQL Server and reopening the Web page to verify that it is updated. There is no need to close your browser. Go into SQL Server, make a change, then reload your HTM page. It is changed also! See Figure 17.36.

Figure 17.35 Viewing your new HTM file.

Figure 17.36 Viewing the changes to the database.

Connecting to SQL Server Using IBM WebSphere

There are many other tools to access SQL Server and publish to the Web. The following pages will not attempt to recreate the example but will show some of the features and functionality that is available in IBM's WebStudio. WebStudio allows the creation of components, some that use the Java Servlet Application Programming Interface (API) and the JavaBean specification. These components collaborate to provide the functionality you require. Generally you will have:

- Html page/s (.html) that will invoke the JavaBean files.
- Configuration files for the servlets.
- Java Server pages (.jsp) that have the tags (html and jsp) for the database columns.
- Servlets (.servlet) that can run on any Java servlet-enabled Web server.
- JavaBeans (.java and .class) that provide the database access layer including the SQL statements.
- WebStudio, which allows you to choose the drivers including JDBC drivers or an ODBC to JDBC driver. (See Figure 17.37.)

After entering the database alias, to facilitate your work, the metadata for the database is provided. (See Figure 17.38.)

SQLStudio comes equipped with several wizards (e.g., the SQL Wizard). Once you enter the correct database alias, WebStudio's SQL Wizard allows you to test the con-

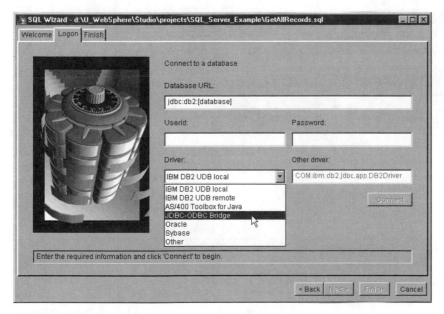

Figure 17.37 Choosing a driver.

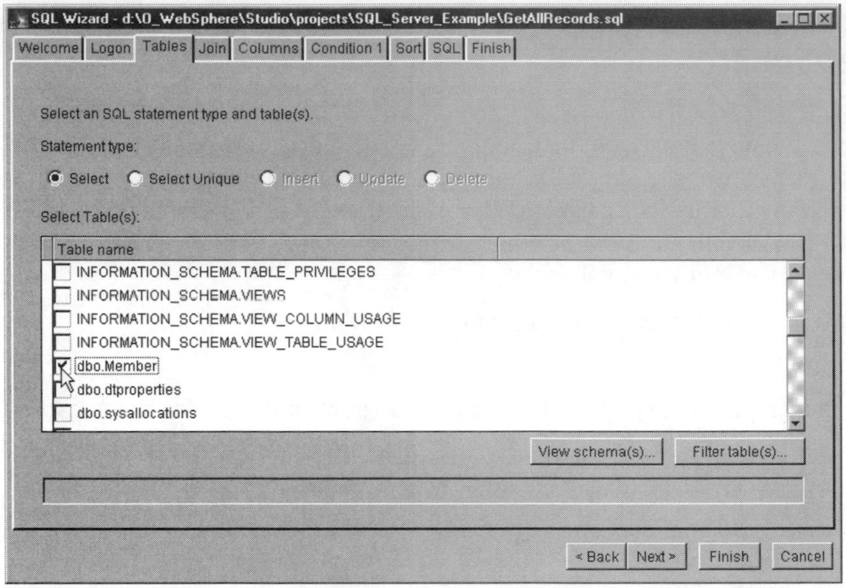

Figure 17.38   Viewing metadata.

nection; if it works it will return the metadata of the database and provide additional tabs for you to manipulate that data (see Figure 17.39).

A nice feature of the Wizard is to use the Run SQL button to test the SQL (see Figure 17.40).

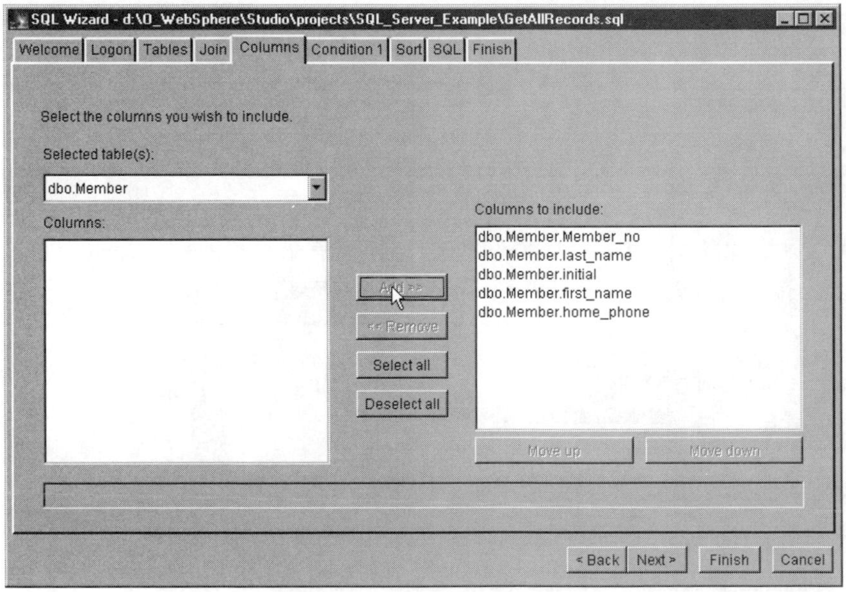

Figure 17.39   Using the SQL wizard.

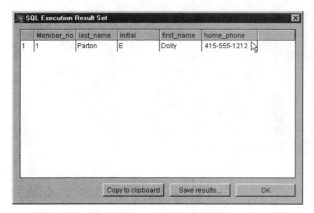

Figure 17.40   Viewing your SQL results.

WebStudio's Database Access Wizard

WebStudio has a Database Access Wizard that will build and compile the following files to perform the database query for our simple example:

- OurFirstDatabaseAccessServlet.class
- OurFirstDatabaseAccessServlet.servlet
- OurFirstDatabaseAccessServletBean.java
- OurFirstDatabaseAccessServletBean.class
- OurFirstDatabaseAccessInputPage.html
- OurFirstDatabaseAccessOutputPage.jsp

These files collaborate to get the data from the database and onto the client's browser.

Source Listing 17.2 is an example of some of the Java code generated for OurFirst-DatabaseAccessServlet.java:

```
// This file was generated by IBM WebSphere Studio Release 1.0 on 06-
Dec-98 7:38:39 PM.

package SQL_Server_Example;

/**
* Our access servlet
*/

public class OurFirstDatabaseAccessServlet extends
com.ibm.servlet.PageListServlet implements java.io.Serializable
{
                                                        (Continues)
```

Source 17.2   OurFirstDatabaseAccess.Servlet.java.

```
/************************************************************************
    * Process incoming requests for information
    *
    * @param request Object that encapsulates the request to the servlet
    * @param response Object that encapsulates the response from the servlet
    */
    public void performTask(javax.servlet.http.HttpServletRequest
request, javax.servlet.http.HttpServletResponse response)
    {
        try
        {

            // instantiate the bean and store it in the request
                    // so it can be accessed by the called page
            SQL_Server_Example.OurFirstDatabaseAccessServletBean
                            ourFirstDatabaseAccessServletBean = null;
            ourFirstDatabaseAccessServletBean =
(SQL_Server_Example.OurFirstDatabaseAccessServletBean)
java.beans.Beans.instantiate(getClass().getClassLoader(),
"SQL_Server_Example.OurFirstDatabaseAccessServletBean");

            // store the bean in the request so it can be
                    // accessed by pages which are accessed with
                    // callPage()
            setRequestAttribute("ourFirstDatabaseAccessServletBean",
                            ourFirstDatabaseAccessServletBean, request);

            // Initialize the bean userID property from the parameters

ourFirstDatabaseAccessServletBean.setUserID(getParameter(request,
                                    "userID", true, true, true, null));

            // Initialize the bean password property from the parameters

ourFirstDatabaseAccessServletBean.setPassword(getParameter(request,
                                    "password", true, true, true, null));

            // Initialize the bean driver property from the parameters

ourFirstDatabaseAccessServletBean.setDriver(getParameter(request,
                                    "driver", true, true, true, null));

            // Initialize the bean URL property from the parameters

ourFirstDatabaseAccessServletBean.setURL(getParameter(request, "URL",
                                    true, true, true, null));

            // call the execute action on the bean
            ourFirstDatabaseAccessServletBean.execute();
```

(Continues)

Source 17.2 *(Continued)*

```
                    // Call the output page. If the output page is not
                    // passed as part of the URL, the default page is
                            // called.
                    callPage(getPageNameFromRequest(request), request, response);
            }
            catch (Exception theException)
            {
                    handleError(request, response, theException);
            }
    }


/*************************************************************************
    * Returns the requested parameter
    *
    * @param request Object that encapsulates the request to the servlet
    * @param parameterName The name of the parameter value to return
    * @param checkRequestParameters when true, the request parameters
                                                            are searched
    * @param checkInitParameters when true, the servlet init parameters
                                                            are searched
    * @param isParameterRequired when true, an exception is thrown when
                                            the parameter cannot be found
    * @param defaultValue The default value to return when the parameter
                                                        is not found
    * @return The parameter value
    * @exception java.lang.Exception Thrown when the parameter is not
                                                                found
    */
    public java.lang.String
getParameter(javax.servlet.http.HttpServletRequest request, java.lang.
            String parameterName, boolean checkRequestParameters, boolean
    checkInitParameters, boolean isParameterRequired, java.lang.String
                            defaultValue) throws java.lang.Exception
    {
        java.lang.String[] parameterValues = null;
        java.lang.String paramValue = null;

        // Get the parameter from the request object if
            // necessary.
        if (checkRequestParameters)
        {
            parameterValues = request.getParameterValues(parameterName);

            if (parameterValues != null)
                paramValue = parameterValues[0];
        }

        // Get the parameter from the servlet init parameters if
        // it was not in the request parameter.
```

                                                                (Continues)

Source 17.2   *(Continued)*

```
        if ( (checkInitParameters) && (paramValue == null) )
            paramValue = getServletConfig().getInitParameter
                                                (parameterName);

        // Throw an exception if the parameter was not found and
        // it was required. The exception will be caught by error
        // processing and can be displayed in the error page.
        if ( (isParameterRequired) && (paramValue == null) )
            throw new Exception(parameterName + " parameter was not
                                                specified.");

        // Set the return to the default value if the parameter
            // was not found
        if (paramValue == null)
            paramValue = defaultValue;

        return paramValue;
    }


/*************************************************************************
    * Process incoming HTTP GET requests
    *
    * @param request Object that encapsulates the request to the servlet
    * @param response Object that encapsulates the response from the
servlet
    */
    public void doGet(javax.servlet.http.HttpServletRequest request,
                      javax.servlet.http.HttpServletResponse response)
    {
        performTask(request, response);
    }


/*************************************************************************
    * Process incoming HTTP POST requests
    *
    * @param request Object that encapsulates the request to the servlet
    * @param response Object that encapsulates the response from the
                                                servlet
    */
    public void doPost(javax.servlet.http.HttpServletRequest request,
                       javax.servlet.http.HttpServletResponse response)
    {
        performTask(request, response);
    }


}
```

Source 17.2 *(Continued)*

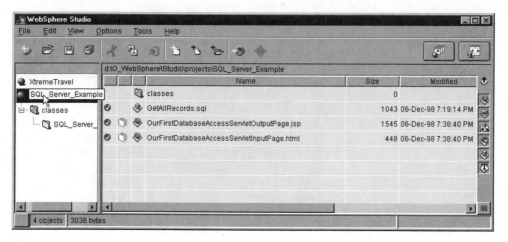

Figure 17.41   The WebStudio environment.

Summary

There are many ways to publish Microsoft SQL Server data to the Web; some methods
are Microsoft-centric, others use SQL or Java. Many do a good job of hiding the complexity, others require that you understand them. OLE DB is a lower-level API than what
Microsoft would like you to use, so that has been wrapped into ADO or ActiveX Data
Objects. ADO was designed to address the needs of Internet developers. Internet developers must be able to access special types of data and traditional relational sources.
ADO was designed to allow the creation of faster, smaller, and more efficient applications. If you are writing new applications, and decide to use Microsoft technology, ADO
is an easy choice, especially now that ADO 2.0 is available. If you decide to use other
methods like Java or SQL, you will have many tools from which to choose.

Deploying Production-Ready N-Tier Applications and System Administration

Part Five provides the reader with information on application testing, optimization, application debugging, system administration, and application implementation. SQL Server wizards and administration utilities are examined in this section of the book. Chapter 18 reviews an approach for testing, optimizing, debugging, and implementing an application during the entire project life cycle. Chapter 19 reviews the administrative tools that are available in SQL Server 7, including the Enterprise Manager, Query Analyzer, and a set of administrative wizards. Chapter 20 examines SQL Server utilities, techniques, and tools for ongoing maintenance of SQL Server–based applications.

CHAPTER

18

Testing, Optimization, Debugging, and Implementation

The application life cycle incorporates activities to test, optimize, and debug application code during the development process. The completeness and efficiency of these activities have a major impact on the timing, costs, and quality of the final application that is delivered to the user community. After these activities are completed it is necessary to deploy or implement the application. The complexity and reliability of this activity depends on the complexity of the production environment and the systems management tools that are available during the deployment or implementation activities.

Learning from SQL Server Experiences

There are a number of recurring factors across development projects that involve SQL Server technology. Knowing these factors in advance allows you to effectively deal with them before application deployment. The following list describes situations that are normally encountered in large development environments that incorporate SQL Server technology:

Overall response time degradation. Overall response time degrades in SQL Server environments because of increasing data volumes, increasing numbers of concurrent users, unexpected bottlenecks, and increased distribution of the application. SQL Server 7 contains features that automatically improve this situation over earlier releases of the product.

User contention. Development is generally done in small teams with limited architecture complexity. There are often unexpected problems when the number of concurrent users is increased. This situation is more acute in distributed environments. The application should be stress tested early in the life cycle to ensure that the technical and application architectures support the maximum number of concurrent users without insurmountable contention problems or performance degradation. It is quite common to neglect this issue because of the assumption that a solution can easily be found and implemented before application deployment. This approach is risky and projects can suffer greatly for it. Even if a solution is found near the end of the project life cycle, there is no guarantee that it can be implemented in a timely manner. The approach can also be costly, requiring consultants to come in at the last minute to rescue the situation. It is highly recommended that the suppliers or vendors be brought in early in the project life cycle to stress test this situation. Product vendors are sometimes in a position to provide access to a test lab or to provide reasonable client references that prove the feasibility of supporting a required number of concurrent users without great expense.

Bottlenecks and data volumes. Applications are often developed in separate and distinct pieces. Each of the pieces are tested individually, with limited amounts of application data. Problems can occur when running an application from start to finish. It is not unusual for an application to perform unreasonably slow when fully loaded with data, even though earlier tests suggested much faster response times. Stress testing is often left to the end of the life cycle, assuming that a solution can always be found easily and implemented in a cost-effective manner. Adding hardware, changing configuration parameters, and tuning the operating system can be effective; however, bottlenecks can also exist due to the inherent architecture and design of the application. Stress testing with high data volumes is another activity that should be conducted near the start of the life cycle with the most complex transactions that need to be processed by the application. This will help to reveal potential bottlenecks that can be resolved before the architecture has driven the overall development of the system. For example, it is not unusual to move some processing activities outside the SQL Server environment (e.g., such as sorting large text lists) and then move the data back into the database environment for subsequent manipulation.

Lack of testing time. Testing activities always appear to be rushed in projects. This is due to an emphasis on functionality development and little emphasis on testing. Spreading testing out over the project life cycle alleviates some of these problems. Testing is an iterative activity that requires a substantial amount of time and resources. Getting a test architect involved at the start of the life cycle can put the testing activities on the right track.

Architecture/design restrictions. The architecture and design that is adopted for an application can have inherent restrictions and inflexibility. It is valuable to invest in a solid architecture and design deliverable and to conduct an external, expert review of the deliverable before investing in development. Leaving this to the end is risky and can have huge impacts to the project.

Lack of tools. Developing a technical architecture at the start of the life cycle and planning to implement tools as they are needed will provide the necessary tuning, testing, and system management tools.

Conflicting priorities. Always ensure that the pieces required to develop, test, implement, and sign off on a project are dedicated or committed to the project. The DBA involved in changing configuration variables and establishing the environment should have a stake in the development project, otherwise the testing environment may not be ready or cleaned up when it is needed. Similarly, users who are committed to operational activities will neglect testing activities unless they are given an incentive and opportunity to do this.

Scalability. This becomes an unexpected problem on many projects, as the application is moved from the test environment to the production environment. The newer releases of Windows and SQL Server are more scalable than previous releases. It is still advisable to establish this at the beginning of the project with the right combination of hardware, software, and tuning to satisfy the requirements of the project.

Backup/recovery. It is not uncommon for development environments to be active with no tested backup and recovery strategy. This means that a hardware problem or error could conceivably destroy many months of work. Dedicated backups are faster than running backups while the CPU is being shared with other tasks. A combination of full backups, followed by daily incremental backups is more resource friendly than full daily backups. However, too many incremental backups will require too much processing to recover a database.

Testing

Testing comes in many types and can have different definitions for different people. It is useful to arrive at a common definition. Some common types of testing, definitions, and resource/responsibility requirements are included in Table 18.1. It is not uncommon to combine some of the testing types to reduce time. It is also possible to add additional types of testing or to enhance the definitions in other situations. Allocating testing resources is generally a challenging activity. The users that are normally required for testing are also urgently needed in operational activities. The owner is responsible for securing the needed users in a timely manner.

Testing Approach

An iterative approach for testing works well in the SQL Server environment. There are a variety of testing/debugging tools that are available for formal testing. An effective approach for development resources is to incorporate the use of scripts to test their code as it is being developed. It is never a good idea to write the entire application without testing as you proceed. Relying on clean compiles does not accomplish this. It is useful to write small pieces of the code and to test them before proceeding. For example, various test constraints were created for user-defined tables in Chapter 7 with the script that follows. In this example, the size of contact_no, that is, 11, is inconsistent with the associated check constraint. The size will need to be increased, but first the tests will find this problem:

Table 18.1 Testing Types

TYPE OF TESTING	DESCRIPTION	OWNER	RESOURCES
Unit	This is a basic type of testing that follows the development of a function.	Team leader	Development resources
System	Test the application functions from a technical perspective and individually.	Project manager	Development resources
Integration	Test the application functions as part of an overall system.	Project manager	Development resources Users
Functional	Test the business functionality of the applications. This is generally done with detailed scenarios and test scripts.	Business manager and stakeholders	Users Application owners
Regression	Test the business application to ensure that new functionality or changes have not broken previous functionality.	Project manager	Development resources
Stress	Test the application with high volumes of data, users, and rigor.	Project manager	Development resources Consultants
Acceptance	The final level of testing that should not uncover any major problems with an application. Signoff is generally followed by system implementation.	Project sponsors	Users Application owners

```
use pubs
go

drop table student
drop table subject
drop table advisor
go
```

```
/* the order of the following create statements is in the sequence of
the foreign keys. */

create table advisor(
      advisor_code             char (10) PRIMARY KEY CLUSTERED,
      advisor_name             char(50),
      contact_no               char (11) CONSTRAINT CK_contact_no CHECK
      (contact_no LIKE '[3-9][0-9][0-9]-[0-9][0-9][0-9]-[0-9][0-9][0-9][0-9]')
CONSTRAINT unique_advisor UNIQUE NONCLUSTERED (advisor_name))
go

create table subject(
      subject_code             char (10) PRIMARY KEY CLUSTERED,
      description              char (50),
      primary_instructor       char (10) REFERENCES advisor (advisor_code))
go

create table student(
      student_id               int     PRIMARY KEY CLUSTERED,
      major_subject            char (10) REFERENCES subject(subject_code),
      advisor_name             char (10),
      admission_date           datetime    DEFAULT getdate(),
      previous_gpa             float           CHECK (previous_gpa > 0 AND
                                                      previous_gpa <=4.3)

      CONSTRAINT FK_major_advisor_name FOREIGN KEY (advisor_name)
              REFERENCES advisor (advisor_code))
go
```

When writing these types of scripts, it is always useful to write them in such a way that they can be rerun to reestablish an environment to a precise state. In the previous script, the tables are dropped before they are created. This allows the script to be rerun without subsequent errors. After running this script successfully, it becomes necessary to unit test its results. This test is not intended to be thorough, or expensive, but rather to ensure that the code being developed has basic integrity and is performing as it is expected to perform.

There are many ways to confirm that the tables were created. The simplest is to trust the success message that SQL Server displays when the code is executed. Another method is to inspect the sysobjects system table. A stored procedure like sp_help can also be used to display the table name and the columns corresponding to the table. In the following example, the placement of the go statement is necessary to include each sp_help statement in a separate batch:

```
sp_help   student
go
sp_help   subject
go
sp_help   advisor
go
```

A series of insert statements can be used to test the datatypes and the column names. Notice that the second insert statement, into the subject table, contains a referentially accurate advisor_code. Our testing strategy is to test a correct insert, followed by some attempts with invalid data. This includes attempting to insert duplicate data rows and referentially incorrect code. It is useful to clear the tables before inserting the data rows. Since the advisor table is independent of the others, it is useful to insert a data row in it, as follows:

```
DELETE advisor
go

INSERT advisor
(advisor_code, advisor_name, contact_no)
VALUES
('joeb', 'Joe Brown', '310-111-9999')
go
```

Attempting to insert the data row into the advisor table generates the following error message:

```
Server: Msg 547, Level 16, State 1
[Microsoft][ODBC SQL Server Driver][SQL Server]INSERT statement
conflicted with COLUMN CHECK constraint 'CK_contact_no'. The conflict
occurred in database 'pubs', table 'advisor', column 'contact_no'.
The statement has been aborted.
```

This error results because the table creation script set the contact_no column as char (11). This is too small to hold the constraint that is also specified for the column. The error can be fixed by increasing the size of the column to, say, 15. The advisor table can be altered; however, modifying the original script is useful to support rerunning it repeatedly. The alter table command is not clean in this case, and is only a temporary fix. Rerunning the alter command after the advisor table is created duplicates effort. The following code drops the advisor table and then creates it with a larger column size for contact_no:

```
drop table advisor
go

create table advisor(
     advisor_code          char (10) PRIMARY KEY CLUSTERED,
     advisor_name          char(50),
     contact_no            char (15) CONSTRAINT CK_contact_no CHECK
   (contact_no LIKE '[3-9][0-9][0-9]-[0-9][0-9][0-9]-[0-9][0-9][0-9][0-9]')
CONSTRAINT unique_advisor UNIQUE NONCLUSTERED (advisor_name))
go
```

Attempting to run this code results in another error because the address and subject tables contain foreign key constraints that reference the advisor table. These other constraints or the tables must be dropped before the advisor table can be dropped. Constraints can be dropped with the alter table command. The following syntax drops the subject and address tables before proceeding to the advisor table:

```
DROP table student
go
DROP table subject
go
DROP table advisor
go

create table advisor(
        advisor_code          char (10) PRIMARY KEY CLUSTERED,
        advisor_name          char(50),
        contact_no            char (15) CONSTRAINT CK_contact_no CHECK
    (contact_no LIKE '[3-9][0-9][0-9]-[0-9][0-9][0-9]-[0-9][0-9][0-9][0-9]')
CONSTRAINT unique_advisor UNIQUE NONCLUSTERED (advisor_name))
go

INSERT advisor
(advisor_code, advisor_name, contact_no)
VALUES
('joeb', 'Joe Brown', '310-111-9999')
go
```

Executing this sequence of commands inserts a record into the advisor table. The data in the code can be displayed with the basic select * from advisor statement. The following statements insert data rows into the other tables as well, but re-create the subject and student tables before attempting these inserts:

```
INSERT subject
(subject_code, description,      primary_instructor)
    VALUES
('CSC101', 'Computer Science 101','joeb')
go

INSERT student
(student_id, major_subject, advisor_name,
 admission_date,previous_gpa)
    VALUES
        (1000, 'CSC101', 'joeb', getdate(), 4.0)
go
```

Reversing the order of these inserts will raise an error because the subject reference constraint is violated. Since the objective is to test the different constraints, it is useful to construct a simple table that identifies the columns and conditions that need to be tested, as illustrated in Table 18.2. This list is not intended to be complete. For example, we may also want to test case sensitivity as well. The Test Status column in the following table is modified as each test is completed.

Table 18.2 Test Script

TABLE NAME	COLUMN NAME	TEST REQUIREMENT AND APPROACH	TEST STATUS
Advisor	Advisor_code	Test code uniqueness across multiple entries Test length of code (<=10 chars)	
	Advisor_name	Unique name Name length (<=50 chars)	
	Contact_no	Check constraint (999-999-9999)	Done
Subject	Subject_code Description	Name length (<=10)	
	Primary_instructor	References advisor-advisor_code	
Student	Student_id	Integer	
	Major_subject	References subject-subject_code	
	Advisor_name	References advisor-advisor_code	
	Admission_date	Valid date	
	Previous_gpa	Must be in the range 0 to 4.3	

Once the test cases are identified, test scripts can be developed to reflect these requirements. The objective is to ensure that the constraints are trapping invalid data while accepting valid data.

The following syntax attempts to insert a duplicate row into the advisor table. Executing the following code displays a primary key violation error:

```
INSERT advisor
(advisor_code, advisor_name, contact_no)
VALUES
('joeb', 'Joe Brown', '310-111-9999')
go
```

Insert a data row with an advisor_code that exceeds 10 characters in length. The command will execute without a syntax error, however, the advisor_code is truncated to 10 characters in length. Since this occurs without warning, there can be unexpected side effects, especially in the cases where the information is returned to called client programs and distributed programs. Such client applications may be programmed to expect a different size for the fields. Since there was no warning in the compile this may go unnoticed:

```
INSERT advisor
(advisor_code, advisor_name, contact_no)
VALUES
('kathBlueWhoToo', 'KathyBlueWhoTooNewKnewKnowwowhow', '333-111-9999')
go

select * from advisor
go
```

Insert a data row into the subject table to test the primary_instructor/advisor_code foreign key constraint. The following statement generates a foreign key constraint violation:

```
INSERT subject
(subject_code, description, primary_instructor)
     VALUES
('BIO101', 'Biology 101','tonb')
go
```

Insert a data row into the student table to test the advisor_name/advisor_code foreign key constraint. The following statement generates a foreign key constraint violation on the advisor_name column and aborts the statement:

```
INSERT student
(student_id, major_subject, advisor_name,
 admission_date, previous_gpa)
     VALUES
          (1001, 'CSC101', 'toneb', getdate(), 4.0)
go
```

Insert a data row into the student table to test the major_subject/subject_code foreign key constraint. The following statement generates a foreign key constraint violation on the major_subject column:

```
INSERT student
(student_id, major_subject, advisor_name,
 admission_date, previous_gpa)
     VALUES
          (1002, 'BIO101', 'joeb', getdate(), 4.0)
go
```

Attempting to insert the following the data row is rejected because it has a duplicate key. Had the duplicate key situation not existed, the data row would have been rejected because of the advisor_name foreign key violation:

```
INSERT student
(student_id, major_subject, advisor_name,
 admission_date, previous_gpa)
     VALUES
          (1000, 'CSC101', 'toneb', getdate(), 4.0)
go
```

The following data rows are rejected because the previous_gpa is not within the data range indicated with the create table command for each of the insert statements:

```
INSERT student
(student_id, major_subject, advisor_name,
 admission_date, previous_gpa)
     VALUES
```

```
            (1003, 'CSC101', 'joeb', getdate(), 5.0)
go


INSERT student
(student_id, major_subject, advisor_name,
 admission_date, previous_gpa)
      VALUES
            (1004, 'CSC101', 'joeb', getdate(), -2)
go


INSERT student
(student_id, major_subject, advisor_name,
 admission_date, previous_gpa)
      VALUES
            (1005, 'CSC101', 'joeb', getdate(), 4.4)
go
```

The following data row tests one aspect of the year 2000 problem by attempting to insert a date value that is past the year 2000 and then displays the contents of the data row in the table. This test simply demonstrates that a date past the year 2000 can be saved in the column. It does not test functionality, which should be done with another set of test cases:

```
INSERT student
(student_id, major_subject, advisor_name,
 admission_date, previous_gpa)
      VALUES
            (1005, 'CSC101', 'joeb', 'Feb 3 2009', 4.0)
go
select * from student
```

These commands display the following information, showing that the admission_ date column can accept dates past the year 2000:

student id	major subject	advisor name	admission date	previous gpa
1000	CSC101	joeb	1998-10-16 02:30:13.320	4.0
1005	**CSC101**	**joeb**	**2009-02-03 00:00:00.000**	**4.0**

Attempt to insert a data row into the student table with an invalid month name, such as FFF. This generates an error message similar to the following: Syntax error converting datetime from character string.

```
INSERT student
(student_id, major_subject, advisor_name,
 admission_date, previous_gpa)
      VALUES
            (1006, 'CSC101', 'joeb', 'FFF 3 2009', 4.0)
go
```

Table 18.3 Test Scripts

TABLE NAME	COLUMN NAME	TEST REQUIREMENT AND APPROACH	TEST STATUS
Advisor	Advisor_code	Test code uniqueness across multiple entries	Done
		Test length of code (<=10 chars)	
	Advisor_name	Unique name	
		Name length (<=50 chars)	
	Contact_no	Check constraint (999-999-9999)	Done
Subject	Subject_code	Name length (<=10)	
	Description		
	Primary_instructor	References advisor-advisor_code	Done
Student	Student_id	Integer	
	Major_subject	References subject-subject_code	Done
	Advisor_name	References advisor-advisor_code	Done
	Admission_date	Valid date	Done
	Previous_gpa	Must be in the range 0 to 4.3	Done

The test case table can be updated as a result of the tests that have been completed, as shown in Table 18.3. These tests have not been exhaustive, but they have been able to prove that the constraints follow some of the expected functionality. Additional tests would still need to be conducted to build more confidence.

Optimization and Performance

Performance measures an application's response time and throughput. Optimization is followed to improve application performance. Application performance is impacted by the following: I/O size, user log cache, locking, disk I/O, deadlocks, lock contention, engine usage, index selection, query optimization, log I/O size, packet size, physical devices, and tempdb contention. Some common methods for improving application performance are the following:

Hardware. Market prices for hardware have dropped so dramatically that it is feasible to attempt throwing hardware at performance problems. This will not always succeed, but multiple, fast processors, lots of RAM, dedicated machines, and powerful client platforms are worth evaluating during stress testing.

Operating system. The operating system, some variation of Windows when utilizing SQL Server, is another place to look to optimize an application. Try changing the application priority using a tool such as the Task Manager. Consider that NT uses processor 0 for I/O and it also leverages the highest processor, in an SMP architecture, for other activities. These should not be included in SMP equations. It is also useful to evaluate the environment using the performance monitor. It is important to avoid paging in order to avoid consuming significant time cycles. NT will generally page with less than 5 MB of free memory.

Indexing. SQL Server 7 offers significant improvements in terms of indexing capabilities. Most of these improvements are available without any special coding. A general rule to consider with indexes is to avoid creating unnecessary ones, say on tables of less than 100 records. Another consideration is to update index statistics regularly and whenever there have been a high number of updates against a table. It is also advisable to minimize the key length in an index. Clustered indexes are more efficient in terms of space usage than nonclustered indexes.

Contention. Locking contention is time consuming and can dramatically impact system performance. This is true whether there are too many locks, too few locks, or inappropriate types of locks. Page level locks in an ERP application significantly impact application performance. SQL Server's new automatic row-locking feature goes a long way toward improving performance in this area. Companies such as SAP and FileNet have dedicated their support for SQL Server due in no small part to this new feature.

Transaction size. Transaction analysis identifies the transaction name, transaction type, transaction frequency, tables affected, and the number of reads/writes. This list can be customized for a specific project and is used to size transactions. Every transaction should be structured to issue locks at the very last instance and to release them as soon as possible.

Transaction log. Appropriate use of the transaction log for recoverability and a consideration for efficiency impacts performance. A minimum amount of data should be written to the transaction log by avoiding uses of NULLs, variable characters, and out-of-place record updates. Similarly utilities such as fast BCP, which do not write to the log, are good alternatives when database recoverability is not an issue.

Partitioning. Partitioning refers to the placement of application logic within a distributed application. In general, place functionality close to the geographic location where it is needed. Static tables can be close to the tier that uses them. Minimize network traffic and calls to the database. This latter point is critical. Do not issue repeated calls to the server in OLTP applications, as each call has an overhead that hits performance negatively. It is better to batch requests and issue a single large request over a network. Proper use of stored procedures also improves performance.

I/O. Improving the efficiency of I/O impacts performance as well. Large I/O is efficient for information type queries. Small I/O is appropriate for OLTP applications.

Tuning. SQL Server is a programmable, tunable database server. Tools such as sp_monitor, sp_sysmon, and the set command can be used to identify ways to improve the efficiency of requests by restructuring code, changing configuration values, and database options.

Implementation

Implementation is the process of deploying an application into a production environment after building the supporting environment. There is also the need to decommission existing applications after a period of parallel activity. Distributed, n-tier environments tend to be somewhat more complicated because of the distinct number of pieces that need to be dealt with. Some fairly standard activities for applications that use database servers in their architecture are defined in this section, as follows:

Signoff. Before starting any implementation activities, ensure that the new application is fully signed off by the project sponsors, and that the business owners have agreed to decommision existing systems.

Data Conversion. It is often necessary to convert data as part of an application implementation. This is usually a subproject within the entire initiative. As such, there should be routines to convert and scrub the data as it is being converted from the previous application to the new application. It is necessary to get the timing just right–perhaps using a month-end or a long weekend to disengage the existing database, transferring the knowledge to the new database, and turning on the application. All this must be done without losing business time.

Communication Plan. The communication plan informs the rest of the organization that an application is being implemented, why it is being implemented, and who is going to be affected. This is a powerful tool for ensuring that the organization is prepared for the application and is ready to deal with the difficulties that could arise. The communication plan should identify who is involved in the communication chain, the deliverables being distributed, and how they are being distributed. Communication deliverables must clearly have the support of the organization executive.

Production Environment. The production environment consists of the servers, networking and the clients/workstations. These are prepared from a hardware and software perspective before the application can be deployed.

Training. A training plan includes different programs for different resources throughout the organization. Training must be supplied to business and technical resources in stages so as not to disrupt the current environment, but to retrain designated resources in a timely fashion.

Application Distribution. Distributing an application in a distributed n-tier environment should be as automated as possible. Tools such as Microsoft SMS can be used to test a remote deployment and to automate the procedure once it is fine-tuned.

Pilot Sites. Instead of deploying an application in one big bang, consider starting with a pilot implementation at one site, and then moving the implementation to other sites.

Contingency Planning. Always have a contingency strategy in case there is a problem with the implementation. This should allow the business to continue running with a minimum of disruption and downtime.

Summary

This chapter examined methods to test, debug, and optimize applications prior to implementation. Various testing phases were discussed in this chapter, including unit, system, integration, stress, and acceptance testing. Roles and ownership within each of these testing cycles were also discussed. A test script was developed and an iterative method of building test scripts and testing table constraints was demonstrated.

This chapter also evaluated factors and problems that are frequently encountered on SQL Server projects. A list of areas to evaluate in order to improve application performance includes hardware, operating systems, indexing, contention, locking, transactions, partitioning, I/O, and server tuning.

The chapter identified some areas that should be included in an implementation plan. This includes data conversion, training, communication plan, pilot sites, technical environment, application distribution, and contingency planning.

System Administration through the Visual Tools and Wizards

Chapter 1 introduced some of the basic visual utilities that are available after SQL Server installation and provided a quick walkthrough of the functionality that is offered. This chapter reviews the administrative wizards and the visual utilities in more detail. The following tools are examined in this section: Enterprise Manager, Query Analyzer, Service Manager, Client Network Utility, Server Network Utility, MSDTC Administrative Console, and Uninstall SQL Server 7.

Visual Tools

The visual tools offer an easy-to-use interface that invokes system procedures and other modules to interact with the SQL Server environment. Many of these functions can be invoked using the ISQL batch utility in character mode. However, I recommend that readers who have built a proficiency with character mode invest the effort to transfer their knowledge base to the Visual Tools toolset.

A drawback with the interactive method of administration is its requirement for manual intervention and the potential need to reenter information to reestablish an environment. A solution to this is to build script files that are invoked by the graphical tool. This method is highly recommended in project environments to increase auditability, quality, and development time.

Enterprise Manager

The Enterprise Manager embodies Microsoft's strategic direction for a central system control panel using the object-based Management Console. The interface is highly componentized, snaps in components for delivering messages to other applications, and launches administrative visual tools such as profiler and Query Analyzer. Figure 19.1 shows that this tool consists of an outside container and a console dialogue that floats inside the container. The console is the primary interface for system administration. Both dialogues contain pulldown menus. The console also offers a tool palette. The console consists of two primary panes. The left pane is a hierarchical view of the physical environment and the database objects. Selecting a node in this hierarchy displays a lower level of detail in the right pane. The right pane also offers menu buttons to access menu options when a registered server is selected.

The Container Options

The container pulldown menu is available at the top of the window and offers three options:

> Two suboptions are offered under the Console button. Options allows settings for the Enterprise Manager to be established. Exit allows you to exit Enterprise Manager.

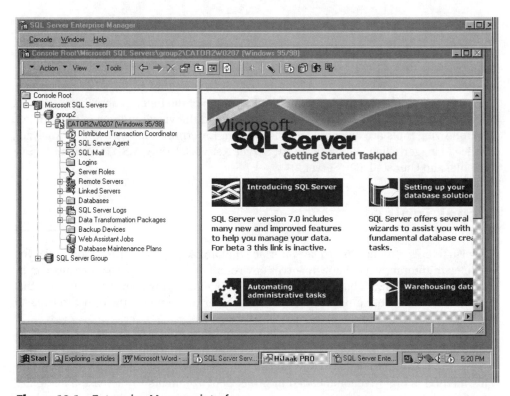

Figure 19.1 Enterprise Manager interface.

In addition to the standard options found in most Windows packages, the Windows option also allows a new console window to be opened. You are free to continue opening console windows, but it is difficult to keep track of more than three or four at any one time.

The Help window offers standard Windows functionality. This option shows the physical memory that is available and the system resource usage.

Console Root

The console root is the top level of the hierarchy in the left side of the console dialogue. This hierarchy provides a logical view of the physical environment related to common administrative functions. It contains folders and nodes that can be expanded or contracted by clicking the mouse button to the left of the object name. The syntax for using this command is as follows:

```
SQL Server
    SQL Server Group 1
            Distributed Transaction Coordinator
            SQL Server Agent
                Alerts
                Operators
                Jobs
            SQL Mail
            Logins
            Server Roles
            Remote Roles
            Remote Servers
            Linked Servers
            Databases
            SQL Server Logs
            Data Transformation Package
            Backup Devices
            Web Assistant Jobs
            Database Maintenance Plans
        SQL Server Group 2
            Repeat instances
```

SQL Server Logs is not a list of transaction log files. This option contains a list of files that contain session histories. The current log is identified as current, and previous log files are labeled archive #1, archive #2, archive #3, and so on.

Console Options

The three buttons, Action, View, and Tools, offer extensive functionality to support administration. The options under the Action button vary with the type of object selected in the hierarchical tree. Some useful options that become available as different objects are selected are described in the following list:

The New Linked Server option is used to establish security for remote servers.

The Tools option provides links to wizards, backup database, restore database, manage SQL Server Messages, Current Activity, External Tools, SQL Server Profiler, SQL Server Query Analyzer, and Options and is the same as the Tools button.

The New option is used to create new instances of the dialogue.

The options Register SQL Server, Edit SQL Server Registration, and Unregister SQL Server are used to identify servers to this tool.

The New Windows option is used to create another instance of the console window.

The View button is used to customize the interface, allowing selection of the types of icons, hierarchy structure, toolbars, status bars, and the description bar.

Some of the common options that are available under the Tools button are described in more detail here. The wizards option allows access to the Database, Data Transformation Services, Management, and Replication wizards. The administrative wizards are described later in this chapter.

The Backup database option offers two panels, as shown in Figure 19.2. The General tab allows selection of a database to back up and a backup type: complete database backup, differential database backup, transaction log backup, or a backup at a file or filegroup level. It is also possible to back up to a disk or a tape, either appending to a media or overwriting to it. A backup schedule can also be identified. The Add button allows the identification of a backup region (e.g., master1098). Clicking the OK button initiates the backup. The Options tab is used to confirm the integrity of the backup.

To test a backup activity, select the Northwind database from the database pulldown list. Click on the Add button and enter a backup file name, for example, C:\MSSQL7\ BACKUP\nw101598, and click on the OK button to complete the backup. The database is

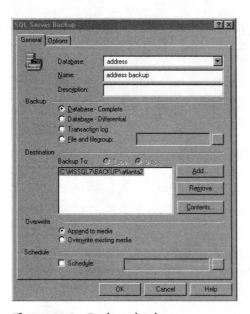

Figure 19.2   Backup database.

small so the backup only requires a few seconds to complete. The backup panel disappears when the backup is complete. Redisplay the backup panel, select the Northwind database, select the backup file_name, and select the contents button to display header information from the backup file. A panel showing the name, server, database, type of backup, date of backup, expiration information, and size of the backup in bytes is displayed. It is necessary to have dbo permissions on the database to complete this example.

The Restore database option offers two panels, as shown in Figure 19.3. The General tab allows selection of the backup for a specific database. The panes allow the selection of a restore type, such as Restore database and transaction logs, Restore filegroups or files, and Restore backup sets from device(s). The Options panel allows interface parameters to be requested. This includes prompting the operator before restoring a backup, overwriting an existing database with a backup, and restoring a backup as a specific database in the server environment. The state of the database after recovery can also be established in this panel.

As an example of a database restore, select the Northwind database, select the C:\MSSQL7\BACKUP\nw101598 Northwind backup, and select the Force restore over existing database from the Options panel. Click on the OK button. The Enterprise Manager displays a message such as "Restore of database 'Northwind' completed successfully." It is necessary to have dbo permissions on the database to complete this example.

The Manage SQL Server Messages option displays a dialogue that contains two tabs, as shown in Figure 19.4. The Search tab is used to find messages containing a specific type of text. The Messages tab is used to define messages with an error number, severity, language, logged, and message text.

The Current Activity option displays a dialogue that contains three tabs, as shown in Figure 19.5. The Server Activity tab displays information similar to that displayed by the sp_who command. The Detail Activity tab displays activity with detailed information, such as the login ID, process ID, status, database, running command, host server, calling application, blocks, lock types, group name, and user name. The Object Locks tab displays information about active locks and the last command issued with respect to the lock.

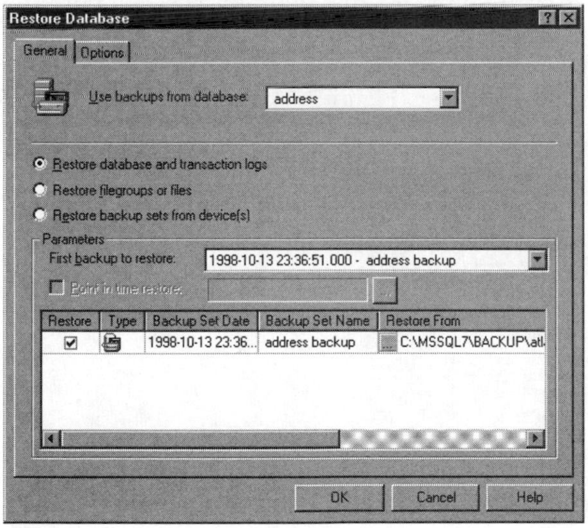

Figure 19.3 Restore database.

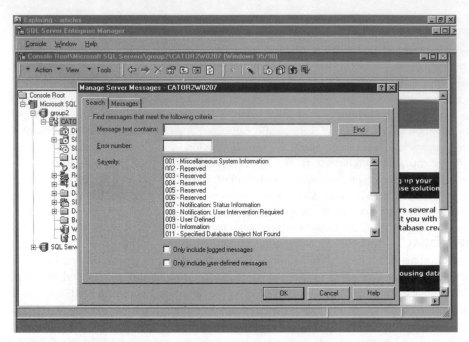

Figure 19.4 Manage SQL Server messages.

The SQL Server Profiler and SQL Server Query Analyzer options launch their respective applications asynchronously. The External Tools option allows external modules to be identified to the environment. Options is used to adjust the Enterprise Manager environment in terms of server state polling, server registration information, and timing settings.

The Properties option is available from three sources when it is relevant: from the Action button, from the tool palette, and by selecting an option, clicking on the right mouse button, and selecting Properties from the list that appears. This is a powerful command and an important window into the SQL Server environment.

Selecting the database object and choosing the properties option in any one of the three ways described here displays the dialogue in Figure 19.6. This allows a subset of

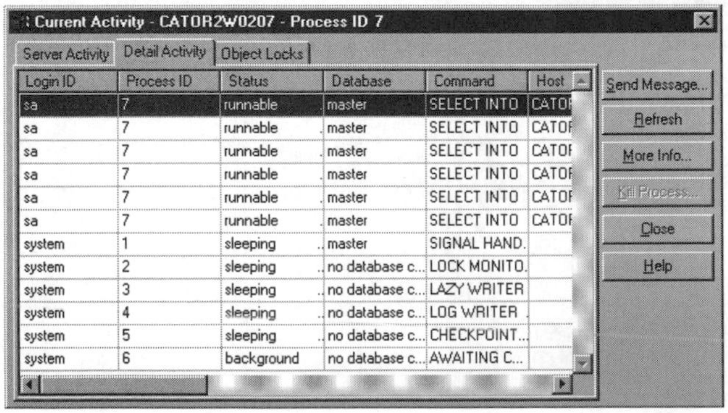

Figure 19.5 Current activity.

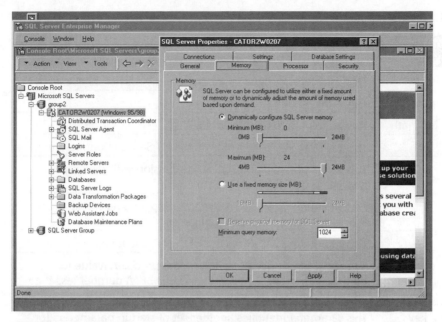

Figure 19.6 SQL Server properties.

configuration values to be modified at the server level. This includes the general environment, memory usage, processor, security, connections, settings, and database settings. These configuration values can also be adjusted using the sp_configure system procedure. The Startup Parameters button displays a Server Parameters dialogue for the database server and accepts a combination of the parameters shown in Table 19.1.

Selecting the SQL Server Agent object and choosing the properties option displays the dialogue shown in Figure 19.7. This allows changes to alerts, e-mail activity, log sizes, and connection information.

Selecting the SQL Mail object and choosing the properties option displays the dialogue shown in Figure 19.8, which allows the definition of mapping with SQL Mail.

Selecting a login user from the logins folder displays the dialogue shown in Figure 19.9. This dialogue allows inspection of the roles and privileges allocated to the login in a specific database as per the user ID. Server roles and specific database access can be identified using this dialogue.

Selecting a database in the databases folder and choosing the properties option displays the dialogue shown in Figure 19.10. Selecting a database name within the Databases folder also displays the same visual information screen. The General tab shows the physical location of the database and the associated file group. It also shows the amount of disk space allocated to the file. The management properties of the file are also maintained through this tab. The file growth can be indicated in terms of increments of disk space that are reserved, either in megabytes or as a percentage of the existing file size. This latter option supports exponential file growth. A maximum file size can also be established. The Transaction Log tab shows the physical attributes of the transaction log associated with the database file. Size attributes for the transaction log can also be established in this panel.

Table 19.1 Startup Options

PARAMETER SYNTAX	DESCRIPTION
-dfile_path	This parameter designates the path to the master database.
-eerrorlog_path	This is the path to the error log.
-lmasterlog_path	This is the path to the master log.
-c	This will start SQL Server outside the NT Service Control Manager.
-f	This parameter starts an SQL Server session with minimal resource requirements.
-m	This parameter is an alternative to the sp_dboption that allows SQL Server to be started in a single-user mode.
-n	This parameter suppresses use of the NT event log.
-pprecision	This parameter is used to establish the precision value for numeric data types. The default value is 38. A number less than 38 can be entered in the parameter.
-sregistry_key	This parameter identifies another set of startup parameters for SQL Server.
/Ttrace#	This parameter is used to start SQL Server with a trace flag. Definitions for specific trace flag values are discussed in Chapter 20.
-x	This parameter creates maximum system performance by suppressing CPU time and cache-hit ratio statistics.

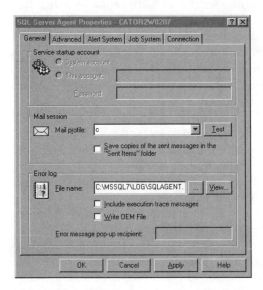

Figure 19.7 SQL Server agent properties.

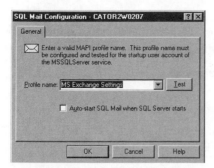

Figure 19.8 SQL Mail properties.

Figure 19.9 Login properties.

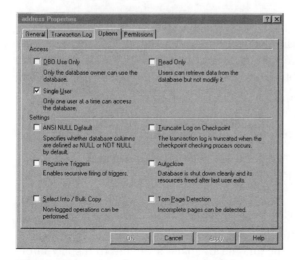

Figure 19.10 Database_Name properties.

The Options tab allows database options to be managed for the database that is selected. The system procedure sp_dboption can be used to conduct this functionality as well. Access database options that are available in this panel include

DBO use only—used to restrict access to a database as a prelude to specific maintenance operations.

Single User—used with operations such as backup/recovery to enable the operation.

Read Only—used to protect data from being updated in a database.

Database settings options that are available in this panel include

ANSI NULL Default—used to toggle between NULL/NOT NULL.

Recursive Triggers—used to enable recursive firing of the triggers.

Select Into/Bulk Copy—used to suppress writing to the transaction log. This is used before using fast BCP.

Truncate Log on Checkpoint—used to drop the log on a checkpoint procedure. Use this option in a development environment only, as it invalidates the transaction log for recovery purposes.

Autoclose—used to free database resources when it is closed.

Torn Page Detection—used to identify physical page inconsistencies.

The Permissions tab retrieves the user IDs in the database and allows permissions to be established for each of these user IDs. These include Create Table, Create View, Create SP, Create Default, Create Rule, Backup DB, and Backup Log. These permissions can also be established using system procedures that were described in Chapter 10.

Tool Palette Options

The tool palette options also vary with the type of object that is selected in the left panel of the hierarchical tree. These options are available under the Action, View, or Tools buttons; however, they are more readily accessible, with fewer keystrokes, from the tool palette. A sample sequence of these options proceeding from left to right include the following:

The Back and Forward buttons are used to traverse the hierarchical tree structure and are used to expand or compress the number of levels that are visible.

The Delete button is used to delete an object that is selected.

The Properties button displays a different window depending on the type of object that is selected.

The Up One Level button is used to traverse the tree structure.

The Show/Hide Console Tree button toggles between hiding and displaying the hierarchical tree, thus adjusting the amount of space available to display information.

Query Analyzer

The Query Analyzer is an interactive utility that replaces the text-based isql/w command as a method to issue requests to SQL Server and to process data result sets. Multiple sessions, each with a different login name can be started at the same time. Performance in mid-range desktop systems is fairly robust with several concurrent sessions. Several windows can also be opened inside the same Query Analyzer session, but each will have the same login name. The Query Analyzer in SQL Server 7 has been enhanced with visually invoked functionality that allows statements to be analyzed for performance and efficiency before they are issued. Figure 19.11 shows an empty window into which commands can be entered. Executing a command splits the window and creates a result window.

The pulldown menu options that are available from this dialogue include file, edit, view, query, window, and help. These are described in this section. Some of the commonly used commands are also available in the tool palette, such as new file, open file, save file, clear window, execute query, execute query with grid, and halt command. The default database can be changed from the pulldown menu.

File Menu

This menu contains options that can be manipulated to save you a lot of time. The basic options include connect/disconnect from a server and exit from the window. The Open command can be used to open text files that contain scripts. This option allows exter-

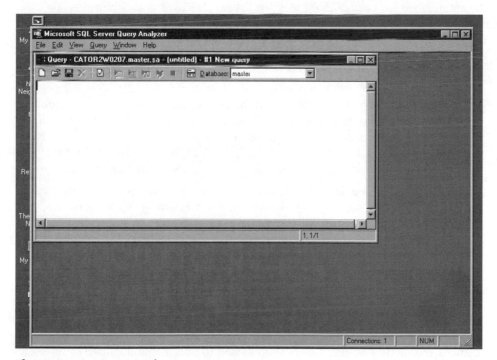

Figure 19.11 Query Analyzer.

nal scripts to be built and maintained and yet be invoked, within this visual environment. The Open command allows a text file to be located and its contents opened directly in the window. The code can now be executed or modified. The code can also be saved into text files using the Save and Save As options. The result sets from the code execution can also be saved into external text files and manipulated as any other text. The Print option prints text in any of the active windows. The Configure options allow adjustment to file extensions, regional settings, and connection information.

Edit Menu

The edit menu options are standard for Windows-type applications, including the find and replace options. Cut and paste options can be used freely within all these visual tools. Even though multiple commands are displayed in the active window, it is possible to select a part of the code and apply functionality only to that part of the code. It is also useful to write a script in a separate file and then copy/paste parts of the script into the Query Analyzer to allow iterative development and testing of the script.

View Menu

The view menu allows adjustment to the visual properties of the interface, allowing changes to such things as text color, foreground color, background color, font style, and font size.

Query Menu

The options available in this menu focus on either executing queries or analyzing the efficiency of executing a query. The options that are available under this menu include the following:

- **Execute query.** This option will execute all the commands in the code window or only the selected code in the window. Using this option divides the code window in half and displays the result set in the lower window. As shown in Figure 19.12, three tabs are also displayed: Results, Results Grid, and SQL Execution Plan. This option is also available from the tool bar and appears as a lightning bold.

- **Execute query into grid.** This option executes the commands in the code window and displays the results in the Results Grid, which contains column formatted output.

- **Display SQL execution plan.** This option displays a visual representation of the query execution plan. The addition of indexes, regeneration of a plan, or selecting a different set of command statements can be used to improve slow execution plans. This command does not execute the statements.

- **Perform index analysis.** This option examines queries and tables to recommend an indexing approach.

- **Cancel executing query.** This option is used to halt a running query. It is useful when queries are run away or extremely slow.

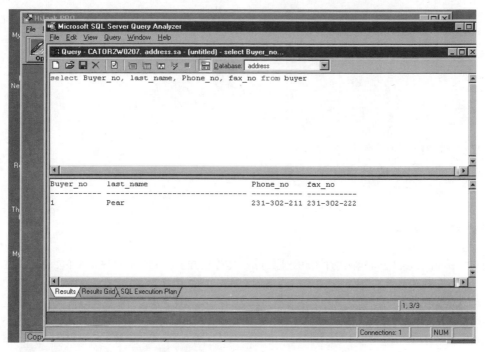

Figure 19.12 Generating a result set.

New query. This option creates another empty window.

Clear window. This option clears the current window. It prompts for unsaved text to be saved in text files. Select the No option to discard the text in the window.

T-SQL help. This option is available when Transact-SQL text is highlighted in the code window. It displays help information pertaining to the statements that are selected.

Object Help. This option is available when an object is highlighted in the window. It displays execution information about an object, such as a system procedure, including a list of input parameters and datatypes.

Set options. This option displays the dialogue shown in Figure 19.13, which contains two panels. The Execution tab allows options to be established for the current query. No Count Display suppresses a numeric count from appearing after a dataset is returned. No Execute is used with Show Options to inspect a query without actually executing it. Parse Query Only is used to inspect the syntax of a query without executing it. Both of these commands are useful in preparing commands that may require an extensive amount of time to execute. Show Query Plan shows details about the query and can be used for fine-tuning. Show Stats Time is used to display statistical information following a query's execution. Show Stats I/O displays information about input/output operations for a running query. These options are also available with the traditional SET command. SET SHOWPLAN ON/OFF (e.g., set showplan on) shows the query optimizer strategy, SET NOEXEC ON/OFF, SET STATISTICS IO ON/OFF (table scan, reads: logical and physical,

Figure 19.13 Set options.

read ahead reads), SET NOEXEC ON/OFF, SET FORCEPLAN ON/OFF, and SET STATISTICS TIME ON/OFF.

The execution dialogue also allows the number of rows (e.g., row count) that are returned from a query to be restricted. A value of zero, the default, means that all rows are returned. The Format tab allows customization of the interface and the format of the information that is returned from a query.

Window and Help Menus

The window menu contains standard Windows options to cascade and tile windows. It also contains commands to manage individual panes. The help menu offers standard windows help functionality.

Service Manager

The SQL Service Manager is used to start, pause, and stop local or remote SQL Servers. A description line at the bottom of the panel displays the status of the SQL Server that is selected. The dialogue also allows different services to be selected, including MSDTC, MSSQLServer, and SQLServerAgent. Figure 19.14 shows the appearance of a running server. A running SQL Server should be stopped before the platform is shut down. SQL Server can also be shut down using a shutdown command from within SQL Server.

MSDTC Administrative Console

This utility contains a set of tabs to examine and administer the distributed transaction environment, as shown in Figure 19.15. The General tab allows the Service Control Status to be started or stopped. The Transactions tab shows the status and work IDs of transactions. The Trace tab displays messages, their source, and their severity. The Statistics tab displays current, aggregate, and response time statistics. The Advanced Tab displays log information and allows parameters to be updated.

Figure 19.14   Service Manager.

Client Network Utility

The Client Network Utility, as shown in Figure 19.16, shows three tabs. The General tab allows network libraries to be selected and added to the environment. The Network Libraries tab displays a list of network libraries, including TCP/IP, Banyan VINES, Named Pipes, and IPX/SPX. The DB Library Options tab displays the location of the DBLIB and allows conversion settings to be established.

Server Network Utility

This utility, shown in Figure 19.17, contains two tabs. The General tab allows network libraries to be maintained. The Network Libraries tab displays a list of server network libraries.

Uninstall SQL Server 7

This option removes SQL Server from the environment. Occasional glitches do occur, especially in terms of locked files for shared applications.

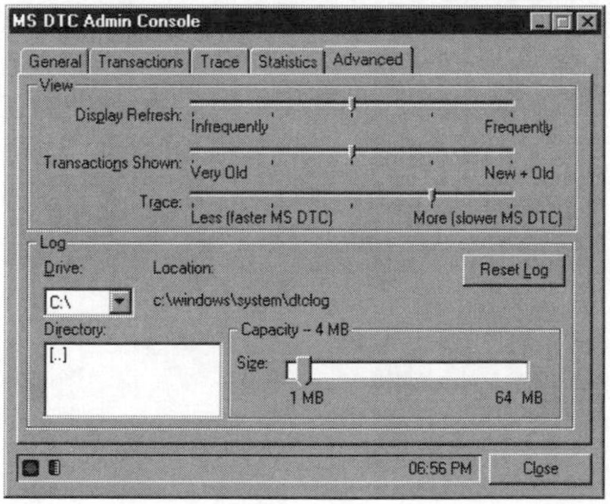

Figure 19.15   MSDTC Administrative Console.

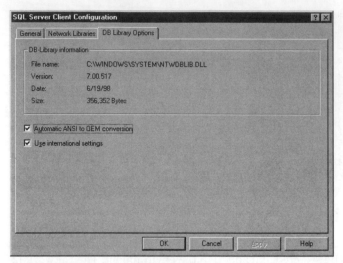

Figure 19.16   Client configuration.

Administrative Wizards

The administrative wizards are used for system administration activities. The wizards available in this category include the following: Backup Wizard, Create Alert Wizard, Create Job Wizard, Create Trace Wizard, Databox Maintenance Plan Wizard, Index Tuning Wizard, and Web Assistant Wizard. These are shown in Figure 19.18.

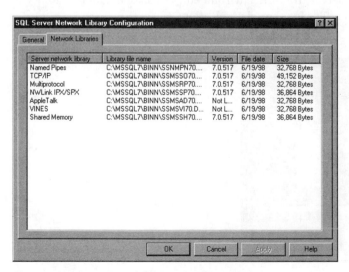

Figure 19.17   Network Library configuration.

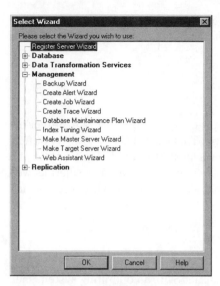

Figure 19.18   Administrative wizards.

Backup Wizard

Backup Wizard can be used in conjunction with the Backup option available under the Tools button. This wizard is used to back up (make copies) information at the database level, transaction log level, or incremental difference level to tape, disk, or some other medium. For example, to make a backup of an entire database, begin by putting the database into single-user format, either by selecting a database property through the Properties option or by using the sp_dboption command. Figure 19.19 shows the results

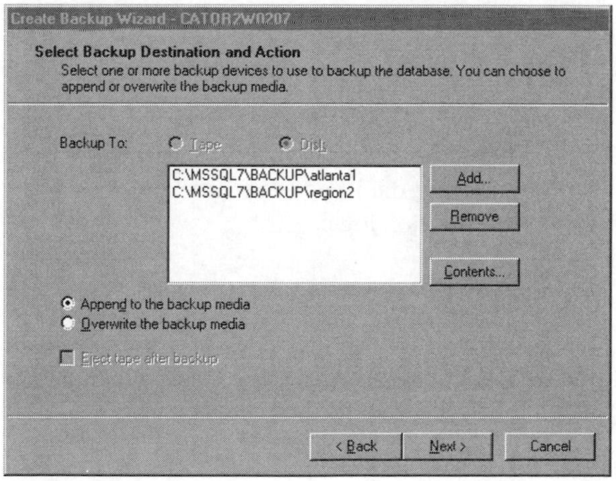

Figure 19.19   Backup Wizard.

after following through several panels. This window allows a backup region to be se-lected or new ones to be added via the Add button. The Contents button shows header information from the selected backup region.

Create Alert Wizard

The Create Alert Wizard is used to define and manage alerts within the SQL Server en-vironment. Alerts are managed at the database level. This wizard also allows a notifica-tion method to be established. The first panel allows an alert to be tied to an error or a severity level. Another panel allows a database to be identified to hold the alert as well as the contents of the alert message. The next panel identifies a job to be executed and notification methods, such as e-mail and pagers.

Create Job Wizard

This wizard is used to create a batch job using Transact-SQL, an operating system shell command, and ActiveScript. Jobs can be programmed to run at different times, such as now, at a specific time, automatically on an SQL Server Agent, when the computer is idle, or on a recurring basis according to a schedule (e.g., daily, weekly, monthly).

Create Trace Wizard

This wizard is used to trace the causes of specific problems, establish filters, and initi-ate trace definitions. Some of the problems that can be traced include Find the worst performing queries, Identify scans of large tables, Identify the cause of a deadlock, Pro-file the performance of a stored procedure, Trace Transact-SQL activity by application, and Trace Transact-SQL activity by user. A trace filters dialogue is customized to the type of trace that is selected. Figure 19.20 shows the final step before a "trace by user" is generated.

Database Maintenance Plan Wizard

This wizard is used to create maintenance plans for one database, a group of databases, or all databases. Some of the DBCC functionality is moved into this wizard. Mainte-nance consists of updating statistics, reorganizing data pages or indexes, recovering empty space, and backing up databases or transaction logs.

Index Tuning Wizard

The Index Tuning Wizard is used to recommend indexes on a table based on statistical information that can be generated using the Trace Wizard. Statistics can be identified using a workload file.

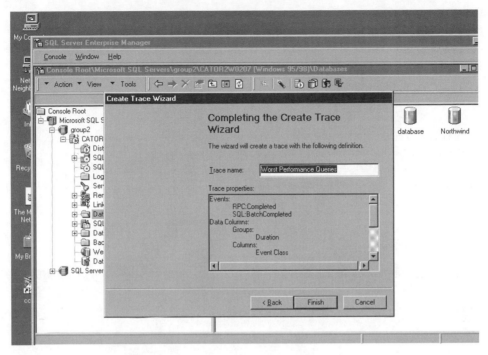

Figure 19.20   Completing the Create Trace Wizard.

Summary

This chapter examined system administration through the visual utilities that are packaged with SQL Server and through administrative wizards. The Enterprise Manager utility is the primary tool for administrating the SQL Server environment. The Query Analyzer utility is used to issue requests to SQL Server and to display the information that is returned from SQL Server. The Query Analyzer offers functionality to inspect queries to improve performance. Other visual utilities reviewed in this chapter include the Client Network Utility, MSDTC Administrative Console, Server Network Utility, and the Service Manager. The administrative wizards discussed in this chapter include the Backup Wizard, Create Alert Wizard, Create Job Wizard, Create Trace Wizard, Database Maintenance Plan Wizard, and Index Tuning Wizard.

CHAPTER

20

Maintaining Your N-Tier COM Applications

This chapter reviews the maintenance and operational requirements for applications once they are built. This chapter also reviews the activities and procedures for this latter phase of the application development life cycle. Three important operational utilities are described in this chapter: Interactive SQL (ISQL), Bulk Copy Program (BCP), and the Database Consistency Checker (DBCC).

Maintenance and Operational Activities

After the application is developed, tested, signed off, and implemented, it is necessary to leverage the lessons learned from n-tier projects in order to ensure that the component/object-based solutions are shared consistently with the rest of the organization. The following activities and deliverables support this goal:

Systems management. The application should be implemented and maintained using a tool such as the System Management Server (SMS) to automate software distribution and asset management in a distributed environment. Tools such as SourceSave should be used to maintain version control of source code and executables even after development activities are completed in a development project. It is not uncommon for environments to lose the integrity between source code and the associated executables over a period of time. This is an expensive situation to be in and should be avoided through the use of these tools.

Future development. Future development should attempt to reuse the technical architecture, deliverables, and lessons learned from past projects. This can be accomplished by maintaining a data repository, say in Lotus Notes, for key deliverables from every project.

Organizational issues. The development team disappears after implementation, so an operations team must be identified and trained to support the system. Operational procedures must be defined to support this unambiguously. Future development projects will also benefit from the experiences of a disbanding project team. A deliberate effort should be made to maximize the reuse of human experience.

Lessons learned. Lessons learned include activities and experiences that worked well on a project as well as those that did not. Both are important and provide benefits on future projects. Proper documentation of these should follow the implementation phase on a project.

Data transfer. N-tier applications rely on the efficiency of LANs and WANs. Data transfer efficiency must be monitored on an ongoing basis and adjusted as the application requirements demand. Expert resources or consultants are useful in optimizing data transfer.

Component libraries. The system should be leveraged to feed reusable component and object libraries. The libraries must be stored in accessible repositories. Component/object interfaces must be clearly defined and published. Quality control procedures must include provisions to ensure that components and objects are reused on other projects.

Reuse. This is facilitated by building the component libraries mentioned in the previous example. It also helps to establish corporate reusability goals over a period of time. It is better to aim for modest and achievable reusability goals than to be too ambitious too soon.

Scalability. The n-tier/COM architecture is popular because of its ability to comfortably scale when resource demands increase on the application. Continue to monitor the system against clear benchmarks and be prepared to increase physical resources, such as adding faster client platforms, adding RAM, adding processors, and upgrading software to maintain consistent performance and throughput for the life of the system.

Training. Maintain an ongoing training strategy that includes up-to-date training materials and courses for both the user and the technical communities. Both groups continue to change over time. Training methods can include strong use of different training and delivery methods, including CD ROM, computer-based training (CBT), intranets, Web sites, self-training, instructor training, and peer training.

Communication plan. A communication strategy that leverages newsletters, Web sites, and intranets to communicate the objectives of a system in a consistent regular manner also supports the reusability objectives of component-based development and object technology.

SQL Server Utilities

SQL Server continues to support utilities that support the operation of the database server in distributed environments. The basic utilities discussed in this section include ISQL, BCP, and DBCC.

ISQL

The batch ISQL utility initiates an interactive session with the SQL Server engine and sends requests from clients and accepts returned results from SQL Server. This command can be initiated from a variety of interfaces including a DOS interface. The Query Analyzer utility incorporates these switches in the Query Options window. Users of older versions of SQL Server may still feel comfortable with the DOS window; however, a move to the Query Analyzer is highly recommended. The basic format of this command requires a login name, password, and a server_name. Each of these can be established as environment variables so that they do not have to be entered with the isql command. An example of the basic syntax is

```
isql -U logon_id   -P password -S server_name
The following example logs on to SQL Server as an 'sa':
    isql -Usa -P
```

Successful execution of this command displays a prompt such as 1>. The following switches can also be appended to the isql utility: -e to echo input to the screen, -p to show statistics, -n for suppress numbering, -c to change end characters, -h to show heads, -w to change the column_size, -m for error_level, -t to set a timeout for query, -l for timeouts on the login, -L for list servers, -a to adjust a packet size, -H for host name, -r to send messages to a standard error device, -E to establish a trusted connection, -I to identify an input file (usually text), and –o to save output into a filename. Other examples of this utility include the following:

The following example uses the ISQL utility to establish a connection with SQL Server for the login id sa on the server specified with the –S parameter:

```
isql -Usa -P -Ssqlserver   /* specifies a server name */
```

The following example uses the ISQL utility to establish a connection with SQL Server for the login id sector with a password of sam:

```
isql -Usector -Psam
```

The following example uses the ISQL utility to establish a connection with SQL Server for the login id sa with the –e parameter to echo input to the screen and the –n parameter to suppress line numbering:

```
isql -Usa -P -e -n
```

The following example uses the ISQL utility to establish a connection with SQL Server for the login id sa. The –o parameter creates or overwrites an operating system file named OUTPUT1 and saves the contents of the ISQL session to this file:

```
isql -Usa -P -oOUTPUT1
```

The following example uses the ISQL utility to establish a connection with SQL Server for the login id sa. The –i parameter identifies an input text file that contains statements which will be compiled by SQL Server and executed. The –o parameter identifies the output text file:

```
isql -Usa -P -iINPUT1 -oOUTPUT2
```

Bulk Copy Program

The BCP continues to be a valuable utility for inserting data into SQL Server and for removing it into external files (load/unload data). The external files can be put into version control and backed up to keep permanent copies of the data. The BCP utility is an executable file that is generally available in the MSSQL\BINN\ directory. The utility is in an executable file called BCP.EXE. This utility is executed from outside the SQL Server environment. It operates at a specific table level.

The BCP utility has two modes of operation, often referred to as slow BCP and fast BCP. Fast BCP requires some database options to be established and does not write records to the transaction log. Fast BCP also overrides rules, constraints, and triggers on the target/source table. The suppression of this latter activity is the primary reason for the faster performance of this mode of activity. SQL Server 7 also offers parallel load operations that also improve the performance of BCP. The database option Select into/bulkcopy must be set to TRUE to support a fast BCP load (e.g., sp_dboption pubs, select into/bulkcopy, TRUE). Single User Mode can also be established for a database using sp_dboption or the Enterprise Manager utility. These options bypass use of the following operations: SELECT INTO, WRITETEXT, and UPDATETEXT.

BCP supports two basic types of data format: native and character format. BCP also supports a variety of data separators. The following syntax is used for the BCP utility, followed by a definition of the option switches that are supported by this utility application:

```
path\BCP dbname.role.database_table_name in | out | format  datafile switches
```

Only one of the in/out verbs is used in this command. The in statement indicates that data is being loaded into the database tables. The out statement is used to extract data from a database table. The format verb indicates the data format; /n indicates a natural data format; /c indicates a character data format; datafile is used to identify an operating system filename. A variety of switches are available as shown in Table 20.1.

BCP Procedure

The BCP procedure requires a few additional activities. Change the database option for the database being examined (e.g., pubs) with the command: sp_dboption pubs, select into/bulkcopy, TRUE. This command should be entered in the Query Analyzer while the pubs database is the default database. The effect of this command can be confirmed by viewing the options panel for the pubs database in the SQL Server Enterprise Manager. The following script re-creates the test table and data to support this example:

```
use pubs
go

drop table test_codetable2
go

create table test_codetable2
(seq_no      int IDENTITY, description     char(50))
go
```

Table 20.1 BCP Switch Types

BCP SWITCH TYPE	SYNTAX	DESCRIPTION
Maximum errors	-m maxerror_no	Indicates the maximum number of errors before BCP aborts.
First row	-F first_row	Specifies an offset from the start of the table to begin the copy operation.
Native data format	-n	Native code data format into and out of the database.
Input file name	-I input_file_name	A name of the input file.
Server name	-S server_name	The server_name of the server being addressed. This is not required if the default server is the target.
Trusted connection	-T trusted_connection	Use if a trusted security connection exists between the operating system (e.g., NT) and SQL Server.
Null values	-k keep_null_values	Specifies that null values should be retained after the copy operation.
Supply hints	-h supply_hints	A list of hints to be used by the optimizer to improve performance of BCP. Use this sparingly.
Format file	-f Format file	This file contains format information for BCP. Use of this file overrides the need to specify column-by-column information interactively. It should be used to enhance batch operations.
Lastrow	-L lastrow	This is a numeric value that indicates the last data row to copy. This provides the end of the data range for the copy operation.
Character datatype	-c	Character code data format into and out of the database.
Field terminator	-t terminator value	Indicates the default field terminator. Valid values can be r for carriage return, n for newline, 0 for null, t for tab, and other mnemonic values.
Output file	-o output_file_name	Specifies the output file name where output from BCP is stored.
User name	-U username	The user name for the user using BCP. Use of BCP requires an implicit login before the operation continues.
Version	-v version	Shows the version number of the product.
Maintain identity values	-E	Inserts values from the input file into identity columns in a table.
Error file name	-e error_file_name	Creates an error file to hold error messages.
Batch file	-b batch_file_name	Specifies rows per batch.
Row terminator	-r row_terminator	Indicates a row terminator.
Packet size	-a packet_size	Network packet size in bytes.
Bulk Copy 6.0/6.5	-6	SQL Server 6 or 6.5 datatypes are maintained in the BCP operation.
Password	-P password	The password corresponding to the username.

```
insert test_codetable2
(description) values ('This first row was updated')

insert test_codetable2
(description) values ('This second row was updated')
go

select * from test_codetable2
go
```

A datatype format must be provided interactively for each column in the table being accessed or within an operating system format file with an extension of .fmt. The format file (.fmt) can be generated on the first invocation of BCP for a table and can be maintained after that. Notice that the prompt for properties for each of the columns in the data row displays a default value delimited by brackets as part of the prompt. Clicking on the Enter key with no data entry accepts the default value. The following steps create a text file containing rows from a user-defined table:

```
BCP pubs..test_codetable2 out codefl1.txt -Usa -P -c
```

The sequence of these verbs is important. Codefl1.txt is the name of the text file that contains the data rows from the BCP utility. BCP responds with a message similar to the following: Starting copy . . . . The utility also displays the network packet size (e.g., 4096 bytes). The clock time and the number of rows copied is also displayed. Running this command again can use the format file if it was generated with this first submission. The contents of the codefl1.txt file consists of two records as follows:

```
1       This first row was updated
2       This second row was updated
```

The text file can be used to insert the data rows back into the table. For the purpose of this test the Query Analyzer can be used to clear the receiving table, which in this case is test_codetable2. The following code will do this:

```
delete pubs..test_codetable2
go
select * from pubs..test_codetable2
go
```

The select statement shows that no records exist in the test-codetable2 table if the delete statement was successfully issued and executed. The following BCP command loads data from the codefl1.txt file into the user-defined table:

```
BCP pubs..test_codetable2 in codefl1.txt -Usa -P -c
```

Successful completion of this command displays a message such as Starting copy, the number of rows copied, network packet size, and clock speed. You will probably notice that copying into the database is slower than copying out of the database. Display the contents of the user table using Query Analyzer using select * from pubs..test_codetable2. Two data rows should be displayed, as follows:

```
3       This first row was updated
4       This second row was updated
```

The number of data rows is correct; however, notice that the first column numbers are different, having changed from 1 to 3 and 2 to 4. This is because of the identity constraint that is tied to the first column. Using the –E switch overrides the identity constraint and uses the values in the input file, which are 1 and 2, respectively. The following example demonstrates the code statement to do this:

```
bcp pubs..test_codetable2 in codefl1.txt -Usa -P -c -E
```

The statistical information displayed as a result of this statement shows that it operates faster without the constraints than it does with them. This is fully expected. The following code sample creates an output file in natural data format:

```
BCP pubs..test_codetable2 out codent1.txt -Usa -P -n
```

Database Consistency Checker

SQL Server 7 moves some of the functionality offered by DBCC into the core engine. However, it is still recommended that DBCC continue to be used as an extra level of protection. DBCC is more efficient than before and has succeeded in running in a fraction of the former time. It is worth benchmarking in your organization to view the time improvements.

DBCC is a large application program that is run in batch as part of the ongoing operation of a system. DBCC displays vital information about the database environment and is used to adjust information in the environment. It is invoked from within the SQL Server environment, as shown in Figure 20.1. The operation is identified through a series of function names and parameters. This is one area where DBCC requires additional improvements. The parameters are not intuitive and some are obscure. Some of the more common ones are described in the following list for your convenience.

The basic syntax for the DBCC function is shown here. It consists of the DBCC verb, followed by a flexible number of functions or parameters:

```
DBCC function_name (parameters)
```

The following list of syntax and examples demonstrates some of the more popular and useful uses of the DBCC utility. To display memory usage, use the following code, which is not case sensitive:

```
DBCC MEMUSAGE
go
```

To display performance statistics such as reads outstanding, writes outstanding, cache hit ratio, cache flushes, free page scan (avg), free page scan (max), min free buffers, cache size, free buffers, network reads, network writes, RA pages found in cache, RA pages placed in cache, and RA physical IO use the following code:

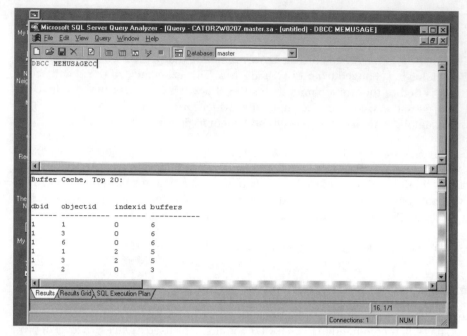

Figure 20.1   Invoking DBCC.

```
DBCC PERFMON
go
```

To reexecute the last command in the buffer, use the following command:

```
dbcc ('inputbuffer')
```

To display page statistics use the following code:

```
DBCC  show_statistics (table_name, key)
go
```

To display performance information, use the following code:

```
DBCC  sqlperf(option)
    Where option = IOSTATS, LOGSPACE, LRUSTATS, NETSTATS,
                            RASTATS, THREADS
e.g. DBCC sqlperf(IOSTATS)
    go
```

To display information about the number of rows in the table and the number of pages that are occupied by the data rows, use the following code:

```
DBCC  checktable (table_name)

e.g. DBCC checktable(test_codetable2)
    go
```

To display information about a database, use the following code:

```
DBCC   checkdb (database_name)

e.g. DBCC checkdb (address)
        go
```

This displays the information that follows about the address database. This information is retrieved for all the system tables in the database; however, the example that follows is reformatted for brevity. This format of the command also displays the consistency of the overall database:

```
DBCC results for ' address'.
DBCC results for 'sysobjects'.
There are 70 rows in 1 pages for object 'sysobjects'.
DBCC results for 'exec_table'.
There are 0 rows in 1 pages for object 'exec_table'.
DBCC results for 'buyer'.
There are 1 rows in 1 pages for object 'automobile_description'.
DBCC results for 'car_units'.
There are 3 rows in 1 pages for object 'car_units'.
DBCC results for 'dealership'.
There are 2 rows in 1 pages for object 'dealership'.
DBCC results for 'dtproperties'.
There are 0 rows in 1 pages for object 'dtproperties'.
CHECKDB found 0 allocation errors and 0 consistency errors in
                                         database ' address'.
DBCC execution completed. If DBCC printed error messages, contact
                                    your system administrator.
```

To display allocation information about the database objects in a database, use the following code. The database can also be enclosed in quotes as in 'address':

```
DBCC   checkalloc(database_name)

e.g. DBCC checkalloc (address)
        go
```

The following information is a partial listing of the results that are returned by this command:

```
DBCC results for -address '.
******************************************************************
Table sysobjects                 Object ID 1.
Index ID 1          FirstIAM (1:4)     Root (1:6)      Dpages 1      Sort 0.
    Data level 1. 3 data pages in 0 extents.
Index ID 2          FirstIAM (1:15)    Root (1:14)     Dpages 1      Sort 0.
    Index ID 2. 2 index pages in 0 extents.
Index ID 3          FirstIAM (1:34)    Root (1:33)     Dpages 1      Sort 0.
    Index ID 3. 2 index pages in 0 extents.
```

```
Total number of extents is 0.
******************************************************************
Table auto_transaction          Object ID 613577224.
Index ID 0         FirstIAM (1:106)   Root (1:105)    Dpages 1      Sort 0.
    Data level 1. 2 data pages in 0 extents.
Total number of extents is 0.
******************************************************************
Table automobile_description    Object ID 629577281.
Index ID 0         FirstIAM (1:108)   Root (1:107)    Dpages 1      Sort 0.
    Data level 1. 2 data pages in 0 extents.
Total number of extents is 0.
******************************************************************
Table car_units                 Object ID 645577338.
Index ID 0         FirstIAM (1:110)   Root (1:109)    Dpages 1      Sort 0.
    Data level 1. 2 data pages in 0 extents.
Total number of extents is 0.
******************************************************************
Processed 36 entries in sysindexes for database ID 8.
Allocation page (1:2). Number of extents = 17, used pages = 116, referenced pages = 75.
CHECKALLOC found 0 allocation errors and 0 consistency errors in database ' address'.
DBCC execution completed. If DBCC printed error messages, contact your system administrator.
```

To shrink a database, use the following code:

```
DBCC  shrinkdb (db_name, revised_size)
```

To check the catalog, use the following code:

```
DBCC  CHECKCATALOG (parameter)
```

To locate open transactions, use the following code:

```
DBCC  OPENTRAN
```

DBCC TRACEON Options

The TraceOn option accepts a variety of parameters to perform different activities. Multiple parameters can be issued in one statement, and are delimited by commas. The general syntax of this instance of the DBCC command is as follows:

```
DBCC TRACEON  (#, #, # list)
```

The # parameter can take on the following values.

3604: display output on client screen.

3605: route to errorlog.

302: display information about usage of the statistics page and index information.

310: join order information.

330: use with showplan. Displays detailed output.

1200, 1204, 1205: display deadlock information.

3609: do not create tempdb on startup.

4022: do not execute boot-up stored procedures.

For example, several codes can be combined as follows: DBCC TRACEON (330, 3605, 302). DBCC trace flags are turned off with the following command:

```
DBCC TRACEOFF (#)

e.g. DBCC TRACEOFF (330)
     go

e.g. DBCC TRACEOFF (302)
     go
```

Distributed Application Considerations

Maintaining a distributed application after implementation requires an understanding of the following considerations:

Components. Update of specific component executables, in-process, out-process, DLLS, without recompiling the entire application.

Version control. A distributed application should still have a central version control repository to ensure that the entire application can be rebuilt at anytime. Change control procedures must be built around this repository. Version control should ensure all the source code in the environment, including VB, C++, stored procedures, batch procedures, and reports.

Security. Must include the internet/intranet, as well as the traditional areas of application security. A combination of security approaches, at the Operating System level, application level, SQL Server environment, and physical security should still be included in the security strategy.

Code reuse. A primary objective of component-based software is reuse. Clear documents (e.g., object models, message contexts), libraries, and procedures must be identified to the development team to ensure that this is done. Walkthroughs should be used to ensure that development teams are reusing components in the environment.

Software upgrades. It will be necessary to update specific software components in the architecture as new releases become available in the market and there is a need to take advantage of new features. This can affect pricing, maintenance agreements, and the interaction of the different software components.

Scaling the application. It may become necessary to scale the application in terms of hardware or software to support increasing numbers of users and widening geography.

Organization. Development teams are generally moved to other projects after an application is implemented. Access must be maintained to key resources on an as-needed basis to correct occasional problems in such things as the components, transaction monitors, architecture, and business rules.

Test/staging environment. A separate test/staging environment should be maintained to allow the entire application or portions of it to be tested. A procedure to test components separately should also be retained. This environment is used for validating software upgrades or scaling the environment.

Summary

This chapter reviewed the maintenance and operational requirements for maintaining applications after they are built, including examining systems management requirements, future development considerations, organizational issues, leveraging lessons learned, data transfer, component libraries, promoting reuse, leveraging scalability, training, and following a communication plan. This chapter also reviewed three SQL Server utilities that are important in the ongoing operational requirements for maintaining an SQL Server–based system.

This chapter also examined some considerations for distributed applications after implementation. This included components, version control, security, code reuse, software upgrades, scaling the application, organization, and a testing/staging environment.

Relational Data Modeling, Normal Forms, and Other Models

This appendix provides a short review of key concepts related to the modeling techniques that were used to build application designs for some of the examples contained in this book:

The Relational Data Model

The relational data model is one of the leading formats for modeling data in the retail database marketplace. Evidence of this dominance is seen in the growing linkages between object databases, data warehouses, and more exotic datatypes. The relational data model is based on mathematical set theory. A set represents an entity. Entities contain attributes that describe properties, such as height, weight, and depth. Entities and attributes are logical descriptions of the physical world. These terms map to tables and columns in a physical implementation. Mathematical operations, such as joins, are applied to two or more entities to produce result sets. Entities contain data rows that are differentiated by primary key fields and foreign key fields. Normal forms are used to categorize attributes and separate them into different entities based on specific rules. The following normal forms are described in the literature:

First Normal Form: removes repeating groups and data redundancy.

Second Normal Form: eliminates functional dependencies.

Third Normal Form: eliminates transitive dependencies. This is the level of normalization required in business projects.

Fourth Normal Form: eliminates multivalued dependencies.

Fifth Normal Form: decomposes tables into projections.

Cardinality represents the types of relationships between entities. These are one-to-one relationships, one-to-many relationships, many-to-one relationships, and many-to-many relationships. Many-to-many relationships can be represented as two relationships, between three tables. These relationships are a one-to-many relationship and a many-to-one relationship. Recursive relationships can also exist between attributes in the same table. For example, consider the examples in Table A.1.

Object-Oriented Models

Object classes contain both data and methods to manipulate the data. Each object instance is uniquely identified by a value generated at run-time. Object methods are invoked by passing messages to object interfaces. Methods can be public or private to an object class. Public methods are available to other objects through the interface, and private methods are visible only within an object class. Object technology is characterized by inheritance, encapsulation, polymorphism, and aggregation.

Object databases are a representation of real life. Object database features include multimedia support, collections, aggregates, complex objects, composite objects, persistence with 3GL, identifiers, object identifiers to pointer conversion, object clustering, instance operations extensibility, class operations extensibility, and type operations extensibility. Some examples of object-oriented databases include GemStone, Illustra, ObjectStore, Java/Depot, Jasmine, ODBMS, Omniscience, ONTOS (Object SQL dialect), OSMOS, Persistence, Poet, UniSQL, Objectivity/DB (SQL++ dialect), and Versant. Folio is an example of a multimedia database.

Pure object-oriented databases integrate Sequel interfaces with their traditional object architectures. Relational databases are being expanded to support complex datatypes, but behavior is still retained in the application. This approach is referred to as a hybrid relational object-oriented database. In this case data records are integrated objects (containing structure and retrieval information).

Work is progressing on an extension to the ANSI/92 database standard, tentatively called the SQL3 standard. SQL3 standardizes embedding SQL into object-oriented databases supporting object/relational capabilities to support the storage of complex data and the management of complex queries. Parallel processing will also be a consideration in SQL3.

Table A.1 Cardinality

CARDINALITY	EXAMPLE OF RELATIONSHIP
One-to-One	Capital-country
One-to-Many	Mother-child
Many-to-One	Seats-train
Many-to-Many	Distributor-product
Recursive	Employee (name, position), where the recursive relationship is on the position attribute. For example, an employee can work for someone and be a manager to someone else at the same time.

Bibliography

Branchek Bob, Peter Hazlehurst, Stephen Wynkoop, Scott L. Warner. *Using Microsoft SQL Server 6.5*. Indianapolis, Ind.: Que, 1996, ISBN 0-7897-0097-2.

Booch, Grady. *Object Solutions: Managing the Object-Oriented Project*. New York: Addison-Wesley, 1996, ISBN 0-8053-0594-7.

Burleson, Donald K. *Managing Distributed Databases: Building Bridges between Database Islands*. New York: John Wiley and Sons, 1994, ISBN 0-471-08623-1.

Chappell, David. *Understanding ActiveX and OLE*. Redmond, Wash.: Microsoft Press, 1996, ISBN 1-57231-216-5.

DiDio, Laura, and Jaikumar Vijayan. NT Scalability Lures Skeptical Customers. *Computer World*, May 19, 1997.

Enck, John, and Mel Beckman. *LAN to WAN Interconnection*. New York: McGraw-Hill, 1995, ISBN 0-07-019614-1.

England, Ken. *The SQL Server 6.5 Performance Optimization and Tuning Handbook*. Boston: Digital Press, 1997, ISBN 1-55558-180-3.

Garms, Jason, et al. *Windows NT Server 4 Unleashed*. Indianapolis, Ind.: SAMS Publishing, 1996, ISBN 0-672-30933-5.

Hipson, Peter. *The Windows NT 4 Server Book*. Research Triangle Park, N.C.: Ventana, 1997, ISBN 1-56604-495-2.

Johnston, Stuart J., and John Foley. Windows NT Sticker Shock. *Information Week*, June 16, 1997, pp. 14–16.

Lang, Curt, and Jeff Chow. *Database Publishing on the Web & Intranets*. Scottsdale, Ariz.: Coriolis Group Books, 1996, ISBN 1-883577-85-3.

Larson, James A. *Database Directions*. Englewood Cliffs, N.J.: Prentice-Hall, 1995, ISBN 0-13-290867-0.

Lhotka, Rockford. *Professional Visual Basic Business Objects*. Chicago, IL: Wrox Press, 1997, ISBN 1-861000-43-X.

Loshin, Pete. *TCP/IP Clearly Explained*, 2nd ed. London: Academic Press, 1997, ISBN 0-12-455835-6.

Microsoft Corp. Microsoft SQL Server training materials. Redmond, Wash.: Microsoft Press.

Nadile, Lisa. Microsoft Adds Tools to SQL Server. *Information Week*, November 11, 1996, p. 100.

Page-Jones, Meilir. *What Every Programmer Should Know About Object-Oriented Design*. New York: Dorset House, 1995, ISBN 0-932633-31-5.

Panttaja Jim, Mary Panttaja, and Bruce Prendergast. *The Microsoft SQL Server*. New York: John Wiley and Sons, 1996, ISBN 0-471-12743-4.

Purba, Sanjiv. *Developing Client/Server Systems Using Sybase SQL Server System 10*. New York: John Wiley and Sons, 1994, ISBN 0-471-06249-9.

Purba, Sanjiv. *Developing Client/Server Systems Using Sybase SQL Server System 11*. New York: John Wiley and Sons, 1996, ISBN 0-471-15338-9.

Purba, Sanjiv. *Using SQL Windows and Centura: Techniques for Building Client/ Server Solutions*. New York: John Wiley and Sons, 1996, ISBN 0-471-13089-3.

Purba, Sanjiv, ed. *The Handbook of Data Management*. New York: Auerbach/CRC Press, 1999.

Rensin, David, and Andrew Fedorchek. *SQL Server 6.5 Secrets*. Foster City, Calif.: IDG Books, 1996, ISBN 1-56884-698-3.

Rogerson, Dale. *Inside COM*. Redmond, Wash.: Microsoft Press, 1997, ISBN 1-57231-349-8.

Index